A GUIDE TO
CHESS ENDINGS

Dr. MAX EUWE
World Champion 1935-1937
and
DAVID HOOPER

DOVER PUBLICATIONS, INC.
New York

Published in Canada by General Publishing Company, Ltd., 30 Lesmill Road, Don Mills, Toronto, Ontario.
Published in the United Kingdom by Constable and Company, Ltd., 10 Orange Street, London WC 2.

This Dover edition, first published in 1976, is an unabridged and corrected republication of the work first published by David McKay Company, Inc., New York, in 1960.

International Standard Book Number: 0-486-23332-4
Library of Congress Catalog Card Number: 75-41882

Manufactured in the United States of America
Dover Publications, Inc.
180 Varick Street
New York, N.Y. 10014

CONTENTS

CONTENTS

INTRODUCTION

TODAY many more tournament games are being played, and club and match games brought more frequently to a finish, so that the ending is not left to the adjudicator but is becoming of increasing importance to the ordinary player. For the expert it has long been an outstanding characteristic of his play, and it is not accidental that the greatest masters of chess have also been the greatest masters of the end-game. In the end-game, unlike the opening, proficiency does not depend on the memory, but upon methodical study, and it is not difficult to acquire a skill that will add its quota of points and half-points to the score table.

Endings are predominantly positional in character, although combinative and tactical manœuvring often enlivens the play. The best endings have their own appeal, one of accurate timing and precision. But the compelling reason for study is surely the practical one: after a long struggle how heart-breaking it is not to reap one's full reward because of poor end-play! In more than sixty examples from play in this book decisive mistakes were made, often by the greatest masters.

In many ways the ending is a different kind of game: the importance of the pawn centre diminishes; the king becomes active; there is the possibility of stalemate; and the pawns, no longer a skeleton clothed by pieces, become powerful in themselves. When the number of pawns is reduced then values change, so that a piece may be worth no more than a pawn.

Rather than a sketchy outline of the whole field, we have made a fairly thorough study of those endings most likely to occur in play, especially those with rooks. The book is best worked through as a course of study, so that the underlying ideas are absorbed, and a sound positional judgment acquired. It is not at first necessary to understand every nuance, far less to try to remember the more difficult and complex variations; indeed, one might well pass over the sub-variations at a first reading. Some of the examples, noticeably in the later chapters, are harder than others. Although considered a suitable textbook for the less skilled player, some more complicated studies, and some recent theoretical discoveries such as the analyses of R+BP+RP v. R, and Q+KtP v. Q, are included. Endings at first difficult yield to further study; the weaker player need never be discouraged, for in time the ideas become clearer, and a logical pattern is revealed.

The examples are for the most part classified according to the kind of pawn-formation, and a dozen or more series of comparative studies, e.g. Examples 223-225, are intended to show the importance of this. Most of the usual conventions are followed. In the diagrams White moves up the board. The player with the advantage, the 'stronger party', is often called White. However, a question mark is used only to indicate a decisive error that changes the course of the game, and is not otherwise used. The first named player is usually the player of the White pieces, although the colours may be reversed for clearer presentation. For the same reason the em—dash is omitted from the moves of sub-variations, e.g. P—K4 becomes PK4.

Acknowledgments are especially given to Cheron's three volume masterpiece *Lehr- und Handbuch der Endspiele*, Berlin, 1955-57; *Rook against Pawns*, by Maizelis, Moscow, 1956; *Chess Endings—Pawns, Bishops, and Knights*, by Maizelis, Averbach, and Chekover, Moscow, 1956; *Koncowa Gra Szachowa*, Vol. 2, 1954, and Vol. 3, 1957, Warsaw, an extensive collection of end-games with pieces, by Gawlikowski.

We should also like to acknowledge the generous help given by Mr. F. W. Allen, who assiduously checked the proofs; by Mr. van den Berg, who assisted with analysis and in various other ways; and by Mr. K. Whyld, whose research was invaluable.

Dr. M. EUWE, Amsterdam.
DAVID HOOPER, Reigate, England.

September, 1958.

CHAPTER I

PAWN ENDINGS

'. . . the Pawns: They are the very Life of this Game. They alone form the Attack and the Defence; on their good or bad Situation depends the Gain or Loss of the Party.'
PHILIDOR, 1749.

1. THE OPPOSITION

Bringing the king into play is the first thing to do in most cases; for in contrast to the earlier phases of the game it is in the ending that the king, instead of hiding himself or playing into safety, becomes an attacking piece.

Its freedom of action as it approaches its rival is controlled by a relationship between their respective positions, which is known as the opposition.

1 The kings stand opposite one another, i.e. in opposition.

White, having to move, can never force his way forward: 1. KQ2 KQ5 2. KK2 KK5—he is directly opposed. Conversely, if Black moves first then he in turn cannot get to his sixth rank: 1... KQ5 2. KQ2 KK5 3. KK2.

The player with the move cannot force the advance of his king; but this is not all, for he cannot prevent his opponent's advance.

We shall suppose it to be Black's move:

| 1... | K—Q5 |

After which White's forward path is obstructed only on two squares (Q3, QB3); but if 1... KKt5 then White outflanks by 2. KQ3.

2 K—Kt3	K—B4
3 K—R4	K—Kt3
4 K—Kt4	

White's further advance, or out-flanking, is restricted by the edge of the board, so he retakes the opposition, and Black, having to move, must again give way.

4 ...	K—B3
5 K—R5	K—Kt2
6 K—Kt5	K—B2
7 K—R6	K—Kt1
8 K—Kt6.	

Black may defend his corner square, 8... KR1 9. KB7 KR2 10. KB8, or his bishop's square, 8... KB1 9. KR7 KB2 10. KR8; but he is powerless to prevent White forcing his way through to the back rank.

Direct opposition

White might as easily have reached the back rank on the king's side. To force this he must first move along the rank, holding the opposition: 1... KQ5 2. KQ2 (After the immediate outflanking 2. KKt3 KQ6, White at best gets to QKt8 or QR8.) 2... KK5 3. KK2 KB5 4. KB2 KKt5 5. KKt2 and now White outflanks by 5... KB5 6. KR3, or 5... KR5 6. KB3, then working his way up the files, as before.

White, then, can force his way to any

1

part of the board, but not to any particular square. He must be careful not to lose the opposition until his objective is in sight. If, for instance, Black commenced by playing 1... KB4, ceding all three squares in front of White's king, then White must reply 2. KB3 retaining the opposition, for either 2. KKt3 KKt4 or 2. KQ3 KQ4 loses it.

Conversely, similar powers accrue to Black if White moves first.

When the kings are thus opposed on the file one square apart it is termed vertical direct opposition. It is usual to say that the player who hasn't the move has the opposition, e.g. White has the opposition if it is Black's move.

Whoever moves first must give ground; or to put it another way: if you have the opposition you can outflank your opponent, and moreover you can choose your moment for doing so.

The player having the vertical opposition may force his way to the farthermost rank. Also, a player having the horizontal direct opposition may get to the farthermost file, e.g. White K at QKt6, Black K at his Q3, which is simply Example 1 turned ninety degrees.

The direct opposition (kings one square apart on the same file or rank) is the most fundamental of all chess manœuvres; and is of consequence in most of the pawn endings in this book.

2 The opposition is here the decisive factor, for it enables White to control the queening square.

1 ...	K—Kt3
2 K—Kt4	K—B3
3 K—B4	

White holds the opposition until his king is in front of (on the same file as) his pawn.

| 3 ... | K—Q3 |
| 4 K—Q4 | K—K3 |

If 4... KB3 5. KK5.

5 K—B5

The right moment for the outflanking movement.

| 5 ... | K—Q2 |

Trying to stop White's king, for if 5... KK4 6. PQ4 ch. KK3 7. KB6, and if 5... KK2 6. KB6.

6 K—Q5

Retaking the opposition, not 6. PQ4? KB2 losing it.

6 ...	K—K2
7 K—B6	K—Q1
8 K—Q6	

Again retaking the opposition.

8 ...	K—K1
9 P—Q4	K—Q1
10 P—Q5	K—K1
11 K—B7.	

White's king controls Q8, and the pawn queens.

White plays and draws
Black plays and loses

But without the opposition White cannot win.

1 K—Kt4	K—Kt3
2 K—B4	K—B3
3 P—Q4	

White must try this as he will make no headway with his king.

| 3 ... | K—Q3 |
| 4 P—Q5 | |

White cannot take the direct opposition because his pawn occupies the relevant square. This always happens when the pawn is beside or ahead of its king. If White is to win he must be able to manœuvre his king clear of obstruction by his pawn, as in the first variation.

4 ...   K—Q2

At this stage Black also draws after 4... KK2 (B2) 5. KB5 KQ2, for White's pawn again prevents his taking the opposition.

5 K—B5   K—B2

Black takes the opposition when White's king advances round the side of his pawn.

6 P—Q6 ch.   K—Q2

Instead, 6... K—Q1 may be played at once.

7 K—Q5   K—Q1

Now that the pawn is on the sixth only this retreat draws. If 7... KK1 (B1)? 8. KK6 (B6) KQ1 9. PQ7.

8 K—B6   K—B1

Black takes the opposition, and White's king is unable to command the queening square.

9 P—Q7 ch.   K—Q1
10 K—Q6 stalemate.

3 The kings are one square apart on the same diagonal, and are said to be in diagonal opposition.

The possession of any form of the opposition means that one can force one's way to any part of the board. If it is Black's move, then White has the opposition, and we may suppose he

Diagonal opposition

wants to get to a square near his KR8 corner. If 1... KKt5 2. KKt2 White moves along to KKt2 and then outflanks; or if 1... KB6 2. KR3 and White moves to QR7 and outflanks. In both these cases the diagonal opposition, which is often transitory, immediately transposes to the direct opposition. Instead, Black might play 1... KQ5 2. KKt2 KK5 3. KB2 KB5 4. KQ2 KKt5 5. KK2 KR5 6. KB2 KR4 7. KB3, etc.

In practice the diagonal opposition is usually seen as a defensive manœuvre, a means of preventing the opponent taking the direct opposition, as in Example 7.

The direct and diagonal oppositions are the only forms of close opposition where the square or squares controlled by one king may also be commanded by the other. There are also long-range forms of the opposition, where the kings are three or five squares apart.

The kings are defined as standing in opposition when (*a*) they are on squares of the same colour, and (*b*) there is an odd number of squares between them by the most direct route or routes.

4 With three squares between them on the same file, the kings are in vertical distant opposition. The player who has the opposition (we shall suppose it to be White) has the power to get to any part of the board, as in Example 1.

1 ...   K—Q3

None of Black's eight possible moves prevents the invasion of his ranks. If he advances, White takes the direct opposition; if he retreats White pursues, maintaining the distant opposition; and if he moves sideways, as here, White outflanks by stepping to the other side.

2 K—Kt3

White outflanks at once. If he wishes instead to penetrate the king's side, he must first play along the rank, 2. K—Q2.

2 ...   K—B2
3 K—R4

There is often a choice, and either

3

3. KB3 or 3. KR3 serves; but White must not cede the vertical opposition, 3. KKt4 KKt3.

3 ...   K—Kt1

If 3... KB3 4. KR5.

4 K—Kt4

Distant opposition

Retaking the distant opposition.

4 ...   K—B1
5 K—R5   K—Kt2
6 K—Kt5.

White has the direct opposition.

One cannot always convert the distant into the direct opposition, and in many positions where the direct opposition is decisive, the distant opposition is of no significance.

Long-distant opposition (kings on the same file or rank with five squares between them) confers similar advantages, but the presence of pawns on the board usually interferes with such extended manœuvring, and examples are rare in practice.

5 White converts the long-distant into the direct opposition. Black submits to this in preference to being outflanked on one wing or the other; but if this position were moved one or two files to the right making a king's side outflanking impracticable, then the long-distant opposition would not be significant, and a draw would come about.

1 K—B2

Taking the opposition. The immediate outflanking 1. KR2? permits 1... KB2 2. KR3 KB3, when 3. KR4? loses, and going to the QKt file cedes the opposition, 3. KKt4 KKt3, or 3. KKt3 KKt2.

1 ...   K—Q1

Black plays towards the centre, else White outflanks on the king's side, 1... KKt1 2. KQ3 KKt2 3. KK3 KB3 4. KK4 KQ2 5. KB4 KK2 6. KKt5 KB2 7. KR6.

2 K—Kt3

The correct moment for outflanking.

2 ...   K—B2

If 2... KQ2 3. KKt4. If 2... KB1 3. KB4 retaking the (distant) opposition, which also happens after the text move.

3 K—B3   K—Q2

If 3... KKt2 4. KQ3 KB2 5. KK3.

4 K—Kt4

Again outflanking.

4 ...   K—B3
5 K—B4

The direct opposition wins, and would do so if the position now reached were moved one or two files to the right.

White plays and wins
Black plays and draws

5 ...   K—Q2

If 5... KKt3 6. PQ5 P×P ch. 7. K×P KB2 8. KK6 KQ1 9. KB7.

6 K—Kt5

The correct outflanking move. Not 6. KB5? KB2, when Black has the opposition, and if 7. KKt5 KKt2 8. KR5 KB3.

6 ...	K—B2
7 K—B5	K—Q2
8 K—Kt6	K—Q1
9 K—B6.	

Soon Black's KP is lost.

With the move Black himself takes the long-distant opposition, and it so happens he can maintain the vertical opposition and thereby draw.

1 ...	K—Kt2
2 K—Kt2	K—Kt3
3 K—Kt3	K—Kt2

The distant opposition. Black must not unwarily advance, 3... KKt4? for he loses the opposition after 4. KB3 KKt3 (4... KB3 5. KB4) 5. KKt4.

| 4 K—B4 | K—B3 |
| 5 K—Kt4 | K—Kt3 |

Black loses the vertical opposition after 5... KQ4? 6. KB3 KB3 7. KB4.

| 6 K—B3 | K—B2 |
| 7 K—Q3 | K—Q2 |

The opposition is not relevant on the Q, K, or KB, files because of pawn-interference, although Black must keep on the same file as White to avoid being outflanked on one wing or the other.

7... KQ1 8. KB4 KB1 also draws after 9. KB5 KB2 10. PQ5 P×P 11. K×P KQ2.

8 K—K4	K—K2(K1)
9 K—B4	K—B2(B1)
10 K—Kt4	K—Kt1
11 K—R5	K—R2.

On neither wing can White get the opposition.

So far we have shown extended forms of the direct opposition with both kings on the same file or rank. Other long-range forms of the opposition can occur —usually however in composed studies.

6 The kings are said to be in oblique opposition, which is compounded of direct + diagonal opposition. The kings are three squares apart by the most direct routes, in accordance with our earlier definition. Another definition also involves odd numbers: visualize the smallest rectangle containing the two kings; and if the sides are both odd numbered (as here 5×3 squares) the kings stand in opposition.

Oblique opposition

The squares marked by dots are those on which Black's king might also stand in opposition of one kind or another to White's king on QR2. Sixteen squares are in this way related, and there are four such sets of squares on the chessboard, as lettered on the supplementary diagram. If one player moves to a B square, the other retains the opposition if he also moves to a B square, and so on. For instance, if White plays 1. KKt1 (a D square) Black may reply 1... KQ6, 1... KB6, 1... KQ4, or 1... KB4 (all of which are D squares), thus retaining the opposition in one form or another.

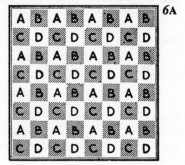

6A This pattern might be termed the natural oppositional field. It may be (and usually is) disturbed locally by pawns, as already seen in Example 2*.

7 A player who has the opposition need never lose it—unless pawns interfere. Here they do not, and Black draws an apparently hopeless position by maintaining the defensive opposition.

The marked-off areas show the lower two ranks as White's domain, and the queen's side area as Black's. White always wins if his king gets into Black's domain—regardless of the opposition. To get there White must move through the transitional area (the 25 squares on the king's side and back rank). If Black moves to the KB file or sixth rank, White advances the RP; and if Black captures White's KtP, White queens the RP and wins against Black's KtP, Example 303.

When White's king is in the transitional area, he wins with and draws without the opposition; when it is on the lower two ranks, the opposition is not significant.

1 ...   K—Q5

Black stays on K5 and Q5 until White plays to the third rank (transitional area) after which Black must take the opposition.

2 K—B2

It is no use sacrificing the RP, 2. PR5 KB4 3. KQ3 KKt4 4. KQ4 K×P 5. KB4 for Black takes the opposition after 5... KR3 6. K×P KKt3.

2 ...   K—K5

After 2... KB6? 3. PR5 White queens first.

3 K—Kt2   K—Q5
4 K—R2   K—K5
5 K—R3   K—Q4.

* Extensive disturbance may cause a whole group of squares in one part of the board to bear a unique relationship to a group elsewhere. The British composer C. D. Locock pioneered such related square problems (1892)—fortunately, perhaps, such things do not occur in play.

Drawn

The only move to draw, and probably the only instance of the oblique opposition in a practical position; for this ending does occur in play, e.g. Spielmann v. Makarczyk, Warsaw, 1934.

Black draws only by maintaining the opposition as in the table below, which also indicates the square letters corresponding with diagram **6A**.

White K.	Black K.
A KKt4	K5
KKt6 K8	K3
KKt8	K1 K3
QB8	QB3
QR8	QR3
B KR4 KB4	Q5
KR6 KB6 Q8	Q3
KR8 KB8	Q1 Q3
QKt8	QKt3
C KKt3 K3 KKt5	K4
KKt7	K2
D KR3 KB3 Q3 KB5 KR5	Q4
KR7 KB7	Q2

The defensive opposition here takes five forms: vertical direct, diagonal, horizontal direct, horizontal distant, and oblique.

8 Triangulation is another frequently used king manœuvre. One king purposefully moves round a triangle of three squares whilst his rival, who is in some way restricted, must shuttle to and fro on two squares. Obviously, one 'loses a move' in this fashion.

1 THE OPPOSITION

In practice a situation arises with, say, White to move, and it is desirable for him that the same position should be brought about with Black to move.

Having to move Black must submit to one of two threats: 1... KQ1 (Kt1) 2. KQ6 (taking the opposition) 2... KB1 3. PB7 KKt2 4. KQ7 KR2 5. KQ8 queening the BP; or 1... KB2 2. KB5 KB1 3. KKt6 wininng the RP.

Triangulation is often the means by which one or other of two closely related threats may be forced. White to play loses a tempo by moving round the triangle Q5-B4-Q4, whilst Black must move from B1 to Q1, or B1 to Kt1, for ... KB2 is always answered by KB5 winning the RP.

White wins

1 K—B4	K—Q1 (Kt1)
2 K—Q4	K—B1
3 K—Q5.	

Triangulation cannot be demonstrated with bare kings, for it is the pawns which restrict the defender. Two separate threats are necessary, and without the RPs this position would be drawn.

9 Quite a different manœuvre, the diagonal march, is peculiar to the kings. In travelling from one part of the board to another, the king may make a considerable detour from the straight path, without taking a greater number of moves.

White plays and wins

In this position White may get to QKt7 in four moves by moving along the rank; he also takes four moves by travelling diagonally via Q5; but in the latter case Black's king is kept out.

| 1 K—K6 | K—B6 |

1... KQ6 2. KQ5 KK6 3. KB6 KQ5 4. KKt7 comes to the same thing.

| 2 K—Q5 | |

A game, Schlage v. Ahues, Berlin, 1921, continued 2. KQ6? KQ5 3. KB6 KK4 4. KKt7 KQ3 5. K×P, with a draw because White's king is imprisoned after 5... KB2, a stock situation with the RP. The same thing would have happened if White had commenced 1. KK7?

2 ...	K—Kt5
3 K—B6	K—R4
4 K—Kt7	K—Kt4
5 K×P	K—B3
6 K—Kt8.	

White frees his king in time, and the pawn queens; the result of marching round two sides of a triangle (K—K6—Q5—B6—Kt7) instead of along the hypotenuse (K—K7—Q7—B7—Kt7).

2. KING AND PAWN v. KING

The circumstances under which the pawn wins are shown in Example 2: White must at least obtain the opposition with his king in front of (clear of obstruction by) his pawn; only thus can

7

he eventually gain control of the queening square.

10 The kings are on the same side of the pawn, but White's is backward. When his king is one file nearer the pawn than Black's, he may be able to gain the opposition by the stratagem of crossing over the queening file in front of his pawn.

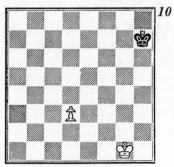

White plays and wins
Black plays and draws

1 K—B2	K—Kt3
2 K—K3	K—B4
3 K—Q4	K—K3
4 K—B5	K—Q2
5 K—Q5.	

Taking the direct opposition. Black to play draws by moving to the knight's file.

11 It is possible to cross the queening file behind the pawn, for which White's king needs to be two files nearer than Black's.

1 K—Q2	K—B2
2 K—B3	K—K3
3 K—B4.	

Only this wins; and after 3. KQ3 4. KQ4, or 3... KQ2 4. KQ5, White takes the opposition. Black draws with the move, by playing to the bishop's file, 1... KB2, or 1... KB1 2. KQ2 KK2 3. KB3 KQ2.

In neither of these examples could White have obtained the direct opposi-

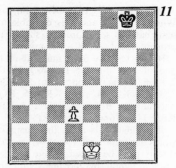

White plays and wins
Black plays and draws

tion by moving up on the same side of the pawn. If here 1. KK2? KB2 2. KB3 White has the distant opposition but it does him no good, 2... KK2 3. KK3 KQ2, and now if White advances to the fourth rank Black takes the opposition.

Examples 2, 10 and 11, show a pawn on Q3; but the same rules apply to any pawn (except the RP) on its second, third or fourth rank.

12 A pawn on the fifth rank wins if the king is in front of it, whether or not White has the opposition, for in either case White gains control of the queening square (except with RP).

With the move, White plays 1. K—Kt6 (taking the opposition; if 1. PKt6? KB1 2. PKt7 ch. KKt1 3. KKt6 stalemate) 1...K—R1 2. K—B7 K—R2

White wins

8

3. P—Kt6 ch. K—R1, and White mates in three.

Black does no better with the opposition:

    1 ...   K—R2

Setting a trap. Instead, 1... KB1, taking the opposition, is answered by 2. PKt6.

    2 K—B7   K—R1
    3 K—Kt6

Not 3. PKt6? stalemate.

    3 ...   K—Kt1
    4 K—R6   K—R1

Black has the opposition, and White cannot outflank, but at this stage a simple pawn advance squeezes Black out.

    5 P—Kt6   K—Kt1
    6 P—Kt7.

13 A pawn on the sixth wins if White obtains the vertical direct opposition with his king alongside his pawn (except with RP).

    1 K—B5   K—B1
    2 K—B6

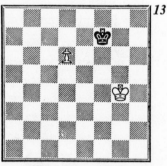

White plays and wins

Taking the opposition. 2. KK6? KK1 3. PQ7 ch. KQ1 4. KQ6 stalemates. If White's king is not controlling the queening square, the pawn checking on the seventh draws.

    2 ...   K—K1
    3 K—K6   K—Q1
    4 P—Q7.

14 The heavy line shows 'the square of the pawn' and if Black's king cannot get into it, he cannot stop the pawn—a rule which, of course, applies to all pawns. After 1. P—R4 Black is unable to enter the square (which has diminished correspondingly) so the pawn runs through without let or hindrance.

With the move Black gets into the square.

    1 ...   K—B4

Threatening to stop the pawn, 2. PR4 KK3 3. KKt4 KQ2 4. KKt5 KB2 5. KR6 KKt1 and 6... KR1. In endings with RP the opposition doesn't matter—if Black's king gets in front of the pawn he always draws.

White plays and wins
Black plays and draws

1... KB5? enters the square, but Black's retreat is then obstructed, 2. KB4 KK4 3. KB5 KK3 4. KB6 KK2 5. PR4 KQ1 6. KKt7, and the pawn queens.

    2 K—B4   K—K3
    3 K—B5   K—Q2
    4 K—Kt6   K—B1

The key square in the ending with RP.

    5 K—R7

White prevents Black from blocking the pawn only by blocking it himself. With the RP this draws, because the crossover stratagem of Example 10 is not possible.

9

| 5 ... | K—B2 |
| 6 P—R4 | K—B3 |

6... KB1 also draws.

| 7 P—R5 |

If 7. KKt8 KKt3; and if 7. KR6 KB2 or even 7... KB4.

| 7 ... | K—B2 |

Not 7... KKt4? 8. PR6 KB3 9. KKt8.

| 8 P—R6 | K—B1 |
| 9 K—Kt6 |

If 9. KR8 KB2 10. PR7 KB1 stalemate.

| 9 ... | K—Kt1 |
| 10 P—R7 ch. | K—R1 |
| 11 K—R6 stalemate. |

The idea of confining White's king to the rook's file also draws when the kings are farther back, e.g. White K at QR3, P at QR2, *v.* Black K at QB6.

3. KING AND TWO PAWNS *v.* KING

With a few exceptions this is usually a simple win.

15 Doubled pawns on the fifth and sixth ranks draw if the defender obstructs them and if he has the opposition.

From here the 13th match game Eliskases *v.* Bogoljubow, 1938, continued:

| 1 K—B1 |

15

Drawn

Not 1. KKt1? KKt6 2. KB1 PB7 3. KK2, when either 3... KKt7 or 3... PB8=Q ch. wins.

1 ...	K—B4
2 K—B2	K—K5
3 K—B1	K—K6
4 K—K1

White takes the opposition.

| 4 ... | P—B7 ch. |
| 5 K—B1. |

A draw was agreed, for if Black guards the PB7 he stalemates, and if he abandons it he cannot win with the other pawn.

16 Doubled pawns (except RPs) win if farther back, for a tempo-move by the extra pawn gains the opposition.

| 1 K—Q4 |

Not 1. KB4? KKt3, when the extra pawn is lost.

| 1 ... | K—Kt3 |
| 2 K—B4 | K—Kt2 |

If 2... KB2 2. KB5 KKt2 3. PKt6 KR3, White gains the opposition by 4. PKt7 KR2 5. PKt8=Q ch., but must not play 4. KB6? stalemate.

16

White wins

3 K—B5	K—B2 (R2)
4 P—Kt6 ch.	K—Kt2
5 K—Kt5	K—Kt1
6 K—R6	K—R1
7 P—Kt7 ch.	K—Kt1
8 P—Kt5.

The decisive tempo-move.

17 United pawns (pawns on adjoining files) always win.

White wins

In this case a pawn must be sacrificed to gain the opposition: 1. K—K4 K—R1 2. K—Q5 K—Kt2 3. P—R8=Q ch. (3. KQ6 KR1 4. KB7? stalemate) 3... K×Q 4. K—B6—diagonal opposition.

United pawns can always defend themselves: if here 1... K×P the other pawn goes on to queen.

18 Disconnected pawns one file apart also defend themselves on whatever rank they stand; but, like united pawns, their advance cannot be forced without the help of their king.

1 ...   K—R3

Black may play instead 1... K—Kt1 2. K—Kt3 (advancing a pawn loses them both, Black attacking the foremost one,

White wins

2. PR6? KR2, or 2. PB6? KB2) 2... K—Kt2 3. K—B4, etc.

If 1... KB3 2. PR6.

2 P—B6   K—R2

If Black captures the rear pawn the other advances to queen.

3 K—Kt3   K—R3

After 3... KKt1 4. PR6, Black is in zugzwang,* for if 4... KR1 5. PB7, or if 4...KB1 5. PR7. Black can be caught in this fashion only when the pawns are on the sixth, for then he has no suitable retreat square.

4 K—B4   K—R2
5 K—K5   K—R3
6 K—Q6.

Avoiding a trap, 6. PB7? KKt2 7. KQ6 KB1, when either 8. PR6 or 8. KB6 stalemates.

19 Curiously, pawns two files apart cannot defend themselves if not beyond the fourth rank. With the move White's king succours his pawns; but Black to play successfully attacks them.

1 ...   K—R4
2 P—K5

After 2. KKt2 K×P 3. KB3 KKt4

White plays and wins
Black plays and draws

* Literally, 'compulsion to move', the term implies that Black must give way to White because he is under the necessity of having to move.

11

White cannot favourably take the opposition.

2 ...	K—Kt3
3 K—Kt2	K—B4
4 K—Kt3	K×P
5 K—Kt4	K—B3.

Black blocks the RP. This position is somewhat artificial—from any other square White's king could aid his QP, and in the event he draws only because he is saddled with a RP.

If White's pawns (two files apart) were on the fifth rank, then one of them queens by force regardless of the kings' positions. Black has not time to stop them both.

The rule for pawns three files apart is mainly of theoretical interest: on the third rank they can defend themselves in the absence of their king, but cannot advance unaided; on the fourth rank one of them queens by force. See Example 88.

4. KING AND PAWN v. KING AND PAWN

A draw is normal, but a few peculiarities must be known.

20 This trap must be watched for when approaching a pair of blocked

Whoever plays wins

pawns. White plays and wins by 1. KK6 (not 1. KK5? KB5) 1... KB5 2. KK5; or Black to play wins by 1... KB6.

21 This shows the inherent advantage of a blocked pawn on the fifth.

1 P—Kt5

Not 1. KK4? PKt4 2. KQ5 KKt2 3. KB5 KR3 4. KB6 KR2 5. K×P, for Black takes the opposition and draws, 5... KKt2, Example 2. If White's blocked pawn is on the second, third, or fourth, rank, an outflanking movement gaining Black's pawn merely draws, because Black always takes the opposition in this way.

1 ...	K—Kt2
2 K—K4	K—B2
3 K—K5	

White plays and wins
Black plays and draws

Outflanking; but not 3. KQ5? KQ2, when Black draws, having the opposition.

| 3 ... | K—Q2 |
| 4 K—Q5 | |

With a blocked pawn on the fifth, White wins when he can outflank and capture Black's pawn. This he can do if he has the vertical opposition with his king also on the fifth, as here.

| 4 ... | K—B2 |
| 5 K—K6 | K—B1 |

Black is eventually squeezed out in all such cases as this.

6 K—Q6	K—Kt2
7 K—Q7	K—Kt1
8 K—B6	K—R2
9 K—B7	K—R1
10 K×P.	

The opposition does not save Black, Example 12.

With the move, Black draws simply by 1... PKt4, taking the opposition after White wins the pawn. Black also draws by 1... K—Kt2 2. P—Kt5 K—B2, for having a pawn on the fifth is not a magic formula, and after 3. K—K4 K—Q3 4. K—Q4 K—K3. White cannot gain Black's pawn.

A blocked pawn on the sixth wins if White can outflank, but if it is a KtP or RP, and Black's king is in the corner, nothing can be done, as shown in Example 24.

Blocked RPs on any rank often draw, because White wins only if, after capturing Black's pawn, he can get his king to its respective Kt7 or Kt8 square, Examples 9, 14.

22 With his pawn on an adjoining file Black has little trouble defending it if his king is near. If he has a RP against a KtP, he may be able to sacrifice it to saddle White with a RP.

Here Black cannot defend his pawn, but may sacrifice it, and thus get the opposition.

1 ...   P—B5

After 1... KKt2? 2. KKt5 PB5 3. P×P, or 1... KKt1 (R2)? 2. KKt5 PB5 3. K×P, White obtains the opposition.

2 P×P   K—Kt1

22

White plays and wins
Black plays and draws

Either 2... KR2? 3. KR5 or 2... KKt2? 3. KKt5 loses.

3 K—Kt4   K—B1
4 K—Kt5

White cannot get the direct opposition; if 4. KB5 (R5) KB2.

4 ...   K—Kt2.

White to play prevents an effective sacrifice, 1. K—Kt5 P—B5 (1... KKt2 2. K×P KB2 3. PKt4) 2. K×P (2. P×P? KKt2) 2... K—R2 (Kt1) 3. K—Kt5 K—Kt2 4. P—Kt4, taking the opposition.

23 When each side has a passed pawn there is often a race between them, and sometimes one player queens whilst his opponent gets his pawn only to the seventh, or both players queen, one subsequently having a mating finish. These possibilities are fully analysed in the chapter on queen endings.

This analysis from the game Cortlever *v.* van Scheltinga, Beverwijk, 1947, shows some other stratagems, available to Black because his king is better placed. Firstly, if White's king goes to QB4, Q3, Q1, or K1, Black may queen with check; secondly, if White's king goes to Q4 or QB3, Black has a skewer check (at QR8) after both players have queened; thirdly, Black may be able to stop White's pawn whilst queening his own pawn.

1 K—B5

23

Black wins

If 1. KB4 KK6 2. PR4 PB5; or if
1. KKt4 KK6 2. PR4 KB5.

1 ...   K—K4

Not 1... KK5? 2. PR4 KB5 3. KQ4
KKt5 4. KK3 PB5 ch. 5. KB2 blocking
the BP.

2 P—R4

If 2. K—Kt4 P—B5? 3. K—B3 K—K5
4. K—Q2 K—B6 5. P—R4 K—Kt6
(5... KKt5 6. KK2) 6. P—R5 (6. KK2?
KKt7 7. PR5 PB6 ch.) 6... P—B6 with
a draw.

To 2. K—Kt4 Black should answer
2...K—K5 3. K—Kt3 (3. PR4 KB5)
3... P—B5 4. K—B2 K—K6 5. K—Q1
K—B7 6. P—R4 P—B6 7. P—R5
K—Kt7, and he queens with check.

If 2. KB4 KK5 3. KB3 KK6, but not
3... PB5? 4. KQ2 KB6 5. PR4 KKt5
6. KK2.

2 ...   P—B5
3 K—B4

After 3. PR5 PB6 4. PR6 KB3 Black
queens his pawn, and stops White's.

3 ...   K—K5
4 K—B3

If 4. PR5 PB6 5. PR6 PB7 6. PR7,
and Black queens with check.

4 ...   K—K6
5 P—R5   P—B6
6 P—R6   P—B7
7 P—R7   P—B8=Q
8 P—R8=Q   Q—R8 ch.

Winning White's queen by a skewer
check, a not uncommon device.

5. KING AND TWO PAWNS v. KING AND PAWN

An understanding of the many
possible blocked positions is essential;
and a fairly thorough examination of
these is therefore given.

There are 35 different kinds of position
where White has a protected passed
pawn, and most of these he can usually
win.

24 Three positions with Black RP or
KtP on the second rank are drawn
because of stalemate threats.

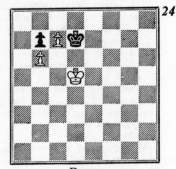

Drawn

Black cannot be winkled out, 1.
P—B8=Q ch. (1. KK5 KB1 2. KK6
stalemate) 1... K×Q 2. K—K6 K—Q1
3. K—Q6 K—B1 4. K—K7 K—Kt1
5. K—Q8 K—R1 6. K—B8 (B7) stalemate.

24A (no diagram). The four basic
positions where Black has a BP or
Centre P on the second rank (the position
of diagram 24 moved one, two, three, or
four files to the right) are easily won.
White may either sacrifice the passed
pawn and squeeze Black out, or outflank
on the other side.

25 Only one position with Black's
pawn on the third rank is drawn—when

Drawn

14

5 KING AND TWO PAWNS v. KING AND PAWN

he has a rook's pawn. 1. K—Q4. (After 1. PKt7 K×P 2. KQ5 White wins Black's RP but his own is useless.) 1... K—Q3 3. K—K4 K—B3 3. K—K5 K—Q2 4. K—Q5 K—Q1 5. K—Q6 (5. KB6 KB1 6. PKt7 ch. KKt1 7. KKt6 stalemate) 5... K—B1 6. K—B6 K—Kt1 7. P—Kt7 K—R2 8. K—B7 stalemate.

26 The other six positions are won for White whose simplest way is to sacrifice one pawn in order to outflank

26

White wins

Black's position: 1. P—Q7 K×P (1... KK2 2. KB5 K×P 3. KB6) 2. K—B5 (not 2. KK5? KK2) 2... K—K2 3. K—K5 K—Q2 4. K—B6, Example 21.

27 Black loses all seven positions where he has a pawn on the fourth. White must not sacrifice his passed pawn as in the preceding example, but should outflank the enemy's position.

White must take more care against a RP, because of stalemate threats.

1 K—B2

Now Black cannot retain the (distant) opposition by playing to QB3—in fact his whole defence is obstructed because White's pawn controls this square; for the same reason, the immediate outflanking also suffices: 1. KQ3 KQ4 2. KK3 KK4 3. KB3 KQ4 4. KB4 KQ3 5. KK4 KK3 6. KQ4 KQ3 7. KB4, gaining the opposition.

27

White wins

| 1 ... | K—Q3 |
| 2 K—Q2 | |

Taking the distant opposition.

| 2 ... | K—K3 |
| 3 K—B3 | |

Outflanking.

3 ...	K—Q4
4 K—Q3	K—K4
5 K—B4	K—Q3
6 K—Q4	K—B2

If 6... KQ2 7. KB5 KB2 8. PKt6 c KKt2 9. KKt5 KKt1 10. K×P; this is the usual winning method.

7 K—Q5

7. KB5 also wins, but not if White continues 7... KKt2 8. PKt6? KR3 9. KB6 stalemate.

| 7 ... | K—Kt3 |

If 7...KKt2 8. KB5 KR2 9. KB6, but not 9. PKt6 ch.?

| 8 K—Q6 | K—Kt2 |
| 9 K—Q7 | K—Kt1 |

9... KKt3 10. KB8 KR2 11. KB7 transposes. 9... KR1 permits mate in 5.

| 10 K—B6 | K—R2 |
| 11 K—B7 | |

11. PKt6 ch. KR1 12. KKt5 wins, but White must avoid the stalemates 12. KB7? or 12. PKt7 ch.? KKt1 13. KKt6.

| 11 ... | K—R1 |
| 12 K—Kt6. | |

15

28 When Black's pawn is on the fifth, two new defensive ideas are possible: the defensive opposition, shown in its most extensive form in Example 7; and the counter attack with the BP now to be illustrated.

With the move Black may choose either defence: 1... K—K2 taking and holding the opposition as in the Example quoted, or 1...K—K4 2. K—Kt6 K—K5 3. K—Kt5 K—Q6 4. P—Kt5 K×P 5. P—Kt6 K—Q7 6. P—Kt7 P—B6 7. P—Kt8=Q P—B7, when the BP on the seventh draws, Example 305.

White is no better off with the opposition:

1 K—Kt6

When Black's pawn is on the fourth, fifth, or sixth, it is no use White sacrificing the passed pawn, 1. PKt5 KQ3 2. KB6 KB4 3. KK5 K×P 4. KQ4 KKt3 5. K×P, for Black takes the opposition, 5... KB3.

28

Drawn

1 ...	K—K4
2 K—Kt5	K—K5
3 K—Kt4	

The outflanking 3. KB6 is answered by 3... KQ6.

| 3 ... | K—K4 |

Albin playing against Charousek, Berlin, 1897, made the mistake of playing 3... KQ6? 4. PKt5 K×P 5. PKt6 KQ7 6. PKt7 PB6 7. PKt8=Q PB7, when White's king was near enough for a mating attack: 8. QKt2 KQ8 9. KB3

KQ7 10. KB2 KQ8 11. QQ4 ch. KB8 12. QQKt4 KQ8 13. QK1 mate.

| 4 K—Kt3 | K—K5 |

Not 4...KB4? 5. KB3 KK4 6. KK3 KQ4 7. KB4 outflanking and winning the BP.

When White's king is on KB3, or K3, Black must be able to take the vertical direct opposition: he has no other defence.

| 5 K—B2 | K—B5 |

If 5 ...KK4? 6. KK3; or if 5... KB4 (Q4)? 6. KB3.

| 6 K—K2 | K—K5 |
| 7 K—Q2 | K—Q4 |

Not 5... KB5(B4)? 6. KB2 outflanking on the queen's side.

| 8 K—Q1 | K—K3 |

Instead he may play 8... KK5 9. KK2 KB5, or 8... KQ3, but not 8...KB3? 9. KK2 KQ4 10. KB3, when he cannot take the direct opposition.

9 K—B1

The distant opposition is no use, 7. KK2 KB3 8. KB2 KK3 etc.

9 ...	K—Q4
10 K—Kt2	K—B3
11 K—R2	K—Kt3

Not 11... KKt4? 12. KR3, when White wins.

| 12 K—R3 | K—Kt4. |

White cannot get through on the queen's side.

In all this, the opposition only really mattered when White's king was on K3 or KB3.

However, the opposition may also be significant when White's king is on K8 or Q8. If in the diagram position White's king is at K8 (instead of KKt7) we get the following play: Black to move loses (White having the opposition) 1... K—Q3 2. K—Q8 (2. KB7? KK4 3. KK7 KK5 4. KQ6 KQ6) 2... K—B3 (2... KK3 or K4 3. KB7) 3. K—K7 K—Kt4 4. K—Q6 K—R5 5. K—Q5 K—Kt6 6. K—Q4. White to move draws:

1. K—B8 K—B3 (the defensive opposition; the counter attack 1... KK4 also draws) 2. K—K8 K—K3 (now 2... KK4? 3. KQ7 KK5 4. PKt5 KQ6 loses) 3. K—Q8 K—Q3 (3... KK4? 4. KB7) 4. K—B8 K—B3 (the only move) 5. K—Kt8 K—Kt4 (the defensive opposition, 5... KKt3, also draws) 6. K—B7 K—R5 7. K—B6 K—Kt6 8. P—Kt5 K×P 9. P—Kt6 K—Q7 10. P—Kt7 P—B6 11. P—Kt8=Q P—B7.

29 If 1... KB5 White outflanks on the queen's side, 2. KB2 KK5 3. KKt2 KQ4 4. KR3 KB3 5. KKt4 KQ4 6. KKt5; whilst if 1... KQ4 White outflanks on the king's side, 2 KK3 KQ3 3. KK4 KK3 5. PQ5 ch. KQ3 6. KQ4. White to play loses a move by a triangulation:

1 K—Q1

29

White wins

The customary outflanking 1. KK2 KB5 2. KB2 KK5 3. KKt3? fails after 3... KQ6 4. PQ5 K×P 5. PQ6 KKt7 6. PQ7 PB6 7. PQ8=Q PB7, and, with Black's king on the knight's file, the BP on the seventh here draws, Example 304.

1 ...   K—Q4

Black's trouble is that he cannot stay on the K-file (White's QP interferes, controlling K5), and if 1... KB5 2. KB2; whilst after 1... KQ6 2. PQ5 K×P 3. KB1 the BP is blocked.

2 K—K2

Threatening 3. K—K3.

2 ...   K—K5
3 K—Q2.

With the kings placed elsewhere Black sometimes draws by getting his BP to the seventh. Sometimes an alternative, the defensive opposition is in two cases the only resource—with White king at QR8(QKt8) and Black king at QR3(QKt) Black draws with or loses without the opposition.

30 When all the pawns are on the centre files, White always wins, except when his king is on the back rank and he does not have the opposition, i.e. 1. KKt8 KKt3 2. KB8 KB3 3. KQ8 KQ3—Black maintains the opposition all along the rank without leaving the square of White's pawn.

30

White plays and draws
Black plays and loses

Having the opposition, White wins easily: 1... KKt3 2. KKt8 KB3 3. KB8 KQ3 4. KQ8 KK3 5. KK8, outflanking after 5... KB3 6. KQ7, or 5... KQ3 6. KB7. Black cannot defend by capturing White's QP, because a centre P on the seventh loses against a queen, Example 303.

31 Regardless of the positions of the kings, this ending is lost for Black. The defensive opposition does not save him because he cannot play his king to the KR file, for then White answers P—B5. After 1. KKt8 KKt3 White wins by

I PAWN ENDINGS

White wins

playing his king via KR8 to KR3 and around to QKt3, a lengthy but simple process.

32 Finally, two other cases with Black pawn on the fifth are always won. This example compares with no. 27.

1 K—B1

The KtP, controlling QB5, prevents Black's maintaining the (distant) opposition. The routine outflanking is more long-winded, 1. KQ2 KQ5 2. KK2 KK5 3. KB2 KB5 4. KKt2 KK5 (4... KKt5 5. PKt5) 5. KKt3.

1 ...	K—Q4
2 K—Q1	K—K4
3 K—B2	K—Q5
4 K—Q2	K—B5
5 K—K3	K—Q4

The counter-attack 5... KKt6 fails, as will be seen later.

White wins

6 K—Q3	K—B3
7 K—B4	K—Kt3
8 K—Q5	

Not 8. PKt5? KR4 9. KB5 stalemate.

8 ...	K—Kt4
9 K—K5	

The same finesse as on the first move, but this time White gains the horizontal opposition because Black's king cannot occupy R4 or B4.

9 ...	K—B3
10 K—K6	K—Kt3
11 K—Q6	K—Kt4
12 K—B7	K—B5

If 12... KR3 13. KB6 KR2 14. KKt5.

13 K—B6	K—Kt6
14 P—Kt5	K×P
15 P—Kt6	K—R7
16 P—Kt7	K—R8
17 P—Kt8=Q	P—R6.

A RP on the sixth is helpless against a queen: 18 Q—K5 ch. K—Kt8 19. Q—K4 ch. K—Kt7 (19... KR8 20. QB2 PR7 21. QB1 mate) 20. Q—Kt4 ch. K—R7 21. K—Q5. Alternatively, White's king is near enough for a mating finish: 18. KB5 PR7 19. KKt4 KKt8 20. QQ6 PR8=Q 21. QQ1 ch. KKt7 22. QQ2 ch. KKt8 23. KKt3.

33 When Black's pawn is on the sixth rank, he draws if he can capture White's rear pawn.

White plays and draws
Black plays and loses

18

5 KING AND TWO PAWNS *v.* KING AND PAWN

This is one of two basic positions which correlate to nos. 7 and 28. To win, White needs to have the opposition with his king on the second rank, 1... KQ5 2. KB3 KB4 3. KK3, etc.

White to play only draws: 1. K—B2 K—B5 2. K—Kt2 K—K6 (2... KKt5 also draws) 3. P—Kt4 (3. KKt3 KQ7) 3... K—Q7 (or 3... KQ5). Instead White may try 1. K—K1 K—K6 2. K—Q1 K—Q5 (not 2...KB6? 3. KB1 KK6 4. KKt1) 3. K—B1 K—B4 4. K—Kt1 K—Kt4 (4... KKt5? 5. KR2) 5. K—R1 K—R4 6. K—R2 K—Kt5.

34 In three basic positions (as diagrammed, or the position moved one or two files to the left) White wins regardless of the opposition, if his king gets to the second rank (one exception: in this position White K at QR2 does not necessarily win).

White plays 1. K—K2 (or 1. KB2) 1... K—B4 2. K—K3 K—K4 3. P—Q4 ch. K—Q4 4. K—Q3.

Black to play:

1 ...   K—B6

White plays and wins
Black plays and draws

In this particular position White has outflanking threats on either wing; consequently 1... KK6? loses after 2. KQ1 KB6 3. KB1 KK6 4. KKt1 KQ5 5. KR2 KB4 6. KKt3.

2 K—Q1

2. KB1 KK6 3. KKt2 KQ7 also draws.

2 ...	K—K6
3 K—B1	K—Q5
4 K—Kt1	K—B4
5 K—R2	K—Kt5
6 K—R1	K—Kt4.

The only move. If 6... KR6 (5, 4)? 7. KKt1 KKt5 8. KB1 KB4 9. KQ1 KQ5 10. KK2; and if 6... KB4? 7. KKt1 KKt4 8. KB1.

34A (no diagram). In two positions, where Black has a blocked centre pawn on the sixth, White will be able to outflank on one wing or the other, and normally wins unless Black's king can attack White's rear pawn.

There are 28 basic positions where White has a backward pawn.

35 Two positions with Black's pawn on the second rank offer stalemate draws because White has a rook's pawn.

Drawn

Here an exchange leaves White a useless RP. 1. P—Kt6 K—Kt1 (1... P×P? 2. PR7) 2. P—Kt7 (2. KKt5 P×P) stalemate.

36 In the other case also Black cannot be dug out of the corner. 1. K—Q5 K—B1 2. K—K6 K—Kt1 3. K—Q7

19

I PAWN ENDINGS

36

Drawn

K—R1 4. P—R6 K—Kt1 (4... P×P?
5. KB7) 5. P—R7 ch. K—R1 stalemate.

37 The five other positions with
Black's pawn on the second rank may be
won by White regardless of whether or
not he has the opposition.

In this particular case White is better
off with his pawn at QB5 than at QB7.

1 K—K5

Not 1. PB6 ch? P×P ch.? 2. KB5
KQ1 3. KQ6 KB1 4. K×P and White
wins; with (four) other pawn configurations this method is decisive, but here
Black should reply 1... KB1 2. PB7
KQ2, Example 24. White must get his
king to Q7 or Q8 before he advances
the BP.

1 ...   K—B3

1... KK2 fails against 2. PB6 KQ1
3. P×P. Black cannot maintain the

37

White wins

opposition when White's pawns are so
far forward.

2 K—Q4	K—Q2
3 K—Q5	K—B1
4 K—Q6	K—Q1
5 K—K6	K—B1

If 5... KK1 6. PB6 KQ1 9. P×P.

| 6 K—K7 | K—Kt1 |
| 7 K—Q7 | K—R1. |

White mates in five: 8. PB6 P×P.
9. KB7, etc.

The results of all 21 positions where
Black's pawn is on its third, fourth, or
fifth rank depend upon who has the
opposition—assuming the kings to be
more or less normally placed.

There are two main groups, according
to the basic pawn-configuration: 12
positions where White has a backward
BP or Centre P; and 9 positions, less
favourable for him, where he has a
backward KtP or RP.

38 The position of this diagram, and
the same moved one file left, or one or
two files to the right, and/or one rank
forwards or backwards comprise the
first group.

38

White plays and draws
Black plays and loses

White wins if he has the vertical direct
opposition with his king abreast of his
backward pawn because of the double
threat: either outflanking, 1... K—Q3

20

5 KING AND TWO PAWNS v. KING AND PAWN

2. K—B4 K—K3 3. K—K4 K—Q3
5. K—B5 soon winning Black's pawn;
or exchanging pawns, 1... K—B4
2. P—Q4 P×P ch. 3. K×P K—K3
4. K—B5 (Example 10) 4... K—Q2
5. K—Kt6 K—B1, and taking the
opposition, 6. K—B6.

Without the opposition White can
only set snares:

1 K—B2

If 1. KB3 KB4 2. KKt3 KK4.

1 ...   K—B3

Maintaining the vertical opposition is
the simpler way, and with blocked
centre pawns (Example 5) it would be
the only way; but here 1... K—K3 also
draws, 2. K—K2 (the distant opposition
is ineffective because there is not enough
space to outflank on the other side of
blocked BPs or KtPs) 2... K—B3
3. K—Q2 (3. KB2 KK3 4. KKt3 KK4)
3... K—K3 4. K—B2 K—Q3 5. K—
Kt3 K—B3 6. K—R4 K—Kt3.

Other replies lose the opposition:
1... KB4? 2. KB3; 1...KQ5? 2. KK2
KK4 3. KK3; or 1... KB5? 2. KK2
KKt4 3. KK3.

2 K—K2   K—K3.

Black can always hold the opposition.

39 Where there are blocked RPs
(Example 38 moved two files to the left)
there is no real threat of exchanging
pawns, for after 1... KQ4 2. PKt4

39

Drawn

P×P ch. 3. K×P, White has a useless
RP.

However, the three basic positions
where Black has a blocked RP on its
third, fourth, or fifth, rank can be won
for White if he has the opposition with
his king one rank farther forward, on a
level with his blocked pawn; and if here
1... K—Kt3? 2. K—Q4 (2. KB4? KB3
draws) K—B3 3. K—B4 a simple outflanking follows, 3... KKt3 4. KQ5
KKt2 5. KB5.

40 The remaining six positions
where White has a backward RP or KtP
are comprised in the diagram position,
and the same moved one file to the left
and/or one rank forwards or backwards.

White lacks the space for outflanking
on the side where the backward pawn is.

Black to play:

1 ...   K—B4
2 K—Q3

If 2. KB3 KK4 3. KKt4 KQ5.

2 ...   K—K4
3 K—B3   K—Q3

40

Drawn

4 K—B2	K—K3
5 K—Kt2	K—Q2
6 K—R3	K—B3
7 K—R4	K—Kt3.

White to play:

1 K—Q3   K—Q3

1... KB3? permits White to advance
his KtP, 2. KB3 KK3 3. PKt4 P×P ch.
4. K×P KQ3 5. KKt5, Example 11.

21

In this last variation, after 3... KQ3 4. PKt5 White wins; but even this would be ineffective if Black's pawn were on the fifth rank, thus correlating to Examples 7 and 28.

White can win if he has the opposition with his king abreast of his foremost (blocked) pawn, if 1... KK3? 2. KK4, following by outflanking, 2... KQ3 3. KB5 KQ2 4. KK5 KB3 5. KK6.

2	K—K4		K—K3
3	K—B4		K—B3.

Without the opposition White cannot make progress, if 4. KKt4 KK4.

When the pawns are not yet blocked, White normally wins. His usual method is to block the pawns at the right moment.

The pawn not directly opposed by an enemy pawn on the same file is termed the candidate, i.e. the candidate for queening, after a pawn-exchange; but in the ending of 2 unpassed pawns *v.* 1 pawn an exchange rarely leaves White the opposition, and the candidate more frequently becomes the backward pawn of Examples 35-40, or 5.

Where the candidate is a Centre P or BP, relating to Examples 5 and 38, White's chances are perceptibly better than where the candidate is a KtP or RP, corresponding to the less favourable Examples 39 and 40.

41 This particular ending BP+ Centre P. *v.* Centre P relates to Examples 24A, 26, 27, 31, 34A, 37, and 38. The general winning idea is to transpose to Example 38; but if White's king were more advanced, he would instead make a direct attack on Black's pawn.

1	K—B2		K—B5
2	P—Q3		K—K4

If 2...P—Q4 3. P—B3 K—K4 4. K—B3 K—B4 (4... PQ5 5. PB4) 5. P—Q4 K—Kt4 6. K—B3 K—B4 7. K—Q3 K—K3 (7... KB5 8. PB4) 8. K—B2 K—Q3 9. K—Kt3 K—B3 10. K—R4, Example 38.

3 K—K3   K—Q4

If 2... PQ4 3. PQ4 ch. KB4 4. KQ3; but not 3. PB3? PQ5 ch. 4. P×P ch. KQ4 5. KK2 K×P—White must always guard against this trap.

4 P—B3

Prematurely advancing the candidate often leads to an unwelcome pawn exchange: 4. PB4 ch? KB4 5. KK4 PQ3 6. KK3 PQ4.

41

White wins

4	...		K—K4
5	P—B4		P—Q3

If 5... PQ4 6. PQ4 ch. KK3 7. PB5, Example 27.

6 P—Q4 ch.   K—K3

6... KB3 7. KK4 transposes; alternatively, White may reply 7. KB4 KK3 8. KKt5, outflanking.

7 K—B4

Not 7. KK4? PQ4 ch.

7 ...   K—B3
8 P—Q5.

White takes care to block the pawns so that he is left with the opposition, Example 38.

The ending of 2 Centre pawns *v.* 1 Centre pawn is as simply won.

42 The ending Centre P+BP *v.* BP is hardly less favourable for White, but a new drawing resource makes its appearance—the BP-on-the-seventh of Examples 29 and 304. For this Black's

5 KING AND TWO PAWNS *v.* KING AND PAWN

pawn must be on the fourth rank, and White's pawns on the third rank; if they are not yet opposed in this way, White should win.

In this position after Dedrle, 1924, White cannot win if he has the opposition!

1 K—B3   K—K4
2 K—K3

The special circumstances that make this position a draw follow the normal outflanking 2. KKt4, when Black has available the counter-attack 2... PB5 3. PQ4 ch. KK5, Example 29.

If 2. PB4 KB4, Black has the opposition, Example 38.

2 ...   K—B4

42

White plays and draws
Black plays and loses

Mason states that sometimes one wants to have the opposition, and sometimes (more rarely) one wants not to have it. Here Black wants not to have the opposition; instead he opposes White's king in knight's move fashion, so that if White plays PB4 Black may then take the opposition and draw.

3 K—Q2

White cannot outmanœuvre Black by temporizing moves, e.g. 3. KK2 KB3 (or 3... KK3 4. KQ2 KK4) 4. KB2 KK3 5. KKt2 KB3.

3 ...   K—K3

3... K—K4 is also sound.

4 K—B2   K—Q3(Q2)

And here 4... K—Q4 5. K—Kt3 (5. KKt2 KB3) P—B5 ch. also draws.

5 K—Kt3   K—B2

Forced, for if 5... KB3? 6. KB4, and White, having the opposition, makes a turning movement round the pawn, 6... KQ3, 7. KKt5 KQ4 8. PB4 ch.

6 K—R3   K—B3

And not 6... KKt3? 7. KR4, for White either outflanks on the queen's side after 7... KB3 8. KR5, or wins on the king's side after 7... KR3 8. KKt3 KKt4 9. KB2 KB3 10. KQ2 KQ3 11. KK3, when Black cannot take the non-opposition, and loses after 11... KK4 12. PB4, Example 38.

7 K—R4   K—Kt3
8 K—R3   K—Kt4

8... KB3, as before, is playable; but not 8... KB2? 9. KKt3 and now: 9... KB3 10. KB4, or 9... KQ3 10. KR4, or 9... KKt3 10. KB2 winning on the king's side.

9 K—Kt3   P—B5 ch.

With the move Black loses because he has the opposition:

1 ...   K—K4

If 1... PB5 2. P×P, Example 16; but not 2. PQ4? which here draws.

2 K—B3   K—B4
3 P—B4.

43 As shown by Keres, 1943, the drawing method of the last example does not apply when the BP is on the fifth rank.

1 K—R2

Either 1. KKt1? PB6 2. PQ3 KB4, Example 34, or 1. KKt2? PB6 ch., draws.

1 ...   K—B4

If 1... KKt4 2. KR3 KR4 3. KKt2-B1-Q1-K2. If 1... PB6 2. PQ3, Example 34.

2 K—Kt2   K—B3

In order to answer 3. KB3 by KB4, or 3. KR3 by KKt4.

23

43

White plays and wins
Black plays and draws

3 K—B1	K—Q4
4 K—Q1	K—K4(K5)
5 K—K2	K—B5

If 5... KK5 6. PB3, Example 38.

6 P—Q4

The double pawn moves makes the difference. 6. PQ3? KK4 draws; whilst the outflanking 6. KB2 KK5 7. KKt3? fails against 7... PB6.

6 ...	K—K5
7 P—B3.	

As Example 29.

With his pawn on the fifth Black has a new drawing resource (available for the five pawn configurations related to Examples 33 and 34) as here with the move: 1... P—B6 2. P—Q3 K—Kt4 (2... KR5? 3. KKt1; 2... KB4? 3. KKt1 KKt4 or Kt5 4. KB1).

44 With BP+KtP *v.* KtP White's chances are not less favourable than in the above examples, but a defensive resource of quite a different kind may sometimes be effective against pawns near the edge of the board.

This is shown in a study by Grigoriev, 1936, in which White's king is poorly placed.

After 1. P—B4? K—B7 2. K—Kt4 P—Kt3 3. K—R3 K—Q6 (the same position occurs after 1. PB3? KB7 2. PB4 KB6 3. KR4 PKt3 4. KR3 KQ6) White cannot escape the 'closed circle'

of moves: 4. K—Kt4 K—B7 (4... KQ5? 5. KKt5) 5. K—R4 K—B6 (5... KKt7? 6. PKt4; or 5. KQ6? 6. KKt5) 6. K—R3 K—Q6 (6... KB7? 7. PKt4; or 6... KQ5? 7. KKt4) 7. K—R4 K—B6 (7... KB7? 8. PKt4 7... KQ5? 8. KKt5) 8. K —R3 K—Q6, etc. If White tries 9. KKt2 KQ5 10. KB2, then 10... PKt4.

The same idea occurs one rank farther forward after 1. P—B4? (1. PB3? KB7 2. KKt4 KQ6 3. PB4 KB7 4. PB5 KQ6 5. KKt5 KB6) K—B7 2. P—B5 K—B6 3. K—R4 K—Q6 4. K—Kt4 K—Q5 5. K—Kt5 K—B6 6. P—Kt4 K—Kt6 7. K—R5 K—B5.

With pawns more centrally placed this attack from the rear would fail, White's king having enough space in which to outmanœuvre Black.

The key move is now clear:

1 K—Kt2	K—Q7
2 P—Kt4	

44

White plays and wins

2. PB4? KQ6 leads to variations already given. A draw follows 2. PB3? KQ6 3. PKt4 PKt3 4. KKt3 PKt4 5. KKt2 KQ7 6. KKt3 KQ6—an unusual use of the opposition in a variant of Example 38.

2 ...	K—K6

If 2... PKt4 3. KKt3 followed by PB4.

3 K—B3	P—Kt4
4 K—Kt2	

Not 4 KKt3? KQ5 5. KKt2 KB5 6. PB3, and the tempo-move with the

BP is prematurely spent. White first wants to get his king into the open.

4 ...   K—K5

If 4... KQ5 5. KKt3 KQ4 (else PB4) 6. KB3 KK5 7. KQ2 KQ5 8. PB3 ch., Example 38.

5 K—B1   K—Q4

5... KK6 is answered by 6. PB4, when Black's king is outside the square of the KtP. White wins because the BP has an option of moving either one or two moves at its first leap; and it would be correct to infer that this position one rank farther forward would be drawn in spite of the tempo-move.

6 K—Q2   K—Q5
7 P—B3 ch.

Winning as Example 38.

45 Of the three basic pawn configurations related to Examples 39 and 40, KtP+BP *v.* BP is the least unfavourable for White, who usually wins.

The critical position occurs when the pawns are about to make contact, the result depending on the opposition.

This position moved one file to the right would be won, White blocking the pawns to get Example 38; but here 1. P—B4 draws, Example 40; and 1. K—B3 K—B4 2. K—Kt3 leads nowhere after 2... K—K5 (2...PB5? 3. P×P).

Black to play: after 1... K—Q4 (1... KB4 2. KQ3) 2. K—B4 K—Q3

45

White plays and draws
Black plays and loses

White may continue his outflanking 3. KB5 KQ4 4. PB4 ch., or take the opposition after 3. KK4 KK3 4. PB4, Example 40.

The position of diagram 45 moved backwards or forwards one rank gives similar results.

Example *45*A (no diagram)—the position of no. 45 moved up two ranks. This is always won because 1. P—B6 transposes to Example 37.

46 Unless White's king is in front of his pawns (when a win is fairly straightforward) he will in general need to manœuvre with some care to win this ending.

We first show that with the move Black cannot save himself:

1 ...   K—B5

If 1... K—B4 (1... KK4 2. KQ3 KQ4 transposes) 2. K—Q3 K—Q4 (2... PB3 3. KK4 KB5 4. KK5) 3. P—B4 ch. K—B4 4. K—B3 P—B3 5. P—Kt3 (5. PKt4 ch.? KQ3 draws) 5... K—Kt3 (5... KQ3 6. KKt4) 6. K—Q4 K—Kt2 7. K—B5 K—B2 8. P—Kt4 K—Kt2 9. K—Q6 K—Kt3 10. P—B5 ch.

If 1... P—B4 (1... PB3 2. KQ3 PB4 3. PB4 ch. transposes) 2. K—K3 K—K4 3. K—Q3 K—Q4 4. P—B4 ch. K—K4 (now White wants this position with Black to play, and triangulates to this end) 5. K—B3 K—Q3 (else PKt4) 6. K—B2 K—K4 (6...KB3 7. KQ3 KQ3 8. KK4 KK3 9. PKt3—the decisive tempo; or 6... KK3 7. KKt3 outflanking) 7. K—Q3 K—Q3 (7... KB4 8. KB3 KK4 9. PKt4) 8. K—K4 K—K3 9. P—Kt3, Example 40.

In this last variation, the option of moving the candidate (KtP) one or two squares at its first move is decisive.

It is good policy to hold back the candidate pawn, because pawn exchanges are thus avoided, and because it may provide useful tempo-moves after the other pawns are blocked. In this particular ending White wins only because his king threatens to operate on both sides of the pawns; and he travels to the queen's side via QB2-QKt3. If the candidate pawn moves to QKt3, this route is blocked.

2 K—B2   K—Kt4

If 2...PB3 a series of triangulations follows, 3. KQ2 KKt6 4. KB1 KB5 5. KB2 PB4 6. KQ2 KKt6 7. KB1 KR5 8. KB2 PB5 9. KQ2 KKt6 10. KB1 KR5 11. KB2 KKt4 12. KQ2 KB4 13. KK3 KQ4 14. KB4.

3 K—Kt3

3. KQ3 KB4 leads nowhere, for if 4. KK4? KB5, and Black's counter-attack is successful when his pawn is unmoved, because it takes White so long to get at it.

46

White wins

3 ...   K—B4

If 3... PB4 4 PB4 ch. as before.

4 P—B4   K—Kt3

If 4... KQ5 5. KKt4 PB3 6. PKt3.

5 K—Kt4   P—B3
6 P—B5 ch.

6. KB3 also wins; but not 6. PKt3? PB4 ch., Example 40.

6 ...   K—B2
7 K—R5   K—Kt2
8 P—Kt3

Forcing Black to the QR file, for if now 8... KB2 9. KR6.

8 ...   K—R2
9 K—Kt4   K—Kt2
10 K—B4   K—B2

If 10... KR3 11 KB3 KR4 12 P Kt4ch
11 K—Q4   K—Q2
12 K—K5   K—K2
13 P—Kt4.

The tempo-move gives White the winning opposition, Example 40.

White to play triangulates, getting the diagram position with Black to move.

1 K—Q1

If 1. K—Q3 (1. KK3 KB5 2. KQ2 KQ4) K—B4 2. K—B2 (2. KK4? KB5) K—B5 3. K—Q2 K—Q4 White travels in circles—or more precisely in triangles.

After 1. K—Q3 K—B4 2. P—Kt3? White's access to the queen's side is barred and he draws, 2... K—Q4 3. K—K3 K—K4 4. P—Kt4 (4. PB4 PB4) 4... K—Q4 5. K—Q3 P—B3 6. P—B4 ch. K—Q3 7. K—K4 (7. KQ4 PB4 ch.) 7... K—K3, Example 45. 1. P—Kt3? also leads to Example 45 after: 1...P—B4 2. K—K3 K—K4 (or 2... PB5 3. PKt4, Example 28).

1. KB1? is the wrong way to tri-angulate, 1... PB4 2. KQ2 PB5 3. KK3 KK4, Example 40.

1 ...   K—B4

A withdrawal, 1... KQ3(B3), is answered by 2. KB2 to which Black cannot answer 2... KB5.

If 1... P—B4 2. K—K2 K—K5 (2... KB5 3. KQ2 KQ4 4. KK3 or 2... PB5 3. KB3) 3. P—Kt3, White has the opposition, 3... K—Q4 (3... PB5 4. P×P) 4. K—B3 K—K4 5. K—K3, Example 45.

2 K—B1   K—Q4
3 K—Q2.

47 The ending RP+KtP v. KtP also corresponds to the comparatively un-favourable Example 40, but is less favourable for White than the preceding example because his king cannot so effectively threaten to operate on both sides of the board.

This position is analagous to Example 45. White draws after 1. P—Kt4, Example 40; or after 1. K—K3 K—K4 2. K—B3 K—Q5. Black to play loses

White plays and draws
Black plays and loses

after 1... K—B4 (if 1... KK4 2. KB3 KQ4 3. KKt4 KB3 4. KR5—a turning movement around the pawn) 2. K—K4, etc., outflanking. The diagram position moved one rank forwards or backwards gives the same results.

48 In contrast to Example 45A where the pawns on the fifth always win, here they only draw because 1. P—Kt6 ch. leads to Example 36.

Nevertheless White wins if his king can make a turning movement round Black's pawn, which means getting it to QB7 or QB8 before advancing the KtP, or to QKt6. Black to play prevents this only by 1... P—Kt3 ch. 2. P×P ch. K—Kt2, Example 15. The following alternatives lose:

1...K—Kt1? 2. K—Kt6 K—R1 3. K—B7 K—R2 4. P—Kt6 ch. (or 4. PR6) 4... K—R1, and White mates in three.

1...K—B1? 2. K—Kt6 K—Kt1 3. P—R6 K—R1 (3... P×P 4. K×P, Example 12) 4. P×P ch. (4. KB7? KR2 5. P×P stalemate) 4... K—Kt1 5. K—R6 K—B2 6. K—R7.

1... K—Q2(Q1)? 2. K—Kt6 K—B1 3. K—R7 (3. PR6? KKt1 4. KR5 KR1 5. PKt6 KKt1 6. PR7 ch. KR1 stalemate) 3... K—B2 4. P—Kt6 ch. (4. PR6? PKt3 5. KR8 KB1 6. PR7 KB2 —a curious stalemate) 4... K—B1 5. P—R6.

Neither can White win with the move:

1 K—Q5	K—Q2

Either 1... KB1 or 1... KQ1 also draws.

2 K—K5	K—B2

Again he may play either 1... KB1 or 1... KQ1, but not 1... KK2? 2. PR6.

3 K—K6	K—Q1

After 3... KB1 4. KQ6 KQ1 5. PKt6 White gains the opposition, but nothing else, Example 36.

4 K—Q6	K—B1
5 K—K7	K—B2
6 K—K8	K—B1

Drawn

Black must not be tempted by 6... KQ3? 7. KQ8, nor must he play 6... K—Kt1? 7. K—Q7 K—R2 8. K—B7 (or 8. KB8 KR1 9. PR6 PKt3 10. PR7) 8... K—R1 9. K—B8 (9. PKt6? or 9. PR6? KR2 10. P×P stalemates) 8... K—R2 9. P—Kt6 ch. K—R1 10. P—R6, and White mates in two.

7 P—Kt6.

Drawing as Example 36.

49 Unlike the preceding examples, White in a general way wins only when his king plays in front of the pawns, which Black with the move prevents:

1 ...	K—B5
2 K—Q2	K—Q5
3 P—Kt3	

If 3. PR3 KB5 4. KB2 PKt4 5. PKt3 ch. KB4 6. KQ3 KQ4, Example 47.

3 ...   K—B4

First given by Sacconi, 1924. After 3... PKt4? 4. PR3 KB4 5. KK3 KQ4 6. KQ3 White has the winning opposition, Example 47.

4 K—B3

If 4. P—R3 K—Q4 5. K—K3 (5. PR4 KB4 6. KB3 PKt3) 5... P—Kt3 6. K—Q3 P—Kt4, Example 47.

4 ...   K—Kt4
5 P—R3

White plays and wins
Black plays and draws

An ingenious draw follows 5. PR4 ch. KR4 6. KB4 PKt3 7. KB3 PKt4.

5 ...   K—B4
6 P—R4

If 6. PKt4 ch. KKt4 7. KKt3 KB3 8. KB4 PKt4 ch.

6 ...   P—Kt3
7 P—Kt4 ch.   K—B3
8 K—B2

White takes the distant opposition.

8 ...   K—B2

The only move, keeping on the same file. White wins if he gets the distant opposition on the queen's file or farther east, e.g. 8... K—Q3? (8... KQ4? 9. KQ3 KB3 10. KK4 or 8... KQ2? 9. KQ3) 9. K—Q2 K—K3 (9... KB3 10. KK3 comes to the same thing)

10. K—B3 (outflanking) 10... K—Q4 11. K—Q3 K—B3 12. K—K4 K—Q3 13. K—Q4, Example 47.

9 K—Q3

White can hold the opposition on the bishop's file but cannot exploit it because of the common trap, 9. KB3 KB3 10. KB4 PKt4 ch.

9 ...   K—Q2

The only move, taking the distant opposition.

10 K—K3   K—K2
11 K—B4   K—Q3

Not 11... KB3? 12. PR5.

12 K—K4   K—K3.

As Example 47.

With the move White gets his king in front of his pawns, and wins by a direct attack upon, and turning-movement around, Black's pawn.

1 K—Kt3

Also 1. KQ3 wins; or 1. KB3 KKt4 2. KQ4 KKt5 3. KQ5 KKt4 4. KQ6 KKt3 5. KQ7, soon attacking Black's pawn—compare Example 48.

1 ...   K—Kt4
2 P—R4 ch.

Not 2. PR3? KR4 3. KB4 KR5 9. KB3 PKt4 10. KB2 PKt5.

2 ...   K—R4

If 2... KB4 3. KB3 PKt4 4. P×P K×P 5. KKt3, Example 2. With his king in front of his pawns White has less reason to fear a pawn exchange, because he may subsequently take the opposition.
If 2... K—B4 3. K—B3 P—Kt3 4. P—Kt3 K—Q4 (4... PKt4 5. PKt4 ch.) 5. K—Kt4 K—B3 6. K—B4 K—B2 (6... PKt4 ch. 7. P×P ch., Example 16) 7. K—Kt5 (the frontal attack) 7... K—Kt2 8. P—Kt4 K—B2 9. K—R6 —the turning-movement.

3. K—R3   K—R3

If 3... P—Kt3 4. P—Kt3 (not 3. PKt4 ch.? nor 3. KKt3? PKt4 4. P×P

28

5 KING AND TWO PAWNS *v.* KING AND PAWN

K×P, when Black has the opposition)
4... K—R3 (4... PKt4 5. PKt4 ch.)
5. K—Kt4.

    4 K—Kt4   K—Kt3
    5 P—R5 ch.

5. P—Kt3 ? seems no less effective but
only draws! 5... K—R3 6. K—B4
(6. KB5 KR4 7. KB4 PKt3 8. KB3
PKt4) 6... K—R4 7. K—B5 P—Kt4
8. P×P—a remarkable stalemate.

    5 ...   K—R3
    6 K—R4   K—R2
    7 K—Kt5   K—R1
    8 K—Kt6   K—Kt1
    9 P—Kt4.

Winning as shown in Example 48.

50 KtP+RP *v.* RP is without
question the least favourable pawn formation from White's point of view.

When Black's pawn is on the third or
fourth rank the critical positions
correspond to Examples 45 and 47.
Here 1. K—K3 K—K4 2. K—B3

50

White plays and draws
Black plays and loses

K—Q5 is pointless; if, instead, White
plays 1. KB2, Black answers 1... KB3,
holding the (distant) opposition. Black
to play loses, not having the opposition:
1... K—B4 2. K—K4 K—B3 3. K—Q4
K—Kt3 (3... KQ3 4. PR4) 4. K—B4
K—B3 5. P—R4, Example 39. The
diagram position moved up one rank
gives similar results.

51 Unlike the preceding cases,
however, Black draws if his pawn is on
the fifth rank, for after 1... K—B5

51

Drawn

2. K—K3 (2. KB2 KQ5 3. PKt4 P×P
e.p.) comes 2... P—R6 3. P—Kt 3 e.p.
ch. K—B6, Example 34.

52 A similar position with Black's
RP unmoved is always drawn unless
White's king can get to R6. After
1. P—Kt6 K—B1 (not 1... P×P?

52

Drawn

2. P×P, Example 13; but he may play
now or later 1... PR3, Example 25)
2. K—B6 K—Kt1 3. P—Kt7 (3. KKt5
P×P) 3... P—R3 4. K—Kt6, stalemate.

53 If White's king is on R6 he
cannot make a turning-movement (as
against a KtP, etc.), but he may win if he

29

can exchange pawns so as to leave himself the opposition as Example 13.

White here wins with or without the move because he has the option of playing the KtP one or two squares at its first leap. This permits him to lose a move if necessary: 1. P—Kt4 K—Kt1

53

White wins

2. P—Kt5 K—R1 3. P—Kt6 P×P 4. P×P K—Kt1 5. P—Kt7 (the pawn on the seventh must not give check); or Black to play, 1... K—Kt1 2. P—Kt3 with play as before.

White could win just as easily if, instead of the KtP, his RP were unmoved; but if neither pawn has this first move option, then the win depends upon whose move it is, White no longer controlling events.

54 In general, against a Black pawn at R2, White cannot win unless he at least has his king on the fourth rank, and one pawn (preferably the KtP) unmoved.

1 P—R4

This tempo-move gains the opposition. If 1. PKt3? White loses the first-move option, Black simply retreating 1... KKt2 2. KKt5 KR1 3. KR6 KKt1, when the eventual exchange of pawns leaves White without the opposition. Black's retreat must be calculated carefully, for if 2... KKt1? 3. KR6 White wins.

1 ...   K—B3

The alternatives are: 1... K—R3

2. P—R5 K—Kt2 3. K—Kt5 K—R1 (3... PR3 ch. 4. KB5 KB2 5. PKt4, Example 39) 4. K—R6, Example 53.

1... PR4 ch. 2. KB4 KB3 3. PKt3, Example 39.

1... P—R3 2. K—B4 K—R4 (2... KB3 3. PKt4, Example 50, or 2... PR4 3. KQ5) 3. P—Kt3, White may move his pawns from the second rank now that Black has done so, 3... K—Kt3 4. K—Q5 K—R4 5. K—B6 (5. KB5? stalemate) 5... K—Kt5 6. K—Kt6 P—R4 7. K—R6.

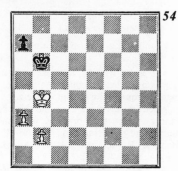

54

White wins

2 K—R5   K—Kt2

If 2... K—B4 3. P—Kt3 (now playable because Black's king cannot get back to the corner. 3. KR6? KKt5 4. PR5 KR5 5. PKt3 ch. KKt5 draws) 3... K—Q5 4. K—R6 K—B6 5. K×P.

3 K—Kt5.

Either 3... K—R1 (B2, B1) 4. K—R6 K—Kt1 5. P—R5, or 3... K—Kt1 4. K—R6 K—R1 5. P—R5, leads to Example 53.

Finally, if 3... PR3 ch. 4. KB5 KB2 5. PR5, Example 39.

55 Against a Black pawn on R2, White cannot in general win with his king only on the third rank.

1 K—Kt3

If 1. KB3, Black draws as shown by Reichhelm, 1873, by 1... P—R4 2. K—Kt3 (2. PR3 PR5, Example 39, or

2. PKt3 KKt4 3. PR3 KB4, Example 50) 2... K—Kt4 3. P—R4 ch. K—B4 4. K—B3 K—Q4, Example 39. White's tempo-move with the backward pawn is of no significance.

If 1. KQ3 KQ4.

1 ...	K—Kt4
2 P—R3	

If 2. PR4 ch. KB4 3. KB3 PR4.

2 ...	P—R3

As shown by von der Lasa and Bilguer, 1843, this draws.

Other moves lose:

2... KB4? 3. KR4 KB5 4. PKt4 KB6 5. KKt5 KKt6 6. PR4 KR6 7. PR5 KKt6 8. PR6.

2... P—R4? 3. K—B2 (only this wins, if 3. KB3? KR5, then 4. KB4 stalemate, or 4. KQ4 KKt6, or 4. KB2 KKt4 5. KQ3 KB4 7. KB3 PR5, Example 39) 3... K—B3 (3... KR5 4. KB3 KKt4 5. KQ4 KR5 6. KB5; or 3... KKt3 4. KB3 KB4 5. PKt3, Example 50; or 3... KB5 4. PKt3 ch. KQ5 5. KQ2 KB4 6. KB3, Example 50) 4. P—Kt3 K—Q3 5. K—Q2. This is Example 50, in which White wins with, or draws without, the distant opposition, 5... K—B3 6. K—K3 K—B4 7. K—K4, etc.

2... K—R4? 3. K—B3 (the only way) 3... K—Kt4 (3... KR5 4. KB4) 4. K—Q4 K—R5 5. K—B4 (5. KB5? KKt6, or 5. KB3? PR4) 5... K—R4 (5... PR3 6. KB5) 6. K—B5 K—R5 7. K—B6.

To 2... K—R4? White must not answer 3. K—B4? when Black stages an instructive counter-attack: 3... K—R5 4. K—B5 (4. KB3 PR4 as before) 4... K—Kt6 5. K—B6 K×P 6. P—R4 K—B6 7. P—R5 K—Q5 8. K—Kt7 K—B4 9. K×P K—B3 10. K—Kt8 (10. PR6 KB2) 10... K—Kt4.

3 K—B3	K—B4
4 P—Kt4 ch.	

If 4. KQ3 PR4 5. KB3 PR5, Example 39, or here 5. PKt3 KQ4, Example 50.

4 ...	K—Kt4

After 4... KKt3(Q3)? 5. KB4 KB3

6. PR4, or 4... KQ4? 5. PR4 KQ3 6. KQ4, White has the opposition, Example 50; but Black may play 4... KB3 5. KKt3 KKt4 6. PR4 ch. KKt3.

5 K—Kt3	K—B3

Not 5... KKt3? 6. KB4 KB3 7. PR4; nor 5... PR4? 6. PR4 ch. and 7. PKt5, Example 27.

6 P—R4	K—Kt2

Black may here play 6... KQ3 (Kt3, Q2) 7. KB3 KB2, or 7. KB4 KB3; but loses after 6... KB2? 7. KB3, or 6... KQ4? 7. KB3.

7 K—B3	K—B2.

55

Drawn

The only move. Black must hold the (direct or distant) opposition when the kings are on the open files, Example 50. If now 8. KQ3 KQ2 9. KK3 KK2 10. KB3 KQ3 (10... KB2? 11. PKt5).

Black also draws with the move:

1 ...	K—B5

1... KKt5 2. KQ3 KB4 3. KK4 KB5 draws; but not 1... K—Q5? 2. K—Kt3 K—B4 (2... KQ6 3. KKt4 KB7 4. PKt3) 3. K—R4.

2 K—Q2

If 2. PR3 PR3 3. PKt3 ch. KB4 4. KB3 PR4, Example 50.

If 2. P—Kt3 ch. K—Kt5 3. K—Kt2 P—R4 4. P—R4 (4. PR3 ch. KKt4 5. KB3 KB4, Example 50) 4... K—B4 5. K—B3 K—Q4, Example 39.

2 ...   P—R4

2... KQ5 also draws.

3 K—B2

Advancing the candidate 3. PKt3 ch. KKt5 leads to an exchange after 4. KB2 PR5.

If 3. PR3 KKt6 4. KB1 PR5.

3 ...   P—R5.

As Example 51.

56 With unpassed disconnected pawns White's chances are less promising. He cannot in general win unless his king is in front of his pawns, and he must also have some spare tempo-moves.

White may win by a pawn-exchange leaving him the opposition, or by a turning movement of his king around Black's last pawn, in which the opposition is also important. A third winning idea, which succeeds only against an unmoved BP or Centre P, is the sacrifice of one pawn so as to queen the other.

1 K—Q3

After 1. K—B3? K—B4 Black having the opposition draws. 2. P—Kt4 ch. (2. KQ3 KKt5 or 2. KKt3 KQ5) 2... K—Kt4 3. K—Kt3 P—B3 4. K—B3 (PQ3) P—B4, and White has not the opposition.

If 1. KKt3? KQ4 2. KKt4 KQ5 3. KKt5 KQ6 4. KB6 K×P 5. K×P KQ6, and the last pawn falls.

White plays and wins
Black plays and draws

If 1. P—Kt4? (1. PQ4 or PQ3, KQ4) 1... K—B3 2. K—B3 (2. KKt3 KKt4 3. KB3 PB4) 2... K—Kt4 3. K—Kt3 P—B3, as before.

1 ...   K—B4

Having the opposition on the queen's file does not save Black: 1... K—Q4 2. P—Kt4 (2. KB3? KB4 draws) 2... P—B3 3. K—B3 K—K4 (3... PB4 4. PKt5) 4. K—B4 K—Q3 5. K—Q4 K—B2(Q2) 6. K—B5 K—Q2(B2) 7. P—Kt5 P×P 8. K×P K—Q3 9. K—B4 K—B3 10. P—Q3, White has the opposition.

1... PB3 2. KB4 PB4 3. PKt3 KB3 4. PQ3 brings about a standard type of position in which White wins with, but draws without, the opposition. If now 4... KQ3 5. PQ4, or if 4... KKt3 5. PKt4; but with the move White could not force a favourable exchange.

2 K—B3

Here, too, White wins with, but draws without, the opposition.

2 ...   P—B3

Black may leave this pawn unmoved, 2... K—Q4 3. P—Kt4 K—Q3 4. K—B4 K—B3 5. P—Kt5 ch. K—Kt3 6. K—Kt4 K—R2 7. K—B5 K—Kt2; when White wins either by a pawn-exchange 8. PQ3 KB1 9. PKt6, or by a pawn sacrifice 8. PQ4 KKt1 9. KB6 KB1 10. PQ5 KQ1 11. KKt7 KQ2 12. KKt8 KQ1 13. PQ6 P×P 14. KR7.

3 P—Kt4 ch.   K—Kt4
4 K—Kt3   K—R3
5 K—B4   K—Kt3
6 P—Q3

A tempo-move; 6. PQ4? KKt2 7. KB5 KB2 draws, Black having the opposition.

6 ...   K—B2

White wins after 6... K—Kt2 7. K—B5 (7. PKt5? KKt3) 7... K—B2 8. P—Q4 K—Q2 (8... KKt2 9. PKt5) 9. P—Q5 exchanging pawns; but he must not attempt a turning-movement, 9. KKt6? KQ3, for Black can maintain

32

the horizontal opposition, 10 KKt7 KQ2 11. KR7 KK2 (distant opposition) 12. KR8 KK1, etc.

7 K—B5	K—Q2
8 K—Kt6	K—Q3
9 P—Q4	

This tempo-move gains the (horizontal) opposition, so that the turning-movement may be completed.

9 ...	K—Q2
10 K—Kt7	K—Q3
11 K—B8	K—K3
12 K—B7	K—Q4
13 K—Q7.	

With the move Black draws by (and only by) taking the distant opposition, 1... K—B3 (1... KQ4? 2. KQ3 or 1... KB4? 2. KB3) 2. K—B3 (2. KQ3 KKt4 or 2. KKt3 KQ4) 2... K—B4 (Black takes the direct opposition on the bishop's file) 3. P—Kt4 ch. (3. PKt3 KKt4, or 3. PQ3 KQ4) 3... K—Kt4 4. K—Kt3 P—B3 5. K—B3 (5. PQ3 PB4) 5... P—B4 6. P×P K×P, Black has the opposition.

57 Black does better with a knight's pawn. He induces White to advance his BP, so that it will most likely be exchanged, a useless RP remaining.

| 1 K—B3 | K—Kt4 |

1... K—B4? permits White to exchange his RP after 2. P—R4 PKt3 3. KKt3 KQ4 4. KKt4 KB3 5. KB4 KKt2 6. KKt5 KB2 7. PR5, or 2... KKt3 3. KKt4 KB3 4. PR5 KQ3 5. KKt5 KB2 6. KB5 KQ2 7. KKt6 KB1 8. PR6.

| 2 K—Kt3 | |

The opposition is here of no account: to have winning chances White must have his king on the fourth rank.

| 2 ... | K—R4 |

Also here if 2... KB4? 3. PR4.

| 3 P—B4 | |

After either 3. PR3 KKt4 4. PR4 ch. KR4 5. KR3 PKt3 6. KKt3 PKt4, or

57

Drawn

3. PB3 PKt4 4. PR3 KR3 5. KKt4 KKt3, Black takes the opposition.

| 3 ... | K—Kt3 |

3... P—Kt3 also draws, 4. P—R3 (4. KR3 PKt4 5. PB5 PKt5 ch. 6. KKt3 KKt4) 4... K—R3 5. K—Kt4 K—R2 (not 5... KKt2? 6. KKt5 KB2 7. KR6 KB3 8. PR4 KB2 9. KR7 KB3 10. KKt8) 6. K—Kt5 K—Kt2 7. P—R4 K—B2 (not 7... KR2? losing the opposition after 8. KB6 KR3 9. KQ6, or 8. PR5) 8. K—R6 (8. PB5 P×P) 8... K—B3, Black has the opposition.

| 4 K—Kt4 | K—B3 |
| 5 P—R3 | K—Kt3 |

5... P—Kt3 6. P—R4 K—B2 also draws.

6 P—R4	K—R3
7 P—B5	K—R2
8 K—Kt5	K—R1

Black may also safely play 8... K—Kt1 9. K—Kt6 K—B1 (not 9... KR1? 10. KB7 KR2 11. PR5 KR1 12. PR6) 10. K—R7 K—B2, and White has no winning plan.

| 9 K—Kt6 | K—Kt1 |
| 10 P—R5 | K—B1 |

10... KR1? loses as in the above note.

| 11 K—R7 | K—B2 |
| 12 K—R8 | K—B1. |

White cannot exchange his RP and win; he cannot outflank; and here the pawn sacrifice 13. PB6 only draws.

58 When White has doubled pawns on the same file as Black's pawn, he usually wins if they are centre pawns, for he may outflank on either side.

1 ...	K—Q4
2 P—Q4	K—K3

If 2... P—Q3 (2... KB5 3. KK4 PQ3 4. PQ3 ch. KB6 5. PQ5) 3. K—Q3 K—K3 4. K—B4 K—K2 5. K—Q5 K—Q2 6. P—Q3 K—K2 7. K—B6 K—K3 8. P—Q5 ch. K—K4 9. P—Q4 ch.

3 K—K4	P—Q3

If 3... P—Q4 ch. (3... KQ3 4. PQ5 KK2 5. KK5) 4. K—B4 K—B3 5. P—Q3 K—K3 6. K—Kt5.

4 P—Q5 ch.

White wins

The tempo-moves of the rear pawn must not be wasted, and here the complete block after 4. PQ3? PQ4 ch. draws.

4 ...	K—B3

White gets through on the king's side after 4... KK2 5. KB5 KB2 6. PQ3 (Q4); but after the text move he goes to the queen's side.

5 K—Q4	K—B4
6 P—Q3	K—B3
7 K—B3	

So as to answer 7... KK4 by 8. KB4 7 KB4? KK4 (8. PQ4 ch. KK5) draws at once, and is the standard form of counter-attack.

7 ...	K—K2

If 7... KB4 8. KKt4 KK4 9. KB4 KB3 10. KKt5.

8 K—Kt4	K—Q2
9 K—Kt5	K—B2
10 K—R6.	

59 It is less easy to outflank on the short side of bishops' pawns which are therefore less favourable to White. In this position after Grigoriev, 1936, White wins only if he gets his king in front of his pawns—which Black with the move prevents:

1 ...	K—B4
2 P—B4	K—Q3
3 K—Q4	P—B3
4 P—B5 ch.	

Instead White may try 4. K—K4 K—K3 (not 4... KB4? 5. KQ3 KQ3 6. KQ4, when White has the opposition) 5. K—Q3 K—K4 6. K—B3 (or 6. KK3 PB4 7. PB3 KB4 8. KB3 KK4) 6... P—B4 7. K—Kt2 (7. KQ3 KB5, or 7. KKt3 KQ5—the standard draw) 7... K—Q3 8. K—R3 K—B3 9. K—Kt3 K—B2 (Black must stay on the bishop's file for if 9... KQ3? 10. KR4, or if 9... KKt3? 10. KB3 KB3 11. KQ3 KQ3 12. KK4 KK3 13. PB3) 10. K—R4 K—Kt3.

4 ...	K—K3
5 K—K4	K—B3
6 K—Q3	K—K3

6... KB4 7. KQ4 KK3 also draws.

7 K—Q4

Black's counter-attack depends on answering White's K—QKt4 by ... K—Q5; and to ensure this he must also be able to answer White's K—QB4 by K—K4, e.g. 7. KB3 KQ4 8. KKt4 KQ5 9. PB3 ch. KQ4, or 7. KB4 KK4 8. KKt3 KQ4 9. KKt4, etc., the standard draw.

By means of the text-move White tries to outmanœuvre Black.

7 ...	K—B4

Not 7... K—B3? 8. K—B3 K—K4 (8...KK3 9. KKt4 KQ4 10. PB3)

9. K—B4 K—K5 (now Black cannot get back in time to prevent a queen's side outflanking, but if 9... KK3 10. KKt4 KQ4 11. PB3) 10. P—B3 K—K4 11. K—Kt3 K—K3 (11... KQ4 12. KKt4) 12. K—R4 K—Q2 13. K—R5 K—B2 14. K—R6, a variation which should be compared to the text play.

8 K—B3	K—K5
9 K—B4	K—K4
10 P—B3	

The best chance, for either 10. K—Kt4 K—Q5 (10... KQ4? 11. PB3), or 10. K—Kt3 K—Q4 (10... KQ5? 11. KKt4 KQ4 12. PB3) draws at once.

10 ...	K—K3

59

White plays and wins
Black plays and draws

Having forced White to expend a valuable tempo (10. PB3) Black hastens to prevent White's entry on the queen's side.

11 K—Kt3	

If 11. KKt4 KQ4.

11 ...	K—Q2
12 K—R4	K—B2
13 K—Kt4	K—B1

The only move, watching both flanks.

14 K—R5	K—Kt2
15 P—B4	K—R2.

A difficult draw, Black's counter-attack, which reached out to the KB file, deprived White of his tempo-moves.

With the move White at first operates on the short side of the pawns, where there is insufficient space for Black's wide-swept counter manœuvres.

1 K—B4	K—B3
2 K—Kt4	K—Kt3
3 P—B4	P—B3

If 3... P—B4 ch. 4. K—B3 K—R4 (4. KB3 5. KQ3 KQ3 6. KK4 KK3 7. PB3 KQ3 8. KB5) 5. K—Q2 (5. KQ3? KKt5) 5... K—R5 6. K—K3 K—Kt5 7. K—Q3 K—R5 8. K—K4.

4. P—B5 ch.	K—B2

If 3... KR3 4. PB3 KKt2 5. KB4 as in the text play.

5 K—R5	K—Kt2
6 P—B3	K—R2
7 K—Kt4	K—Kt2

If 7... KR3 8. KB4 KR4 9. KQ3 but not 9. KQ4? KKt4.

8 K—B4	K—B2
9 K—Q4	K—Q2
10 K—K5	K—K2
11 P—B4	K—Q2
12 K—B6.	

The tempo-moves are prettily used.

60 Efforts to outflank are useless against an unmoved KtP, and Black may simply stay in the corner (QR1, QR2, QKt1) until White stalemates him (PKt6, KB7).

Even so, there are many drawing positions with the KtP on other ranks, because White's attempts to outflank are limited to one side of the pawns, e.g.

60

Drawn

1. K—Kt4 K—Kt3 2. K—B4 K—B3
3. P—Kt4 P—Kt3 4. K—Q4 K—Q3 (not
4... KKt4? 5. KB3 KB3 6. KB4
PKt4 ch. 7. KQ4 KQ3 8. PKt3) 5.
K—Q3 K—Q4 6. K—B3 P—Kt4,
drawn.

Doubled RPs are not usually more
significant than single ones.

61 When the doubled pawns are on
an adjoining file, the essence of Black's
play is counter-attack (except against
doubled RPs).

White to play pins Black to the
defence, and soon forces a favourable
pawn exchange: 1. KQ6 KB1 2. PB4
KQ1 3. PB5 KB1 4. PB6.

Against doubled BPs or Centre Ps,
Black usually has enough space for
counter-attack, as here with the move:

1 ...   K—B2
2 K—B5

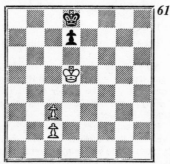

61

White plays and wins
Black plays and draws

If 2. P—B4 K—Kt3 (if 2... KKt2?
3. KQ6 KKt3 4. PB3 Black is in
zugzwang) 3. K—Q6 (3. PB5 ch. KKt4)
3... K—R4 4. P—B3 (4. KB5 KR5)
4... K—Kt3 (4... KR5? 5. K×P)
5. P—B5 ch. K—Kt4 6. K—Q5 K—R5
(6... KR4? 7. PB6) 7. PB6 (7. KQ4
KKt6) 7... P×P ch. 8. K×P K—Kt6.

2 ...   K—Kt2
3 P—B4

If 3. KQ6 KKt3 4. PB4 KR4 as
before.   3. K—Kt5 K—B2 (not 3...

KR2? 4. PB4 KKt2 5. PB5) 4. P—B4
transposes to the text play.

3 ...   K—B2

Not 3... K—R3? 4. K—Kt4 K—Kt3
5. P—B5 ch. K—R3 (5... KB3 6. KB4)
6. K—R4 K—R2 7. K—R5 K—Kt2
8. K—Kt5 K—B2 (8... KR2 9. PB6)
9. K—B4 K—B3 10. P—B3 K—Kt2
11. K—Q5 K—B2 12. P—B4 K—Kt2
13. K—Q6 K—B1 14. P—B6 K—Q1
15. P—B5.

4 K—Kt5

If 4. KQ5 KKt3, or if 4. PB3 KKt2
5. KQ6 KKt3.

4 ...   K—Q3
5 K—Kt6

If 5. PB5 ch. KQ4 6. PB3 KK5 7.
KB4 KK6 8. KQ5 KQ6 9. PB4 KB6.

5 ...   K—K4
6 K—B5   K—K5
7 K—Q6   K—Q5
8 P—B5   K—B5
9 P—B3   K—Kt4.

The play is not subtle. Black strives at
all times to counter-attack White's
pawns.

62 In the preceding example, the
defending king ranged from the QR to
the K files. With KtPs White's chances
are somewhat better because Black may
be restricted on one side of the pawns.

If Black's king were already aggressively placed (say at Q6) he would draw

62

White wins

5 KING AND TWO PAWNS v. KING AND PAWN

easily enough, but as things are he hasn't a chance: 1... K—Kt2 (1... KQ2 2. PKt4 and 3. KB6) 2. P—Kt4 K—Kt1 (2... KR2 3. KB6 KR3 4. PKt3) 3. K—B6 K—B1 4. P—Kt5 K—Kt1 5. P—Kt6 K—B1 6. P—Kt4.

This position moved five files to the right (KKtPs v. KRP) is also won for White.

63 Black simply stays in the corner. In this case only he plays defensively, for

Drawn

an exchange of pawns cannot help White.

64 White's chances are always very good if he has a passed pawn—a standing threat which hinders the Black king's movements.

Here Black threatens to break up the pawns, and indeed draws after 1. KB2?

White wins

PQ4, for if 2. KKt2 PQ5 3. P×P K×KtP, or if 2. KQ2 PQ5 3. P×P K×QP.

White triangulates to lose a move:

1 K—Q1

Not 1. KK2? PQ4 3. KK3 K×P 4. PKt5 PQ5 ch.

1 ...   K—Kt4

White answers 1... PQ4 by 2. KB2 PQ5 3. P×P, so that if 3... K×QP 4. KKt3, or 3... K×KtP 4. KQ3, Example 11.

2 K—B2   K—B5
3 K—Q2   P—Q4
4 K—B2   K—Kt4
5 K—Q3

The blockade is relieved, and a win soon follows 5... KB3 6. KQ4 KQ3 7. PKt5.

White is fortunate in having the right kind of pawns. If this position were moved one file to the left or four files to the right the break-up would leave a RP; on the other hand if the position were nearer White's side of the board a triangulation is not feasible, the result then depending on the move.

65 A passed pawn usually deflects or decoys the enemy king, and if it is only one file away it is not very effective for this purpose.

When Black has a BP or Centre P on its home square, stalemate threats will hamper White. In this position, and the same moved one or two files to the right, White wins only because his passed pawn is unmoved.

1 K—Q5

White depends on the option of moving his KP one or two squares at its first leap, and failing this he draws, 1. P—K3? K—B2 2. K—B5 (2. KQ5 KB3 3. KB5 KK4 4. KKt4 KQ3 5. KKt5 KQ4 6. PK4 ch. K×P) 2... K—K2 3. K—Kt6 K—Q3 (3... KK3? 4. PK4 KQ3 5. KB7) 4. P—K4 K—K3, Black takes the horizontal opposition, and 5. K—Kt7 K—K2 6. P—K5 K—K1

37

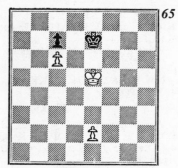

65

White wins

66

White wins

7. K—B6 K—B1 8. P—K6 K—K1
9. P—K7 is stalemate.

1 ...	K—B3
2 K—B5	K—K3(K4)
3 K—Kt5	K—Q4

If 3... KQ3 4. PK4.

4 P—K3	K—Q3
5 P—K4	K—K4
6 K—R6.	

White could not outflank in this way
if the position of this example were
moved one or two files to the left, when
Black would have a blocked KtP or RP.
A draw would then be normal, although
a win is sometimes possible, as in
Example 69.

66 With blocked BPs and passed
RP Black has less space for counterplay,
and White wins providing his RP is not
beyond the fourth rank.

1 K—R5

The immediate outflanking fails,
1. K—B5? K—R3 2. K—K4 (2. KK5
KKt3) 2... K—R4, and Black has time
to capture the RP. Therefore White first
triangulates, forcing Black to retreat.

| 1 ... | K—Kt1(R1) |
| 2 K—Kt4 | K—R2 |

If 2... K—R1(Kt1) 3. K—B5.

3 K—Kt5	K—Kt1(R1)
4 K—B5	K—R2
5 K—K4	

White wants to answer Black's ...

KKt3 by KK5—in fact 5. KK5? KKt3
draws.

5 ...	K—R3
6 K—Q5	K—Kt3
7 K—K5	K—R3
8 K—Q6	K—R4
9 K—K7	K—Kt3
10 P—R5 ch.	

With BP+RP *v.* BP White can win
only by outflanking, both here, and in
the position of this example moved down
the board one or two ranks.

67 In other cases where Black's
pawn is on the third or fourth rank
White wins in a different way: the king
and passed pawn advance together,
White finishing as in Example 8.

There is one exception, here shown.
Black may sometimes capture White's

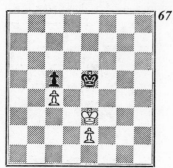

67

White plays and draws
Black plays and loses

BP, and draw by getting his own BP to the seventh rank:

1 K—Q3	K—B4

1... K—B5   2. P—K3 ch. (2. PK4 KKt4   3. KK3 KKt5)   2... K—B6   3. K—Q2 K—K5 transposes.

2 P—K3

If 2. K—B3 K—K5   3. K—Kt2 (3. KKt3 KQ5) 3... K—K6.

2 ...	K—K4
3 K—Q2	K—K5
4 K—K2	K—B4

Not 4... KK4?   5. KB3 KB4   6. PK4 ch. KK4   7. KK3, and White wins.

5 K—B3	K—K4
6 P—K4	K—Q5
7 K—B4	K×P
8 P—K5	K—Kt6
9 P—K6	P—B5
10 P—K7	P—B6
11 P—K8=Q	P—B7.

The queen cannot win. Example 304. Having the opposition White wins by 1... KB4   2. KB3 KK4   3. PK3 KB4   4. PK4 ch. KK4   5. KK3 KB3   6. KB4 KK3   6. PK5, etc.—Black is given no chance to counter-attack.

68 When Black's pawn is on the fifth or sixth rank he will at least draw, and sometimes win, if he is permitted to capture White's blocked pawn, his own pawn then becoming dangerous.

Having the opposition White wins as before, 1... KQ4   2. KQ3 KB4   3. PB4 soon picking up Black's RP.

Without the opposition White must lose a pawn:

1 K—Q2	K—Kt6
2 K—Q3	K×P
3 K—B2	

After 3. PB4 KKt6   4. PB5 Black queens first. After the text-move he has a stalemate defence.

3 ...	K—R7
4 P—B4	P—R6
5 P—B5	K—R8
6 P—B6	P—R7.

White plays and draws
Black plays and loses

The position of this example moved 1, 2, 3, or 4, files to the right, and/or one rank nearer to White's side of the board gives the same results, although the play varies slightly.

69 When the pawns are not yet blocked White wins unless his king is very backward, as happens here with Black to play:

1 ...	K—B6
2 K—Q1	P—R3

Black blocks the pawns to suit himself. He may instead play 2... P—R4   3. K—B1 P—R5   4. K—Kt1 (4. PR3 KQ5   5. KQ2 KB5)   4... K—Kt5   5. K—Kt2 P—R6 ch.   6. K—Kt1 K—B5   7. K—B1 K—B6, Example 68.

3 K—B1	P—R4
4 K—Q1	P—R5
5 K—B1	

If 5. P—R3 K—Kt7.

5 ...	P—R6
6 K—Kt1	K—B5

Not 6... KQ7?   7. PB4.

7 K—B1	K—B6.

As Example 68, where, having the move, White draws.

The win requires care because it is difficult for White to get at Black's rook's pawn if he leaves it where it is. This ending is not uncommon, see Examples 86 and 286.

I PAWN ENDINGS

1 K—Q2	K—B5
2 P—B3	K—B4

Unless he can force a favourable blockade, Black does best to leave his RP unmoved.

If 2... PR3 3. KB2 PR4 4. PR4 KQ4 5. KQ3 KB4 6. PB4 KKt5 7. KQ4 K×P 8. KB3 White queens first.

3 K—Q3	K—Q4
4 P—B4 ch.	K—B4
5 K—B3	K—B3

White has two ways of winning, both depending on the option of moving his RP one or two squares at its first leap. After 5... K—Kt3 6. K—Kt4 K—B3 White may win by 7. PB5 as in the next note, or by 7. P—R3 (7. PR4? draws) 7... K—Kt3 8. P—R4 as in the text.

69

White plays and wins
Black plays and draws

6 K—Kt4	K—Kt3
7 P—R4	

The text variation is shown by Valles, 1949.

7. P—R3? draws, but White may win instead by 7. P—B5 ch. as shown by Bauer, 1911, 7... K—B3 8. K—B4 K—B2 9. K—Q5 K—Q2 10. P—B6 ch. K—B2 11. K—B5 K—B1 12. K—Q6 (because of the RP the normal method 12 KKt5 KB2 13. PR4 KB1 14. KR6 KB2 15. K×P draws) 12... K—Q1 13. P—B7 ch. K—B1 14. K—B6, and Black loses the tempo struggle, 14... P—R3 (14... PR4 15. PR3 PR5 16. KKt6) 15. P—R4 P—R4 16. K—Kt6.

7 ...	K—B3
8 P—R5	K—Q2
9 K—Kt5	

9. K—B5? K—B2 draws, Black having the opposition, 10. P—R6 (10. KQ5 KQ2 11. KK5 KB3, or 10. KKt5 KKt2 11. PB5 KB2 12. PB6 KKt1 13. KB5 KB2 14. KQ5 KQ1) 10... K—Q2 11. K—Q5 K—B2 12. K—K6 (12. KK5 KQ2 13. KB5 or B6 KB3) 12... K—B3 13. K—K7 K—B2 14. K—K8 K—B1.

9 ...	K—B2
10 K—B5	K—Q2
11 K—Q5	K—B2
12 K—K6	K—B3
13 P—R6	

Taking the horizontal opposition, and thus outflanking Black.

13 ...	K—B2

If 13... KB4 14. KQ7 K×P 15. KB6.

14 K—K7	K—B3

If 14... KB1 15. KQ6 KQ1 16. KB6 KB1 17. PB5.

15 K—Q8	K—Q3

If 15... KKt3 16. KQ7, or 15... KB4 16. KB7.

16 K—B8	K—B3
17 K—Kt8	K—Kt3
18 P—B5 ch.	

Whichever pawn Black takes, the other queens.

70 When the passed pawn is farther away, White normally has no difficulty in sacrificing it to decoy the enemy king, by this means capturing Black's last pawn.

Black may have drawing chances when there are RPs.

1 K—B2

Here White wants not to have the opposition; if 1. K—Q2? KB5 2. K—B2 (2. KK3 KKt6, or 2. PB4 KQ5) 2... K—Q5, with repetition of moves.

1 ...	K—B5

Black cannot get back in time after

40

1... KK6 2. KB3 K×P 3. KKt4 KK5
4. K×P KQ4 5. KKt5.

2 K—Q2

The disadvantage of the rook's pawn
is plain after the diversionary 2. PB4?
KQ5 3. PB5 KK4 4. KB3 K×P 5.
KKt4 KK3 6. K×P KQ2, for now it is
blocked.

2 ...   K—Q5

The presence of rooks' pawns may
sometimes be in White's favour, as after
2... K—Kt6 3. P—B4 K×P 4. P—B5
K—Kt7 (4... KKt6 5. KB1 KR7
6. PB6) 5. P—B6 P—R6 6. P—B7
P—R7 7. P—B8=Q P—R8=Q 8.
Q—Kt4 ch. K—R7 9. K—B2, when
White's mating threats are unanswerable, Example 306.

3 K—K2   K—B5

If 3... KK4 4. KQ3 KB5 5. KB4
K×P 6. KKt4 KK5 7. K×P KQ4
KKt5.

If 3... KB6 4. PB4 KKt6 5. PB5 K×P
6. PB6 KKt7 7. PB7 PR6 8. PB8=Q
PR7, and again White's king i near
enough for a mating finish, 9. KQ2
PR8=Q 10. QKt4 ch. KR7 11. KB2.

4 P—B4

Not 4. K—K3? K—Kt6 5. P—B4 (or
5. KQ3 K×P 6. KB3 KR7 7. PB4 PR6
8. KB2 KR8) 5... K×P 6. P—B5
K—Kt7, Black safely queening.

4 ...   K—Q4

If 4... K—Q5 (4... KKt6 5. PB5)
5. K—B3 K—Q4 (5... KB6 6. PB5)
6. KKt4, and White queens the BP.

5 K—Q3

If 5. K—B3(K3)? K—K3 6. K—K4
K—B3, Black captures the BP and gets
back to QB1 or QB2, 7. KQ4 KB4
8. KB4 K×P 9. KKt4 KK4 10. K×P
KQ3. Advancing the passed pawn makes
no difference, 7. PB5 KB2 8. KK5 KK2
9. KQ5 KB3.

With the text-move White wins
because he gains a tempo on these
variations.

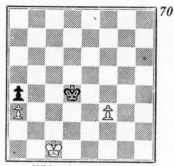

White plays and wins

5 ...	K—K3
6 K—B4	K—B4
7 K—Kt4	K×P
8 K×P	K—K4
9 K—Kt5	K—Q3
10 K—Kt6.	

And the RP queens.

The note to White's fifth move shows
that there are conditions under which an
outside passed pawn does not win if
there are blocked RPs, because the
defender's king may capture the passed
pawn and have time to get back to his
QB2 or QB1 square.

With Black's pawn on its fifth rank as
diagrammed, White wins if his passed
pawn is not beyond his KKt2, KB3, K4,
or Q5, squares; with the Black pawn on
QR6, White needs to have his extra
pawn no farther advanced than KB2,
K3, or Q4; and if Black's pawn were at
QR4 White's passed pawn should not be
more forward than KR2, KKt3, KB4,
K5, or Q6.

There are, of course, circumstances in
which White may win if his passed pawn
is beyond these limits, for he may simply
be able to queen it, or he may gain an
extra tempo when sacrificing it, as in the
example given.

As a general principle one should
block RPs with one's own as far forward
as possible. As to the passed pawn, text-
books often say that one should advance
it as far and fast as one can, but rather
we should say: advance the passed pawn
only as far as is necessary.

In this study of basic pawn endings we see that the most important principle is that of getting the king into play, as far forward as possible, and in fact this is nearly always the first thing to be done.

6. MORE PAWNS: MATERIAL ADVANTAGE

A pawn up nearly always wins unless one has a serious positional weakness.

71 Najdorf *v.* Kotov, Saltsjobaden, 1948. As there are RPs, White should take care to avoid the drawn endings of 2 pawns *v.* 1 pawn, which Grandmaster Najdorf failed to do!

| 1 P—Kt4 | K—B2 |
| 2 P—Kt5 | |

Advancing the candidate 2. PB4 KK2 3. PB5 is best, creating a passed pawn after 3... P×P 4. P×P, Example 69, or 3... KB2 4. PB6.

| 2 ... | K—K2 |
| 3 K—Q5 | |

This and the following few moves are aimless. 3. PB4 KB2 4. PB5? now draws after 4... P×P; but White wins simply by 3. PB4 KB2 4. KQ6 KB1 5. KK1 6. KB6 KB1 7. PR3 KKt1 8. KK7 KKt2 9. PR4 KKt1 10. PR5, exchanging the drawish RP, 10... KKt2 11. P×P.

71

White wins

3 ...	K—Q2
4 K—K4	K—K3
5 K—B4	K—Q4
6 K—Kt4	K—K4
7 P—B4 ch.	K—K3

If 7... KK5 8. PR4 KQ4 9. PB5.

8 K—B3

White now wins only because he has the option of moving his RP one or two squares at its first leap, and if this is wasted a dead draw results, 8. PR4? KB2 9. PR5 KK2 10. P×P (10. PR6 KB2-Kt1-R1) 10... P×P, Example 38.

8 ...	K—K2
9 K—K3	K—Q2
10 K—K4	K—Q3

If instead 10... KK3 11. PR3 KQ3 12. PR4, as in the next note.

11 P—R3?

He should play 11. P—R4 K—K3 12. P—R5 P×P (12... KQ3 13. P×P P×P, Example 38) 13. P—B5 ch. (the decisive gain of a tempo) 13... K—Q3 14. K—B4 P—R5 (14... KQ4 15. PKt6 P×P 16. P×P KK3 17. KKt5 PR5 18. KR6) 15. K—Kt4 K—K4 16. P—B6 K—K3 17. K×P P—R3 18. K—R5 P×P 19. K—Kt6.

11 ...	K—K3
12 P—R4	K—Q3
13 P—B5	

If now 13. P—R5 Black may draw by either 13... KK3 14. P×P P×P, Example 38, or 13... P×P 14. PB5 PR5 15. KB4 PR6 16. KKt3 KK4 17. PB6 KK3 18. K×P PR3.

13 ...   P×P ch.

There followed 14. K×P KK2 15. KK5 KB2 16. PR5 when Kotov settled matters by 16... PR3 17. PKt6 ch. KKt1, Example 25.

72 Alatorzev *v.* Kirova, Correspondence, 1934-5. White's king is backward, but he wins by a triangulation not unlike that of Example 64.

1 K—K1

Not 1. KQ1(Q2)? PQ5 2. P×P

72

White wins

K×QP 3. KB2 KK5 4. KB3 K×P 5. KB4 KK4 and Black's king returns in time. Also 1. KB1(B2)? fails after 1...PQ5 2. P×P K×BP.

1 ...   P—Q5

After 1... KB4 2. KQ2 KK5 3. KK2 Black must relieve the blockade, or play P—Q5 as in the text.

2 P×P   K×BP

If instead 2... K×QP 3. KB2 KK5 4. KKt3 KB4 5. KB3 KB3 6. KK4 KK3 7. KQ4.

3 K—Q2   K—K5
4 K—B3   K—Q4.

And White won after 5. KQ3 KQ3 6. KB4 KB3 7. PQ5 ch. KQ3 8. KQ4 KQ2 9. KB5 KB2 10. KKt5.

73 Szabo v. Pirc, Hastings, 1938-9. White's king is backward, his queen's side pawns weak; but he wins, not least because Black's blocked king side pawns are a sitting target.

1 P—B3

The usual winning idea is to create a passed pawn which decoys the enemy forces. Having a wing majority (4 pawns v. 3) on the king's side, White will there make his passed pawn; but if 1. PK3? P×P 2. P×P PR5 3. KB3 KQ4 4. KK2 KB5 5. KQ2 K×P, the KP is not distant enough to be menacing.

A passed pawn is effective in proportion to its distance from the scene of

action, and with the text-move (1. PB3) White plans to get a passed pawn on the KKt or KR files, sacrificing to that end if necessary.

1 ...   K—Q4

If 1... KQ5 2. KB2 PR5 3. PK3 ch. P×P ch. 4. KK2 KB5 5. K×P KKt6 6. PB4 P×P ch. 7. KB3 K×P 8. PKt5 PR6 9. P×P.

2 K—B2

Bringing the king into the game.

2 ...   K—Q5
3. K—K1   K—B5

After 3... KK6 White gains the opposition with the tempo-move 4. PKt3, and if 4... KQ5 5. KQ2.

4 K—Q2

The game continued 4. P—K3? P×P 5. K—K2 K—Q5 6. P—Kt3 (although here necessary, it is generally inadvisable to move the pawns on that side of the board which is being defended. Ideally White should here manœuvre only with his king's side pawns, and Black with his queen's side pawns) 6... K—B6 7. P—B4 P×P 8. P—Kt5 K—Q5 (White had overlooked this) 9. P×P P—B6 ch. 10. K×P K—Q6 11. P—R7 P—K7 12. P—R8=Q P—K8=Q 13. Q—Q8 ch. K—B6 14. Q×P ch. K×P 15. P—Kt6 Q—Q8 ch. 16. K—Kt3. Now Black carelessly played 16... Q×P? (16... QK8 ch. is correct) resigning after 17. PKt7 QKt4 ch. 18. KB3 QB4ch.

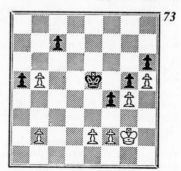

73

White plays and wins

19. KK3 QKt4 ch. 20. KQ4, because White's king finds a haven at QR7.

4 ...   P—R5

4... K×P 5. PK3 transposes; and if 4... KQ5 5. PKt3 (again this tempo-move is necessary) 5... KQ4 6. PK3.

5 P—K3   P×P ch.
6 K×P   K×P

If 6... KKt6 7. PB4 P×P ch. 8. KB3, sacrificing pawns to save time, 8... K×P 9. PKt5 PR6 (now 9... P×P does not give check) 10. P×P PR7 11. PR7 queening with check.

7 P—B4   P×P ch.
8 K×P   P—B4
9 P—Kt5   P×P ch.
10. K—K3

Not 10. K×P? P—B5 11. P—R6 (11. KB4 PB6 12. P×P PR6) 11... P—R6 (11... PB6? 12. P×P PR6 13. PR7 PR7 14. PB4 ch.) 12. P×P P—B6.

10 ...   P—B5
11 P—R6.

White, who after all obtained a passed pawn on the KR file, queens first.

---

74 In king and pawn endings a backward pawn is in general less of a handicap than in other kinds of ending. This is because the enemy king cannot usually hold a blockade indefinitely, and because of the possibility of sacrificing the backward pawn.

If White has the opposition he wins easily after 1... K—Kt3 (1... KR4 2. PB4) 2. K—Kt4 K—B3 (otherwise White outflanks, 2... KB2 3. KB5, or 2... KKt2 3. KKt5) 3. P—B4 (after 3. K—R5? K—B2 4. K—Kt4 K—Kt3 5. K—Kt3, Black takes the distant opposition and draws, by 5... K—Kt2, and if 6. KR3 KB2) 3... P×P 4. K×P, Example 5. White offers the pawn exchange when Black retreats to QB3.

Without the opposition, White has a combination. Sacrifices of backward pawns are common in pawn endings because the king is a slow-moving piece,

and often cannot get back to stop the newly-created passed pawn:

1 K—R3   K—R4

If 1... K—B5 2. K—Kt2 Black cannot maintain the blockade, and loses the opposition, after 2... KKt4 3. KKt3 or 2... KQ6 3. KKt3 (3... KK6 4. KB2 KK7 5. PB4).

If 1... KB3 2. KR4 KB2 3. KR5 KB3 4. KR6 KB2 5. KR7 KB3 6. KKt8 KKt4 7. KB7 KB5 8. KQ6, etc.

2 P—B4   P×P
3 P—Q5   P×P
4 P—K6

Nimzowitsch writes that backward pawns have a natural lust to expand, and indeed break through sacrifices of this kind are by no means uncommon.

74

White wins

If White plays 1. PB4 ch. P×P ch. 2. KB3 he regains his pawn 2... KKt3 3. K×P, but loses the opposition 3... KB3, Example 5. This idea wins, however, if the diagram position is moved up one rank, when exchanges lead to Example 37.

Similar positions with RPs are often drawn, exchanges transposing to Examples 35, 36, or 39; whilst if the pawns are nearer White's side of the board a sacrifice is not feasible, so that White wins only with the direct opposition.

75 Persitz *v.* Paffley, Southend, 1955. Here White's backward pawn takes no part in the proceedings, its mere presence ultimately ensuring victory.

1 ...   K—Q2

There is to be a struggle for the horizontal opposition, and the alternative is 1... P—R4 2. K—Kt3 K—Q2 (2... PQ5 3. KB4 KK4 4. KKt5 KQ4 5. PB6) 3. K—R4 K—B3 4. K×P K×P 5. K—R6 (not 5. PB3? KB5 and Black wins) 5... P—Q5 (or 5... KB3 6. PB3) 6. K—Kt7 K—Q3 7. K—Kt6 (not 7. KB8? KB3, Black holding the vertical opposition).

75

White wins

2 K—Kt4   K—B3
3 K—R5   K×P

If 3... K—Kt2 4. P—B3 (not 4. PB6 ch.? K×P 5. K×P PQ5 for Black has the opposition) 4. K—B2 5. K×P K—B3 6. K—R7 K—B2 7. P—B6 K×P 8. K—R6 (not 8... K—Kt8? 9. K—Kt3) 8... K—B4 9. K—Kt7.

4 K×P   K—B3

If 4... PQ5 5. KKt7, or if 4... KB5 5. KKt6 KB6 6. KB5.

5 P—B3

This tempo-move gains the opposition.

5 ...   K—B4
6 K—Kt7   P—Q5

If 6... KQ3 7. KKt6, but not 7. KB8? KB3.

7 P×P ch.   K×P
8 K—B6   K—K4

9 K—Q7   K—B3
10 K—Q6.

Finally not 10. KK8? KK3. After the text-move White wins the KtP, 10... KB2 11. KK5 KKt3 12. KK6 KKt2 13. KB5 KR3 14. KB6 KR2 15. K×P, and the two pawns win.

76 G. A. Thomas commenting on a game in the Boys' Championship at Hastings, 1949, shows that Black wins in spite of having doubled pawns.

1 ...   P—K5 ch.
2 P×P ch.   K—B4

Not 2... KK4? 3. KK3, when White has the opposition.

3 K—B3   P—K4

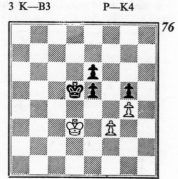

76

Black wins

Gaining the opposition, and outflanking White's position.

4 K—Q3   K—Kt5
5 K—K2   K—B5
6 K—K3   K—B6
7 K—B2   K—Q5
8 K—B3   K—Q6.

White fares no better with the move, 1. KK3 PK5 2. PB4 (if 2. P×P ch. KK4, Black has the opposition) 2... P×P ch. 3. K×P KQ5 4. KKt5 PK6 5. PKt6 PK7 6. PKt7 PK8=Q 7. PKt8 =Q QB7 ch. 8. KKt5 QKt6 ch.

77 Teichmann v. Blackburne, Berlin, 1897. Here the doubled pawn provides a decisive tempo-move. Black's

I PAWN ENDINGS

king's side pawns are slightly better than White's because of the prospect of a passed pawn on the KR file. It is remarkable that these two slight advantages suffice for a win.

Having the move, White cannot defend against P—R5:

Variation A:

1 K—B2	P—R5
2 P—B4 ch.	K—B4
3 P×KtP	

If 3. P×RP P×RP Black's passed pawn is stronger than White's because it is farther away. If 3. KB3 PKt5 ch. 4. KB2 P×P ch. 5. K×P PB4.

3 ...	P—R6

A move made possible by White's playing to the KB file (1. KB2). 3...

77

Black wins

P×P ch.? 4. K×P K×P draws because Black's king is only on the fourth rank; whereas after the text it gets to the fifth rank.

4 P—Kt4 ch.	K×P(Kt4)
5 K—Kt3	P—R7
6 K×P	K×P
7 K—Kt2	K—B5
8 K—B2	K—K5
9 K—K2	P—B4

Taking the opposition and outflanking.

Variation B:

1 K—R2	P—R5
2 P—B4 ch.	P×P
3 P×P	

Now White's passed pawn is the stronger, but he loses because his king is poorly placed; indeed, if it were at KKt2 he would turn the tables on Black.

3 ...	K—B4

This important finesse (instead of 3... KK5? at once) inveigles White's king to KR3, so that Black threatens to queen with check.

4 K—R3	K—K5
5 K—Kt2	

After 5. PR5 KK6 6. PR6 PB6 7. PR7 PB7 8. PR8=Q P—B8=Q ch. Black easily wins the queen and pawn ending.

5 ...	K—Q6
6 K—B3	

If 6. P—R5 K—K7.

6 ...	K×P
7 P—R5	K—Kt6
8 P—R6	P—B6
9 P—R7	P—B7
10 P—R8=Q	P—B8=Q.

Here too the queen and pawn ending is won for Black.

Variation C:

1 K—R3	P—R5
2 K—Kt2	

For 2. P—B4 ch. see Variation B. If 2. P×P P×P 3. KKt4 PB4 4. PB4 ch. KK5 5. PB5 PR6 6. PB6 PR7 and Black wins

2 ...	P×P
3. K×P	K—B4
4 K—Kt2	K—B5
5 K—B2	P—B4

Again the tempo-move wins the opposition.

6 K—K2	K—Kt6
7 K—K3	K—R6

Blackburne had foreseen this move, although the game took a different course. White cannot now maintain the (distant) opposition because he cannot play KQ3.

8 K—K4	K—Kt7

Taking the diagonal opposition, and outflanking next move.

46

9 K—K3	K—B8
10 K—K4	K—B7
11 P—B4	P×P
12 K×P	K—K7.

These three variations show that in the diagram position White's king is on its best square; and that Black wants to have this position with White to move. This he achieves by a triangulation.

1 ...	K—K3

Not of course 1... PB4? prematurely using his tempo-move. Neither can he win by 1... PR5? 2. PB4 ch. KB4 3. P×KtP P×P 4. K×P K×P, for the tempo-move is no help when his king is only on the fourth rank.

2 K—R3

The game continued 2. K—R2 K—B3 (2... PR5 would be simpler) 3. K—Kt2 eventually leading to Variation C. If 4. KB2 PR5 5. PB4 PR6.

2 ...	K—B3
3 K—Kt2	

If 3. KR2 PR5. If 3. PKt4 PR5 4. PB4 P×P 5. K×P KK4 and Black wins the queen endings after 6. PKt5 KK5 7. PKt6 PB6, or 6. KR3 KK5 7. KKt2 KQ6!

3 ...	K—K4

And not yet 3... PR5? 4. PB4 P×BP 5. P×RP KB4 6. KB3, when White wins; but after the text-move White, having to move, must submit to one of the given variations. A difficult ending composed of well-known elements: spare pawn-moves, triangulation, opposition.

78 A position from the game Bender v. Bahr, Freiburg, 1932. Black has an extra and protected passed pawn, a great advantage; but his problem is how to get his king into White's half of the board.

By carefully conserving spare pawn-moves, whilst inducing White to spend his, Black wins by a tempo.

1 ...	K—Q2

The first phase is to deprive White's KRP of spare moves.

2 K—Q4	K—K2
3 K—B5	P—R3
4 K—Q4	K—B2

Not yet 4... PKKt4? (which the text-move threatens) because of 5. PKR4 P×RP 6. P×P KB2 7. PR5 closing this wing, and leaving Black no tempo-moves. White's next move is forced because Black is now threatening to open this wing.

5 P—KR4	K—K2

The second phase begins—depriving White's QRP of spare moves.

Black wins

6 K—Q3	K—Q2
7 K—B3	K—B2
8 K—Q3	K—Kt2

A tempo-move, or finesse. The point is that White has an answer to each of the two immediate attempts to force ... PQR4:
8... KB3 9. KQ4 PQR4? 10. P×P PKt5 11. PR6 KKt3 12. PR7 K×P 13. KB5 KR3 14. K×P, and White's QRP sufficiently compensates for Black's QP.
8... K—Kt3 9. K—K3 P—QR4? 10. P—Kt4 (this breakthrough is feasible only when White's king is on the K-file or further east, and when Black's is on the QKt or QR file) 10... BP×P (10... PR4 is safe, but leaves Black no spare pawn moves, and so draws; whilst if

47

10... RP×P 11. PR5 P×RP 12. PKt5)
11. P—R5 P×RP 12. P—B5 P—Kt6
13. P×P ch. K—B3 14. P—B6 P—Q5
ch. 15. K—B3 P—Q6 16. P—B7 P—Q7
17. K—K2 P—Kt7 18. P—B8=Q, with
drawing chances.

9 K—Q4

White wants to answer ... KKt3 by
KK3, and ... KB3 by KQ4, as in the
variations given; but, having to move, he
cannot maintain the status quo.
If 9. K—K3 (9. KK2 KB3) 9...
K—Kt3 10. K—K2 (10. KQ4 PQR4)
10... K—B3 (10... PQR4? 11. PKt4)
11. K—K3 P—QR4 12. P×P (the
sacrifice 12. PKt4 is of no avail when
Black's king is on the QB file, 12...
RP×P 13. PR5 P×RP 14. PKt5 P×P
15. P×P KQ2) 12... P—Kt5 13. P—Kt4
P—KR4, with a safe king's side, and
entry for his king via QKt4.
If 9. KB3 KKt3 10. KQ4 PQR4.

```
 9 ...              K—B3
10 K—B3
```
If 10. KK3(Q3) PQR4.
```
10 ...              K—Kt3
```
Not 10... PQR4? 11. P×P KKt2
12. KKt4.
```
11 K—Q4
```
He can no longer delay Black's PQR4.
```
11 ...              P—QR4
12 P—R3
```
The breakthrough fails when White's
king is on the Q file, 12. PKt4 BP×P
13. PR5 PKt6 14. KK3 PQ5 ch. 15. KB3
PQ6 16. P×P PQ7, and Black queens
with check.
```
12 ...              P×P
13 P×P
```
Black now has one tempo-move,
White none. In the third phase Black
sacrifices his QP and gets his king to Q4,
then plays P—KR4, thus forcing entry
for his king at QB5 or K5.
```
13 ...              K—B3
14 K—Q3             K—Kt2
```
Not 14... PQ5? 15. K×P, when Black
cannot get to his Q4 except by pre-

maturely spending his tempo-move,
15... PR4 16. KB3 KQ4 17. KQ3, and
White having the opposition draws.
After sacrificing his pawn (... PQ5)
Black wants to answer K×P by ...KB3
—another example of manœuvring for a
square (a kind of triangulation) as was
seen on the 8th move.

```
15 K—Q4             K—Kt3
16 K—B3(K3)         P—Q5 ch.
17 K—Q3             K—B2
18 K×P              K—B3
19 K—B3(K3)         K—Q4
20 P—R5
```
20. KQ3 PR4 is also hopeless.
```
20 ...              P×P
21 K—Q3             P—R5
22 P×P              P—R4.
```
And Black's king enters White's
terrain, with decisive results.

7. MORE PAWNS: POSITIONAL ADVANTAGE

With level pawns there are winning
possibilities only when one side has some
kind of positional advantage.

79 Botwinnik, 1952, shows that
here the better position of Black's king
ensures victory.

```
 1 K—B3
```
White cannot prevent Black's out-
flanking him. The main idea follows
1. K—Kt1 (1. KR1 KQ6 2. KKt1 KK7
3. KKt2 PB5) 1... K—Q6 2. K—B1
K—Q7 3. K—Kt2 (3. KKt1 KK7)
3... K—K8 4. K—Kt1 K—K7 5. K—
Kt2 P—B5, when Black wins because he
now has the opposition, 6. P×P (6.
PKt4 KK8, or 6. KKt1 PB6) 6... P×P
7. P—B3 (7. KKt1 PB6) 7... K—K6,
Example 21.
1. K—R2 (if 1. KR3 KK5, not 1...
KQ6? 2. PB4) 1... K—Q6 2. K—R1
K—Q7 3. K—R2 K—Q8 4. K—R1
P—B5 transposes to the text play.
White could draw this position if he
could get his king to K2 under favour-

able circumstances, but the attempt fails:
1. K—B1 K—Q6 2. K—K1 P—B5
3. P—Kt4 K—B7 4. K—K2 K—B8
5. K—Q3 (5. KK1 PB6) 5... K—Q8,
outflanking after 6. KK4 KK7 7. PB3
KB7.

1 ...	K—Q6
2 K—Kt2	K—K7
3 K—Kt1	K—Q7

The immediate 3... PB5? leaves White
the opposition, 4. P×P P×P 5. KKt2,
and a draw.

4 K—R2

White plays to the rook's file, because
after 4. K—Kt2 K—K8 5. K—Kt1
(5. KB3 KB8 6. KK3 PKt5 7. PB3
KKt7) 5... P—B5 it is Black who has
the opposition.

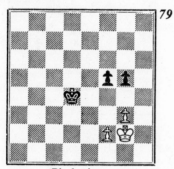

79

Black wins

4 ...　　　　　K—Q8

White must be forced into the corner,
or 4... PB5? permits 5. P×P P×P 6.
KR3.

5 K—R1

5. KR3 KK8 6. KKt2 loses as before.

5 ...　　　　　P—B5

Obviously Black cannot force the win
by 5... KK7 6. KKt1, or 5... KK8
6. KKt2.

6 P×P

If 6. K—R2 (6. KKt2 KK7) 6...
P—B6 7. P—Kt4 K—K8 (7... KK7?
8. KKt3) 8. K—Kt3 K—K7.

6 ...	P×P
7 K—R2	K—K8
8 K—Kt2	

It is too late for White to seize the
opposition, if 8. KKt1 PB6.

8 ...	K—K7
9 P—B3	K—K6

As Example 21.

80 Euwe *v.* Pirc, fifth match game,
1949. White's king is better placed (this
usually means more advanced) and he
has a greater number of spare pawn
moves. Even so Black should draw.

1 P—R4

White uses his spare pawn moves to
force his king's advance, a familiar idea.

1 ...　　　　　P—R3

In the game Black lost after 1... PR4?
2. PKKt3 PR4 ch. 3. KR4 KR3 4.
PKKt4 P×P 5. K×P KKt3 6. KB4
KB3 7. PKt3, and having the opposition
white won the QP.

2 P—Kt4　　　　P—Kt4

Black will lose the tempo struggle, but
his manner of doing so is of consequence,
and the pawns must be blocked in the
right way. After 2... PR4? 3. PKt5 KB3
4. KR5 KB4 5. K×P play continues
much as in the text, White queening
whilst Black gets his QP only to the
seventh. The queen then wins against the
passed pawn as exemplified in chapter
IV.

80

Drawn

3 P—R5   K—B3

Best, for either 3... KKt2? 4. KR5 KR2 5. PKt4 KKt2 6. PKt5, or 3... PR4 ch.? 4. KR4 KR3 5. PKt3 KKt3 6. PKt4, leaves White the opposition, so that the QP falls.

4 K—R5   K—B4
5 K×P   K—B5

A clever finesse. Black must try and queen his QP, and wants to do so with check, by drawing White's king to KR5.

6 P—Kt3 ch.   K—B6

After 6... K×P? 7. KKt5 White wins the QP.

7 K—R5   K—K5

The race is started.

8 P—Kt4   K×P
9 P—Kt5   K—B6
10 P—Kt6   P—Q5
11 P—Kt7   P—Q6
12 P—Kt8=Q   P—Q7

The game is drawn. If 13. QB8 ch. KKt7 14. Q×P P—Q8=Q ch., Black does not come out two pawns down, because he queens with check.

On the other hand, because the square QB4 is not available for White's queen it cannot win against the QP on the seventh (see notes to Example 303). It is for this reason that 2... PKt4 is superior to 2... PR4?.

81 Taubenhaus v. Pollock, Bradford, 1888. White's king's side pawns are under restraint, whilst Black has active centre pawns. Nevertheless White draws, because a central majority is both here, and in general, much less effective than a wing majority.

If Black creates a passed pawn in the centre, not only does it fail to decoy White's king which anyway wants to be in the centre, but the passed pawn may even be hard to defend, as happens in Example 83.

Against Black's central phalanx White naturally seeks counterplay on one wing or the other.

1 ...   P—Q4

After 1... P—R5 White has time to free his king's side pawns, when his passed KKtP gives him some initiative, 2. K—Kt2 P—Q4 3. P—R4 P×P e.p. ch. 4. K×P P—Q5 (4... P×P 5. KKt2 KB4 6. KB2 KKt5 7. PKt4) 5. P×P P×P 6. K—Kt4 K—K4 7. K—B3 P—B4 8. P—KKt4 P—B5 9. P—Kt5, although Black gets a drawn queen-ending after 9... PR6 10. P×P PB6 11. KK2 K×P 12. PKt6 PQ6 ch. 13. KQ1 KK6, etc.

The game continued 1... P—B4 2. K—K3? (White should block the position by 2. PB4) 2... P—Q4? (Black wins by 2... PB5 3. KB2 PQ4) 3. P×P

81

Drawn

ch.? (3. PB4 is still correct) 3... K×P 4. K—Q3 P—B5 ch. 5. K—K3 P—R5 6. P—QR3, and Black, having more spare pawn-moves, forced his king's advance, 6... P—B3 7. K—B2 K—K5 8. K—K2 P—B4.

2 P—QR4

As shown by Castaldi, only this move, threatening to obtain a passed QRP, draws. After 2. KK3? PR5 White is deprived of play on the wings, and can only mark time whilst Black's king manœuvres its way through on the queen's side, 3. KQ3 KQ3 4. KK3 KB4.

2 ...   P—Q5

White is threatening a queen's side advance, and if 2... P×P 3. P—Kt4 P×P 4. P×P P—B4 5. P—R5 P×P (5... KQ4? 6. PR6 KB3 7. P×P)

6. P—R6, he has a perpetual check after queening.

If Black prevents this by 2... P—B4 he has no entry for his king after 3. P—B4 P×KP (3... P×BP 4. KK3 PB6 5. P×P) 4. K—K2 P—K6 5. K×P K—B4 6. K—Q3 P—K5 ch. 7. K—K2 K—K4 8. K—K3 P—B3 9. P—Kt3.

If Black's king tries an immediate advance, 2... KQ3 3. KK3 KB4 4.KQ3, he can make no further progress, for 4... P×P ch.? loses.

3 K—K2.

White renews his threat of PQKt4, and Black does best to take the simple draw by 3... PB4 blocking the position. After 3... K—Q3? a dramatic race leads to a hairsbreadth win for White, 4. P×P P P×P 5. P—Kt4 P×P 6. P—R5 P—Kt6 7. K—Q1 P—Q6 8. K—B1 P—B4 (8... KB4 9. PR6) 9. P—R6 K—B3 10. P—R7 K—Kt2 11. P—K5 P—B5 12. P—K6 P—B6 13. P—K7 P—Kt7 ch. 14. K—Kt1.

After 3... P×P 4. P×P Black is on the defensive but can draw, 4... K—Q3 5. K—B2 (5. KQ3? KB4 6. KQ2 KB5 7. KB2 PB4) 5... K—K3 (5... KB4? 6. PR3) 6. K—Kt2 K—B3 7. P—B4 P—B4 (7... KKt3? 8. PB5) 8. P—R3 P×P ch. 9. K—R2 K—Kt3 (9... KKt4? 10. K×P PB3 11. PKt4 KB5 12. KR4 K×P 13. PKt5 KQ6 14. PKt6 PK5 15. PKt7 PK6 16. PKt8=Q PK7 17. QQ8 ch. KB7 18. Q×P) 10. K×P K—Kt4 11. P—Kt4 K—B5 12. K—R4 K×P 13. P—Kt5 K—Q6 14. P—Kt6 P—K5 15. P—Kt7 P—K6 16. P—Kt8=Q 17. P—K7, and because White's queen cannot use her Q4 square she cannot win against the KP on the seventh.

82 Barcza v. Gawlikowski, Marianske Lazne, 1948. White has the advantage of a wing (queen's side) majority. Black has a majority of pawns on the king's side, but this is not as valuable. A majority portends a passed pawn, and the value of a passed pawn depends on its distance from the centre of the board and/or its distance from the positions of

the kings. It seems here that White might get a passed pawn on the QB file, or even the QR file, which is better than the one which Black might establish on the king's file.

There are other factors: the weakness of White's queen's side pawn nearly deprives him of victory; Black's king is better placed; but White has one thing in his favour, Black's advanced KP, itself an object of attack, leaves weak squares to be invaded by White's king (Q4, KB4).

White naturally first endeavours to bring his king into play.

| 1 K—B1 | K—Q3 |
| 2 P—QKt4 | |

This and the next three moves are forced, if White is not to lose a pawn.

White plays and wins

2 ...	K—K4
3 P—B5	P×P
4 P×P	K—Q4
5 P—B6	K—Q3
6 K—K2	P—B5

Black prevents the White king's immediate entry. If 6... PQR3 7. P×P K×P 8. KK3 KKt3 9. KB4 PKt3 Black's pawns are broken up, 10. PKt4 P×P 11. K×KtP K×P 12. KKt5 KKt4 13. KR6 KB5 14. K×P KQ6 15. K×P KK7 16. KB5.

7 P—Kt3

A race follows, Black liquidating White's queen's side pawns and returning, if he can, before his own are gobbled up.

The text is the quickest way to break up Black's pawns. If 7. K—Q2? (Black may safely give up a pawn after 7. PR4 PQR3 8. P×P K×P 9. PKt3 KKt3 10. P×P K×P 11. KK3 KKt3) 7... P—QR3 8. P×P K×P and now:

(a) 9. K—B3 P—B6 10. P×P (10. PKt3? PK6) 10... P×P 11. K—Q4 K—Kt3 12. P—R4 K×P 13. K—B5 K—R4 as in the game, when a draw was agreed.

(b) 9. PKt4 (commended by the tournament book) 9... KKt3 10. KB3 K×P 11. KQ4 PK6 13. P×P P P×P 12. K×P KKt3, drawn.

(c) 9. PKt3 KKt3 10. P×P K×P 11. KK3 KKt3 12. K×P KB3, drawn.

| 7 ... | P—Kt4 |

White wins by a tempo after 7... PQR3 8. P×RP K×P 9. P×P KKt3 10. KK3 K×P 11. K×P KKt3 12. KK5.

8 P×P	P×P
9 K—Q2	P—QR3
10 P×P	K×P
11 K—B3	K—Kt3

The exchange of pawns on the KKt file deprives Black of the counterthrust PKB6 that was played in the game.

12 K—Q4	P—K6
13 P×P	P×P
14 K×P	K×P
15 K—B4	K—Kt3
16 K—Kt5	K—B3
17 K—R6.	

There may follow 17... KQ4 18. K×P KK5 19. KKt6, or 17... KQ3 18. K×P KK2 19. KKt7.

83 Eliskases v. S. Rubinstein, Vienna, 1932. Black has the queen's side majority, but he is at a disadvantage because of two pawn-weaknesses: firstly, his P at QR4 hampers the mobilization of his majority—it would be better placed at QR3 to support the QKtP; secondly, his P at KB4 (it would be better at KB2) permits White quickly to

get a passed pawn if he so wishes—see note to Black's third move. If Black were rid of either of these weaknesses he would draw; if rid of both he would have winning chances.

1 P—QR4

This breaks up Black's queen side pawns. Such a 'minority' attack would be positively bad in many cases, but is here justified, for it is the means of exploiting Black's pawn weaknesses.

| 1 ... | K—B3 |
| 2 K—Q3 | P—QKt4 |

White plays and wins

Necessary, for White threatened K—B4 fixing the backward QKtP.

3 K—B3

After 3. PB3? PB5 ch. 4. P×P PKt5, the protected passed pawn ensures a draw for Black. And if here 4. KB3? BP×P 5. P×P ch. K×P 6. K×P Black wins because of his outside passed pawn.

| 3 ... | P×P |

Under normal circumstances the remote passed pawn created after 3... PQB5 4. P×P ch. K×P 5. P×P ch. KB4 would suffice; but here the weakness of Black's king's side fails him, for after 6. PB3 PR5 7. PK4 P×P 8. P×P PR6 9. PK5 the disconnected passed pawns, which can defend themselves, are superior to Black's QRP.

| 4 P×P | K—Q4 |
| 5 P—B3 | |

Black's passed pawn is a liability rather than an asset, for it is isolated and needs defending, and is not distant enough to be menacing.

| 5 ... | P—R3 |
| 6 K—Q3 | P—B5 ch. |

A bold and ingenious defence follows; but cautious play is no better:

6... P—Kt4 7. P—Kt4 P×P 8. RP×P K—K4 (8... KQ3 9. KB4 KB3 10. PK4) 9. K—B4 K—Q3 10. P—K4 K—B3 11. P—K5, and White wins the QBP.

6... PR4 7. PR4 KQ3 8. KB4 KB3 9. PK4 P×P 10. P×P KQ3 11. PK5 ch. K×P 12. K×P KB5 13. KKt5, and White queens the QRP.

| 7 K—B3 | K—B4 |
| 8 P—K4 | P—B5 |

If 8... P×P 9. P×P, Black runs out of tempo-moves, losing the BP.

9 P—R4

This finesse deprives Black of tempo-moves with his KRP. A curious draw follows 9. PK5 KQ4 10. PK6? K×P 11. K×P PKt4 12. KKt5 KQ4 13. K×P KB4 14. KR6 KB3 15. PR5 PR4 16. KR7 KB2 17. PR6 PR5, when White's king is incarcerated.

9 ...	P—R4
10 P—K5	K—Q4
11 P—K6	K×P
12 K×P	P—Kt4
13 K—Kt5.	

Black resigns. He may have hoped for 13. P×P? K—B4 14. K—Kt5 (14. KQ5 K×P 15. KK5 KR5 16. K×P stalemate) 14... K×P 15. K×P K—R5 with counterplay.

White's passed KP proved more valuable than Black's passed QBP; but White's real advantage was that he could dictate the moment for creating the passed pawns.

84 Analysis from the game Botvinnik *v.* Smyslov, Sverdlovsk, 1943. Black's pawns are very weak (four are isolated), and White's king is better placed. White

may expect to win, but it is not so easy for his king to get at Black's pawns, and once again tempo-moves are the decisive factor.

1 ...	K—Q2
2 K—K4	K—K3
3 P—KKt4	

Securing his king's position.

3 ... P—QB3

Preventing White's king entering via Q5.

84

White wins

If 3... K—B3 (3... KQ3 4. KB5 KQ4 5. PR4 KQ5 6. PKt5 P×P 7. PKR5) 4. K—Q5 K—Kt4 (else PKR4) 5. K×KP K—R5 6. P—KB4 K×P 7. P—Kt5 P×P 8. P×P K—Kt5 9. K—B6 K—B5 10. P—B4 K—Kt5 11. K×P K×P 12. K—K6.

4 P—KR4 P—B5

A sacrifice to obstruct the entry of White's king, for if 4... KB3 5. KQ3 KK3 6. KB4.

5 P×P	K—B3
6 P—Kt5 ch.	P×P
7 P×P ch.	K—K3

After 7... K×P 8. K×P White wins the QBP.

| 8 P—R5 | P—R3 |
| 9 P—KB3 | P—B3 |

If 9... PQB4 10. PB3 KQ3 11. KB5.

10 P×P	K×P
11 PB4	P×P
12 K×P	K—K3

13 K—K4	K—Q3
14 K—Q4	P—B4 ch.
15 K—K4	K—K3
16 P—B3	K—Q3
17 K—B5.	

85

Black to play:

1 ...	K—B2

Black wins because of his powerful outside passed pawn which decoys White, and because of White's backward QBP—Black's one pawn at QKt4 holds two.

2 K—K3

There is no time to exchange the weak pawn, 2. KQ3 KK3 3. PB4, because of 3... PKt6.

85

Whoever plays wins

2 ...	K—K3
3 K—K4	P—Kt6
4 K—B3	K—Q4
5 K×P	K—B5
6 K—B3	K—B6
7 K—K3	K×BP
8 K—Q4	

8. KK2 KKt6 9. KQ1 K×P also loses.

8 ...	K—Kt6
9 K—B5	K—R5.

White to play:

1 P—B4

The characteristic breakthrough sacrifice, often seen with backward pawns when the enemy king is far away.

1 ...	K—B2

If 1... P×P 2. PKt5, and although Black's pawns can force their way forward, it so happens that White gets there first, 2... PKt6 3. PKt6 PKt7 4. KB2 PB6 5. PKt7 PB7 6. PKt8=Q ch.

2 P—B5

White wins because of the great strength of the protected passed pawn, which restricts the Black king's freedom.

2 ...	K—K3
3 K—B2	K—B3
4 K—Kt3	K—B4
5 K—R4	K—B5

Here Black cannot both protect his KtP and remain within the square of White's passed pawn (but he could do so if the passed pawn were at KKt4 instead of KKt5).

6 P—B6	P—Kt6
7 K—R3	K—B6
8 P—B7	P—Kt7
9 P—B8=Q	P—Kt8=Q
10 Q—B5 ch.	K—K7
11 Q×P ch.	K—K8

A queen exchange cannot be avoided. If 11... KB6 12. QB5 ch. KK7 13. QKt4 ch., and if 11... KQ7(Q8) 12. QQ5 ch. KB6(B7) 13. QB5 ch.

12 Q—K5 ch.	K—Q7
13 Q—Q5 ch.	K—K8(K7)
14 Q—K4 ch.	K—Q7
15 Q—Kt2 ch.	

86 Although there are occasions when an outside passed pawn is the equal of a protected passed pawn, the latter is usually stronger, as in this study by Fine, 1941. The extra pawns create additional threats for White.

1 K—Kt4

In the first phase White positions his king for the inevitable exchange of passed pawns, and here 1. KQ4 KB2 2. KB5 KQ2 3. KQ5 PQR3 4. KB5 comes to the same thing.

1 ...	K—Kt3
2 K—R4	K—B3

2... PQR4 3. PR5 leads to play as in the text.

If Black moves his KRP, White exchanges passed pawns, takes the horizontal opposition, outflanks Black, and wins his vulnerable KKtP: 2... P—KR4 (or 2... PQR3 3. KKt4 KB3 4. KB4 KQ2 5. KQ5 PKR4 6. KB5 KB2 7. KKt4 KKt1 8. KR5 KKt2 9. PK6) 3. K—Kt4 K—B3 4. K—R5 K—Kt2 5. K—Kt5 K—B2 6. K—R6 K—Kt1 7. P—K6 K—B2 8. K×P K—Q3 9. K—Kt6 K×P 10. K—B6 K—K2 11. K—B7 K—K3 12. K—Q8 K—B2 (12... KQ4 13. KK7 KK5 14. KB6 KB6 15. K×P K×P 16. KKt5) 13. K—Q7 K—B3 14. K—K8 K—Kt2 15. K—K7 K—Kt1 16. K—B6 K—R2 17. K—B7 K—R3 18. K—Kt8.

86

White wins

3 K—R5	K—Kt2
4 K—Kt5	K—B2
5 K—R6	K—Kt1
6 P—R5	

The second phase, weakening Black's pawns. After the immediate exchange 6. PK6? KB2 7. K×P KQ3 8. KKt6 K×P 9. KB6, Black takes the opposition and draws, 9... PKR4.

| 6 ... | P×P |
| 7 P—K6 | |

The third phase, exchanging the passed pawns.

7 ...	K—B2
8 K×P	K—Q3
9 K—Kt6	K—K2

10 K—B7

The position eventually transposes to Example 69. Certain squares are correlated, and White must move carefully—here 10. KB6? K × P draws.

10 ...	K × P
11 K—B6	K—B2
12 K—Q7	

Either 12. KQ6? KB3, or 12. KQ5? KK2 draws.

| 12 ... | K—B3 |
| 13 K—Q6 | K—Kt2 |

If 13... PR3 14. KQ5 KKt3 15. KK6 KKt2 16. K×P KB2 17. KK5 KK2 18. PB5 KB2 19. PB6 KK1, and White wins by triangulating, 20. KB4 KB1 21. KK4 KK1 22. KK5.

14 K—K7

Here 14. KK5? KB2, or 14. KK6? KKt3 draws.

| 14 ... | K—Kt1 |
| 15 K—K6 | |

Not 15. K—B6? K—B1 16. K—Kt5 (16. K×P PR5 17. P×P KK2) 16... P—R5 17. K×P (17. P×P KB2) 17... P—R3 and Black draws.

| 15 ... | K—B1 |
| 16 K—B6 | |

Not 16. K×P? PR5 17. P×P KK2.

16 ...	K—Kt1
17 K×P	P—R5
18 P×P	

White wins as Example 69.

87 The ending of a game Schweda v. Sika, Brno, 1929. Neither side appears to have any positional advantages in the normal sense.

It is obvious that a move by either king loses a pawn. It is therefore a battle of pawns, and the player with the move is able to arrange the pawn-moves to his own advantage in each case. It is difficult to say why this should be so, although the option of moving a pawn one or two squares at its first leap is a significant factor.

White to play:

1 P—KR4   P—QR4

After 1... P—KR4 2. P—R3 the pawns are arranged symmetrically. In all such cases the player who has to move first cannot lose a move, and there might follow 2... P—Kt3 (2... PKt4 3. PKt4) 3. P—Kt3 P—R4 4. P—R4 (if 4. PKt4? an exchange is seen to lose a move, 4... P×P 5. P×P PKt4).

2 P—R5

Depriving Black's KRP of its first move option. After 2. PR4? PR4, or 2. PKt3? PR4 3. PR3 PKt4, Black wins.

2 ...   P—R5

87

Whoever plays wins

If 2... PR3 3. PR4; if 2... PKt4 3. PR6; and if 2... PKt3 3. PR4.

3 P—R6   P—Kt3

The attempt to lose a move by a sacrifice usually fails, e.g. 3... PR6 4. P×P PKt4 5. PR4 P×P 6. PR3, when Black still has the move.

4 P—Kt4

The first-move option decides the issue. 4. PKt3? PR6 loses.

4 ...   P×P e.p.
5 P×P   P—Kt4
6 P—Kt4.

Black to play wins by 1... P—QR4 2. P—Kt3 (2. PQR4 PR3 makes a symmetrical arrangement of pawns, whilst if 2. PKR4 PR5 3. PKt3 P×P

4. P×P, Black's first-move options decide) 2... P—Kt4 3. P—R3 P—R3, with, in effect, symmetry; and if 4. P—Kt4 P—R5, but not 4... P×P?, the exchange losing a move.

A tempo struggle in a very clear-cut form.

88 A kind of positional advantage sometimes occurs when both sides have passed pawns, but one set of them is more dangerous. This means they are nearer to queening, or more mobile, or there is a mating threat involved.

This study by Guy, 1951, shows the idea in simple form.

1 K—B4   K—Kt1
2 K—B5   K—B2
3 K—B6

White loses a move. Black cannot do the same, his king must oscillate from QKt1-QB2, or from QKt1-QR2.

3 ...   K—Kt1

As long as White's king remains on KB4, KB5, or KB6, Black will lose his pawns if he dares to advance them, e.g. 3... PR4 4. KKt5 PQ4 5. K×P, and White's king is in time to stop the other pawn.

88

Whoever plays wins

4 K—Kt6

If endings of this kind are to be won, there comes a moment when the enemy pawns must be permitted to advance, and the risk must be calculated carefully.

4 ...   P—Q4

Otherwise Black loses his pawns.

5 K—B5   P—R4

Forced, for the same reason.

6 K—K5   P—R5
7· K×P   P—R6

If now 7... KB2 8. KK4, and the KRP falls.

8 K—B6.

An advanced pair of united passed pawns may contain two kinds of threat, the pawn-mate 8... PR7 9. KKt6 PR8=Q 10. PR7, or the queen-mate (which occurs on the edge of the board, that is with KtP+RP as here) 8... KR2 9. KB7 PR7 10. PKt8=Q ch. K×P 11. QKt6.

With the move Black plays 1... PR4 2. KB4 PQ4, and one of his pawns will queen.

89 Another kind of advantage is the possibility of a breakthrough sacrifice when the defending king is too far from the scene.

In the finish of the game Ermolaev *v.* Karpinsky, Ukraine, 1950, Black's position (or should one say combination?) is worth more than a pawn.

1 ...   P—R5

Not 1... PKt5? 2. PR4, when Black's pawns are blocked.

2 P—B4

White sees but cannot avert the threat of ... PKt5.

If 2. KK4 PKt5 3. K×P P×P 4. KB3

Black plays and wins

White's king is tied down (blocked by the QBP), and Black captures White's QP and KKtP, after 4... KK4 5. PQ4 ch. KB4, as in Example 19, for they are not forward enough to be dangerous.

If 2. KB5 PKt5 3. PKt6 KK2.

2 ...   P×P e.p.

Not 2... PKt5? 3. PB5 ch.—with pawns three files apart on the fifth rank White will queen one of them, 3... KK2 4. PB6 P×P 5. PB7 KQ2 6. PKt6, etc.

3 K—K3   P—Kt5
4 P—Kt6   K—K2
5 P—Q4   P×P

Avoiding the queen ending which follows 5... PKt6 6. PQ5 PKt7 7. PQ6 ch. K×P 8. PKt7.

6 P—Q5   P—B7
7 K—Q2   P—R7

White resigned after 8. P—Kt7 (if 8. PQ6 ch. K×P) 8... P—B8=Q ch. 9. K×Q P—R8=Q ch.

CHAPTER II

MINOR PIECE ENDINGS

'Here I'm amazed at th' actions of a knight
That doth bold wonders in the fight;'
ABRAHAM COWLEY,
Pindaric Odes: To Destiny, 1656.

We shall not consider knights and bishops separately, but will show in a comparative study their differing characteristics. The bishop has more mobility for it may cross the board in one move, and a greater range for it may control squares at a distance. The knight may take as many as six moves to reach a given destination, but is less easily obstructed, and has greater scope, being able to control squares of either colour.

In open positions with only a few pawns the bishop is stronger, whereas the knight is the better piece in positions where the bishop is obstructed by its own pawns.

1. MINOR PIECE *v.* PAWN

This is normally drawn, the piece sacrificing itself for the pawn if necessary. Against an advanced pawn the knight may find this difficult.

90 Against a BP or Centre P the knight operates at full strength on either side of the pawn.

1 K—B8

If 1. PB8=Q KtQ3 ch. The fork is the theme of Black's defence.

If 1. KKt6(Kt8) KtK2, or if 1. KB6 KtK2 ch. 2. KQ7 KtQ4, attacking the pawn, and forking if it queens.

1 ...   Kt—K2 ch.

Not 1... KtQ3 ch.? 2. KQ7 KtB5 3. KB6 KtK4 ch. 4. KKt5 KtB2 5. KB5.

2 K—Q8	Kt—B3 ch.
3 K—Q7	Kt—R2

4 K—Q6	K—Kt7
5 K—B5	K—B6
6 K—Kt6	Kt—B1 ch.

Drawn

The knight draws if it can occupy a square immediately in front of the pawn, except against a rook's pawn on the seventh.

If now 7. KKt7 KtQ3 ch., or 7... KtK2.

White plays and wins

58

91 The knight is less effective against a KtP.

1 K—Kt8	Kt—Q2 ch.
2 K—B8	

Not 2. KB7? KtB4.

2 ...	Kt—Kt3 ch.
3 K—Q8(B7).	

And the pawn will safely queen.

92 Against a RP the knight operates at little more than half-strength, and, as here shown by Grigoriev, 1932, it has some difficulty drawing against a RP as far back as its second rank.

1 P—R4	Kt—B6

After 1... KtB2 ch.? 2. KB7, or 1... KtK5 ch.? 2. KB6, the pawn goes through.

Drawn

2 K—Q5

If 2. PR5 KtQ5 3. PR6 KtKt4 ch. 4. KB6 KtR2 ch. From here the knight safely moves around the circuit QB1-Q3-QKt4-QR2, i.e. 5. KKt7 KtKt4 6. KKt6 KtQ3, or 5. KKt6 KtB1 ch. 6. KKt7 KtQ3 ch.

2 ...	Kt—R5
3 P—R5	Kt—B4

The key square, from which the knight threatens to get on to the above-mentioned circuit in three different ways: ... KtQ3; ... KtK2—QB1; or KtQ5—QKt4.

4 K—B6	Kt—Q5 ch.

Not 4... KtK2 ch.? 5. KQ7 KtQ4 6. PR6 KtKt5 7. PR7 KtQ4 8. KB6.

5 K—Kt6	Kt—B4
6 P—R6	

If 6. KB7 KtQ5 7. PR6 KtKt4 ch.

6 ...	Kt—Q3.

Black's knight plays to QB1 or QKt4.

White plays and wins

93 A well known stratagem which occurs only with the RP: 1. Kt×P ch. Kt×Kt 2. PR6, and if 2... KB2 3. PR7.

2. MINOR PIECE *v.* TWO PAWNS

This ending is normally drawn, but there are winning chances for the pawns if the defending king is far away.

94 As a rough guide Black draws if his king is within the square of the united pawns, and if his minor piece is reasonably well placed, as here, where the knight effectively operates from behind the pawns.

1 K—Q6

White tries to hold off Black's king. If 1. K—Q5 K—B4 2. P—B5 Kt—Kt5 ch. 3. K—Q6 (3. KB4 KtB3 4.KKt5 KtQ5 ch. 5. KKt6 KK4 6. PB6 KtK3, or 3. KB4 KtB3 4. PKt4 KK3 5. PKt5 KQ2) 3... K—K5 4. P—B6 Kt—Q4 5. K—B5 (5. PKt4 KQ5 6. PKt5 KB5) 5... K—K4 6. P—Kt4 Kt×P.

If 1. P—Kt4 (1. KKt6 KB4 2. PB5
KK4 3. PB6 KtKt5) 1... K—B4
2. P—Kt5 K—K3 3. K—B6 Kt—Q5 ch.
4. K—B7 K—K4 5. P—Kt6 Kt—K3 ch.
6. K—B6 K—Q5 7. P—Kt7 Kt—Q1 ch.

1 ...   K—B4
2 P—B5   Kt—R6

Not 2... KtKt5? 3. PB6.
3 P—B6

Drawn

If 3. P—Kt4 Kt—B5 ch., by means of
this check Black's king forces its way
nearer, 4 K—Q5 (4. KB7 KK3 5. PKt5
KQ4 6. PKt6 KtK4) 4... Kt—K6 ch.
5. K—B6 K—K3 6. P—Kt5 Kt—B4
7. P—Kt6 Kt—Q5 ch. 8. KB7 KQ4.
If 3. KB6 KK3 4. KKt6 KQ2.

3 ...   Kt—Kt4 ch.
4 K—B5

If 4. K—Q7 K—K4 5. P—B7 (5.
PKt4 KQ4) 5... Kt×P; or if 4. KQ5
KB3.

4 ...   Kt—B2
5 P—Kt4

If 5. KKt6 KtQ4 ch. 6. KKt7 KK4
7. PKt4 KQ3 8. PKt5 KB4.

5 ...   K—K4
6 P—Kt5   Kt—K3 ch.
7 K—Kt6   K—Q3
8 K—Kt7   Kt—Q1 ch.

In these variations Black draws by
setting up a kind of blockade, with his
knight and king at the side of or behind
the pawns.

95 A minor piece also normally
draws against two disconnected pawns,
the king holding back one of them, and
the piece the other. This is not always
easy for the knight, whose versatility is,
however, well shown in this ending by
Grigoriev, 1934.

1 ...   K—K3
2 K—B2   K—B4
3 K—Kt3

3. KKt2 traps the knight, but only
draws after 3... K×P 4. K×Kt KB4,
Example 14.

3 ...   Kt—B8 ch.

Not 3... K×P? 4. PR4 KtB8 ch.
5. KB4 KtK7 6. PR5 KtB5 7. PR6
KtK3 8. PR7 KtB2 9. KB5 KtR1
10. KB6 KB3 11. KKt7. Black is unable
to hem White in after sacrificing the
knight.

Black plays and draws

4 K—B4   Kt—K7
5 P—R4   Kt—B5
6 P—R5   Kt—Kt3

6... KtK3 loses as before.

7 P—R6   Kt—K2
8 K—B5

If 8. PR7 KtB1 9. PR8=Q KtKt3 ch.

8 ...   Kt—B1
9 K—B6   K×P.

96 Isolated pawns may win if the
defending king cannot play his part; then
the minor piece, trying to hold both
pawns, is overburdened.

96

White plays and wins

1 K—Q5

Threatening PKt7. The immediate advance draws, 1. PKt7? BK4 2. KQ5 BKt1.

1 ...	B—K4
2 P—Kt3 ch.	K—B4
3 P—Kt4 ch.	K—B5(B3)
4 P—Kt5 (ch.)	K—B4
5 P—Kt6	K—B3
6 P—KKt7.	

96A For the twin brother of this amusing study (no diagram), place a knight at Black's KKt5 and remove the bishop—White wins in a similar way after 1. KQ5 KtK4 2. PKt3 ch. KB4 3. PKt4 ch. KB5 4. PKt5 KtQ2 5. PKt6 Kt×P ch. 6. KK6. Both studies were fathered by Rinck, 1937.

3. MINOR PIECE v. THREE PAWNS

Chances are often in favour of the pawns, and values are approximately as follows: the knight is equal to three united pawns on the fourth but loses if they are farther forward; if the three pawns are widely separated they win against the knight. The bishop normally draws against three united pawns; and also draws against disconnected pawns unless they are well advanced.

Four pawns usually defeat a piece—no examples are given.

97 Laroche v. Greville, Paris, 1848. Played at the famous Café de la Régènce in its heyday, this is, as Kieseritsky remarked, a very interesting ending.

1 K—Kt4	K—B3
2 P—R4	K—Kt3
3 K—B4	Kt—Q4 ch.

Not fatal, but the systematic move 3... K—R4 draws without trouble. The king should oppose the most advanced pawn, thus hindering the advance of its neighbour. If then 4 KK5 KtB3 ch. 5. KQ5 KtKt5 ch. 6. KK6 KtB3 7. PB4 KtQ5 ch.; or 4. PB3 KtQ4 ch. 5. KK4 KtB6 ch. 6. KB5 KtK7.

In these variations the knight plays away from and behind the pawns, thus tending to draw off White's king.

4 K—K5	Kt—Kt5
5 P—B3	

White advances his pawns roller fashion, more or less abreast, so as to keep out Black's king and avoid blockade.

5 ...	Kt—Q6 ch.

5... KtB3 ch. 6. KK4 KR4 is still the simple course.

6 K—K4	Kt—B4 ch.
7 K—Q4	Kt—K3 ch.

This and the following retreat entice White's king where it wants to go. Black should play 7... KtKt6 ch. getting into the wide open spaces.

97

Drawn

8 K—K5   Kt—B1?
9 P—Kt4

The alignment of the pawns on the fourth rank is the danger moment for Black. He should then be ready to attack them effectively with his knight, which he cannot do here.

9 ...   Kt—Q2 ch.
10 K—B4?

This gives Black another chance. White should invade the enemy camp by 10. K—Q6; if 10... KtB3 11. KK6, and if 10... KtB1 11. KK7 KtR2 12. PB4 KKt2 13. PR5.

10 ...   Kt—B4
11 K—K3   Kt—K3
12 P—B4   Kt—Kt2?

A far from bold knight.

12... Kt—B4 draws, 13. K—Q4 (13. KB3 KtQ6 14. KKt3 KtK8) Kt—Q2 14. K—K4 (14. PB5 ch. KB3 15. KK4 KtB4 ch.) 14... Kt—B3 ch. 15. K—B3 Kt—Q4 16. P—B5 ch. (16. PR5 ch. KR3 17. KK4 KtB3 ch. 18. KB5 KtQ4 19. KK5 KtK6) 16... K—B3 17. K—K4 Kt—B6 ch. 18. K—Q4 Kt—K7 ch. 19. K—K3 Kt—Kt6 20. K—B4 (20. KB3 Kt×P) 20... Kt—K7 ch.

After the text-move White gets his pawns to the fifth, and Black is crushed by the pawn roller.

13 K—K4   Kt—K1
14 P—B5 ch.   K—B2
15 P—Kt5   Kt—Q3 ch.
16 K—B4   Kt—K1
17 P—R5   Kt—Kt2
18 P—R6   Kt—K1
19 K—K5   K—Kt1
20 P—Kt6   K—B1
21 P—B6   Kt—B2
22 P—R7.

Black resigns.

A bishop in circumstances similar to the last example would draw with ease. The same principles apply: the king blocks the foremost pawn, the bishop attacks from behind.

98 Duhrssen *v.* Seibold, Correspondence, 1930. The pawns are too advanced, and even the bishop cannot hold them.

98

Black wins

1 B—B6   P—Kt5
2 K—R2   P—R6
3 K—Kt3   K—Kt3
4 B—Q4   K—B4
5 B—K3   K—K5
6 B—Q2   K—Q6
7 B—B4   P—B6
8 K×P   K—K5.

White resigns.

To summarize: in all these basic examples of minor piece *v.* pawn or pawns the bishop proves itself superior to the knight.

4. MINOR PIECE AND PAWN *v.* LONE KING

This is a win, with a few exceptions as shown below.

99   99A

White plays and wins   Drawn
Black plays and draws

4 MINOR PIECE AND PAWN *v.* LONE KING

99 White plays 1. Kt—R6, and his king escapes; but if it is Black's move he plays 1... KB2, and as White's knight can never lose a move it cannot force Black's king from QB1 and QB2.

99A The other draw with a knight also involves a RP on the seventh. Black can never be dug out of the corner. When White's king guards the pawn, hoping to free the knight, he stalemates.

100 Black to play moves 1...KR2 and 2... KR1, after which his king is not dislodgeable, because the bishop does not control the queening square. This is referred to as RP with bishop of the wrong colour, a well known draw.

However, Black must be able to reach the queening square, and merely blocking the pawn is not good enough. White to play wins by keeping Black out of the corner.

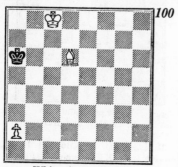

100

White plays and wins
Black plays and draws

1 K—Kt8	K—Kt3
2 P—R3	K—R3
3 B—B5	K—Kt4
4 B—K3	K—R3

If 4... KR5 5. BB1.

5 K—R8	K—R4
6 K—Kt7	K—Kt4
7 B—Q2	K—R5
8 B—Kt4	K—Kt4
9 B—Q6	K—R4
10 B—B5	K—Kt4
11 B—Kt4	K—R5

12 K—Kt6	K—Kt6
13 K—Kt5	K—B7
14 P—R4.	

5. MINOR PIECE AND PAWN *v.* PAWN

Although normally a win, there are a few exceptions.

101 A sacrifice is necessary for White cannot outflank, but he mates in five by 1. KtB6.

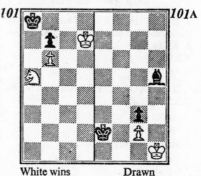

101 *101A*

White wins   Drawn

101A After 1... BB6 2. KKt1 no progress is possible. A KB instead also draws. If there are blocked RPs, with the defender's pawn unmoved, neither the knight nor the bishop can win.

102 When the king is absent the knight (more rarely the bishop) may have difficulty in preventing the loss or exchange of the last pawn.

This beautiful study by Prokes, 1946, shows most of the possible stratagems.

1 P—Q4

Not 1. Kt×P? KB7 2. PQ4 KQ6 3. KtKt5 KB5 4. KKt2 K×Kt 5. KB3 KB3 6. KK4 KQ3.

1 ...   K—B7
2 Kt—K5

A sacrifice which is possible because Black's king is outside the square of the pawn. 2. KtKt5? permits 2... KQ6

63

102

White plays and wins

3. KtB3 KK6 4. KKt2 KK7, Black has the opposition and draws, 5. KKt3 KK6 6. KKt4 KK5 7. KKt5 K×Kt 8. KB5 KK6.

| 2 ... | K—B6 |

If 2... KQ7 3. PQ5 KK6 4. KtB6 KK5 5. KtK7.

| 3 Kt—B3 | K—Q6 |
| 4 K—R2 | |

Not 4. KKt2? KK7.

4 ...	K—K7
5 K—Kt2	K—K6
6 K—Kt3	K—K5
7 K—Kt4	K—K6

If 7... PQ4 8. KKt5.

8 K—B5	K×Kt
9 K—K6	K—K5
10 P—Q5.	

103 The most frequent exception with a bishop occurs when it is of the wrong colour for a RP. In this study by Rauser, 1928, after Teichmann, 1899, the win is simple in principle but not easy in execution.

With the move Black draws by going to the queening square 1... KKt1 and 2... KR1, after which no harm befalls him.

White to play keeps Black from the queening square:

1 B—Kt3	K—Q2
2 K—Kt7	K—Q1
3 K—B6	K—K2

White next drives Black's king outside

the drawing area, the 30 marked-off squares. This the king and bishop are able to do because Black has a tempo move with his RP, but for which he could stay in the area and be stalemated. Thus 3... KB1 fails because of 4. BB7 forcing 4... PR6, and White captures the pawn with his bishop, winning as Example 100.

4 B—B7	K—K3
5 B—Q6	K—B4
6 K—Q7	K—B3
7 B—R3	K—K4
8 B—K7	K—B4
9 K—Q6	K—Kt3
10 K—K6	K—Kt2
11 B—Q8	K—Kt3

103

White plays and wins
Black plays and draws

If 11... KKt1 12. KB6 KB1 13. BK7 ch. KK1 14. KK6, forcing ... PR6.

12 B—B6	K—R3
13 K—B7	K—R4
14 B—K7	K—Kt5
15 K—K6	K—B5
16 B—B6	K—K5
17 B—K5	

It would be premature to play 17. PR3? because Black can get back into the marked-off area by 17... KB5.

17 ...	K—B6
18 B—R2	K—Kt5
19 K—B6	K—R6

If 19... KB6 20. KB5 KK6 21. KK5 KQ6 22. KQ5.

20 B—B4	K—Kt5
21 B—Kt5	K—Kt6
22 K—B5	K—B6
23 B—B4	K—Kt7
24 P—R3	

Now that Black is firmly barred from the drawing area this move may be played. White next captures the RP with his king, whilst still keeping out Black's king.

24 ...	K—B6
25 B—R6	K—Kt6
26 B—Kt5	K—B6

Horwitz and Kling showed the win from here (1851).

27 B—B4	K—Kt7
28 K—Kt4	K—B7
29 B—B1	K—K7
30 K—B4	K—Q8

If 30... KQ6 31. BK3 KB5 32. KK5 KKt6 33. BB5 as in the text play, and if 30... KB7 31. BK3 ch. KKt7 32. KKt4 KR7 33. BB4 ch. KKt8 34. BKt3 KKt8 35. KB3 KR8 36. BKt8 KKt8 37. KK4 KKt7 38. KQ5 KB6 39. KB6 KK5 40. KKt5 KQ4 41. BR2 KK3 42. K × P, Example 100.

31 B—K3	K—B7
32 K—K5	K—Kt6
33 B—B5	K—B5
34 K—Q6	K—Kt4
35 K—Q5	K—R4
36 K—B6	K—R3
37 B—K3	K—R4
38 K—Kt7	K—Kt4
39 B—Kt6	K—B5
40 K—B6	K—Kt6
41 B—B5	K—B5
42 B—K3	K—Kt6
43 B—B1	K—B5
44 B—Kt2	K—Kt6
45 K—Kt5.	

104 When both players have a passed pawn White normally wins, his king supporting his own pawn, his piece holding up Black's pawn.

Difficulty arises only when Black's pawn is very advanced, where White has

Drawn

a RP, and where the minor piece is a knight.

White to play: 1. Kt—Kt4 K—Kt1 (1... KR1? loses, 2. KKt6 KKt1 3.KtB6 PR7 4. PR7 ch. KR1, and White mates in two) 2. K—Kt6 K—R1 3. Kt—B6 P—R7, and both players queen.

With the move Black must retreat just as carefully: 1... K—R1 (1...KKt1? loses) 2. K—Kt6 K—Kt1 3. Kt—Kt4 K—R1, as in the first variation.

The knight here shows one of its weaknesses—it cannot lose a move.

With the kings and the KRP as diagrammed Black draws if his pawn is on one of the following squares: QR6 (as shown), QR7 QKt7 Q7, KB7, KKt6, KKt7, or KR7, and if it is blocked by a knight.

6. MINOR PIECE AND PAWN
v. TWO PAWNS

This is normally a won ending, as might be expected.

105 Where there are no passed pawns White forces a blockade, drives off Black's king, and attacks and captures the pawns.

1 K—B4	K—Kt3
2 B—K2	

Not 2. KKt4? PB4 ch. Black's chief drawing resource is of course an exchange of pawns.

White wins

2 ...	K—R4
3 K—Kt3	K—Kt3
4 K—R4	K—Kt2
5 K—R5	K—R2
6 B—B3	K—Kt2
7 B—Kt2	K—B2
8 K—R6	K—Q2
9 K—Kt7.	

Either blockade loses, 9... PQ4 10. KKt6 KQ3 11. BR3, or 9... PB4 10. PQ5.

It is much the same with a knight, which in compact positions like this is not inferior to the bishop.

106 Pawns nearer the edge are in consequence a better match for the piece, a fact already shown with the knight. The same applies to a bishop, although not in so marked a degree.

An exchange is inevitable after

Drawn

1. K—Q4 (1. KKt4 is profitless) 1... K—R3 2. K—K5 P—B4 3. K—Q6 P—Kt4.

107 When White has a RP with bishop of the wrong colour he draws unless he has other advantages: his pieces must be well advanced and Black's king unable to reach the queening square; or there must be a favourable blockade.

Black with the move gets to the queening square.

1 ...   P—Kt3

Keeping the KtP ahead of the RP is a safe rule.

2 B—K5   P—R3

Not 2... KB1? 3. KB6.

3 B—Kt3	P—Kt4
4 P—R5	P—Kt5.

White plays and wins
Black plays and draws

This pawn decoys White either by 5. KB4 KB3 6. K×P KKt2, or 5. BB4 PKt6 6. BK5 PKt7 7. B×P KB2.

White to play:

1 P—R5

Not 1. B×P? PKt3 2. B×P(BKt8) KB1.

1 ...   K—B1

If 1... P—Kt3 2. P—R6 (the point; not 2. B×P? KB1) 2... K—B1 B—K5.

If 1... P—Kt4 2. P—R6 P—Kt5 (attempting to decoy White's pieces, if

2... KB2 3. B×P) 3. K—B4 K—B3
4. K×P (not 4. B×P? PKt6 5. K×P
KKt4) 4... K—B2 5. B×P.

If 1... P—R3 submitting to a backward pawn, White may even allow Black
into the corner! 2. B—Kt6 (a simple win
follows 2. KB5) 2... K—B1 3. K—Q6
K—Kt1 4. K—Q7 K—R1 5. K—Q8
K—Kt1 6. B—Q4 P—Kt4 (6... KR1
allows mate in three) 7. P×P e.p., con-
verting the moribund RP into a live
KtP.

   2 B×P   K—B2

If 2... PKt3 3. PR6 KB2 4. KQ4 KB3
5. KB4.

   3 K—Q4

3. KB5? PKt3 ch. 4. P×P ch.,
incarcerating the bishop, draws; a
mistake made by L. Paulsen in his game
against Metger, Nuremberg, 1888.

3 ...	K—B3
4 B—Kt6	K—Q3
5 K—B4	K—B3
6 K—Kt4	K—Q2

If 6... KQ3 7. KKt5 KQ2 8. BB2.

7 K—B5	K—B1
8 B—R7	K—B2
9 K—Kt5	K—Q2
10 B—Kt8	K—B1
11 B—R2.	

108 Fleischmann *v.* Mieses (Monte
Carlo, 1904). When Black has an outside
passed pawn White may have difficulty
with the short-ranged knight, but may
expect to win if the pawn is not too
dangerous.

White cannot leave the knight (as he
could a bishop) to take care of the
passed pawn, 1. KK3 KB8 2. KB3
KKt7 3. KtKt5 KKt6 4. K×P KB5,
because the need for a continuous series
of knight-moves leaves him no time to
advance his own pawn, 5. KtR3 ch.
KKt6 6. KtKt1 KB7 7. KtR3 ch., etc.
Therefore White must stop the passed
pawn with his king, whilst the knight
guards the KKtP. An alternative idea is
the sacrifice of the knight for the RP,
thus obtaining a winning pawn-ending.

1 Kt—B4	K—B8

If 1... KK8 2. KK3 KB8 3. KB3 KK8
4. K×P KK2 5. KB4 KQ3(Q!) 6.
KtKt2 ch., a fortunate tactical resource.

2 K—B3	K—Q8
3 Kt—Q6	K—K7
4 Kt—B5	K—B7
5 Kt—R4.	

White captures the RP and returns to
the king's side.

With Black to play it takes longer to
prepare this manœuvre, because the
knight cannot lose a move.

108

White wins

1 ...	K—K8

If 1... K—B8 2. Kt—B4 K—Kt8
(2. KQ8 3. KtQ6 KK8 4. KtB5) 3.
K—Q2 K—R7 4. K—B2, duly giving
up the knight for the RP. The game was
agreed drawn after 1... KB8 2. KtKt5
KKt7 3. KtQ6 KKt6, although White
could still have won.

2 K—K3	K—Q8

If 1... KB8 2. KB3 KK8 3. KtB4.

3 Kt—B4	K—B7
4 K—Q4	K—Kt6
5 K—Q3	K—Kt5
6 Kt—K3	K—Kt6
7 Kt—B2	

White gradually brings his king
towards the RP, whilst keeping Black
from the king's side.

7 ...	K—R7

If 7... K—Kt7 8. K—Q2 K—Kt6

(8... KKt8 9. KB3) 9. K—B1 K—B6
10. Kt-K3 K—Q6 11. Kt—B5, and
White's king blocks the RP, whilst the
knight either takes Black's KtP, 11...
KB6 12. Kt×P, or defends his own
KtP, 11... KK7 12. KKt2 KB7 13.
KtR4.

8 K—B3	K—Kt8
9 Kt—R3ch.	K—B8
10 Kt—B4	K—Q8
11 Kt—Q6	K—K7
12 Kt—B5	K—B7
13 Kt—R4.	

White takes the RP and returns to the
king's side.

109 From a game played at Kishi-
nevsk University, U.S.S.R., 1949, with
analysis by Ganshin. Black's chances of
a draw are better than in Example 108
chiefly because of the possibility of a
pawn exchange on the king's side.

With a knight a draw would be certain;
but having a bishop, White to play just
scores: 1. K—K4 K—R2 2. K—B5
P—R6 3. K—Kt5 P—R7 4. B—Kt2.
Here the superiority of the bishop is
apparent, for it guards QR1 holding
Black's QRP; it attacks KKt7 soon
winning the KKtP; and then controls
KR8 so that White's pawn will promote.

With the move Black strives for a
pawn-exchange:

1 ...	K—R2

Not 1... KB2? 2. KK4 PKt3 3. PR6
PKt4 4. B×P PR6 5. KB5 PR7
6. BB6.

2 K—B4	

White has two winning plans. In the
first and more usual one, given above,
his bishop holds the passed pawn whilst
the king helps his KRP; but here 2. KK4
PKt3 3. PR6 PR6 draws quickly.

The other (or reverse) plan is for
White's king to stop the passed pawn,
and this he now attempts.

2 ...	K—Kt1

As 2... PKt3? 3. PR6 plainly loses,
Black alters course, now steering via
KB2 to attack the KRP with his king.

The shufflings of Black's king seem
meaningless, but are in fact carefully
designed to meet White's various winning attempts.

3 K—Q4	

3. K—Kt4 K—B2 4. B—Kt2 (4...
K×P 5. KB3) 4... P—Kt4 5. K×P
K—Kt1 transposes back to the text
variation.

3 ...	K—R2
4 K—Q3	

White temporizes, for neither winning
plan can be forced.

White plays and wins
Black plays and draws

4 ...	P—R6
5 K—B2	P—R7
6 K—Kt2	K—Kt1
7 K×P	K—B2
8 B—Kt2	

If 8. KKt3 KB3, making for the KRP.

8 ...	P—Kt4
9 K—Kt3	K—Kt1

No time must be lost in renewing his
attack on the KRP. 9... PKt5? loses
after 10. KB4 PKt6 11. KQ3 PKt7 12.
BQ4 KKt1 13. KK4 KR2 14. KB5
KR3 15. KKt4.

10 B—B1	

Else Black plays 10... KR2 and
11... KR3.

10 ...	P—Kt5
11 K—B4	P—Kt6
12 K—Q3	P—Kt7

6 MINOR PIECE AND PAWN v. TWO PAWNS

13 B—K3	K—R2
14 K—K2	P—Kt8=Q
15 B×Q	K—R3.

White's king, commencing midstream, was unable to decide which side to make for. By using both his pawns for decoys, Black finally liquidated the KRP.

110 If Black has two united passed pawns, the normal winning idea is to block them with the minor piece, whilst using the king to assist the lone pawn, as happens here with White to play:

1 K—Q3	K—B3

If 1... KK3 2. KB4 KB4 3. KQ5 preventing counter-attack.

2 K—B4	K—Kt3
3 P—Kt5	K—R2
4 K—B5	K—Kt2
5 P—Kt6	P—Kt6

Desperation, but if 5... KR1 6. KB6 PKt6 7. PKt7 ch.

110

White plays and wins
Black plays and draws

6 B×P	K—R1
7 K—B6	P—R7.

Instead of 8. B×P? stalemate, White mates in three. See also Example 113.

Here White's king helped his pawn to queen. But suppose in the diagram position that White's king and bishop changed places (White K at KR2, B at QB3), then the game is drawn for the bishop cannot assist the pawn's advance; and White's king cannot cross over

without being caught midstream by an advance of Black's pawns, as happened in Example 109.

Black's other counterchance is to assist his pawns with his king:

1 ...	K—K5
2 P—Kt5	K—B6
3 P—Kt6	P—Kt6

Not 3... K—Kt7? 4. P—Kt7 K×B 5. P—Kt8=Q ch. P—Kt6 6. KQ3, and the queen wins after 6... KR8 7. Q×P PR7 8. QB3 ch. KKt8 9. KK2 PR8=Q 10. QB2 checkmate, or here 6... KKt7 7. KK2 PR7 8. QR8 ch. KKt8, when White mates in two.

4 P—Kt7	

If 4. B×P K×B 5. PKt7 PR7.

4 ...	P×B
5 P—Kt8=Q	K—Kt7.

Lastly, not 5... P—R8=Q? 6. QR8 ch.

In this kind of ending, too, the bishop is somewhat the superior piece.

7. MINOR PIECE AND PAWN v. THREE PAWNS

This ending is normally drawn with a knight, but there are often winning chances for a bishop.

111 With one unpassed pawn v. three united pawns the knight draws because it cannot force an effective blockade.

1 K—K3	K—B3
2 K—B4	

If 2. Kt—B3 (2. KK4 KKt4 3. KK5 KKt5) 2... K—B4 3. P—R3 (it is wrong to move this pawn before the enemy pawns are blocked, for an exchange of pawns is thus facilitated) 3... P—Kt4 4. Kt—Q4 ch. K—Kt3 5. K—K4 (5. KB3 PB4) 5... P—Kt5 6. P—R4 (6. P×P PR4) 6... K—R4 7. Kt—B5 P—Kt6 8. K—B3 P—Kt7 9. K×P K—Kt5. The knight, unlike the bishop, cannot move away and yet maintain its guard.

69

111

Drawn

2 ...   P—Kt4 ch.

In all endings of this kind Black has a choice of directly attacking White's pawn as in the last note, or of advancing his mass of pawns so that an exchange of White's last pawn is eventually forced.

3 K—K4   K—K3
4 Kt—K2

If 4. KtB3 PB4 ch. 5. KK3 KB3.

4 ...   P—B4 ch.
5 K—Q4   P—R4
6 Kt—B1

If 6. KtKt3 PB5 7. Kt×P KB2 trapping the knight. 6... PR5 is also good.

6 ...   K—B3
7 K—K3

White wants to answer the threatened ... PKt5 by KB4, firmly blocking the pawns with his king.

7 ...   K—K4
8 Kt—Q3 ch.   K—B3.

If White temporises Black maintains the status quo, but must not try and force matters, for after 9. KB3 PKt5 ch.? 10. KB4 White wins.

If White tries anything Black soon forces a pawn exchange, 9. KQ4 PKt5 10. KtB4 KKt4 11. KK3 PR5 12. KtK6 ch. KB3 13. KtQ4 KKt4 14. KtK2 PR6 and now 15. KB2 PB5, or 15. KtB4 PKt6.

112 Kashdan *v.* Flohr, Hamburg, 1930. If a blockade already exists (or can

be forced) the knight wins against the pawns when they are united or close together.

1 Kt—B3   K—B5
2 K—Kt5

112

White wins

Not 2. Kt—R4 K—Q4 3. Kt×P? P×Kt 4. K×P P—R5 5. P—K6 K—Q3 (5... PR6? 6. PK7 PR7 7. PK8=Q PR8=Q 8. QR8 ch.) 6. K—B6, when both players queen.

2 ...   K—Q4
3 K—B6   P—B5
4 Kt—R4   K—K5
5 K×P   P—B6
6 Kt×P.

The sacrifice of the piece for a winning pawn-ending is a well known theme. After queening Black falls into a mating net, 6... K×Kt 7. KB5 PR5 8. PK6 PR6 9. PK7 PR7 10. PK8=Q KKt7 11. KKt4 PR8=Q 12. QK2 ch. KKt8 13. KKt3, Example 306.

113 If Black has a pair of united passed pawns White usually wins if they are neither too forward nor too far away, and if he has a bishop, as in this position by Averbach, 1954.

Under favourable circumstances a knight might also win, but a draw would be more likely.

1 B—B2

Preventing ... KKt6. 1. B—R2? is less clear, for Black's king stays on his fifth

rank and cannot be driven back, 1...
K—R5 2. B—B7 (to answer 2... KKt5
by 3. BQ6, for if 2. BQ6 KKt5 3. KK3
PB4 4. KB2 PB5 5. BK5 KB4 6. BKt7
KK5) 2... K—R4 3. K—K3 K—Kt5
4. K—B2 P—B4 5. B—Kt6 P—B5
6. B—Q4 K—B5.

1 ...	K—B5
2 B—K1	

White's bishop safeguards his pawn,
and his king maintains the blockade—
not the best arrangement. No progress
can be made this way for if 2. KB5
KKt5 3. K×P? Black draws by 3...
PQ5 decoying the bishop. White therefore regroups.

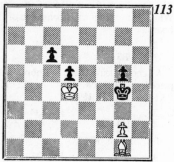

113

White plays and wins

2 ...	K—B4

Black's king has a choice of defences:
it may harass White's pawn, as now; or
support his own passed pawns as later.
There is no such counterplay after
2... KKt5 3. KK5 KR4 4. KB5 PB4
5. PKt4 ch., blocking and thereby safeguarding his pawn.

3 B—Kt3	K—K3
4 B—Kt8	K—B4
5 B—B7	K—Kt5

White is tempo-manœuvring. If now
5... KK3 6. PKt4.

6 B—Q6	K—B4
7 K—K3	K—Kt5
8 K—B2	K—B4

If 8... PQ5 9. KK2 KB4 10. KQ3
KK3 11. BB5.

9. K—B3	P—Q5

White's pieces are now correctly
placed, and continued defensive play is
hopeless: 9... KK3 10. BB5 KB4 11.
PKt4 ch. KKt3 12. KK3 KB3 13. KQ4
KKt3 14. BKt6 KB3 15. BQ8 ch. KKt3
16. KK5.

Black therefore advances his pawns, a
counter-attack not to be underrated.

10 P—Kt4 ch.	K—K3
11 B—B5	K—Q4
12 B—K7	P—B4
13 B×P	P—B5
14 B—B6	P—B6
15 B—Kt7	K—B5
16 K—K2	

The pawns fall to a combined assault.
There is a natural tendency for White's
king to go to the same part of the board
as Black's king, thus foiling his schemes.

16 ...	P—Q6 ch.
17 K—K3	P—Q7

If 17... PB7 8. BKt2.

18 K—K2	K—Kt6
19 K—Q1	K—B5
20 B×P.	

114 When Black has three united
passed pawns, such a phalanx may well
draw against a knight. For a bishop
however there are good winning chances
if the pawns are not beyond the second
or third rank, but a probable draw if
they are farther forward. There are
rarely any winning prospects for Black,
unless White overreaches himself.

1 K—K4

The normal winning method follows,
the king supporting the KKtP, the
bishop blocking Black's pawns.

1 ...	P—B4
2 P—Kt4	P—Kt3

If 2... PKt4 3. BK3 KQ3 4. PKt5
PKt5, and there follows a sacrifice,
5. B×P ch. K×B 6. PKt6 PKt6
7. KQ3.

3 B—B4	P—R3

A blockade also follows 3... PB5 4. BQ2 PR4 5. BB3 PR5 6. BKt4.

| 4 B—B7 | P—Kt4 |
| 5 B—Kt6 | P—B5 |

If 5... KQ3 6. PKt5 PKt5 7. B×P ch.

6 B—R5.

The rest is easy, the bishop making tempo-moves if necessary. 6... KB3 7. KB4 KKt3 8. PKt5 KKt2 9. KB5 KB2 10. PKt6 ch. KKt1 11. KB6 KB1 12. PKt7 ch. KKt1 13. BKt4.

Black with the move avoids a fatal blockade.

1 ...   K—K4

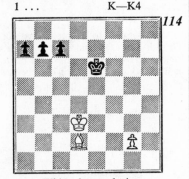

114

White plays and wins
Black plays and draws

Preventing the enemy king's advance, for the time being.

Black's king must be within reach of the KKtP, yet able to assist his own pawns. If he at once plays 1... KB4 2. KK3 KKt5? then after 3. KB2 PB4 4. PKt3 PKt3 5. BB4 his unsupported pawns are soon blocked.

After 1... P—B4 2. K—K4 P—Kt4 3. B—K3 K—Q3 4. P—Kt4 P—Kt5 5. K—B5 P—R4 6. P—Kt5 (6. KB6 PKt6 7. BB1 PB5 8. BKt2 KB4) 6... P—Kt6 7. B—B1 P—B5 8. B—Kt2 K—K2 9. K—Kt6 P—R5 10. K—R6 K—Q2 11. P—Kt6 P—B6 12. B×P P—R6, White queens first, although it is doubtful whether he can win.

2 K—K3

White's first task is to attack and block the enemy pawns, so he frees his bishop from the need of defending the KKtP, for if 2. BB3 ch. KB5 3. BK1 PR4, or if 2. PKt4 PB4 3. BK3 PKt4.

If 2. P—Kt3 P—B4 3. B—B4 ch. K—Q4 4. P—Kt4 P—Kt4 5. P—Kt5 P—B5 ch. 6. K—B3, Black draws by 6... K—K3. He must avoid the fiendish trap 6... PR4? 7. PKt6 PKt5 ch. 8. KKt2 KK3 9. BKt5, when his king dare not move whilst the pawns, having to do so, fall like ninepins, 9... PR5 10. BR4 PR6 ch. 11. KR2 PB6 12.KKt3.

If 2. B—K3 P—R4 3. P—Kt3 P—R5 4. B—B4 ch. K—B4 5. B×P (5. BB1 PB4) 5... P—R6 6. K—B3 (6. BKt6 PR7 7. BQ4 KKt5) 6... P—Kt4 7. K—Kt3 P—Kt5 8. B—Q6 K—Kt5, White's king is on the wrong side of the board.

2 ...   P—B4
3 K—B3

A check leaves the bishop badly placed, 3. BB3 ch. KB4, or 3. PKt4 PKt4 4. BB3 ch. KK3.

3 ...   P—Kt4
4 B—K3

If 4. BB4 ch. KK3.

4 ...   K—Q3
5 P—Kt4

The attempt to force a queen, 5. KKt4 PKt5 6. KR5? fails because Black does so first, 6... PKt6 7. BB1 PB5 8. BKt2 KB4 9. BB3 PR4.

5 ...	P—Kt5
6 K—K4	P—R4
7 P—Kt5	

7. KB5 PR5 is even dangerous for White.

7 ...   P—Kt6
8 B—B1.

Black draws after 8... PB5 9. BKt2 PR5 10. KB5 KK2 11. KKt6 KQ2; or after 8... KK3, when White cannot do more than liquidate all the pawns, 9. BR3 PB5 10. BKt2 PR5 11. KQ4 KB4. White's blockade is not effective, Black's pawns being too far forward.

7 MINOR PIECE AND PAWN v. THREE PAWNS

115 Black's best chances occur when his pawns are widely spread.

If advanced they may defeat a knight and pawn, otherwise they draw. As usual the bishop is stronger, and may win if Black's pawns are far back.

In the ending Thomas v. Flohr, Hastings, 1935-36, White's king is badly placed outside the square of Black's passed pawns, yet the game should be drawn.

1 B—Q2

Controlling the advance of the QRP and QP from one diagonal, K1-QR5. Thomas lost after 1. KQ6? PR4 2. PKt4 PR5 3. PKt5 PQ6 4. KK7 PR6, Black queening first.

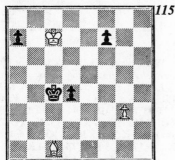

115

White plays and draws
Black plays and wins

1 ...	K—Q6
2 B—R5	K—K7
3 K—Kt7	P—Q6

If 3... KB6 4. K×P K×P 5. KKt6 PB4 6. KB5.

4 K×P	P—Q7
5 B×P	K×B
6 K—Kt6	K—K7
7 K—B5	K—B6
8 K—Q5	K×P
9 K—K5.	

Much depends on where the pawns are. With the move a rapid advance wins for Black, because White's king is out of the play, 1... PR4 2. KQ6 PR5 3. KK7 PQ6 4. K×P PR6, etc.

According to how widely spaced or far advanced they are, four pawns tend to be somewhat better than a minor piece and pawn.

8. MINOR PIECE AND PAWNS v. PAWNS

116 In the preceding examples Black's defence hinged upon the exchange of White's last pawn. If White has two or more pawns his prospects are therefore a great deal better. In general two pawns will not then be sufficient compensation for the piece.

1 K—K3

The first phase, centralizing the pieces.

1 ...	K—Q2
2 Kt—Q3	K—Q3
3 K—K4	P—B4
4 Kt—B4	

The second phase, forcing some kind of pawn weakness. Black will have to move his KKtP.

4 ...   P—QKt4

As weaknesses will be induced anyway, Black takes the bull by the horns, and advances his queen's side pawns in an attempt to get counterplay.

5 Kt—R5	P—Kt3
6 Kt—B4	P—QR4

If 6... PKt5 7. KtQ3 PQR4 8. PQKt3, or if 6... PB5 7. KQ4.

7 P—KKt4

116

White wins

73

The third phase: to fix or block
Black's weakened pawns.

7 ...   P—Kt5

If 7... PKR4 the typical sacrifice
8. Kt×RP P×Kt 9. P×P leaves a won
pawn ending.

8 P—Kt5   P—B5

White answers ... PR5 the same way.
In fact Black cannot avoid the blocking
of his queen's side pawns.

9 Kt—Q5

9. KQ4 PB6 10. P×P P×P 11. K×P
KK4 12. KtR3 also wins.

9 ...   K—K3

Seeking entry on the king's side. If
9... KB4 10. KK5 PR5 11. Kt×P or
11. PR3

10 P—R3

Not 10. KtB6? PR4, when Black has
threats on both wings.

10 ...   P—Kt6

If 10... P×P 11. P×P KQ3 12. KtB6,
or if 10... PB6 11. Kt×BP.

11 P—R4   K—Q3
12 Kt—B3.

The last phase, mopping up the fixed
pawns. Play might continue 12... KK3
13. KtKt5 KQ2 14. KQ5 KK2 15. KK5
KB1 16. KB6 KKt1 17. KtR3.

117 Iljin-Genevsky *v.* Myasoedov,
Leningrad, 1932. Colours reversed. The
pawns save the game only when dangerously advanced, and it is rarely possible
to force such a situation. Here Black's
sporting try succeeds.

1 ...   P—Q5

If 1... KK3 2. BR7 KB4 3. PB3 PR6
4. BQ4 PKt3 5. P×P K×P 6. PK4
P×P 7. P×P, White wins.

2 B—Q6?

White should first fix the king's side
pawns 2. PB5, and then deal with Black's
passed pawns, 2... PR6 3. BR7 P×P
4. P×P PR7 5. BQ4, winning in due
course.

2 ...   P—Q6
3 K—B1   P—Kt3

Black now obtains threats on both
sides of the board, and he must at least
draw.

4 P—B5?

White wins

White overlooks Black's brilliant fifth
move. An interesting draw follows
4. P×P ch. K×P 5. KK1 PR4 6. KQ2
PR5 7. K×P PKR6 8. PB5 ch. K×P
9. PB3 KK3 10. BB4 PR6 11. KB3
PQR7 12. KKt2 KQ4 13. K×P KB5
14. KKt2 KQ6 15. KKt3 KK7 16. KB3
K×P 17. KQ3 PB4 18. KQ4 KK7.

4 ...   P×RP
5 K—K1   K—K1

White yet wins after 5... PR5?
6. KQ2 PKR6 7. K×P PR6 8. KB3.

6 K—Q2

White resigned after 6. PK4 KQ2
7. PK5 PR5 8. BKt8 PQR6.

6 ...   K—Q2.

The bishop must move from its key
square. Whether he plays 7. BR3 PR5
or 7. BR2 PR6, White has not time to
take the queen's pawn.

118 Botvinnik *v.* Thomas, Nottingham, 1936. Black's passed pawns are
unlikely to be dangerous when they are
close together. Here they are already
blocked, so White is ready for the
mopping-up phase, which requires more

care than usual because of Black's advanced protected passed pawn.

1 ...   K—Q2

White threatened the break-through 2. Kt×P ch. P×Kt 3. PB6.

118

White wins

2 Kt—R5	K—Q1
3 Kt—B6	P—R3
4 Kt—Kt4	P—R4
5 Kt—B2	K—Q2
6 K—R4	K—Q1
7 K×P	K—K2
8 K—Kt4	K—K3
9 K—Kt3	K—Q2
10 Kt—Kt4	

Botwinnik won in another way, by driving Black's king to QR1 and leaving it without a move, thus forcing PB7, when White's king returns and captures it.

| 10 ... | K—K2 |
| 11 Kt—K5 | K—Q1 |

White threatened Kt × QBP.

12 Kt×KBP

The familiar sacrifice, breaking up the blocked position.

12 ...	P×Kt
13 K×P	K—K2
14 P—K4	P×P ch.
15 K×P	K—K3
16 P—Q5 ch.	P×P ch.
17 K—Q4	K—Q2
18 K×P.	

As Example 37.

A knight is sometimes the better piece

in a blocked position. Here White could have won with a KB instead; but a QB would have been useless, Black running to his funkhole at QR1.

119 Macht *v.* Batik, Correspondence, 1927. When White has a bishop of the wrong colour for the RP, Black may be able to bring about a draw by exchange of pawns, providing their numbers are already sufficiently reduced.

1 B—Kt5 ?

A mistake, because the bishop comes under attack on its K3 square later on. Instead, White should play 1. B—R4 P—Kt5 2. B—B2 P×P 3. P×P K—Q6 (if 3... KKt4 4. B×P as in the game) 4. K×P K—K5 5. B—Kt3 K—B4 (Black is in the drawing area of Example 103, but too far east) 6. K—Kt5 K—K3 7. K×P K—Q2 8. K—Kt5 K—B1 9. K—Kt6, Example 100.

1 ...   P—Kt5

2 B—K3

If 2. P×P P×P White's last pawn soon falls.

| 2 ... | P×P |
| 3 P×P | K—Q6 |

The position relates to Example 103, and the result depends on whether Black's king can be kept out of the drawing area there shown. In the game he lost after 3... KKt4? 4. B×P KR4 5. KB6 KR3 6. BKt1 KR4 7. KKt7, Example 103.

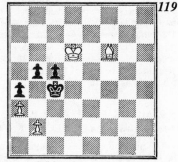

119

White plays and wins

4 B×P	K—K5
5 K—K6	K—B5
6 B—Q6 ch.	

Although 6.BK7 drives Black from the drawing area, White's pieces are not so placed that they can keep him out.

6 ...	K—Kt4

Not 6... KK5? 7. BR2, for in this way Black can be forced permanently out of the drawing area, 7... KQ5 8. KQ6 KB5 9. KB6 KKt6 10. BQ6 KB5 11. BB5.

7 K—Q5	K—B3
8 K—B5	K—K3
9 K—B6	K—B2.

A draw follows 10. K—Kt5 K—K3 (10. KK1? K×P 11. KQ2 KKt5) 11. K×P K×B.

It has been stated that four pawns are generally a little superior to a minor piece and pawn. However, when there are more pawns on the board the piece is about equal in value to three pawns. For instance, an ending with minor piece and two pawns *v.* five pawns is normally drawn. If either side has a positional advantage he may win: if the enemy pawns are or can be blocked, the minor piece may lead to victory; but if the player with the pawns has them well advanced and mobile, then he will probably win.

The relative merits of the knight and bishop when opposed to one another have been debated for many years; but there is no doubt that the bishop is a superior alternative to the knight when combating an enemy superiority of pawns, and especially when those pawns are widely spaced. Only in blocked positions is the knight sometimes a superior piece as in Example 118, but even there a bishop of the right colour would do as much.

9. MINOR PIECE AND PAWN *v.* MINOR PIECE

The position of Black's king is of first importance in this ending. If it blocks the pawn a draw is normal. Otherwise

Black will try to give up his piece for the pawn, and will succeed, except against an advanced RP or KtP, if his king is not too far off. But if the defending king is on the far side of the board, then there are sometimes winning chances for an unmoved KtP or RP, or for a well advanced BP or Centre P.

As to the pawn, the nearer the edge the better, the KtP and RP having the best prospects.

Finally, as to the piece, the bishop is stronger than the knight in these open positions.

Endings with bishops of opposite colour are treated separately, Examples 174-188.

120 For White the least favourable permutation of pieces is Kt+P *v.* B. Black mostly draws if his king is not too far away. The most favourable pawn is the RP or KtP, and this critical position with RP on the seventh relates to Example 99.

1 Kt—Kt7 ch.

If 1. Kt—B4 B—R8 2. Kt—Kt6 (2. KtQ6 or R5 BR1) 2... B—Kt7 3. Kt—R4(B4) B—R8.

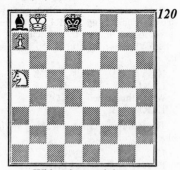

White plays and draws
Black plays and loses

1 ...	K—Q2
2 K×B	K—B1

Black plays to a square the same colour as that on which the knight stands. 2... KB2? loses to 3. KtQ6.

3 Kt—Q6 ch.   K—B2

The knight cannot lose a move; and
having to play neither can Black:

1 ...   K—Q2

If 1... BR8 2. KtKt7 ch. screening the
pawn's advance.

2 Kt—Kt7   K—B3
3 K×B   K—B2
4 Kt—Q6.

121 Even when Black's king is as
far away as it can be White has winning
chances only when the pawn is well
advanced. As a rough guide this means a
RP on the fourth as in Example 145,
a KtP on the fifth, a BP on the sixth as
in this example by Kosek, 1910, or a
Centre P on the seventh.

1 Kt—Q6   B—Kt8
2 P—B6   B—Kt3
3 K—K6   B—B2

One long diagonal (Black's QKt1-
KR7) and one short diagonal (Q1-QR4)
intersect on QB2, across which the pawn
has yet to move.

The result is largely determined by the
length of the shorter diagonal, and here
four squares is not sufficient for the
bishop which is eventually driven away.
If for instance the pawn had yet to cross
White's QB6, in which case the shorter
diagonal has five squares, the bishop
could hold it back.

Pawns nearer the edge of the board
have better chances of winning because
the diagonals are there shorter, and the
defending bishop proportionately less
effective.

4 K—Q7   B—Kt1
5 Kt—K8   K—Kt7
6 Kt—B7   B—R2

If 6... K—B6 7. K—B8 B—R2
8. Kt—Kt5 B—Kt3 (8... BK6 9. KtQ6
BKt3 10. KtbB4 BKt8 11. KQ7) 9.
Kt—Q6 K—K7 10. Kt—B4 driving off
the bishop, 10... BB7 11.KQ7 BKt6
12. KtQ6.

7 Kt—R6   B—Kt3
8 Kt—B5   K—B6

White plays and wins
Black plays and draws

9 Kt—R4   B—R4
10 Kt—Kt2   K—K5
11 Kt—B4.

The knight on QB4 chases away the
bishop. Black to play may control this
vital square with his king:

1 ...   K—Kt7
2 Kt—Q6   B—Kt8
3 P—B6   B—Kt3
4 K—K6   B—B2
5 K—Q7   B—Kt1
6 Kt—K8   K—B7

The king must choose his route care-
fully. After 6... K—B8? 7. Kt—B7
K—K7 (he runs into an awkward check
on this square, but if 7... BR2 8. KtR6
BKt3 9. KtB5 KK7 10. KtR4 BR4
11. KtKt2 and Black's king cannot play
to Q6) 8. K—B8 B—R2 9. Kt—K6
B—B7 (9... BKt3 10. KKt7 BR4 11.
KR6) 10. Kt—B4 ch. K—B6 11.
K—Kt7.

7 Kt—B7   B—R2
8 Kt—R6

A cyclic repetition follows 8. KB8
BQ5 9. KtKt5 BK4 10. KQ7 BKt1
11. KtB7 BR2. If 8. KtKt5 BKt1.

8 ...   B—Kt3
9 Kt—B5   K—K6
10 Kt—R4   B—R4
11 Kt—Kt2   K—Q5.

Preventing 12. Kt—B4.

122 Reshevsky *v.* Rossolimo. Amsterdam, 1950. Kt+P *v.* Kt is a more favourable arrangement of pieces for White, and the RP is then much the strongest pawn. Here White wins with a RP on the fourth.

1 ...	Kt—K3 ch.
2 K—B6	Kt—B4
3 P—R5	Kt—K5 ch.
4 K—B7	K—B6

In the game, Black lost after 4... KtKt4 ch.? 5. KKt7 KK5 6. PR6 KB4 7. KtB8 KKt5 8. KKt6 KR5 9. KtQ7 KKt5 10. KtK5 ch. KB5 11. KtB7 KtK3 12. KB6 KtB1 13. KKt7 KtK3 ch. 14. KKt8.

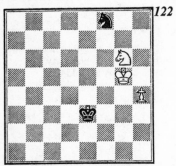

Black plays and draws

5 P—R6	K—Kt5
6 K—Kt7	Kt—Kt4

Black's knight holds back the pawn by moving on the 'circuit' KKt4, K3, KB1, and KR2. White's knight plays via KKt8, KB6, Q7, and K5 to KB7, thus controlling Black's KKt4 and interrupting the circuit.

From time to time White's knight guards the pawn, thus making it possible for his King to move freely, and to gain time whilst avoiding harassment from the black knight.

7 Kt—K7

7. KtK5 ch.? KR4 8. KtB7 KtK3 ch. 9. KR7 KtB2 draws (Reti). The pawn is blocked and Black frees his knight, threatening checks at K1, KB3, and

KR4; but if 9. KKt8 KtKt4.

7 ...	K—R4

Or 7... KtK3 ch. 8. KB6 KtB1 9. KB7 KtR2 10. KKt7 KtKt4 11. K—Kt6 Kt—K3 12. KtKt8 KtB1 ch. 13. KB7 KtR2 14. KKt7 KtKt4 15. KtB3 ch. KB5 16. KKt6 KtK3 17. KtQ7 KtKt4 18. KtK5 KtK3 19. KtB7. The method is the same, here, in the game, and as follows.

8 Kt—Kt8	Kt—K3 ch.
9 K—B7	Kt—Kt4 ch.
10 K—B6	Kt—R2 ch.
11 K—Kt7	Kt—Kt4
12 Kt—B6 ch.	K—R5
13 K—Kt6	Kt—K3
14 Kt—Q7	Kt—Kt4

Or 14... KtB5 ch. 15. KB7 KR4 16. PR7 KtKt3 17. KKt7 KKt4 18. KtK5.

15 Kt—K5	Kt—K3
16 Kt—B7	K—Kt5
17 K—B6	Kt—B1
18 K—Kt7	Kt—K3 ch.
19 K—Kt8.	

In general a KtP is not so favourable, although it has some winning chances; but against a BP or Centre P the defending knight operates at full strength on either side of it, and in consequence usually draws.

When Black's king is on the far side of the board White has winning chances with an unmoved RP, or a not too backward KtP; but has chances with a BP or Centre P only if it is already far advanced.

123 There are exceptions to all generalizations about knights because if one is badly placed several moves may be needed for regrouping. This study is by Halberstadt.

1 Kt—B4	Kt—R2
2 Kt—K6	

A great weakness of the knight: if on the edge of the board it may become trapped.

2 ...	K—R1
3 P—B3	

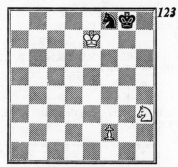

123

White plays and wins

A tempo-move, for if 3. PB4? KKt1
4. PB5 KR1 5. KB7 KtKt4 ch. 6.
Kt×Kt stalemate; or if 3. KB7?
KtKt4 ch. 4. KK7 KtB6.

3 ...	K—Kt1
4 P—B4	K—R1
5 K—B7	Kt—Kt4 ch.
6 P×Kt.	

124 White's prospects with bishops
are somewhat better still. If the defending king is unable to block the pawn but
can attack it from the rear, then White
wins with a pawn at R5, R6, Kt6, or
Kt7; sometimes wins with a pawn at
Kt5, B5, B6, B7, or a Centre pawn on the
sixth or seventh; but draws if the pawn
is farther back, or at R7.

The KtP is the strongest, followed by
RP, BP and Centre P in that order.

Here a rook's pawn on the fourth
draws.

124

Drawn

1 B—Kt6	B—K8
2 B—R5	B—R5
3 B—Kt4	B—Q1
4 B—B5	

If 4. BQ6 BKt3.

| 4 ... | B—B2. |

Black's bishop cannot be driven off
the diagonal Q1-QR4. The length of this
diagonal is the critical factor, and four
squares is just sufficient.

125 Centurini, 1856. A RP on the
fifth wins because the critical diagonal
has only three squares.

| 1 B—Kt7 | B—Kt4 |
| 2 B—R6 | B—B3 |

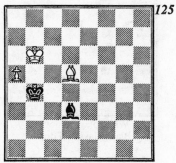

125

White wins

If 2... BQ2 3. BB1 BB1 4. BKt5
BKt2 5. BQ7.

3 B—B1	B—Kt2
4 B—Kt5	B—B1
5 B—B6.	

Black is now in zugzwang. If 5... BR6
6. PR6, or if 5... KB5 6. BKt7.

A RP on the sixth will win; but if the
diagram position is moved up two ranks
(RP on seventh) White draws because he
has no means of opposing bishops on the
long diagonal.

126 A KtP on the fifth draws if
Black has the direct opposition, which
with the move he takes, 1... K—Kt6
2. B—Kt6 B—Kt4 3. B—B2 (3. KKt7
KR5 4. KB6 KKt6 5. BB5 BQ1 6. BQ6

79

KB5) 3... B—Q1 4. B—K1 K—R5, preventing 5. B—R5. The four-square diagonal Q1-QR4 suffices.

If White has the diagonal opposition, which is more favourable for him, he may win with a pawn on Kt5, B6, or a centre pawn on the sixth or seventh; whereas the direct opposition only draws in these cases.

1 B—Kt6	B—Kt4
2 B—B2	B—Q1
3 B—K1	B—B2
4 B—R5	

126

White plays and wins
Black plays and draws

This key manœuvre is only possible with diagonal opposition.

4 ...	B—Kt6
5 P—Kt6	K—B4
6 P—Kt7	

A KtP on the seventh always wins, as shown by Centurini, 1856.

| 6 ... | K—B3 |

If 6... BKt1 7. BKt6 ch. KB3 8. BK3 KQ2 9. KKt6 KQ1 10. KB6 KK2 11. BKt6 KK3 12. BB7 BR2 13. KKt5 KQ2 14. KR6.

7 K—R7	K—Kt4
8 B—K1	B—R7
9 K—R8	K—R3
10 B—B2	B—B5
11 B—R7	B—R7
12 B—Kt8	B—Kt8
13 B—Kt3	B—R2
14 B—R2.	

127 Centurini, 1856, shows the win with the KtP on the sixth.

| 1 ... | K—R3 |

If 1... BR3 2. KB6 BKt4 ch. 3. KB7 BR3 4. BB5 KKt5 5. BQ3.

| 2 B—B6 | B—B1 |
| 3 B—K4 | B—Kt2 |

If 3... BQ2 (preventing KB6) 4. PKt7 KR2 5. KQ6.

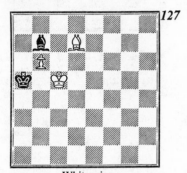

127

White wins

4 B—Q3 ch.	K—R4
5 B—Kt5	B—B1
6 K—B6	K—Kt5

If 6... BQ2 ch. 7. KB7 BB1 8. BB4.

7 B—Q3	B—R6
8 B—K4	B—B1
9 K.--B7	K—Kt4
10 B—Q3 ch.	K—B4(R4)
11 B—K2.	

White to play moves 1. B—Kt5 (see 5. BKt5 above).

A position similar to the diagram but with White's king at QR5 and Black's at QB4 would be drawn; White could not force Dehler's position (see Example 132) with Black to play.

128 A BP on the seventh wins only if White's king is on the knight's file (Kt6 or Kt8).

A BP on the fifth has winning chances only if White's king has the diagonal opposition, and is on the knight's file (Kt6).

White plays and wins

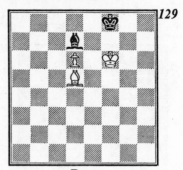

Drawn

Lipnitsky should have won this ending *v.* Sokolsky, Moscow, 1950.

| 1 P—B6 | B—B4 |
| 2 P—B7 | K—Q3 |

Horizontal opposition.

3 B—B3	B—B1
4 B—Kt2	B—Kt5
5 K—Kt7	K—B4
6 K—Kt8	K—Kt3

This is the equivalent form of vertical opposition.

7 B—Kt7	B—B4
8 B—B8	B—Q6
9 B—Kt4	B—R3
10 B—B3	K—B4
11 B—Kt7.	

White's king has to be on the knight's file. If it were here at Q8 there would be no effective way of driving Black's bishop off the short diagonal QB1—QR3.

129 When Black's king cannot block the pawn he must try to attack it from behind, and to obtain the direct opposition.

Against a centre pawn, however far advanced, this ensures the draw.

1 B—B7

Preventing ... K—K1—Q1 blocking the pawn.

1 ...	B—R5
2 B—Kt6	B—Q2
3 B—R5	B—R6
4 K—K5	K—Kt2

Black's king follows White's, taking the direct opposition in due course.

5 K—Q5	B—Q2
6 K—B5	K—B3
7 K—Kt6	K—K4
8 K—B7	B—B4

Not 8... BR5? for the diagonal opposition loses after 9. BB3 threatening 10. BB6.

9 B—K8	K—Q5
10 B—Q7	B—B7
11 B—Kt4	B—R5
12 B—B3	K—B4.

Both of the diagonals intersecting at Black's Q2 are sufficiently long for a proper defence.

130 Teichmann *v.* Marshall, San Sebastian, 1911. Colours reversed. The RP on the fifth wins if the defending king attacks from the rear; but special to the RP is a different drawing idea, Black's king approaching from the side.

1 ...   B—R6

Teichmann resigned after 1... KQ4? 2. BB1 KQ3 3. BK2, for if 3... KQ4 4. BB3 ch. KQ3 5. B×P.

2 B—K2

After 2. K×P K—B4 (preventing White's king playing to QKt6, as Example 125) 3. B—K2 B—Kt7 ch. 4. K—B7 (if 4. KR7 BK5 5. PR6 BKt7 6. KKt8 KKt3, Black's bishop cannot be driven from the long diagonal) 4...

B—B6 5. B—R6 (5. B×B KKt4)
5... B—Kt7 6. B—Kt7 B—B8.

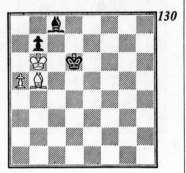

130

Drawn

2 ...	B—Kt7
3 B—Kt4	B—K5
4 B—B8	B—Kt7
5 B×P	B—B8
6 B—R6	B×B
7 K×B	K—B2(B3).

131 When Black's king is far behind, White has winning chances with an un-moved RP, as shown by Cheron (1956).

With the move Black draws by 1... BKt3 2. PR4 BQ1 3. BQ6 BKt3 4. BK7 BB2 5. BB5 BQ1 6. KB4 KR7 7. KKt5 KKt6, Example 124.

White to play circumvents this defence.

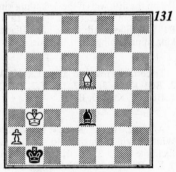

131

White plays and wins
Black plays and draws

1 B—B7	B—B7
2 P—R4	B—K8
3 B—Kt6	B—Q7
4 B—B5	B—R4

Forced, because 5. BKt4 is threatened, but now White gains a vital tempo by attacking the bishop on this square.

5 K—B4	K—B7
6 K—Kt5	B—Q1
7 B—Kt6.	

And the pawn goes through.

132 Grigoriev, 1931, shows how a KtP on the fourth may win when the enemy king is far away.

| 1 B—Q5 | K—Kt4 |

If 1... BKt4 2. KQ4 KKt4 3. KB5 BR3 4. BB4.

| 2 B—B4 | |

The bishop shields the pawn's advance.

| 2 ... | B—Kt5 |

If 2... BB6 3. PKt5 KB3 4. KKt4 KK2 5. KR5.

| 3 P—Kt5 | K—B3 |
| 4 P—Kt6 | B—B1 |

If 4... BB6 5. KQ4 BKt2 6. BQ5.

5 K—Q4	K—K2
6 K—B5	K—Q2
7 B—Kt5 ch.	K—Q1

If 7... KK2 8. KB6 KQ1 9. BB4.

| 8 K—B6 | |

The continuation given by Fine, 8. KQ6? BKt2 9. BQ7 BKt7 10. BK6 BKt2 11. KB5, draws, for after 11... BB6 12. BQ5 Black is not forced to exchange bishops but plays 12... BK7 13. PKt7 KB2.

| 8 ... | B—Q2 ch. |

If 8... BR6 9. KKt7 as in the text.

| 9 K—Q6 | B—B1 |

If 9... B—B4 (9... B×B 10. PKt7) 10. P—Kt7 B—B1 11. P—Kt8=B, the only move, 11... B—B4 12. B—B7 ch. K—B1 13. B—R6 mate.

10 B—B4	B—Kt2
11 B—K6	

As shown by Dehler (1922) White can win this crucial position only if it is Black's move.

132

White plays and wins

11 ...	B—R3

If 11... BB6 12. BQ5 B×B 13. K×B, Example 13.

12 K—B6	B—B1

If 12... BK7 13. KKt7 BB6 ch. 14. KR7.

13 B—B4	B—B4
14 K—Kt7	B—K5 ch.
15 K—R7	K—Q2
16 B—R6	K—Q3(Q1)
17 B—Kt7	B—B4
18 B—B3	B—B1
19 B—Kt4.	

Finishing with the customary sacrifice —Black's bishop must leave the short diagonal.

Black to play draws by 1... KKt4, swiftly getting his king back, or by 1... BQ8 2. PKt5 BR5.

With a BP or Centre P not beyond respectively the fourth or fifth rank, a win is unlikely even though the defending king is absent. Dehler's position (see move 11) is drawn except with the KtP, as is clear from Example 129.

133 B+P *v.* Kt compares with B+P *v.* B; but if the knight is awkwardly

situated White's prospects are somewhat better.

The RP is strongest, followed by KtP, BP, and Centre P, in that order.

As before, Black draws if his king blocks the pawn, unless his knight can be trapped on the edge of the board.

With Black's king attacking from the rear a RP on the sixth or seventh wins, but on the fifth it may be held, as in this position from a game played in Holland, 1953.

1 B—K8	K—B5
2 K—Kt6	K—Q5

In this kind of ending White cannot shield the pawn's advance, as he does when Black has a bishop; nor can he challenge the knight when it is on a square of the wrong colour. White's chief weapon is zugzwang, which comes about after 2... KKt5? 3. BKt5, for the knight, unable to lose a move, must forego control of QR3.

3 B—B7	Kt—Q2 ch.

This and his next move draw off White's king, so that Black's may approach. If 3... KtR5 ch? 4. KB6 KtB4 5. KKt5 squeezing out the knight.

4 K—B6	

4. KB7 KtB4 5. KB6 KtR3 6. KKt6 KtKt1 comes to the same thing.

4 ...	Kt—Kt1 ch.
5 K—Kt5	

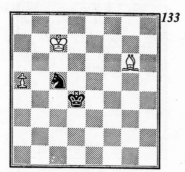

133

Drawn

If 5. K—Kt7 K—B4 6. B—K8 (6. K × Kt KKt4) 6... K—Kt5.

5 ...	K—B6
6 B—K6	K—Kt7

An attack on two fronts, the knight from base and the king from the rear.

7 K—Kt6	K—R6
8 K—Kt7	K—Kt5.

134 A somewhat similar attack on two fronts usually draws against a centre pawn, as here with White to play:

1 B—B7 ch.

If 1. BR5 KB4.

1 ...	K—B3

Not 1... KB4? 2. BR5.

2 B—K8 ch.	K—Q4

Again not 2... KB4? 3. BR5.

3 B—R5	K—B4

On the critical diagonal (White's KR5—K8) the squares used by the bishop, KR5, KB7, and K8, correlate respectively to the squares used by Black's king, QB4, QB3, and Q4; and neither player can lose a move.

4 B—B3

This avoids the cyclic repetition, but when the bishop leaves the diagonal in question, the knight can harass White's king.

134

White plays and draws
Black plays and loses

4 ...	Kt—Kt3 ch.
5 K—Q7	Kt—B1 ch.
6 K—B7	Kt—K3 ch.

Black to play is caught on the wrong foot.

1 ...	K—B4
2 B—R5	K—B3(Q4)
3 B—B3 ch.	

The bishop changes diagonals with a check.

3 ...	K—B4 (K4)
4 B—K4.	

The knight on the edge of the board is trapped.

If the position of this diagram were moved to the left (White QBP cr QKtP) the critical diagonal is longer, and the bishop can lose a move and outmanœuvre Black. On the other hand White also wins if the diagram position were moved two files to the right (White KBP) because then the knight is trapped in the corner.

If Black's knight were here at QB4 or QKt3 he would draw with or without the move.

There are few examples showing Black's king on the far side of the board, but it seems that White's chances are not less promising than with B+P *v*. B, and that an unmoved RP, or a KtP on the fourth, might win in comparable circumstances.

10. MINOR PIECE AND TWO PAWNS *v*. MINOR PIECE

In all normal circumstances the pawns win. Black sometimes draws if the pawns cannot be defended; if he can establish a blockade; or when White has a bishop of the wrong colour for a RP.

135 In this study after Butler, 1889, White's bishop is badly placed.

1 P—B6

After 1. BR5 KQ2 2. KKt6 KtB3 the knight shuttles to and from QB3. This

Drawn

kind of blockade always draws except when the knight is on the edge of the board or on the second rank, where, not having a sufficient choice of squares for its oscillations, it will be trapped.

| 1 ... | K—Q4 |

Both pawns now fall.

2 P—Q7	Kt×BP
3 K—Kt6	Kt—Q1
4 B×Kt	K—Q3.

Compare Example 140 for another case where the pawns cannot be held.

136 White must try to support the advance of the more forward pawn, here the QP.

1 K—Q3	B—K1
2 K—B4	B—Q2
3 K—B5	B—R5
4 P—Q6	B—Q2
5 B—B3	B—R5

If 5... BK1 White may offer a piece, 6. BR5, and if 6... BQ2 7. BKt6 BR5 8. BB7 as in the text-play.

| 6 B—K2 |

Instead, White offers a pawn.

| 6 ... | B—Q2 |

If 6... K×P 7. B—Kt5.

| 7 B—Q3 | B—K1 |
| 8 B—B4 | B—R5 |

If 8... K×P 9. BQ5 ch. KK4 10.BB6.

| 9 B—R2 |

A tempo manœuvre.

| 9 ... | B—K1 |
| 10 B—Kt3 | B—Q2 |

Black's K1—QR5 diagonal is too short, and the bishop is forced to play to this square.

| 11 B—Q5 | B—R6 |

Black is in zugzwang, if 11... BK1 12. BB6.

| 12 K—B6 | K—B3 |
| 13 K—B7. |

Not 13. PQ7? KK2, but after the text-move Black loses his bishop for the QP.

Black to play prevents an effective outflanking movement:

| 1 ... | B—K1 |
| 2 K—Q3 |

White cannot outflank on the king's side, if 2. KB2 KB5.

| 2 ... | B—Kt4 ch. |

White's king must not be allowed to play to QB4.

3 K—B3	B—K7
4 K—Kt4	K—Q3
5 K—R5	B—Kt5
6 K—Kt6	B—Q2
7 K—Kt7	B—Kt5
8 K—R6	B—K7 ch.

Not 8... BB1 ch.? 9. KKt5 BQ2 ch. 10. KB4 KK4 11. KB5.

| 9 K—Kt7 | B—Kt5 |
| 10 K—Kt6 | B—Q2 |

White plays and wins
Black plays and draws

Not 10... BB1? 11. KKt5.

| 11 P—K5 ch. | K×P |
| 12 K—B7 | B—Kt5 |

Not 10... BR5? 13. PQ6 KQ5 14. BB6.

| 13 P—Q6 | K—Q5 |
| 14 B—B6 | K—B4. |

If the diagram position were moved two files to the left White would win even without the move, either by out-flanking on the king's side, or by advancing the KtP to Kt6 as Example 127. Otherwise a blockade with pawns on the fourth and fifth generally draws.

The win depends on a sacrifice, of either a pawn or the bishop, and a blockade with pawns farther back therefore draws; whilst if they are farther forward White wins in most cases.

In a general way the two pawns win without any real difficulties, regardless of the kind of minor pieces on either side. When White has a bishop he should avoid placing both his pawns on squares of the same colour as those controlled by his bishop.

137 Vajda *v.* Alekhine, Kecshemet, 1927. B *v.* Kt+RP+KtP is for Black a relatively favourable assortment of pieces and pawns.

1 P—R5?

We have examined the knight's blockade of bishop and pawns, and the blockade when both sides have bishops. It is also possible for the bishop to blockade a knight and two pawns, as in the following play.

In this case a blockade is best avoided by keeping at least one pawn on a square of the same colour as those controlled by the enemy bishop. Here this means advancing the KtP first, 1. Kt—Kt2 K—Kt3 (preventing 2. KB5) 2. K—B3 B—K2 3. K—Kt3 B—Q1 (3... BQ3 ch. 4. KtB4 ch. KB3 5. KB3 KK4 6. PKt5 KB4 7. KtK2) 4. Kt—B4 ch. K—B3 (4... KR3 5. KtK6 BK2 6. PKt5 ch.) 5. K—R3 (not 5. PKt5 ch.? KB4 6. KtR3 BK2, and White is stopped in

his tracks) 5... K—K4 6. Kt—K2 B—K2 7. P—Kt5 K—B4 8. Kt—Kt3 ch. K—B5 (else White plays KKt4) 9. P—Kt6.

| 1 ... | K—Kt4 |
| 2 K—B3 | |

If 2. KtK6 ch. K×P.

| 2 ... | B—R4 |
| 3 Kt—R3 ch. | |

In the game a draw was agreed here.

3 ...	K—R3
4 K—B4	B—Kt5
5 K—B5	B—K2

Not 5... BQ7? 6. KtB4 cutting off the bishop.

137

White plays and wins

| 6 Kt—B2 | B—R6 |
| 7 Kt—K4 | B—Kt5 |

Not 7... BK2? 8. KtB6—the other way of cutting off the bishop.

8 Kt—Kt5

If 8. Kt—B6 B—Q7 9. Kt—Q5 B—Kt4 (9... BR4? 10. PKt5 ch. K×P 11. PKt6).

8 ...	B—R6
9 Kt—B7 ch.	K—Kt2
10 K—K6	B—B8
11 P—R6 ch.	

If 11. PKt5 B×P.

11 ...	K—Kt3
12 K—K7	B—Q7
13 K—B8	B×P ch.

See also Example 150.

10 MINOR PIECE AND TWO PAWNS v. MINOR PIECE

In passing it may be noted that in the ending Kt+2 P v. Kt the defender can also sustain a blockade.

138 A fine analysis by Cheron, 1945, shows the correct play when the bishop is of the wrong colour for the RP. Black will try to sacrifice his bishop for the KtP, whilst White in his turn must shield its advance with his bishop.

1 ...	B—R6
2 P—Kt3	K—B3

If 2... KR3 3. BB1 BKt5 4. PR4 BB4 5. KB2 BKt5 6. KK3 BK3 7. KB4 BQ2 8. BQ3 BR6 9. BB5, the bishop shields the advance of the KtP, 9... BB8 10. PKt4 BK7 11. PKt5 ch. KR4 12. KKt3.

3 B—B1	B—K3
4 K—B2	K—K4
5 K—K3	B—Q2
6 P—R4	B—Kt5
7 B—K2	B—K3
8 B—Q3	

White next tries to get his king to KB4. If 8. P—R5? K—B4 Black establishes his king at KKt4, and the pawns are blocked after 9. BQ3 ch. KKt4 10. BKt6 BKt5, or 9. KQ4 BB2 10. BQ1 BK1 11. KQ5 BB2 ch. 12. KQ6 KB3 13. KQ7 KKt4.

8 ...	B—B2

White threatened P—R5. The alternative is 8... B—Kt5 9. B—Kt6 B—Q8 10. P—R5 K—B3 (else 11. PR6) 11.

K—B4 B—K7 12. B—K8 K—Kt2 (12... KK2 13. PR6 KB3 14. PKt4 B×P 15. K×B, Example 100) 13. K—Kt5 B—Q6 14. B—Kt6 B—K7 15. P—R6 ch. K—Kt1 16. K—B4 B—Q8 17. B—K4 B—K7 18. B—B3, when the KtP advances after all.

9 P—Kt4	B—K3

If 9... BR4 10. P×B KB3 11. PR6 KB2 12. BR7, Example 100.

10 P—Kt5	B—B2
11 K—B3	B—R4 ch
12 K—Kt3	K—Q5

Black is in zugzwang, if 12... BK1 13. KKt4 BQ2 ch. 14. KR5, or if 12... BQ8 13. BKt6 followed by PR5.

13 B—Kt1	K—K4
14 B—B2	K—K3
15 K—B4	K—B2
16 B—B5	B—Q8
17 B—Kt4	B—B7
18 P—R5	B—Q6
19 B—B5	B—K7
20 P—R6	B—R4
21 K—K5	K—B1
22 K—B6	K—Kt1
23 B—K6 ch.	K—R1
24 B—B7	B—Q8.

White mates in four.

White also wins if Black has a knight instead of a bishop in this ending.

139 Black's only hope against disconnected pawns is that of leaving White a rook's pawn with bishop of the wrong colour, but White can often avoid this.

1 B—K8

The correct plan is first to shield the advance of the 'good' pawn as far as possible. If the RP is moved up it becomes a less effective decoy, Black capturing it sooner.

1. PR5? BK7 2. BK8 BKt5 brings about a position which occurred in the game Goglidze v. Kasparyan (Tiflis, 1929) 3. KQ8 KR3 4. BQ7 B×P 5. PK6 KKt2 6. PK7 KB3 7. BK8 BQ8 8. BB7 (the bishop cannot at once play to KR5,

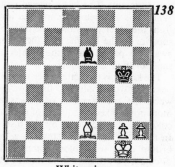

138

White wins

87

and loses a vital tempo) 8... BR5
9. BR5 KK4 10. BKt4 KQ3.

Another line is 1. PR5? BK7 2. BK8
BKt5   3. KQ6 KR3   4. BQ7 B×P
5. PK6 KKt2   6. PK7 KB3   7. BR4
BKt3 8. KQ7 KK4 9. KQ8 KQ3.

In both variations Black has time to
capture the RP, and to return and take
the vertical opposition, as Example 129.

1 ...   K—R3

If 1... BKt5 2. KQ6 KR3 3. BQ7.
1... BKt6 2. BR5 KR3 3. BKt4 transposes.

139

White wins

2 K—B6

If 2. KQ6 BKt6 3. BB6? prematurely
ceding the decoy pawn, then 3... KR4
4. BQ5 BB7 5. PK6 K×P draws.

Instead White manœuvres his bishop
to the better square KKt4, and when he
finally gives up the RP he gains a tempo
on the above variation.

2 ...	B—Kt5
3 B—Kt6	B—Q2
4 B—B5	B—R5
5 B—Kt4	B—Kt6
6 K—K7	B—B5

Black can only mark time whilst
White regroups his king.

7 K—Q6	B—Kt6
8 B—B3	B—B5
9 B—Q5	B—Q6
10 P—K6	B—Kt3
11 P—K7	K—R4

This fails by a tempo, but if 11... KKt2
12. KQ7 KB3 13. KQ8 KK4 14. BB6

KQ3 15. BK8 BB7   16. BB7 BR5
17. PR5.

12 K—Q7	K×P
13 K—Q8	K—Kt4
14 B—B6	K—B3

The diagonal opposition here loses,
but if 14... BR4 15. BK8 BQ8 16. BB7
BR5 17. BK6.

15 B—K8	B—B7
16 B—R5	B—R5
17 B—Kt4	K—K4
18 B—Q7.	

Black almost certainly draws against
KBP+KRP with bishop of the wrong
colour; but if instead the pawns were
more widely spaced (e.g. QP+KRP),
then White wins more easily.

In the general case with disunited
pawns Black will be forced to block one
with his king and the other with his
piece. White takes his king over towards
the enemy piece, which usually has to be
sacrificed for the pawn it blocks.

11. MINOR PIECE AND TWO PAWNS *v.* MINOR PIECE AND PAWN

Unlike the comparable pawn endings
nos. 35-63, a draw is normal when there
is no passed pawn, and when the defending king is present; it is then of little
consequence whether one has a bishop
or a knight.

In a general way White has winning
prospects only if he has a passed pawn.
When this is three or more files away
from the other pawn then the bishop is
superior to the knight; and the farther
away the passed pawn the greater the
superiority of the bishop.

The knight is the better piece when the
passed pawn is only two files away, or
when the enemy pawn or pawns are
more or less fixed on squares of the same
colour as those covered by the bishop.
In the latter case the enemy has a 'bad
bishop' or 'a weak colour complex', for
of course he will have little control over
squares of the opposite colour.

11 MINOR PIECE AND TWO PAWNS v. MINOR PIECE AND PAWN

140 Taimanov v. Spassky, Leningrad, 1952. The defender usually loses if his king cannot block the pawns, but here an ingenious counter-attack draws.

1 K—Kt6	Kt—Q4
2 K—B7	K—B4

2... Kt×P 3. K×P also draws.

3 Kt—Kt1	Kt×P
4 Kt—B3	P—K4

140

White plays and draws

If 4... KK5 5. KtQ2 ch. KQ6 6. KtB1 PB4 7. KB6 threatening KtKt3 followed by Kt×P. The king attacks from the rear, the knight from base, much as in Examples 133 and 134.

5 Kt—R4 ch.	K—Kt4
6 Kt—B3 ch.	K—B4
7 Kt—R4 ch.	K—Kt5

How else make progress?

8 K×P	P—K5
9 Kt—B5.	

A draw was agreed, for the defending knight has sufficient manœuvring space around a centre pawn.

141 Analysis by Botwinnik from the game Boleslavsky v. Bondarevsky, Leningrad, 1941. The defending king is too far away, so White's king may control the queening square; there is also a weak colour complex to be exploited by White's two pieces. Here the knight is superior to the KB.

1 K—B5	K—K2
2 K—Kt6	K—B1
3 K—R7	K—B2
4 P—Kt5	B—B6

If 4... BQ3 5. PR4 BKt6 6. PR5 BB5 7. PKt6 ch. KB3 8. KtK5, threatening PR6.

5 P—R4	B—Kt7

If 5... P—Kt3 (5... KK3 6. KKt6) 6. Kt—R2 (threatening 7. KtKt4 and 8. KtR6) 6... B—K8 7. P—R5.

6 P—R5	B—B6
7 Kt—R4	B—Q7

Else White plays KtB5 and Kt×P.

8 P—Kt6 ch.	K—B3
9 Kt—B5	

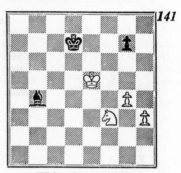
141

White plays and wins

A sacrifice typical of minor piece endings.

9 ...	K×Kt
10 K×P	K—Kt4
11 K—R7	

Not 11. PR6? KR4 12. PR7 BB6 ch. 13. KB7 KR3 with blockade.

11 ...	B—B6
12 P—R6.	

And White queens.

142 Capablanca v. Fine, Semmering 1937. This kind of pawn formation is also usually drawn because the passed pawn, which is only one file away, does not form an effective threat.

89

1 K—Kt3	K—B3
2 Kt—B3	B—K5
3 Kt—K5	B—B7
4 K—R4	P—R3

142

Drawn

It is best to have one's pawns on squares of the opposite colour from those controlled by the bishop, which can here chase away White's king if it attacks the RP, 5. KR5 KKt2 6. KtB4 BKt3 ch. (not 6... BK8? 7. KtK3).

5 Kt—Q7 ch.	K—Kt2
6 P—B5	B—R5
7 Kt—B5	B—Q8
8 K—Kt3	

If 8. KR5 BB7 9. KtK6 ch. KB3 10. KtQ4 BQ8.

| 8 ... | K—B2 |
| 9 K—B4 | B—K7 |

The bishop always attacks from the rear.

10 Kt—K4	B—Q8
11 Kt—B3	B—Kt6
12 K—K5	B—B5.

If 13. KQ6 BQ6 threatening 14... B×P, whilst if 13. KtQ1 BK7 14. KtK3 BB6.

143 Analysis by Grigoriev of a position from the 5th match game Sultan Khan *v.* Tartakower, 1931.

A passed pawn two files away often wins if the stronger party has a knight, but wins much less frequently if he has a bishop. The kind of piece the defender

has is less important: here a bishop loses; in Example 158 a knight loses a similar ending.

In the present case White has taken care to block the king's knight's pawns in such a way that his own cannot be attacked by Black's bishop, and it is important for him not to have it otherwise.

With an outside passed pawn there are two winning motifs: capturing Black's last pawn; or, if he defends this with his king, winning his piece for the passed pawn, which eventually happens here.

| 1 Kt—B6 | B—Kt4 |
| 2 P—Q6 ch. | K—B2 |

If 2... KQ1 3. KtK4 KK1 4. KB6 BQ6 5. KtB5 BB4 6. PQ7 ch. KQ1 7. KB7 BB7 8. KK6.

3 Kt—Q5	B—B3
4 Kt—B7	B—B6
5 K—Q4	

143

White wins

Having deprived Black's king of counterplay, White obtains entry for his king on the queen's side, thus supporting the advance of his QP and winning the bishop for it.

5 ...	B—B3
6 K—B5	B—Q2
7 K—Kt6	B—R5
8 K—R7	B—B3
9 K—Kt8	B—Q2
10 K—Kt7	B—B4
11 Kt—Q5	K—K3

12 K—B6   K—K4
If 12... BK5 13. PQ7.
13 Kt—B6   K—B5
14 Kt—R7.

144 Botvinnik v. Lissitzin, Moscow, 1935. Colours reversed.

When the passed pawn is three or more files away, and the defending king is blocking it, White normally draws if he has a knight.

1 ...   Kt—K1

The knight hold's White's other pawn under attack, an essential part of the defence.

Drawn

2 K—Q5   Kt—Kt2
3 K—K4   K—Kt3
4 K—B4

If 4. Kt—B4 K—Kt4 5. Kt—K6 (5. KtQ5 KB4 6. Kt×P Kt×P 7. K× Kt KKt5) 5... Kt—R4 (5... Kt×P 6. K×Kt KKt5 7. KtQ4 KB6 8. KK4 PB4 ch. 9. KQ5 KKt5 10. KK5 KB6 also draws) 6. Kt—Q4 ch. K—Kt5 7. K—Q5 Kt—Kt2. Unlike the bishop the knight cannot simultaneously maintain control of squares in different places, here KB5 and QKt3.

4 ...   K—R4.

A draw was agreed, for if the knight moves Black answers K—Kt5.

However, White sometimes wins when he has a knight: (a) if his passed pawn is blocked by the minor piece which has to be given up for it; or (b) if the defender's bishop cannot counter-attack the blocked pawn, as in the preceding and next examples.

145 That this position after Fine, 1941, can be won for White is really due to a number of positional advantages: his QRP on a white square cannot be attacked; his knight is centrally placed and as it happens has tactical threats; Black's king is a long way from the passed pawn; and finally, the blocked pawn is a RP.

It is often the blocked pawn that White eventually tries to queen, and a RP or KtP is more favourable than a Centre P or BP in the ending of minor piece and pawn v. minor piece, Examples 120-134.

1 ...   K—Kt3
2 K—Q3

White wins

It is no use trying to queen the passed pawn; indeed its advance merely facilitates its capture. White's correct plan is to go for Black's pawn, only moving the KRP to decoy Black's king if this becomes necessary.

2 ...   K—Kt4

Black must first win the passed pawn, and then try to draw the B v. Kt+ QRP ending, but in the event he is a tempo short.

3 K—B4   B—K8

Both on this and his next move Black
must avoid a fork, if 3... KR5 4. KtB5
ch.

4 K—Kt5	B—B6
5 Kt—B6	K—R5
6 Kt×P	K×P
7 Kt—B6	K—Kt5
8 Kt—Kt4	K—B4
9 P—R5	K—K3
10 P—R6	B—Q5
11 K—B6	B—B7
12 Kt—Q5	B—R2
13 K—Kt7.	

146 Santasiere *v.* Kashdan, Boston,
1938. An outside passed pawn three or
more files away (the farther the better)
often wins when White has a bishop.
It makes less difference what kind of
piece Black has. Of course all these
positions correlate to Examples 120-134,
and after the usual pawn exchange B+P
v. minor piece is more likely to win than
Kt+P *v.* minor piece.

Black's king is as favourably placed
as it can be, blocking the passed pawn;
but his bishop is on too short a diagonal: were it at QB7 he could draw.

1 K—K7	P—B4
2 K—B6	B—R6
3 K—K5	

The B+P *v.* B ending must be carefully assessed, for after 3. KKt5 KB1
4. BK6 ch.? Black will eventually take
the vertical opposition, 4... KKt2
5. B×P BKt7 6. BQ3 BR6 7. BK2 K×P
8. BKt4 BB8 9. PB5 KB4 10. PB6 BB5
11. KKt6 KQ3 12. KKt7 KK4 13. BR5
KB5, etc.

3 ...	B—Kt5

Now if 3... KB1 Black gains a tempo
on the last note because of his better
king position, 4. BK6 ch. KKt2 5. B×P
BB8 6. BK6 K×P 7. PB5 KB2 8. PB6
KQ1 9. BB7 BQ6 10. KB4 KQ2 11.
KKt5 KQ3 12. KR6 KK4 13. KKt7
BKt4 14. BKt3 BK1 15. BB2.

4 B—Kt2	

The only way, for after 4. BK6? KKt2

White wins

5. B×P BK7 6. BK6 K×P 7. PB5 KB4
8. PB6, Black has a better square for his
bishop than in the last note, 8... BR4.

4 ...	K—B1
5 K—B6	K—Kt1
6 K—Kt5	K—B1
7 B—K4	

Thus capturing the BP with gain of
tempo.

7 ...	K—Kt1
8 B×P	B—B6
9 B—R7	K—Kt2
10 P—B5	K×P
11 P—B6	B—Q4
12 K—Kt6	K—B4
13 K—Kt7	K—Q3
14 B—Kt8.	

147 Seibold *v.* Keres, Correspondence, 1930. When the bishop is of the
wrong colour for his RP a win is still
possible if the other pawn is far enough
away (three or more files) and circumstances are favourable.

1 ...	K—Kt6
2 K—B3	

White prepares to take the vertical
opposition, else the KP queens. If 2.
KQ2 KB7 3. KB3 PK6 4. KQ4 BK7
5. BK6 BB8 6. BKt4 BKt7.

2 ...	K—B7
3 K—Q4	P—K6
4 K—K5	B—K7
5 B—B7	B—B8
6 B—R5	B—Kt7
7 K—B4	

Preventing in time 7... BB6.

7 ...	P—R4
8 P—R3	

If 8. PR4 BB3 9. BQ1 B×P.

8 ...	P—R5
9 B—Kt4	B—B3
10 B—R5	P—K7
11 B×P	K×B.

White cannot get back to the queening square.

147

White plays and draws
Black plays and wins

With the move White draws by blocking the passed pawn:

1 K—Q2

The game continuation 1. B—Q5? P—K6 2. K—Q3 should have lost after 2... B—Q2 3. K—K2 (3. BB4 4... KB6 and 5... KB7) 3... B—Kt4 ch. 4. K—K1 P—R4 5. P—R3 K—K4 6. B—Kt3 K—Q5 7. P—R4 (7. BB2 KB6 8. BQ1 BB5 9. PR4 BKt6) 7... B—Q2 8. K—K2 (8. BB2 KB6 9. BQ1 BK1) 8... BKt5 ch. 9. K—K1 K—B6 10. B—Q5 B—Q2 11. K—K2 B×P 12. K×P B—Kt4 13. K—B2 P—R5 14. K—K1 P—R6 15. K—Q1 K—Kt7 16. K—Q2 B—R5 17. B—K6 B—Kt6. In this, White's bishop was forced to guard his RP from the diagonal Q1—QR4. In the following play he can protect it from the diagonal QR4—K8.

1 ...	P—K6 ch.
2 K—K1	K—K5
3 B—Kt5	K—Q5

4 B—R6	K—B4
5 P—R4	

Else Black plays his king to QR6, attacking White's pawn.

5 ...	K—Kt5
6 B—Kt5	K—R4
7 B—K8	P—R3

For the time being this keeps White's bishop off its QKt5 square.

8 B—B6	K—Kt3
9 B—K8	K—B4
10 K—B1	B—K3
11 K—K2	K—Q5
12 B—B6	B—B5 ch.

Thus Black's bishop has changed sides.

13 K—K1	K—B4
14 B—Q7	K—Kt5
15 B—B6	P—R4
16 B—Q7	B—Kt6

The idea behind Black's careful manœuvring; but only a draw comes about.

17 K—K2	B×P
18 B—Kt4	K—B6
19 K×P	B—Kt4

If 19... KB7 20. BB5 ch. KB8 21. BK6, or here 20... KKt7 21. BKt4.

20 B—Q1.

Black cannot get his pawn to the fifth without permitting White's king to block it, 20... KKt5 21. KQ2 BB5 22. KB1. See also Example 161.

148 Marshall *v.* Marco, Monte Carlo, 1904. Having two passed pawns against one passed pawn, White cannot normally win with knight against bishop, unless all the pawns are close together as in Example 152.

1 K—Kt4	P—B5
2 K—B3	P—B6
3 Kt—Q3	K—B5
4 Kt—K1	K—Q4
5 P—R4	B—Q3

Black's correct plan is to use his advanced QBP to tie down the knight, and his king to stop the passed pawns—

the bishop attacking them as occasion demands. 5... KK4 6. PKt4 KB3 is therefore simpler, and if White then goes for the QBP Black at least blocks, and probably wins, the united pawns.

6 P—Kt4	B—K2
7 P—Kt5	K—K4
8 K—Kt4	B—B1
9 Kt—B2	K—K5 ?

Black has illusions of counterplay. 9... KK3 is indicated.

| 10 P—R5 | K—Q6 |

148

Drawn

After 10... KK4 11. PR6 KK3 12. KR5 KB2 13. PKt6 ch. KKt1 14. PR7 ch. KR1 Black threatens, in time, to move his knight to KB7.

11 Kt—R1

Not 11. KtK1? KQ7.

11 ...	K—K5
12 P—R6	K—K4
13 K—R5	K—B4
14 Kt—B2.	

Black has no good waiting move, and resigned after 14... BQ3 15. KtQ4 ch. KK5 16. KtK2 PB7 17. PKt6 BR6 18. PKt7 KQ6 19. PKt8=Q K×Kt 20. QR2. If 14... KK3 15. KKt6 BQ3 16. KR7.

149 Yanofsky v. Golombek, Hastings, 1951-52. White's chances are somewhat better when Black too has a knight, but he still draws if the lone pawn can be made a real threat.

| 1 K—Q2 | Kt—Q5 |

1... KtR6 is also playable, and after the best continuation, 2. KQ3 PKt5 3. KtK4 KtB7 4. KtB6 KtK8 ch. 5. KQ4 KtB7 ch., may simplify to Example 94, 6. KB5 KKt4 7. Kt×P K×Kt. White's problem is always the same: what to do about Black's passed pawn. When he sacrifices the knight for it, the result of the knight v. two pawns ending is of consequence, and here 6... PKt6? loses after 7. KtR5 ch. KKt5 8. Kt×P K×Kt 9. PKt4, because Black's king is one square farther away.

| 2 K—Q3 | Kt—B3 ? |

This fails because Black's king is forced into a bad position. Instead a draw follows 2... Kt—B6 3. Kt—Q7 (White's knight must try to stop the KKtP. If 3. KtK6 ch. KK4 4. KtKt7 PKt5 5. KtR5 then 5... KtQ5 6. PKt4 KtB4 7. PKt5 PKt6) 3... K—B4 (simpler than 3... PKt5 4. KtB6, which however probably leads to Example 94) 4. Kt—Kt6 P—Kt5 5. Kt—Q5 P—Kt6 6. Kt—K3 ch. K—K4 7. Kt—Kt2 Kt—Q5 8. P—Kt4 Kt—K3.

This is the normal way of drawing: the lone pawn ties down White's knight, and Black's pieces stop White's pawns. If White's king goes over to capture the KKtP, Black sacrifices his knight for White's pawns.

| 3 Kt—K6 ch. | K—Kt5 |

If 3... KB4 White exchanges knights and wins the pawn ending.

| 4 K—K4 ? | |

A move difficult to assess. 4. P—B5 certainly wins, for White then establishes his knight on the central square Q4 from where it influences the play on both sides of the board. There may follow:

4... K—R5 (if 4... KtR2 or 4... KtK2, then 5. KK4) 5. Kt—Q4 Kt—K2 (if 5... Kt×Kt the pawn ending is lost, if 5... KtK4 ch. 6. KK4 KtQ2 7. PB6 KtKt3 8. PB7 KtB1 9. PKt4, or if 5... KtKt1 6. PKt4 KtR3 7. KB4) 6. P—Kt4 P—Kt5 7. P—Kt5 P—Kt6

8. K—K2 K—R6 (8... KtQ4 9. PKt6 KtB5 ch. 10. KQ2) 9. K—B1 K—R7 10. Kt—B3 ch. K—R8 (10... KR6 11. PKt6 KtB3 12. PKt7 KtKt1 13. KKt1 KtB3 14. KR1 KtKt1 15. KtK5) 11. P—Kt6 Kt—B3 12. P—Kt7 Kt—Kt1 13. K—K2 K—Kt7 (13... KtB3 14. KK3 KtKt1 15. KtQ4 KtB3 16. KB4) 14. Kt—Q4 K—R6 (14... KR8 15. KB3) 15. P—B6 P—Kt7 (15... Kt×P 16. Kt×Kt, PKt7 17. KB2) 16. K—B2 K—R7 17. Kt—B3 ch. K—R8 18. P—B7. In this variation Black loses because his king is badly placed.

4 ...   Kt—R4?

The knight alone cannot stem the pawns' advance. Instead, Black could put up a tough and possibly adequate defence by 4... K—R5, as follows:

5. K—Q5 is not a real threat because of a characteristic weakness of the knight for after 5... PKt5 6. K×Kt PKt6 7. KtB4 KKt5 8. KtK2 PKt7 9. KQ5 KB6 10. KtKt1 ch. KB7 11. KtR3 ch. KKt6, or 5... P—Kt5 6. Kt—B4 P—Kt6 7. Kt—Kt2 ch. K—Kt5 8. Kt—K1 (8. K×Kt KB6 9. KKt5 K×Kt leads to Example 315) 8... K—B5 9. K×Kt K—K6 10. K—Q5 K—B7 11. Kt—Q3 ch. K—K6, White's knight cannot sacrifice itself for the KKtP, nor can it pause. In general this kind of draw by repetition occurs with a KtP on the sixth or seventh as here, or with a RP (Example 108). Around a Centre P or BP the knight has sufficient manœuvring space (Example 148).

5. Kt×P K×Kt 6. KQ5 KtKt5 ch. is similar to Example 94.

The best continuation is 5. Kt—Kt7 P—Kt5 6. Kt—B5 ch. K—Kt4 7. P—B5 (7. KtKt3 KtR4, or 7. KtK3 PKt6) 7... K—B3 8. Kt—Kt3 K—K3 (not 8... KKt4?) and Black's king is back in play. The White knight alone holds up the KKtP by operating on the squares KB1, KKt3 and KR5. Even so it is not clear how White can force his pawns' advance in the face of Black's two pieces.

5 P—B5

Failing to see Golombek's ingenious defence. 5. Kt—Q4 wins quickly, White sacrificing his knight after 5... KtKt2 6. KQ5 KB5 7. KtK6 ch., or queening first after 5... KR5(R6) 6. PB5 PKt5 7. PB6.

5 ...	Kt×P
6 P—B6	Kt—R4
7 P—B7	Kt—B5
8 K—Q5	Kt—Kt3 ch.
9 K—B6	Kt—B1
10 K—Kt7	

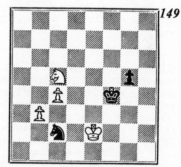

149

Drawn

10. K—Q7? Kt—Kt3 ch. (not 10... KtR2? 11. KtQ4 KR6 12. KtKt5) 11. K—Q8 K—R5 12. Kt—B5 P—Kt5 13. Kt—Q7 P—Kt6 draws.

10 ...   Kt—K2

Or 10... Kt—Q3 ch. 11. K—Kt8 K—R5 (11... KB4 or R4 12. KtKt7 ch. KKt3 13. KtK8) 12. Kt—Kt7 P—Kt5 13. Kt—B5 ch.

11 Kt—Q4	K—B5
12 Kt—B6	Kt—B4
13 K—Kt8?	

White could win by 13. KB8! KtQ3 ch. 14. KQ7 KtB5 15. KtK7 KK4 16. KtB5! If 16... K×Kt 17. KB6, or if 16... KtKt3 ch. 17. KB6 KtB1 18. KKt7.

13 ...	Kt—Q3
14 Kt—Q4	P—Kt5
15 Kt—Kt5	P—Kt6
16 Kt×Kt	P—Kt7
17 P—B8=Q	P—Kt8=Q

18 Q—B5 ch.	K—Kt6
19 Kt—K4 ch.	K—Kt7
20 Q—Kt4 ch.	K—R7?

This slip has drastic consequences. 20... KB8 draws, but after the text-move comes 21. QR4 ch. KKt7 22. QKt3 ch. KR8 23. QR3 ch. QR7 ch. 24. KtKt3 ch. KKt8 25. QB1 mate.

In contrast, a bishop and two united pawns generally win easily against minor piece and pawn, because the bishop can maintain control of squares at a distance.

It is the same if White's two passed pawns are disconnected: with a bishop they frequently win; with a knight, rarely.

Sometimes with only two or three pawns left on the board the players may have two or more minor pieces each. In such cases the basic positional ideas are the same as in the above examples, but more pieces in a general way increase the drawing propensities, and offer more tactical and combinative chances.

One characteristic of a plurality of minor pieces is the strength of two bishops as opposed to two knights; for a pair of bishops working together can control squares of either colour, and in this sense two bishops are more than twice as strong as one.

12. MORE PAWNS: MATERIAL ADVANTAGE

With a total of five or more pawns spread over five or more files a pawn up normally wins. Exceptions may occur when the stronger party has a knight and the defender a bishop, and there is a total of seven or fewer pawns on the board; or when there is no way for the king to enter the defender's position.

If the pawns are spread over four files a pawn up usually draws when the stronger party has a bishop because its chief advantage, its long range, is at a discount. He sometimes wins if he had a

knight, which may control squares of either colour, and is suited to infighting.

With 3 united pawns opposed by 2 pawns, the game should be drawn.

So much for inherent factors. Other positional considerations such as strong or weak pawns, or badly placed king or minor piece, will as usual influence and modify these general propositions.

The usual winning procedure is outlined in the notes to Example 154.

150 Fine v. Reshevsky, Semmering, 1937. White has some disadvantage in that his king cannot get far forward, but he has an outside passed pawn, the QKtP. Even so Black's bishop holds the passed pawn on one side and confines White's king on the other side, and although White does everything possible by weakening Black's pawns, and advancing his own passed pawn as far as he can, he cannot break through.

White's difficulty is that his knight cannot oppose or dislodge the enemy bishop. If instead of a knight on K5 White had a bishop on, say, Q2, he would win easily.

1 P—QKt3	B—Q5
2 Kt—B4	K—B2
3 K—B1	K—K3
4 Kt—K3	B—B4
5 K—K2	P—R4

This move keeps White's knight out of his KKt4 square.

6 Kt—B2	P—Kt4
7 P—QKt4	B—Q3
8 P—Kt3	K—K4
9 P—Kt5	B—B4
10 Kt—K3	K—Q5

White was threatening PKt6.

| 11 Kt—B5 ch. | K—K4 |
| 12 Kt—Kt7 | |

Fixing Black's pawns on black squares.

12 ...	P—R5
13 P—Kt4	B—Kt3
14 Kt—B5	B—B4
·15 Kt—K3	

150

White to play

If 15. PB3 KB5. the text-move again threatens PKt6.

15 ...	K—Q5
16 Kt—B5 ch.	

As pointed out by Reshevsky, if 16. PB3 BKt3 17. KtB1 (threatening 18. KtQ2) 71... P×P ch. 18. K×P KQ6 White's king is still hemmed in, and his passed pawn a bystander, for if 19. KtR2 BK6 20. KKt2 KB5.

16 ...	K—B5
17 Kt—R6	K×P
18 Kt—B7	K—B5
19 Kt×P	K—Q4
20 P—B3	P×P ch.
21 Kt×P	K—K5

A very fine move which leads to a curious blockade of White's pawns, whereas 21... BK2? liberates White's king, 22. KK3, and he later captures the RP and wins.

22 Kt×P	K—B5
23 Kt—B5	

Forced, else one of the pawns is lost.

23 ...	B—Kt3.

White cannot relieve the blockade. If 24. KB1 KB6 25. PKt5 BQ1 26. PKt6 BB3 27. PKt7 B×P 28. Kt×B KKt6. After the game continuation 24. KQ3 BQ1 25. KQ4 BB3 ch. 26. KQ5 BR1 27. KQ6 BK4 ch. 28. KK6 BR8 29. KK7 BKt7 30. KB7 KKt4, a draw was agreed.

151 Sherbakov *v.* Averbach, Moscow, 1950. The knight's limited range is well shown. In spite of his extra pawn Black must play carefully to draw.

1 P—Kt4

If 1. K×P? Kt×B 2. PR5 KtQ6 3. PR6 KtK4 ch. (the check gains a tempo) 4. KKt7 KB4 5. PR7 KtKt3. Also if 1. B—Kt2? P—Kt5 2. P—Kt4 (2. K×P PR5 3. PR5 PR6 4. BKt7 KtB5 ch.) 2... Kt—B5 3. B—B1 P—Kt6 4. B—R3 P—R5 5. B—B1 K—B6 6. B—R3 Kt—R6 ch. 7. K×P K×P 8. K—B6 Kt—B5, and Black wins.

1 ...	Kt×B

If 1... KtKt6? 2. K×P, and White's pawns move faster. Black therefore accepts the sacrifice, but the knight is at its worst trying to combat an advanced RP, as is well known.

2 P—R5	P×P

Not 2... PKt5? 3. P×P

3 P×P	P—Kt5

If 3... KtQ6 4. PR6 KtK4? both players get a queen, but White's is skewered, 5. PR7 KtB2 ch. 6. KB6 KtR1 7. KKt7 PKt5 8. K×Kt PKt6 9. KKt8, etc.

4 P—R6	P—Kt6
5 P—R7	P—Kt7
6 P—R8=Q	Kt—Q6

After the race to queen the nature of the position is changed completely. As

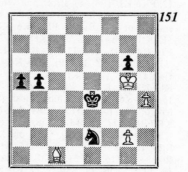

151

White to play

it happens Black draws, although such results are not easy to foresee.

7 Q—R1 ch.	K—K6
8 Q—Kt1	P—R5
9 K—B5	P—R6
10 Q—R2	K—Q7
11 K—K4	Kt—B8.

Drawn.

In this and the preceding example the pawns are spaced over seven or eight files, and their numbers are few, so that the bishop moves freely about the board, whilst the knight has few points of anchorage.

152 Capablanca *v.* Reshevsky, Nottingham, 1936. The play takes place over a limited area, when the knight is not at such a disadvantage. Even so, and having also the advantage of a well centralized king, the win is a close-run thing.

1 ...	K—Kt6
2 P—B4	P—KKt5
3 P—B5	B—B1
4 K—K5	B—Q2
5 P—K4	B—K1

5... K—B6, freeing the passed KKtP, sets White a harder problem, which can be solved only by meticulous play, 6. P—B6 B—K1 7. P—Kt4 P—Kt6 8. Kt—B4 K—Kt5 (8... BB2 9. KB5 BKt6 10. KtKt6) 9. KtKt2 K—B6 (9... BB2 10. KQ6 KB6 11. PK5 K×Kt 12. PK6 KB7(B6) 13. P×B, and White can just win a difficult queen and pawn ending, or 9... BKt3 10. KK6 KB6 11. KtR4 ch. KKt5 12. Kt×B) 10. Kt—R4 ch. K—Kt5 11. Kt—B5 B—Kt3 (11... KB6 12. Kt×P) 12. K—Q6 P—Kt7 (12... B×Kt 13. PB7) 13. Kt—K3 ch. K—B6 14. Kt×P K×P 15. K—K6, the only move, losing a tempo, 15... B—K1 (15... BB4 ch. 16. KK7 BKt3 17. KtKt1 KQ5 18. KtB3 ch. KB6 19. KtKt5 BR4 20. KtB6, or 15... BR4 16. KK7 KB6 17. PB7) 16. Kt—R4 K—Q5 (16... BB3 17. KtB5 BQ4 ch. 18. KQ6 BKt6 19. KtK7) 17. K—K7 B—R4 18. Kt—B5 ch. K—B6 19.

Black to play

Kt—Kt7 B—Kt3 20. Kt—K6 K×P 21. Kt—B4, and the BP queens.

6 K—Q4

An easier way than 6. PB6 KB6 transposing to the above variation.

6 ... K—B6

If 6... B—B2 7. P—K5 K—B6 8. P—K6 P—Kt6 (8... BKt1 9. KK5 PKt6 10. KtB4 KKt5 11. PB6 B×P 12. K×B) 9. P×B P—Kt7 10. P—B8=Q P—Kt8=Q ch. 11. K—K5.

| 7 P—K5 | P—Kt6 |
| 8 Kt—K3 | K—B5 |

There are two ways in which Black's bishop may force a blockade of the pawns on the fifth, but neither saves him:

8... B—R4 9. P—K6 B—Kt5 10. P—Kt4 K—B5 (10... PKt7 11. Kt×P, or 10... KK7 11. KK4) 11. Kt—Kt2 ch. K—Kt4 (after 11... KB6 12. KtR4 ch. the bishop occupies the square needed for Black's king, and if 12... KB5 13. PK7 BR4 14. KtKt6 ch.) 12. P—K7 B—R4 13. K—K5 K—Kt5 (13... BB2 14. KtK3) 14. K—K6 K—B6 15. P—B6 B—Kt5 ch. 16. K—B7 K×Kt 17. K—Kt7.

8... B—Q2 9. P—K6 B—B1 10. P—K7 B—Q2 11. P—B6 B—K1 12. Kt—B5. With the knight on this key square the KKtP cannot escape, 12... P—Kt7 (12... BB2 13. KK5, or 12... KKt5 13. Kt×P K×Kt 14. KK5 BB2 15. KQ6) 13. Kt—R4 ch. K—B5 (or 13... KKt6 14. Kt×P) 14. Kt×P ch.

98

K—B4 15. Kt—K3 ch. K×P 16. Kt—Q5 ch. K—B2 17. Kt—B7.

9 P—K6　　　　　　P—Kt7

The bishop can no longer hold White's pawns, but the text is a forlorn hope.

10 Kt×P ch.　　　　K×P
11 K—Q5　　　　　　K—Kt5
12 Kt—K3 ch.　　　　K—B5
13 K—Q4.

And Black resigns.

Where there are more pawns, which obstruct the bishop but do not much hinder the knight; or where the pawns are closer together, spread over five or at most six files; then a pawn up should win even though the stronger party fights with a knight against a bishop. With a greater concentration or number of pawns there are generally more squares on which the knight may be firmly based. The general winning plan for all such endings is the same as that delineated in Example 154.

153 Goldenov v. Szilagyi, Minsk, 1957. When both players have knights a pawn up generally wins. The greater number of pawns favours the stronger party because some of the drawing resources of the basic endings are not available—notably those variations in which the defender sacrifices his piece so as to liquidate all the pawns.

1 ...　　　　　　　　Kt×P

Black's extra pawn, the KP, is neither easy to defend nor much of a threat in itself, so he exchanges it for White's QRP. He thereby gets a queen's side majority, and eventually a passed QRP which diverts White's pieces from the defence of his king's side.

2 Kt×KP　　　　　　P—R4
3 Kt—Q7 ch.　　　　K—Kt4
4 P×P

4. Kt×P P×P 5. KtR4 PKt6 is even stronger for Black.

4 ...　　　　　　　　P×P
5 Kt—B5　　　　　　Kt—Kt8

Threatening to attack White's KBP, and indirectly securing the advance of his passed pawn, the QRP.

6 K—K5　　　　　　P—R5

The passed pawn ties down White's knight.

7 Kt—K6 ch.

The immediate diversion 7 Kt×P leads to the loss of all his pawns after 7... KtQ7.

Black to play

7 ...　　　　　　　　K—R5
8 K×P　　　　　　　P—R6
9 Kt—Q4　　　　　　P—R7
10 Kt—B2　　　　　　Kt—Q7
11 Kt—R1　　　　　　K—R6
12 Kt—B2

After 12. KK3 KKt6 13. K×Kt K×P Black wins easily on the king's side. With the text-move White attempts to exchange off all Black's pawns. If 12. PKt5 KR5 13. P×P P×P 14. KK3 Kt×P 15. K×Kt K×P, and the two rook's pawns win.

12 ...　　　　　　　　Kt—Kt6
13 K—K4　　　　　　K—Kt6

Black must not yet accept the sacrifice, 13... PR8=Q? 14. Kt×Q Kt×Kt 15. KB5, when all his pawns are exchanged. Instead, his king outmanœuvres White's king. To retain one pawn will be sufficient for victory. There is a natural tendency for the rook's pawns to be left on the board, which is to the advantage of the knight, for then the RP is as good

II MINOR PIECE ENDINGS

as, in fact rather better than, any other pawn.

| 14 K—K3 | K—R6 |
| 15 K—K4 | K—Kt7 |

The turning movement induces White to weaken his pawns, for if now 16. PKt5 P×P 17. KB5 KtQ5 ch., or if 16. KK3 KKt6 17. KK4 KtQ7 ch.

16 P—B4	K—Kt6
17 P—Kt5	K—Kt5
18 P×P	P×P
19 K—K5	K×P
20 P—B5	K—Kt4.

White resigns, for if 21. PB6 KKt3 22. KK6 KtQ5 ch. Black never queened his QRP, a case of the threat being stronger than its execution. In the event White's knight was tied down whilst Black's had active threats.

154 Botvinnik *v.* Bondarevsky, Moscow, 1941. When both sides have bishops a pawn up wins both more certainly and more directly than is the case with any other pieces, with the possible exception of bishop *v.* knight. Not long before in this game each player had a rook, a queen, and a bishop. Black exchanged for preference the major pieces, leaving a bishop and pawn ending.

In most endings the winning processes are the same. First the king and the other pieces must be centralized, brought to good squares where they have the greatest mobility, and be ready for active service on either flank.

1 K—K2

The defender also centralizes.

1 ...	P—B3
2 K—Q3	P—Q4
3 P—R3	

White correctly puts his pawns on White squares, where they do not impede the bishop.

3 ...	K—B2
4 P—B3	K—K3
5 B—B2	K—Q3
6 B—Kt1	

Keeping out Black's king.

| 6 ... | B—K4 |

Centralizing the bishop.

| 7 B—B2 | K—B3 |
| 8 B—K3 | |

When the passed pawn is in the centre, or when there is a large number of pawns on the board, the attacker may have difficulty getting his king into the game, a problem especially prone to occur in bishop endings. Here Black's king cannot easily support the further advance of the passed pawn, nor otherwise get round to attack White's QRP.

| 8 ... | P—B4 |

Centralization is now complete.

The next stage is usually to make the extra pawn a real threat. This means making a passed pawn, or threatening to do so. In this case the passed pawn (QP) already exists.

As the passed pawn can rarely be forcibly queened, it is used to decoy the enemy pieces, or one of them. In the preceding example Black's QRP decoyed White's knight. If instead the passed pawn decoys or is blocked by the defending king, then the attacking king goes to the other side of the board and there mops up the pawns (cp. Example 156). Thus positions with pawns on both sides of the board are easier to win—the decoy draws the defender's forces farther away.

154

White to play

12 MORE PAWNS: MATERIAL ADVANTAGE

In the present case the passed pawn, which is always least favourable when in the centre, does not at the moment form an effective decoy, but might do so if the kings were elsewhere. With the text-move, 8... PB4, Black therefore plans to move his king over to the king's side with this end in view; and indeed this is the most systematic method, if not in this instance the quicker.

The player with the extra pawn has the inherent advantage that he may offer an exchange of pieces, on the supposition that he can win the pawn ending; whilst if the defender declines to exchange, and withdraws his piece, then the attacker accordingly advances and improves his position. Botwinnik indicates how this factor may here lead to a direct win: 8... BQ3 9. BB2 BB4 10. BK1 KKt3 11. BQ2 BQ3 12. KQ4 KB3 13. BK1 BK4 ch. 14. KQ3 KB4, Black has slightly improved his king's position, but entry is not yet assured, 15. BQ2 BR8 16. BK1 PQ5 17. BQ2 BB6, and now White must allow Black's king to attack the QRP, or play 18 B×B P×B 19. K×P PQR4, after which Black wins the tempo-struggle, thereby gains the opposition, and finally advances his king into the enemy position. Although not always available, opportunities of returning the extra pawn must not be overlooked.

To summarize, the player with the pawn up has in consequence two positional advantages: his pawn may itself be a threat; or he may offer to exchange pieces, the declension of which improves his game.

9 B—B2	K—Q3
10 B—R7	K—K3
11 B—K3	K—B3
12 B—Q2	K—Kt3
13 K—K2	K—R4
14 B—K1	K—Kt4
15 B—Q2 ch.	K—R5
16 B—K1 ch.	B—Kt6
17 B—B3	P—Kt4
18 B—Q4	P—Kt5

Whether he likes it or not Black will have to exchange some pawns to force

his king into the game. In one way at least this suits White, who may yet hope to draw by exchanging off all the pawns.

19 B—B6 ch.	K—R4
20 RP×P ch.	P×P
21 B—Q8	B—B5
22 B—K7	P×P ch.

In the game Black played 22... PKt6? He was seduced by the tactical possibilities of a sacrifice of his KRP (PKR4-5-6) creating a passed KKtP. The game went on for 21 moves before a draw was agreed, White stopping the QP with his king 23. KQ3 KKt3 24. KQ4, and holding up Black's KRP with his bishop 24... KB2 25. BR4 KK3 26. BQ8 PKR4 27. BR4. Black's play was inconsistent, for the move he chose deprived his king of the chance of entering White's half of the board, which was surely the main purpose of his previous manœuvring.

23 K×P	B—K4
24 B—Q8	K—Kt3
25 B—K7	K—B4
26 P—Kt4 ch.	

Else Black plays ... PKR4.

26 ...	K—Kt3
27 B—Q8	B—B3
28 B—R5	K—Kt4
29 B—K1	P—Q5

The culmination of Black's plan. Now that the kings are on the king's side, the passed centre pawn becomes an effective decoy.

| 30 B—Q2 ch. | |

If 30. KKt3 BK4 ch. 31. KB3 BB5 32. BR5 PQ6

30 ...	K—R5
31 B—K1 ch.	K—R6
32 B—Q2	P—Q6
33 P—Kt5	B—Q1
34 K—K4	

After which Black's king decisively enters, but if 34. BB4 BR4, followed by 35... PQ7.

34 ...	K—Kt5
35 K×P	B×P
36 B—K1	P—KR4.

And Black wins.

101

155 Keres *v.* Lilienthal, Tallinn, 1945. White's king has no way of entering Black's game, and can neither assist the advance of his passed pawn, nor effectively attack Black's pawns.

1 K—Kt3

White tries the king's side. He cannot do anything on the queen's side, for there the black squares are resolutely blocked.

1 ...	B—K1
2 K—R4	K—B3
3 B—K6	B—Kt3
4 B—Kt3	K—Q3
5 B—Q1	

To make a way for the king via KR5.

5 ...   K—K2

155

White to play

Opposing the king's entry is more important than snatching the queen's pawn, if 5... KQ4? 6. BR5 BR2 7. BB7 ch. K×P 8. KR5 KK5 9. K×P K×P 10. P—R4 K—Kt5 11. P—R5.

6 B—R5	B—R2
7 P—Q5	

If 7. BK8 K×B 8. KR5 KB2 9. K×P BKt1 10. KKt5 KK3 11. PR4 BB2 12. PR5 BKt1 13. PR6 BR2 14. PQ5 ch. K×P 15. KB6 KQ3 16. KKt7 KK2 17. K×B KB2, a drawn variant of Example 66.

7 ...   K—Q3

Lilienthal played 7... BKt1? which permitted White's king to enter, 8. BKt6

B×P 9. KR5, and the KRP falls, 9... KB3 10, K×P, when Black loses chiefly because his KBP obstructs his bishop, 10... BK3 11. KR7 BQ4 12. PR4 BB5 13. PR5 BQ4 14. BK8 BK3 15. PR6, now White's problem is that of extricating his king, 15... B—B2 16. B—Q7 B—B5 17. B×P (the not untypical sacrifice) 17... KB2 18. BQ7 BQ6 ch. 19. PB5 KB1 20. BK6, and Black resigned.

8. B—K8

White's king, limited by the edge of the board, cannot get into the game without this sacrifice, which however only draws. 8. BB7 KK2 comes to much the same thing.

8 ...	K—K2
9 K—R5	

Of course if 9. BKt5, then 9... BKt3.

9 ...	K×B
10 K×P	B—Kt1
11 P—Q6	K—Q2
12 P—R4	B—B2.

Not 12... K×P? 13. KKt6 BB5 14. PR5, but after the text-move the game is quite drawn.

156 Bonch-Osmolovsky *v.* Konstantinopolsky, Moscow, 1949. When the stronger party has a bishop against a knight he wins easily; always excepting those cases where there is a weak colour complex (pawns on the same coloured squares as his bishop, so that he is very weak on squares of the other colour).

Here the positional factors balance, and White wins simply because of the inherent advantage of bishop *v.* knight and a plus-pawn.

1 P—Kt5

White's pieces are already centralized. He next creates a passed pawn to tie down Black's pieces.

1 ...	RP×P ch.
2 P×P	P×P ch.
3 K×P	K—K4

The player with the knight sets up a typical strongpoint defence, in this case

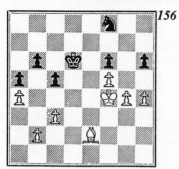

156

White to play

on his KB3 square; but White outflanks it, in the best military tradition.

If 3... KtQ2 4. PB6 KK4 5. PB7 KK3 6. BKt4 ch.

4 B—Q3

The pawn cannot advance, 4. PB6? KtR2 ch., but is a sufficient decoy where it stands.

4 ...	Kt—Q2
5 K—Kt6	Kt—B3
6 K—B7	Kt—Q4
7 B—B4	

Instead, 7. KK8 may be played at once.

7 ...	Kt—K6
8 B—K6	Kt—Kt5

The pawn ending is lost after 8... Kt×P 9. B×Kt K×B 10. KK7.

9 K—K7	Kt—B3
10 B—B8	Kt—K5
11 K—Q7	K×P
12 K—B6 ch.	

The passed pawn has diverted Black's king so that his queen's side pawns may be mopped up.

12 ...	K—K4
13 K×P	Kt—Q3
14 B—R6	K—Q4
15 B—Kt5	Kt—B1 ch.
16 K×P.	

Black resigned after 16... KQ3 17. BR6 KtK2 18. KKt6 KtQ4 ch. 19. KKt7 KtK6 20. BK2 PB5 21. PR5.

157 Smiltiner *v.* Portisch, Moscow, 1956. The bishop shows itself to be better than the knight when holding up a passed pawn. Here Black's bishop not only protects his own pawns, and prevents the advance of the KP, but may do so from many different squares; whereas the knight can only shuttle to and from its QKt2 square.

We first show that White to play loses.

1 Kt—Kt2

If 1. KK3 KKt7 winning the KKtP.

1 ...	K—K8
2 K—K3	P—Q5 ch.

After this useful check, Black's king emerges.

3 K—Q3	K—B7
4 K—K4	

If 4. KB4 KB6 5. K×P K×P 6. KB4 KB4 7. KQ5 PKt5 8. KtQ3 PKt6 9. KtK1 PQ6. The knight alone is no match for the disconnected passed pawns.

4 ...	K—K7
5 K—B5	B—K2
6 K—K4	K—Q7
7 K×P	K—B7
8 Kt—R4	P—Kt7
9 Kt—B3	

If 9. Kt×P K×Kt 10. K—Q5 K—B6 11. K—B6 K—Q5 12. K—Q7 B—Kt5 13. P—K7 B×P 14. K×B KK4, winning the pawn ending.

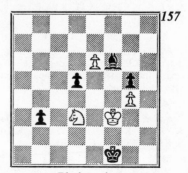

157

Black to play

103

II MINOR PIECE ENDINGS

9 ...	B—B3 ch.
10 K—B4	B×Kt.

White resigns, for after 11. PK7 PKt8=Q 12. PK8=Q Black forces a queen exchange, and then wins with his KKtP.

Having to move, Black cannot directly win; but another facet of the bishop's superiority, its ability to lose a move enables him to obtain this position with White to play.

1 ...	K—Kt8

At present Black cannot get his king into the game, for if 1... BQ1 2. KK3 (threatening the QP) 2... BB3 3. KB3, or 1... BK2 2. KK3 BB4 ch.? 3. Kt×B PKt7 4. KtKt3.

The idea behind the text-move is to hold White's king to the defence of his KKtP.

2 Kt—Kt2	

If 2. K—Kt3 (foregoing his threat of KQ4) 2... B—Q1 and after 3. KB3 BK2 4. KKt3 BB3, or 3. KtKt2 BK2 4. KtQ3 BB3, Black has lost a move with his bishop.

2 ...	K—R7
3 Kt—Q3	

After 3. KB2 BQ1 White's king cannot leave his post, 4. KK3 KKt6 5. KQ4 K×P 6. K×P KB4 7. KB4 PKt5 8. K×P PKt6 9. KtQ1 KB5 10. KtB3 KB6, and the KtP queens. Also if 3. KtQ1 BQ1 4. KK3 KKt6 5. KQ4 K×P 6. K×P KB6 7. KB4 PKt5 8. K×P PKt6.

3 ...	B—Q1

Black's bishop loses a tempo on the diagonal KB3 to Q1, although the process is interrupted, being completed on his eighth move.

4 Kt—Kt2	

And if here 4. KK3 KKt6 5. KQ4 K×P 6. K×P KB6 7. KB4 KK6 8. KtKt2 PKt5 9. K×P PKt6.

4 ...	B—K2
5 K—B2(K3)	B—B4 ch.
6 K—B3	K—Kt8

7 Kt—Q3	B—K2
8 K—K3	

8. KtKt2 KB8 9. KtQ3 BB3 transposes.

8 ...	B—B3
9 K—B3	K—B8.

158 Chernikov v. Chekover, Leningrad, 1948. In all endings with pieces and pawns the defender has excellent drawing chances when all the pawns are on one side of the board, spread over four or fewer files.

If the stronger party has a bishop a pawn up generally draws, and it is the same in rook or queen endings; but if the stronger party has a knight, then a pawn up often wins. The knight's short range is here no handicap, whilst its ability to control squares of either colour is a distinct asset. It makes little difference whether the defender has a knight or a bishop.

1 Kt—Q2	Kt—Q3
2 Kt—Kt3	K—B3
3 Kt—Q2	K—Q4
4 K—Q3	P—B4

Having centralized his pieces Black creates a passed pawn. In the nature of things this will not be far from the other pawns, a circumstance which favours the knight, whereas it would be to the disadvantage of the bishop.

5 P×P	P×P
6 Kt—B1	

The pawn ending is easily won after 6. KK3 KtB5 ch.

6 ...	P—K5 ch.
7 P×P ch	P×P ch.
8 K—K3	K—K4
9 Kt—Q2	Kt—B4 ch.
10 K—K2	P—K6

Black now advances his passed pawn, winning the knight for it. With a knight he can sometimes do this even when the pawn is directly opposed by the enemy's king and minor piece, a procedure impossible with bishops—or for that matter any other pieces.

11 Kt—B3 ch.	K—B5
12 Kt—K1	K—K5
13 K—B1	Kt—Q5
14 K—Kt2	Kt—K7
15 Kt—B3	

If 15. KB1 KtB5   16. KKt1 KtQ6
17. KtKt2 PK7.

| 15 ... | K—Q6 |
| 16 Kt—K5 ch. | K—Q5 |

Not 16... KB6? 17. KB3 KQ7 18.
KtB4 ch.

| 17 Kt—B3 ch. | K—B6 |
| 18 Kt—K5 | |

158

White to play

If 16. KB1 KtB5   17. KK1 KQ6
18. KtK5 ch. KK5   19. KtB4 KB6
20. KtK5 ch. KKt7 21. PR4 PR4.

18 ...	Kt—B5 ch.
19 K—B3	P—K7
20 K—B2	Kt—Q6 ch.
21 K×P	

White resigned after 21. Kt×Kt
K×Kt 20. KK1 KK6. He loses the
tempo struggle, 21. PR4 PR3, or 22.
PR3 PR4.

21 ...	Kt×Kt
22 K—K3	Kt—Kt3
23 K—K4	K—Q7
24 K—B5	K—K6
25 K—Kt5	

The game is not to be saved.
If 25. KB6 KB6 26. KKt7 KtB1.

25 ...	K—B6
26 P—R4	K—Kt6
27 P—R5	Kt—B1

28 P—R6	Kt—Q2
29 K—B5	K—R5
30 K—K6	K—Kt4.

With 5 united pawns v. 4 pawns the
stronger party may expect to win
whether he has a bishop or a knight. The
method is the same, a passed pawn is
created, and either forced through or
used as a decoy.

159 Fine v. Najdorf, New York,
1949. With 3 united pawns opposed to
2 pawns the game is drawn regardless of
the kind of minor piece, although
knights do offer some chances of a win
if the defender is at all careless.

| 1 ... | Kt—K2 |
| 2 Kt—K4 | |

2. KtK2 KtQ4 3. KtKt1 is simpler.
The knight keeps out Black's king,
guards the BP, and leaves White plenty
of elbow room for his own king; and a
draw might honourably be agreed.

| 2 ... | Kt—B4 |
| 3 P—R3? | |

159

Black to play

This extra weakness is fatal. Instead
he should play 3. Kt—B2 Kt—K6 ch.
(3... KtQ5 4. KtR3 PKt4 5. KtKt1)
4. K—Kt1 Kt—B7 3. Kt—Q3 P—Kt4
4. K—B2 K—R6 5. K—Kt1, when
White's knight firmly prevents Black's
intended 5... Kt—K8.

105

3 ...	Kt—K6 ch.
4 K—R2	Kt—B7
5 K—Kt2	Kt—K8 ch.
6 K—B2	K×P

A neat sacrifice. Once again a rook's pawn is shown to be very strong against a knight.

7 K×Kt	K—Kt7
8 K—K2	P—R4
9 Kt—Kt5	P—R5
10 Kt—K6	P—Kt4.

White resigns because he cannot stop the RP. If 11. Kt×KtP PR6 12. Kt×P K×Kt 13. KQ3 KKt7, but not here 13... KKt6? 14. KK4.

160 Guldin *v.* Averbach, Baku, 1955. Here three pawns win against two pawns because they are spread over four files.

1 ...   P—Kt4

To fix White's pawns, so that later the KKtP becomes a target.

2 P—R5

In general White would prefer to exchange, but here 2. P×P ch. K×P exposes his KtP too much, and leads to a lost pawn ending after 3. KB3 PK5 ch. 4. KKt3 KtB5 5. KtR2 KtQ7 6. KB2 KB5 7. KK2 KKt6, or 3. KtR2 PK5 4. KQ4 KB5 5. KtB1 KtKt4 ch. 6. KB5 PK6.

2 ...	K—K3
3 K—Q3	K—Q4
4 Kt—K3 ch.	K—B4
5 Kt—B2	P—K5 ch.
6 K—K3	K—B5

Black's king makes a tempo-move before guarding his KP, for if at once 6... KQ4? 7. KtKt4 ch. KK4 8. KtB6 ch., and White's knight is aggressively placed.

7 Kt—Q4	K—Q4
8 Kt—K2	

If 8. KtB5 Kt×Kt, Black wins, Example 32.

8 ...   Kt—B5 ch.

Black to play

As in Example 158, the knight removes the blockading king.

9 K—B2	Kt—K4
10 K—Kt3	K—B5

White resigns, for his knight will be lost for the KP.

13. MORE PAWNS: POSITIONAL ADVANTAGE

The two most important factors are: the inherent potentialities of the pawn formation, one player having a passed pawn, a wing majority, or in some way better actual or potential passed pawns; and the position of one's king, Either may be decisive.

Weaknesses such as isolated, doubled, or backward pawns, although troublesome, are not so serious as they are in rook and pawn endings.

The position of the minor piece is rarely vital. A bishop can re-position itself in a move or so—except for those special cases where there is a bad bishop (Example 166). Sometimes the knight is a little misplaced, requiring several moves to reach this or that square.

Of the powers of the bishop opposed to those of the knight the concensus is as follows:

Open positions, pawns spread over 6-8 files: the bishop is superior, but not decisively so; if the player with the bishop has also some other advantage a better placed king or a more favourable

13 MORE PAWNS: POSITIONAL ADVANTAGE

pawn structure, he often wins (Examples 170-172). If on the contrary his position is otherwise inferior, the bishop may afford sufficient compensation to avoid defeat (see notes to Example 168).

Open positions, pawns confined to 5 or at most 6 files: the knight and bishop are about equal in value (Example 169).

Pawns confined to 4 or fewer files: the bishop's chief advantage, its long range, is of no account; and the knight is superior, for its ability to cover squares of either colour is useful in close warfare.

Twelve or more pawns, close but not blocked positions: in general the knight is not greatly inferior to the bishop; but pawns tend to be exchanged, and the position thereby opened up, when the bishop comes into its own. The player with the knight must therefore avoid opening up the game too much. This sometimes makes it difficult for him to exploit an advantage (Example 168).

Blocked positions: if the player with the bishop has pawns on the same colour as those used by his piece, then he has a bad bishop, or weak colour complex, when the marked superiority of the knight is well known. In many cases this single factor suffices for victory (Example 167).

The pawn-structure is said to be balanced when, as in Examples 163 and 166, neither player has an actual or potential passed pawn or pawn majority. An unbalanced pawn-structure, Example 161 *et al.*, often leads to the creation of passed pawns, which in general are more effectively handled by the bishop than by the knight; but it does not follow that unbalanced pawns necessarily favour the bishop. The way in which the pawns are unbalanced is more important: in Example 172 the unbalance favours Black, who has a bishop, and who wins; whereas in Example 168 the unbalance favours White, who has a knight, and he takes good care not to create passed pawns too hastily, but rather to maintain the threat of doing so, and he too wins.

The most usual difficulty for the

attacker is that of getting his king into the enemy's lines—the problem of king-entry. The function of a passed pawn (as one can rarely queen it) is usually to decoy the enemy king so that one's own king enters, as in Example 161.

A knowledge of certain peculiarities of the knight may assist one's calculations. For instance, a knight on Q4 can reach any square in three or fewer moves, except QKt2, QKt6, KB2, KB6, and KR8. An adverse king, on the same diagonal as the knight with one square between them cannot be checked in under three moves: in effect the king is as far away as possible. Another useful distance is to have one's king on the same line, rank or file, with two squares between them. These relationships are commonly seen, as, for instance, in Example 165.

161 Averbach *v.* Veresov, Moscow, 1947. White's queen's side majority leads to a passed pawn which is farther away and therefore of more value than Black's passed pawn. This advantage, and the fact that the KP is vulnerable, and even to some extent hampers its own bishop, are sufficient for victory.

1 B—R3   P—QKt4

Seeking liquidation, as good a chance as any. To move the king would let in White's king.

The winner analyses the 'wait and see' policy, 1... B—R1 2. B—Q7 B—Kt2 3. P—Kt4 P×P 4. P×P B—R1 5. P—B5 P×P 6. P×P K—Q4 (if 6... BQ4 7. BK8 KB4 8. PB6 KKt5 9. PB7 BK3 10. B×P K×P 11. B×RP K×P 12. BB7 BB1 13. K×P, Example 128) 7. B—K8 P—Kt4, doubling White's pawns, 8. P×P K×P 9. BKt6 BQ4 else the bishops are forced off), 10. B×KP B—Kt1 11. K—B4 K—Q3 12. K—B5 K—K2 13. K—Kt6 K—B1 14. K—R6.

2 P×P	B×P
3 B—B8	B—B3
4 P—QKt4	P×P
5 P×P	B—Kt4
6 B—Kt7	P—Kt4

If 6... B—Q6 7. B—B6 K—B4 (7...
PKt4 8. P×P KB4 8. PKt6) 8. P—Kt5
K—Kt5 9. P—Kt6 B—R3 10. K—B2
P—K6 ch. 11. K—Kt2 P—K7 12.
B—B3 ch. K—B4 13. B×KP.

7 B×P	P×P
8 P×P	B—R5

This compares with Example 147,
where the bishop is of the wrong colour
for the RP. Black's king has held his
ground, but sooner or later it must go
over to the QKtP.

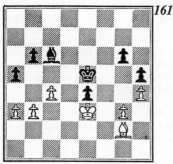

White to play

9 B—Kt6	B—Q8
10 P—Kt5	K—Q4
11 K—B4	K—B4
12 K—Kt5	B—K7
13 B—K8	

Not 13. B×P? B×P 14. BKt4 BK1
15. BB5 KQ3 16. BKt6 KK2, Black gets
back in time to block the RP.

13 ...	K—Kt3

The king is decoyed one square
farther away. If 13... BQ8 14. B×P.

14 B×P	B×P
15 B—Kt4	B—K1
16 B—B5	K—B2
17 B—Kt6	K—Q1
18 K—B6	

Black resigns. The winning method is
always the same: a passed pawn is
created, and used to decoy the enemy
king away from his other pawns, which
may then be attacked.

162 Balogh v. Barcza, Budapest,
1946. Black's king's side majority fore-
shadows the making of a passed pawn;
but owing to the doubled pawns White
cannot evaluate his own majority. In
effect Black is a pawn up on the king's
side, and in the usual way this decoys
White's king. Also, Black's king is
better placed, for he can get it to the
fourth or fifth rank.

1 ...	K—B3

Centralization is first completed.

2 K—B2	K—K4
3 P—R4	

If 3. KK3 PKKt4 4. BB1 PB5 ch.
5. P×P ch. P×P ch. 6. KQ3 BK5 ch.
7. KB3 PB6.

3 ...	K—Q5
4 B—K2	B—K5
5 P—B5	P—R3

Black's two queen's side pawns hold
three. Now he mobilizes his majority.

6 B—B1	P—KKt4
7 P×P	P×P
8 B—K2	P—B5
9 P×P	P×P
10 B—B1	B—B3
11 B—K2	K—K5

Black's king seeks entry on the queen's
side.

12 B—B4	P—B6
13 B—K6	

After 13. BB1 KQ5, White must move
his king or his bishop, letting Black in.

Black to play

13 ...	K—Q6
14 B—Kt3	K—Q7.

White resigns because of 15... KB8, followed by mopping up operations.

Here the doubled pawn is weak because the pawn majority is thereby crippled; but in a balanced pawn structure doubled pawns, if not isolated, are no great handicap.

163 Alekhine *v.* Turover, Bradley Beach, 1929. White has the better king position, for he cannot be kept out of the fifth rank. Black might survive with one weakness, but four weak pawns is too many.

1 K—Kt5	Kt—Q4
2 P—B4	

Fixing White's doubled pawns. By successively attacking different pawns White endeavours to tie up Black's pieces.

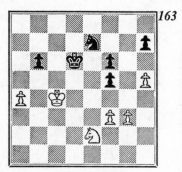

White to play

2 ...	K—B2
3 Kt—Q4	Kt—B6 ch.
4 K—Kt4	Kt—Q4 ch.
5 K—B4	Kt—K2
6 K—Kt5	K—Kt2
7 Kt—K6	Kt—B1

White threatens Kt—B8 attacking the RP. If 7... KtB3 8. KtKt7 KtK2 9. KtK8 attacking the pawn on B3, 9... KtKt1 10. KtQ6 ch. winning the pawn on B4.

8 K—B4	Kt—Q3 Ch.
9 K—Q5	Kt—K5
10 P—R6	

Fixing Black's RP. Now if 10... Kt×P 11. Kt—B8 Kt—K7 12. Kt×P Kt×P ch. 13. K—Q4 Kt—Kt3 14. Kt×P White wins because of his powerful KRP.

10 ...	Kt—B7
11 Kt—B8	Kt—Kt5
12 K—K6	

The king decisively enters.

12 ...	Kt×P
13 K×P	K—R3
14 K—Kt5	Kt—Kt1
15 K×P	K—R4
16 Kt—Q7	K×P
17 Kt×P ch.	K—Kt4
18 Kt—Q5	K—B3
19 K—K6	

Here the king is safe from check, and White threatens an exchange of knights.

19 ...	Kt—R3
20 Kt—B6.	

Black resigns, for his knight is trapped.

164 Flohr *v.* Zagorovsky, Minsk, 1952. In general a protected passed pawn is more powerful than a pawn-majority. Here Black dare not exchange bishops for the pawn ending is lost. White also has the advantage that his king can enter on the king's side: he has the better king position, or Black's king side pawns are weak—whichever way one chooses to look at it.

1 B—Q3

This threatens P—QR4, when Black's bishop has no moves.

1 ...	P—R5
2 P—Kt4	P—R6
3 P—Kt5	

After this Black can only move his king, and is therefore forced to give way before the advances of White's king. However, the vulnerable White pawn at QKt5, combined with the pawn majority on the king's side, offers Black counterplay.

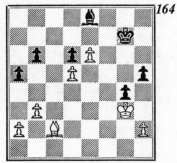

164

White to play

3 ...	K—Kt1
4 K—B4	K—B1
5 K—B5	K—Kt1
6 K—B6	P—R5
7 K—K7	

In the game Black's counter-thrust drew, 7. PK7? PKt6 8. P×P P×P 9. BB1 BQ2, for White could only win this position without the move, and if 10. BKt2 B×P 11. KK6 BK1 12. K×P KB2.

7 ...	P—Kt6
8 P×P	P×P
9 B—K4	B×P
10 K×P	K—B1
11 K—B7	K—K2
12 B—Kt2	B—K1
13 B—R3.	

And White wins.

165 Tartakower *v.* Botvinnik, Groningen, 1946. Sometimes one player's passed pawns are more dangerous than those of his opponent, generally because they are farther advanced.

| 1 ... | P—R4 |
| 2 Kt—B4 ch. | |

Unless this piece succours the imprisoned king, an immediate breakthrough decides, as shown by Bronstein, 2. PR4 KtQ7, keeping out White's knight, 3. PR5 PR5 4. PR6 PKt6 5. P×P P×P 6. PR7 PKt7 ch. 7. KR2 KtB6 ch. 8. K×P PKt8=Q 9. PR8=Q and White is in a mating net, 9... QR7

ch. 10. KKt4 KtK4 ch. 11. KB5 QKB7 ch., etc.

| 2 ... | K—Q4 |
| 3 Kt—K3 ch. | K—K5 |

Black can renew the mating threats only by capturing the KBP. This would be impracticable if White's passed pawns were more advanced.

    4 P—R4

If 4. PKt4 KtQ5 5. PR4 KB6 6. PKt5 K×P.

| 4 ... | K—Q6 |
| 5 Kt—Q5 | |

The advance of the RP is too slow, 5. P—R5 K—K7 6. P—R6 K×P 7. Kt—K1 ch. (7. KtB5 PR5 8. Kt×P Kt×Kt 9. PR7 PKt6 10. PR8=Q PKt7 ch., with mate in 3) 7... K—K7 8. Kt—B3 ch. (8. PR7 PKt6 with mate in 2) 8... K—B8 9. Kt—K4 P—R5 10. P—R7 P—Kt6 11. Kt—Q2 ch. Kt×Kt 12. P—R8=Q, and Black mates in 4.

165

Black to play

5 ...	K—K7
6 Kt—B4 ch.	K×P
7 Kt×P ch.	

After 7. Kt×P Black mates in 6, commencing 7... PKt6 8. Kt×P K×Kt 9. PR5 PR7.

    7 ...   K—B8

Not 7... P×Kt? crippling his pawns; for their steady advance now wins. Meanwhile Black's king evades the checks as much as possible.

8 Kt—B4	P—Kt6
9 Kt—Kt2	K—B7
10 P—R5	P—R5
11 Kt—B4	K—B8

Threatening 12... PR6   13. Kt×P PKt7 mate.

12 Kt—Kt2	P—R6
13 Kt—K3 ch.	K—B7
14 Kt—Kt4 ch.	K—K7.

White resigns, for he is mated in 2.

166 Smyslov *v.* Keres, U.S.S.R. Championship, Moscow, 1951. Because his queen's side pawns are on white squares, and have to be defended by, whilst they also obstruct, his bishop moving on white squares, White is said to have a bad bishop. This is not in itself fatal, but his pawn-structure shows another disadvantage: the isolated KP, which permits Black to occupy a fine square at his K4, and eventually to penetrate the position with his king, as Keres shows with flawless technique.

1 ...	B—Kt8

First Black fixes the queen's side pawns, which leads to the immobilization of White's bishop at Q1.

2 P—R3	P—QR4
3 B—Q1	

To prevent ... BB7, which remains a standing threat for the rest of the game.

3 ...	K—Kt3

Next Black centralizes his king.

4 K—Kt2	K—B4
5 K—B3	K—K4
6 P—QR4	

After 6. K—K2 B—B4 7. P—KKt4 (7. PKR4 BKt5 ch.) 7... B—Kt8 8. P—KR4 (else 8... PKKt4 fixing the king's side pawns on White squares) 8... K—K5 9. K—Q2 B—Q6, and now if 10. PR5 PR5, whilst otherwise Black's well-placed king ensures a won pawn ending:
10. PR4 PKt3 11. PR5 P×P 12. P×P

PB4 13. BK2 B×B 14. K×B PB5; or 10. BK2 B×B 11. K×B PKt3 12. PR4 PB4 13. P×P P×P 14. PR5 PB5.

6 ...	P—KKt4

Black wants to fix White's king's side pawns on White squares, thus further restricting his bishop. The immediate king advance, 6... KB4 7. KB2 KK5 is answered by 8. BR5 KQ6? 9. BKt6 ch.

7 K—K2	

7. PR4 avoids what follows, but the game is opened up so that Black's king enters, 7... P×P 8. P×P PB4 9. KB2 PB5 10. KB3 P×P 11. K×P BKt3.

166

Black to play

7 ...	B—B4
8 P—KKt4	B—Kt8
9 K—B3	

9. KQ2 loses the KRP, 9... BK5 and 10. BKt7.

9 ...	P—B4
10 P×P	

Now his KRP becomes vulnerable, and Black has threats on both wings; but if 10. KK2 BK5 11. KB2 PB5, and Black's king forces its way through.

10 ...	K×P
11 K—B2	B—K5
12 K—Kt3	K—Kt3

White's KRP is to be fixed on KR3.

13 K—B2	P—R4
14 K—Kt3	P—R5 ch.
15 K—B2	B—B4
16 K—Kt2	

Both White's king and bishop are tied to their defensive posts. Black now prepares the decisive king-entry.

16 ...	K—B3
17 K—R2	K—K3

If at once 17... KK4 18. KKt2 BKt8 19. KB2 KK5 20. BR5, threatening BKt6 ch.

The text-move is a tempo-move, after which White resigned, for if 18. KKt2 KK4 19. KR2 BKt8 20. KKt2 KK5 21. KB2 KQ6 22. KB3 KQ7 23. BK2 BB4.

167 Averbach *v.* Lilienthal, Moscow, 1949. Against a bad bishop a knight is even more effective. Here this advantage is alone sufficient for victory, more than outweighing the force of Black's protected passed pawn. With a KB Black would have a satisfactory game; but as it is he is hopelessly weak on the black squares.

First White fixes Black's pawns on white squares.

White to play

1 P—Kt5	P×P

If 1... PB4 2. KtB3 BK1 3. KtK5 KQ1 4. KB3 KK2 5. KK3 KK3 6. KQ4 KK2 7. KtQ3 KK3 8. KtKt4 PR4 9. KtQ3 BQ2 10. PR4 BK1 11. PKt4, and the passed QRP is decisive.

2 P×P	B—B1
3 K—B4	P—R4
4 K—K5	B—R3

Also after 4... B—Kt5 White's king forces its advance towards Black's QBP, 5. K—B6 B—R4 6. Kt—K6 ch. K—Q2 7. Kt—B4 K—K1 (7... KQ1 8. Kt×B P×Kt 9. PKt6) 8. K—K6 (not 8. Kt×B? when Black wins) 8... B—B6 9. K—Q6.

5 K—B6	B—Q6
6 K—K7	B—Kt8
7 P—R3	B—K5
8 Kt—K6 ch.	K—Kt2
9 K—Q6	B—B7
10 Kt—Q4	B—Q8
11 Kt×P.	

And White wins.

Note the comparative ease with which the king enters the game via the squares which neither the bishop nor its pawns control; and getting the king forward as far as possible is the principal winning motif. If the defender has more than one vulnerable pawn (here he has two, the QBP and KKtP) he generally loses.

168 Reshevsky *v.* Woliston, U.S.A. Championship, 1940. The unbalanced pawns are in White's favour, the queen's side majority being of greater value than Black's potential of a passed KP. Also, Black's king side pawns are somewhat weak.

On the other hand the natural superiority of the bishop might in part compensate for these disadvantages if the position were opened up. For this reason White does not hurry to create a passed pawn, but holds this as a threat. He keeps the position close and tries to block the pawns so that Black has a bad bishop.

1 K—Q3	K—B3
2 Kt—K2	B—B4 .
3 P—KB4	P—Kt4?

The ideas behind this move, provoking exchanges and putting his pawns on white squares, are sound enough; but it now becomes easier for White to get a passed pawn on the queen's side.

The text-move is also a sin of omission for White's reply both secures a powerful central square on the fourth rank for his king, and prepares the investment of Black's king's side. Black should have played ... P—KB4, either here or at an earlier stage.

4	P—KKt4	P—QR3
5	K—K4	B—B1
6	Kt—Q4 ch.	K—Q3
7	Kt—Kt3	B—K2
8	Kt—Q2	B—B1
9	P—B4	K—B4

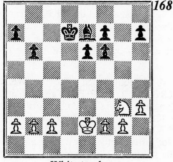

White to play

After the following pawn exchange White's majority becomes more of a real threat; but Black would do better to play 9... P×P (or on the next move 10... K×P) for the pawn on QKt4 provides another target for White's pieces.

| 10 | P×P | P×P |
| 11 | Kt—Kt3 ch. | K—Q3 |

11... KB5 offers no king-entry after 12. PB5 PK4 13. KtQ2 ch.

| 12 | Kt—Q4 | K—B4 |
| 13 | P—B5 | P—K4 |

Black gets a protected passed pawn which is useless; but 13... P×P ch leaves his pawns weak, and after 14. Kt×P Black's bishop cannot move because of the threatened KtR6, so that White's king soon forces entry via Q5, 14... K—B3 15. P—R3 K—B4 16. P—Kt3 K—B3 17. P—Kt4.

| 14 | Kt—B3 | P—KR3 |

White has two separate threats, the

advance of the KKtP (which the text-move temporarily prevents) and the queen's side majority. Having a knight against a bishop, White does not create a passed pawn on the queen's side: indeed it might be a liability, to be defended; or Black's king might enter on the wing and capture it, returning in time to the king's side, as in Example 150. White's knight could not simultaneously support a passed QRP and a passed KRP.

15	P—KR4	B—K2
16	P—R5	B—Q3
17	P—R3	

White prepares to close this wing. The pawn majority has served its turn by keeping Black's king from the king's side, where the breakthrough now comes.

| 17 ... | K—B5 |

In the game Black tried 17... PKt5, resigning after 18. PR4 PKt6 19. KtQ2 KKt5 20. PR5 K×P 21. KtB4 ch. Reshevsky gives the following continuation:

18	Kt—Q2 ch.	K—B4
19	P—Kt4 ch.	K—B3
20	Kt—B3	B—B1
21	P—Kt5	RP×P
22	Kt—R2	B—Kt2
23	Kt—Kt4	K—Q3
24	P—R6	B—R1
25	P—R7	B—Kt2
26	Kt—R6	K—K2
27	K—Q5.	

And the king-entry decides.

169 Levenfish v. Ragosin, Moscow, 1939. White has an outside passed pawn. Before this falls his king gains a decisive entry. The knight is here the equal of the bishop because the manœuvres are short-ranged, and because, as it happens, it can attack the king's side pawns effectively.

| 1 | K—B3 | B—K2 |

If 1... KQ2 2. KK4 KB3 3. KtB4 K×P 4. Kt×P, and White wins because Black's king is too far off, compare Example 141.

2 P—B6

Better than 2. KtKt3? Tied to the
defence of a pawn the knight, unlike the
other pieces, is immobilized.

2 ...   K—Q1

If 2... PB4 3. P×P P×P 4. KtB4
BB3 5. KtQ6 ch. KQ1 6. PB7 ch. Play
with the knight always involves various
tactical continuations. This sense of
immediacy contrasts with the deliber-
ately prepared manœuvres of the bishop.

3 K—K4   K—B2
4 K—Q5   P—B4

White wins easily after 4... PB3
5. KtK4.

169

White to play

5 P×P   P×P
6 K×P   K×P
7 Kt—Kt3   B—Q3 ch.

7... KQ2 is more logical, but in any
event his KRP cannot be defended.

8 K—K6

Holding off Black's king.

8 ...   B—R7
9 Kt—Q4 ch.   K—B4
10 Kt×P   P—R4
11 Kt—Kt3   K—Q5
12 K—B5   P—R5
13 Kt—R5   B—Kt8
14 P—B3   B—B7
15 Kt—B4   B—K8
16 Kt—Kt6   K—Q4
17 K—Kt4.

Black resigns.

170 Konig v. Smyslov, Great Britain
v. U.S.S.R., Radio match, 1946. Other
considerations apart, the unbalance of
pawns should favour White, who has
a queen's side majority, whilst Black has
only a central majority; but Black's
king is much better placed, and in the
event enters and captures the queen's
side pawns whilst his own passed pawn
holds White's king in the centre—a
reversal of the normal procedure which
only just succeeds. In addition White's
king's side pawns are weak, so that his
knight must defend the KRP and cannot
manœuvre freely. Finally, in this open
position the bishop has a natural
superiority over the knight.

1 ...   P—Kt4

A correctly timed attack on White's
KRP, for 2. P×P P×P gives Black a
dangerous king's side majority, e.g.
3. KK2 PR5 4. P×P P×P 5. KB1 PR6
6. KKt1 KK4 7. KR2 KB5, and wins.
Not infrequently the attacker may alter
the nature of the pawn-structure in his
favour.

2 K—K2   P×P

Black exchanges before White can
defend by KtKt2.

3 P×P   P—B4
4 Kt—Kt2   K—K4
5 P—R3

White's pieces are tied to the king's
side: if the king moves, then ... PB5
threatening ... PB6; if the knight moves
far, then ... BK2 wins the KRP. If
5. PB4 ch. Black's protected passed
pawn wins the day, 5... KK3 6. KtK3
BK2 7. KtKt2 BB3 8. PKt3 BQ5
9. KtK3 B×Kt. Lastly, if 5. PKt3 BK2
6. KK3 PB5 ch. 7. Kt×P BB4 ch. winning the knight.

5 ...   B—Q3

Not 5... PR4? 6. PKt4 liquidating
Black's future plunder, 6... P×P 7. P×P
B×KtP, and now 8. PB3, with drawing
chances because the bishop is of the
wrong colour for the RP.

6 P—Kt4

170

Black to play

If 6. Kt—K3 B—K2 7. Kt—Kt2 P—R4 8. P—Kt4 P—R5 9. P—B3 (9. KQ2 PB5) 9... P×P ch. 10. K×P K—Q5.

6 ...	P—B5
7 P—B3	K—Q5
8 P×P	

If 8. PR4 PK6 9. PKt5 PR4, and White is still tied up.

8 ...	K×P
9 Kt—K1	K—Q5
10 K—B3	

Black's king enters one way or the other. If 10. K—Q2 K—B5 11. K—B2 B—B2 12. Kt—B3 B—Kt3 13. Kt—Kt5 (after 13. KtK5 ch. KQ5 14. KtQ7 BQ1 15. KtKt8 B×P 16. Kt×P Black's passed pawns win, because they are farther from the enemy king, and because the bishop is here superior to the knight) 13... B—K6 14. Kt—B3 B—B7.

10 ...	K—B5
11 K—K4	

The pawn ending is lost by a tempo after 11. KtKt2 KKt6 12. Kt×P B×Kt.

11 ...	K—Kt6
12 Kt—Q3	K×P
13 Kt—B5	

If 13. KQ5 BK2 14. Kt×P K×P 15. Kt×P PR4 16. KtB4, the QRP cannot be stopped.

13 ...   K×P.

White resigns, for after 14. Kt×P ch.

KKt4 the knight is trapped on the edge of the board.

171 M. Vidmar v. Ulvestad, Yugoslavia v. U.S.A., Radio match, 1950. Each party has a pawn majority but Black's is under restraint, and the three pawns are for the time being held by two. Also, his QKtP is a vulnerable target. The position is open, and the bishop therefore inherently stronger than the knight.

1 ...	Kt—Q3
2 B—Q5	

The liquidation 2. BB3 PB5 3. P×P Kt×P 4. B×P Kt×P 5. B×P? draws because all the remaining pawns are on the side of the board; but here 5. BQ5, trapping the knight, is to be considered.

2 ...   P—R4

Hoping to exchange some king's side pawns. A sturdier resistance follows 2... P—KKt3 3. K—B2 K—Kt2 4. K—K3 K—B3 5. K—Q3 K—K2 6. P—KKt4 P—R3 (6... KQ2? 7. PKt5 threatening 8. BKt8) 7. P—R4 K—B3 (7... KQ2? 8. BK4) 8. K—B3 K—K2 9. P—Kt4 P×P ch. 10. K×P, although White's prospects remain good.

3 K—B2

Each player centralizes his king.

3 ...	K—R2
4 K—K3	K—Kt3
5 B—B3	

171

Black to play

Forcing Black's hand, and avoiding a pawn exchange. If in reply 5... PB5 6. PQKt4.

5 ...	P—R5
6 P—KKt4	K—B3
7 P—Kt5 ch.	K—K3
8 B—Kt4 ch.	K—K2

If 8...KQ4 9.PB5 KK4 10. PB6 P×P 11. PKt6 KtK1 12. BB8 winning the fixed queen's side pawns.

9 P—B5	Kt—B2
10 K—B4	K—Q3
11 B—B3	Kt—K4

Black cannot both defend his QKtP and hold up White's majority. If 11... KB2 12. PB6 P×P 13. PKt6 KtR3 14. PKt7 threatening 15. BQ5.

12 B×P	P—B5
13 P×P	Kt×P
14 P—B6	P—Kt3

If 14... P×P 15. PKt6 KK2 16. PKt7 KB2 17. BQ5 ch. winning the knight.

15 B—Q5

A charming touch. If 15... K×B 16. PB7, or if 15... Kt×P the knight is trapped.

15 ...	Kt—K4
16 P—B7	Kt—Q2
17 B—B4	K—K2
18 B×P	K×P
19 B—Kt7.	

And Black resigns. White made full use of his active majority.

172 Golombek *v.* Keres, Margate, 1939. That a wing majority is often a sufficient advantage to defeat an isolated passed centre pawn is seen in Example 161. When in addition the attacker has a bishop for a knight, the task is somewhat easier, for king-entry is not in general so difficult.

1 ...   B—B7

It is of course a general principle to weaken the opponent's pawns if and when possible. It may pave the way for one's king to enter—in this case White's KB4 square is weakened.

2 P—KKt4

A pawn cannot indefinitely be guarded by a knight, 2. KtK2, for the piece is thereby immobilized, and here after 2... KB3 3. KQ3 KK4 it must soon move.

2 ...	K—B3
3 K—K2	B—Q5
4 K—B3	

Black's king threatens to enter White's game, and cannot be kept out by 4. KQ3 BKt3 5. KtK2 KK4, for the knight must sooner or later give way, ceding the square KB4.

Black to play

4 ...   P—QR4

Black mobilizes his majority. As usual the passed pawn, here the QBP, will draw off one or both of White's pieces, permitting Black's king to enter the game, or a decisive attack to be made in another part of the board.

5 P—Kt5 ch.

Hoping for some play on the king's side later on. Of course if 5... K×P? 6. KtK6 ch.

5 ...	K—K4
6 Kt—Q3 ch.	K—Q3
7 P—KR4	P—QKt4
8 Kt—K1	

It is useless to advance the KP, 8. KB4 PB4 9. PK5 ch. KQ4 followed by ... PB5.

116

13 MORE PAWNS: POSITIONAL ADVANTAGE

8 ...	B—B4
9 Kt—Q3	B—Kt3
10 Kt—B4	B—Q5
11 Kt—Q3	P—B4
12 Kt—B4	P—B5
13 P×P	P×P
14 Kt—Q5	K—K4
15 Kt—B6	

If 15. KK2 K×P 16. KtB6 ch. KB4 17. Kt×P BKt2 (preventing KtB8) 18. KQ2 KKt5 19. KtB6 ch. K×P with a safe pawn up.

15 ...	P—KR4
16 Kt—Q5	P—B6
17 Kt—B4	P—B7
18 Kt—Q3 ch.	K—Q3
19 K—K2	B—Kt7?

A curious blunder. After 19... BK4 20. KQ2 BKt6 Black wins the king's side pawns and the game.

20 Resigns?

A more curious blunder. After 20. KQ2 PB8=Q ch. 21. Kt×Q B×Kt ch. 22. K×B KK4 23. KKt2 K×P the pawn-ending is drawn, 24. KB3 KB5 25. KQ4 KKt5 26. KK5 K×P 27. KB6 KKt6 28. K×P PR5 29. KB6 PR6 30. PKt6, and White queens with check.

173 Clarke v. Milner Barry, Bognor, 1958. Black's king is better placed, but White has a passed pawn, and his knight is suited to the blocked position. The amusing finish shows the remarkable combinative powers of the knight. White first brings up his king.

| 1 K—Kt2 | P—B5 |
| 2 K—B2 | |

Not 2. P×P'ch. when Black's king enters.

| 2 ... | B—R4 |
| 3 P—R5 | |

A risky winning attempt. The safe 3. KtK2 maintains the balance.

| 3 ... | P×P |
| 4 Kt—R4 | B—Q8 |

This looks good, but fails against White's following combination. Black

has excellent winning chances after 4... KQ3 5. P×P BQ8 6. KtB3 BB7 7. KK3 PR5 8. KQ2 BQ6.

| 5 Kt×P | P—B6 |
| 6 Kt×P | |

This kind of sacrifice, when the defending king is drawn outside the square of the passed pawn, is often possible in minor piece endings. If now 6... K×Kt? 7. PQ6.

White to play

| 6 ... | P—R5 |

Getting the bishop into play, 6... BB7, is probably best.

7 P—Q6	K—K3
8 P—B5	P—R6
9 P—B6	P—R7
10 P—B7	K—Q2
11 Kt—B6 ch.	K×P?

It is curious that this loses, whereas 11... K—B1 12. Kt—Q5 (12. PKt6 P×P) P—R8=Q 13. Kt—K7 ch. K—Q2 gives good drawing chances.

| 12 P—B8=Q | P—R8=Q |
| 13 Q—B6 ch. | K—K2 |

If 13... K—K4 14. Kt—Kt4 ch. K—B4 when the quiet move 15. K—Kt3 leaves Black helpless, for if 15... QR5 16. PK4 ch. Q×P 17. QB6 mate, or here 16... KKt4 17. QR6 mate.

| 14 Q—K8 ch. | K—Q3 |

If 14... K×Kt 15. QR8 ch. skewering Black's queen on the diagonal.

| 15 Kt—K4 ch. | K—B2 |

117

And a skewer also follows 15... KQ4
16. QB6 ch. KK4 17. QB6 ch.

16 Q—K7 ch.

Black resigns. If 16... KB1 17. KtQ6
ch. KKt1 18. QKt7 mate, or if 16...
KKt1 17. QQ8 ch. KKt2 18. KtB5 (Q6)
mate, or 16... KKt3 17. QB5 ch. KKt2
18. KtQ6 ch. KKt1 19. QB8 mate.
Finally, if 16... KKt3 17. QB5 ch. KR4
Black's queen is skewered, this time on
the file, 18. Q×P ch.

14. BISHOP AND TWO PAWNS v. BISHOP OF OPPOSITE COLOUR

Many of the ordinary rules do not
apply. The bishops cannot attack the
same squares, and are not easily exchanged. One player may control all the
squares of one colour, whilst those of the
opposite colour are inviolate. Such
endings are less subtle, and refinements
like triangulation and the opposition are
at a discount.

A pawn up does not generally win.
Even the basic ending bishop and two
pawns v. bishop is often drawn, White
winning only if the pawns are widely
separated or far advanced.

174 United pawns draw if the
bishop is of the wrong colour for the RP.

1 ...   B—B3

The bishop stays on the long diagonal.

2 B—K5 ch.   K—B1

Black plays and draws

After 2... KR1? White's king goes to
QB7 supporting the advance of the KtP,
3. KKt4 BKt7 4. KB5 BB6 5. KQ6
KKt1 6. KQ7 ch. KR1 7. KB7 BKt7
8. PKt7 ch.

3 K—Kt4   B—Kt7.

Black temporises with his bishop,
which White can win for two pawns by
4. PKt7 ch., but in the absence of other
material this is meaningless.

175 In all other cases pawns on the
sixth win.

1 ...   B—Q3

If 1... BQ1 2. BB5 ch. KKt1 3. BKt4,
Black is in zugzwang, and cannot
prevent PB7.

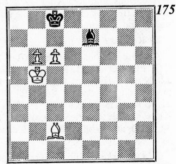

White wins

2 B—B5 ch.

After which White's king will support
the advance of the BP from either Q7
or QKt7.

2 ...   K—Q1

If 2... KKt1 White's king goes to Q7.

3 K—R6   B—R7
4 K—Kt7   B—Kt6
5 P—B7 ch.

176 This and its counterpart (pawns
at KB5 and KKt5 with queen's bishops)
are the only positions with pawns on the
fifth which cannot be drawn.

If 1... BR2 2. BK4 ch. KB2 3. BB3
with zugzwang (4. PKt6 follows) whilst

176

White wins

if 1... BB2 2. BK4 ch. KR2 3. KQ5 BR4 4. KB6 BQ1 5. PKt6 ch.

177 All other positions with united pawns on the fifth, and all positions with united pawns abreast on the fourth or farther back can be drawn if Black's king and bishop are correctly placed.

1 ...   B—Kt2

Not 1... BQ2? 2. BB4 ch. KKt2 3. KK5.

2 B—B4 ch.   K—Q2.

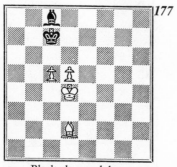

177

Black plays and draws

If 3. PB6 ch. B × P. If 3. PQ6 BB3 with an absolute blockade. If instead White plays his bishop or king, Black temporizes by shuttling his bishop from QKt2-QR1, from which diagonal it both prevents PB6, and holds the QP under fire thus trying down White's king.

This is the standard drawing position,

but if the diagram position were moved one rank forward or one file to the left Black's bishop could not mark time, which explains why the two preceding examples are won for White.

178 In practice pawns farther back often win because it is not always easy for Black to get his pieces, especially the bishop, correctly placed. Here with the move he gets the standard drawing position by 1... KB3 2. PB4 BB2 3. PQ4 BK3; but without the move he cannot prevent the pawns' advance.

1 P—B4   B—K3

The diagonal from which the bishop wants to oppose pawns on the fourth (KKt1, KB2, K3) is not the same as the diagonal for opposing pawns on the fifth (QKt2, QR1, as in the preceding example). The bishop must choose, and White plays accordingly; if 1... BB3 2. PQ4 BKt2 3. PQ5 transposing to the text variation.

2. K—B5

Not 2. PQ4? KB3 with the standard draw.

2 ...   B—B1

If 2... BKt1 3. PQ4 BB2 4. PQ5 BKt1 5. KQ4 BB2 6. PB5 aligning the pawns on the fifth, after which the defending bishop is misplaced, and PB6 cannot be prevented.

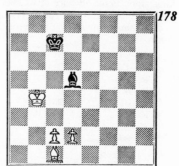

178

White plays and wins
Black plays and draws

3 P—Q4	B—R3
4 P—Q5	K—B1
5 B—B4	K—Q1
6 K—Kt4	K—Q2
7 B—Kt3	

Not 7. PB5? BKt2, for then Black's bishop is on its correct diagonal for the standard draw.

7 ...	B—B1

Black is in zugzwang, if 7... KK2 8. PB5 followed by 9. PB6. If this position were moved one or more files to the right Black's bishop would have a tempo move at this point, but now it is squeezed out.

8 K—Kt5	B—Kt2
9 K—Kt6	K—B1
10 K—R7.	

In a general way some pawn-groupings are more favourable than others. With king's bishops, White does best with QKtP+QBP, or KP+KBP; and with queen's bishops the reverse formations are best, QBP+QP as here, or KBP+KKtP.

179 Disconnected pawns one file apart draw if they are blocked.

If the pawns are two files apart the result depends on the files the pawns are on. KBP+QBP is often won because there is sufficient manœuvring space for White's king to penetrate the position.

There is only one winning plan, the king supports the advance of whichever pawn is blocked by the enemy bishop, in due course winning that piece for the pawn.

1 P—B4	B—B3
2 K—Q5	B—B6
3 K—K6	K—Q1
4 P—B5	B—Q5
5 P—B6	B—B6
6 K—B7	B—Q5
7 K—Kt6	B—B4
8 P—B7	

If 8. KKt7 BQ5.

8 ...	B—B1
9 K—R7	

White wins

To ensure entry for his king White needs two files to the side of the pawn.

9 ...	K—K2
10 K—Kt8	B—R3
11 B—K8	K—Q1
12 P—B8=Q.	

180 As shown by Averbach, 1950, pawns two files apart draw, whatever files they are on, if their advance is blocked by a bishop from one and the same diagonal, and if Black's king can oppose the entry of White's king.

1 K—Q5	K—B3
2 B—Kt4	B—Kt6

Not 2... K—K2? (2... KKt4? 3. KK6) 3. K—K4 followed by P—B4.

3 K—B5	B—B2
4 K—Kt5	K—K2
5 K—R6	K—Q1
6 K—Kt7	B—Kt6.

Drawn

181 With KKtP+QP (or QKtP+ KP) the game is drawn when Black's king blocks the centre pawn, but otherwise may be lost.

1 K—B4	B—B3
2 P—Kt4	B—Kt7
3 P—Kt5	K—K2
4 K—K4	

White's king cannot force an entry on the king's side, for if 4. KB5 BB6 5. KKt6 BQ7 6. KR5 BB6 6. KR6 BQ7 7. KR5 BB6 8. PKt6 BKt2.

4 ...	K—Q3
5 K—Q3	B—B8
6 P—Kt6	B—R3
7 K—B4	B—Kt2
8 K—Kt5	K—B2

Drawn

It is important to keep White's king out.

8... BK4? loses, as shown by Cheron, 1954. 9. KKt6 BKt2 10. KKt7 BK4 11. KB8, threatening to move along the back rank, 11... KK2 12. BB7 BB5 13. KKt7 BKt6 14. KB6 BK4 15. KB5 BQ3 ch. 16. KKt5 BB5 17. BK6 BK4 18. KB5 KB3 19. BB7 KK2 20. KB6 BB5 21. BK6 KB3 22. BB5 KK2 23. BKt4 BKt6 24. BR5, the winning manœuvre (which, however, is not possible with a RP), 24... BK4 25. PQ6 ch. B×P 26. PKt7.

9 K—B5	B—B1 ch.

Black checks whenever White plays K—QB5.

The ending with KRP+KP, or QRP +QP, is drawn if the bishop is of the wrong colour for the RP. In other cases Black draws if his king blocks the centre pawn, but may lose if his king blocks the RP.

182 Analysis from the game Kotov *v.* Botvinnik, Moscow, 1947. Colours reversed. Pawns three or more files apart normally win unless there is a bishop of the wrong colour for the RP. Black then draws if his king can block this pawn—here the QRP.

1 K—Kt8

Drawn

If 1. PR5 BR2 2. PR6 KKt4 3. KKt7 BK5 ch. 4. KR7 BR2.

1 ...	K—Kt3
2 B—Q2	B—B4
3 B—K1	K—B3
4 P—R5	K—Kt4
5 K—B7	K—R3.

White may gain the enemy bishop for the KRP, which draws. He would win only if it were possible to gain the bishop for the QRP.

Black's QP makes no difference. In endings with bishops of opposite colour this is not unusual; it is not the number of pawns that matters, but whether they are dangerous, and an isolated passed pawn unsupported by its king is rarely an imminent threat.

II MINOR PIECE ENDINGS

15. BISHOPS OF OPPOSITE COLOUR: MORE PAWNS

Other things being equal a pawn down or a pawn up draws, and all that matters is how effective the passed pawns are. Pawn sacrifices, either to get passed pawns, or to prevent the opponent's getting them, are the rule rather than the exception.

A material advantage of two unblocked pawns will win; but if White is only one pawn up the game is drawn unless he also has some positional advantage.

There are two basic winning methods: getting a pair of mobile united passed pawns, for which the opponent will at least have to give up his piece; or getting threats on both sides of the board, which generally results in widely separated passed pawns, for one of which the opponent will lose his bishop.

More rarely one might win by a combination, or because the defending bishop is too constricted.

183 Nejmetdinov *v.* Livshin, U.S.S.R. Championship, 1954. White has an extra and passed pawn, but has no real threats on the other side of the board—the queen's side. In the event he wins because he obtains a pair of united passed pawns.

| 1 B—Q8 | B—Kt6 |
| 2 P—B5 ch. | K—B2 |

This endangers his KRP, which he should guard by 2... K—Kt2. After 3. K—Kt3 (3. KK3 BQ8 4. KB4 PB5 5. BKt6 BK7 6. BK3 BQ6 transposes) 3... B—B7 4. B—Kt6 P—B5 5. B—Q4 ch. K—R2 6. K—B4 B—Q8 7. B—K3 B—B7 (not 7... BK7? 8. KKt3, 9. KR4, and 10. KR5 winning the KRP) 8. K—K5 (now if 8. KKt3 BK5 9. KR4 BB3 10. KR5 Black may chase the king away, 10... BK1 ch.) 8... B—Q8, 9. K—Q6 (9. PKt5 P×P 10. B×P BKt5) 9. B×P 10. K—B5 B—Q8 11. K×P B—Kt6, and Black's queen's side is quite safe, whilst his king blocks the KBP.

| 3 K—Kt3 | B—Q8 |

3... BQ4 is simpler.

| 4 B—Kt6 | P—B5? |

183

White to play

After this Black cannot maintain his KRP at R3, and White gets a pair of united passed pawns. Black yet draws by sacrificing his QBP, 4... B—B7 5. B×P B—Kt6 (not 5... PR4? 6. F×P B×P 7. BK3 KKt2 8. PR6 ch. KR2 9. KB4 BQ6 10. KK5 BK7 11. KQ5 BQ6 12. KB5 BK7 13. BB1 BQ6 14. KKt4 BB5 15. PKt3 P×P 16. PR4, and White gets united pawns on the queen's side) 6. B—K3 K—Kt2 7. P—Kt5 P×P 8. B×P K—B2 9. K—B4 B—B7 10. K—K5 B—Q6 11. P—B6 B—K7, etc.

| 5 B—K3 | P—R4 |

Otherwise White wins this pawn after 6. K—R4 and 7. K—R5.

6 P—Kt5	B—B7
7 K—B4	P—R5
8 P—Kt6 ch.	K—Kt2
9 K—Kt5	P—R6
10. B—B4.	

Black resigns. He cannot even give up his bishop for the pawns, one of which must queen. His passed KRP is useless.

184 Euwe *v.* Yanofsky, Groningen, 1946. If the united pawns can be blocked by the defending king, they will only draw.

| 1 K—K3 | B—Kt7? |

After 1... KB4 2. BB8 PKt3 3. KQ4

BKt7 4. KB5, Black blocks the passed pawns with his king, 4... KK3 5. KKt6 KQ2 6. KB5 KB1 7. KQ6 KKt2, and guards his pawns on the other side with his bishop, 8. KK5 BB6 9. KB6 BK5 10. KK5 BKt8. This is the normal drawing method when there are pawns on both sides of the board.

Here Black's king and bishop changed sides, the king retreating to the queen's side via the Black diagonal KB4-K3-Q2-B1. After the text move Black's king is drawn off this diagonal to protect his king's side (5... KB2) and by a combination (11. PR5) is prevented from returning.

White to play

2	K—B4	P—Kt3
3	P—KKt4	P×P
4	K×P	B—R8
5	K—Kt5	K—B2

Necessary, for if 5... BK5 6. PKt4 KQ2 7. PR4 KB1 8. PR8=Q ch. B×Q 9. K×P, and the disconnected pawns win.

6 B—Q4

White first prepares everything thoroughly, before breaking through.

6	...	B—Kt7
7	P—R4	B—R8
8	P—Kt4	B—Kt7
9	P—Kt5	B—R8
10	B—B6	B—Kt7
11	P—R5	P×P
12	K—B5	

The point of the sacrifice—this move prevents Black's king returning to K3.

12	...	B—R8
13	B—R4	B—Kt7
14	K—K5	K—K1
15	K—Q6.	

White wins because the pawns are blocked only by the bishop.

185 Rubinstein *v.* Grunfeld, Carlsbad, 1929. In the preceding examples White had threats on one side of the board only. Here White wins because he can create widely separated passed pawns.

1 K—B2

In the game White made another passed pawn one move too soon, 1.PKR5 P×P 2. B×P KK2 3. KB2 PB5 4. BK2 KB2 (Grunfeld lost after 4... PB6? The draw is shown by Becker) 5. B×P ch. KKt3 6. KKt3 B—K8 7. BQ5 K×P 8. KB4 KB3 9. KKt5 KK2 10. PR5 KQ1 11. KKt6 KB1, and Black returns just in time to prevent the loss of his bishop for the QRP.

1 ...   B—K8

If 1... K—K2 2. K—Kt3 B—K8 (2... KB2 3. KB4) 3. KB4) 3. P—KR5, or if 1... PB5 2. B×P BK8 3. PKR5.

| 2 | P—KR5 | P×P |
| 3 | B×P | B—R5 |

If 3... PB5 trying to keep out White's king, then 4. PKt6 KK2 5. PKt7, a neat

White to play

tactical point. If 3... KK2 4. KKt3 KB1 5. KB4.

The winning method is the usual one, White's king gaining the enemy bishop for the pawn it blocks.

4 P—Kt6	B—B3
5 K—Q3	K—B2
6 K—B4	K—B3
7 P—R5	B—Kt2
8 B—Q1	B—B1
9 B—R4 ch.	K—Q3
10 P—R6	K—B2
11 K—Q5	K—Kt3
12 B—Kt5	B—Kt2
13 K—K6.	

White wins the bishop for the KKtP.

186 Nimzowitsch *v.* Tarrasch, Kissingen, 1928. Besides the queen's wing majority, which eventually means a passed pawn there, White has an advantage on the other side because his king can attack Black's weak pawns.

White has threats on both wings; and the king's side threat means either that Black's king will be drawn away from the queen's side, or that White will get a second passed pawn on the king's side—else it means nothing; for a pawn majority on one wing cannot win unless there are also threats on the other wing. Here Black would draw if his king's side pawns could be defended by the bishop alone.

1 K—R2?

The correct route is 1. K—B1 B—Kt4 ch. 2. K—K1, and if 2... B—R3 3. P—QKt3 K—B3 4. P—QR4.

1 ... P—QB5?

Black safeguards these pawns before moving his king away. If instead 1... PKB5? White gets a king's side majority by 2. BKt5 PB6 3. PKKt4.

However a draw follows 1... B—Kt4 2. K—Kt3 (2. KKt1 BK7) B—B8 3. P—KR4 P—R4 4. K—B4 B×P 5. K×P B—B6, again showing the standard drawing procedure: the defending king blocks the pawn majority, and

the bishop guards the pawns on the other side of the board.

2 K—Kt3	K—B1
3 K—B4	K—Q2
4 B—Kt4	K—K3
5 B—B3	B—Q2

The bishop cannot by itself defend the king's side, if 5... BKt3 6. KKt5 KQ4 7. PKR4 PKt4 8. PQKt3 P×P 9. BP×P KB4 10. PR4 P×P 11. P×P KKt3 12. PKR5 BK1 13. PR5 ch. KR3 14. K×P B×P 15. K×P.

6 P—KKt3	P—Kt4
7 K—Kt5	K—B2
8 P—KR4	

186

White to play

White prepares everything carefully.

8 ...	B—B1
9 K—R6	K—Kt1

The end of the first phase, Black's king has been drawn as far as possible from the queen's side.

10 P—Kt3	P×P
11 BP×P	B—Q2

White is now trying to create a passed QRP, and Black to prevent this. In the game Tarrasch played 11... PB5 at once giving White a passed pawn on the king's side, and lost after 12. P×P BQ2 13. KKt5 KB2 14. PB5 BB3 15. KB4 KK2 16. KK5 (zugzwang) 16... BK1 17. K×P BB3 ch. 18. KK5 BK1 19. KQ5.

12 B—K5	B—K1

If 12... BB1 13. PR4 P×P 14. P×P

BQ2 15. PR5 BB1 16. BQ6 BR3 17 KKt5 BB1 18. KB6, duly winning the bishop for the QRP.

13 K—Kt5	B—Q2
14 K—B6	K—B1
15 B—Q6 ch.	K—Kt1
16 K—K7	B—B3
17 K—K6	K—Kt2
18 K×P.	

And White wins, 18... KB2 19. BB5 KKt2 20. KK6 KKt3 21. PKKt4 KKt2 22. PR5 KKt1 23. KK7 KKt2 24. BQ4 ch. KKt1 25. PR6 BKt2 26. PR4, at last getting a passed pawn.

187 Szabo *v.* Bronstein, Budapest, 1950. A pawn up, White strives for victory by means of one of the basic methods. Having a passed KBP he may try to create another threat on the queen's side; or he may instead try and get a pair of connected passed pawns, QKtP+QRP.

White fails because, apart from Bronstein's skill, he has no positional advantage to supplement his material advantage. The two passed pawns are too close together, and do not form effectively separate threats.

| 1 K—Q2 | K—K3 |
| 2 B—K5 | |

Safeguarding the pawns, for if 2... K×B? 3. PB7. White hopes to continue with 3. KB3, 4. PKt4 P×P 5. K×P, and 6. KR5 attacking the QRP, when the threats on both sides of the board promise victory; a plan which is promptly nipped in the bud.

| 2 ... | P—QR4 |
| 3 K—B3 | |

If 3. B—B3 Black eliminates the weak QRP, 3... P—R5 4. P×P (4. KB2 P×P ch. 5. K×P BK1 6. BK5? K×B) 4... B×P 5. B—K5 B—Kt4 6. K—B3 B—K1, and now either 7. KKt3? or 7. KB4? is answered by 7... K×B 8. PQ7 B×P 9. PB7 BK3 ch. It is this resource that prevents White's king advancing via the white squares.

In endings with bishops of opposite colour it is often difficult to get the king into the enemy lines, because the bishops cannot be opposed with a view to forcing a way through. In the event White gives up one of his advanced pawns to get his king into active play.

3 ...	B—Kt4
4 P—QR4	B—K1
5 B—Kt3	

Here too if 5. KB4? K×B.

| 5 ... | K—Q2 |

White to play

After 5... K×BP? 6. BB2 KK3 7. B×P KQ4 8. BKt6 White gets connected passed pawns, for which Black would ultimately have to give up his bishop; and White then wins, for his own bishop is of the correct shade for his KRP.

| 6 K—Kt2 | |

If 6. KB4 KB3 threatening 7... BB2 ch

| 6 ... | K—K3 |
| 7 K—B2 | |

7. BK1 wins a tempo but not the game.

| 7 ... | P—B5 |

Not 7... KQ2? 8. BK1 K×P (8... KK3 9. B×P K×BP 10. KB3) 9. B×P when White has a passed pawn on each wing.

8 B—K1	P×P ch.
9 K×P	K×BP
10 B×P	

White's passed pawns are not far enough apart to be really dangerous. Given enough time he could win Black's bishop for them, but in the meanwhile his remaining pawn, the KRP, would be liquidated.

10 ...	K—K3
11 B—B7	P—Kt4
12 P—R5	P—Kt5
13 K—B4	P—R4
14 P—R6	P—R5

A routine draw follows 14... BB3 15. KB5 KQ2 16. BQ8 BR8 17. BR4 BKt7 18. BKt3 BR8 19. KKt6 BQ4 20. KR7 KB1 21. PQ7 ch. K×P 22. KKt8 KK3 23. PR7 KB4 24. PR8=Q B×Q 25. K×B KK5 26. KKt7 KB6 27. KB6 KKt7 28. KQ5 PR5, but not 28... KR6? 29. KK4 PR5 30. KB4. Instead Bronstein concocts some traps, impartially for his opponent and for himself, in a highly diverting finish.

15 K—B5	P—Kt6
16 P×P	

Not 16. PR7? BB3 17. K×B P×P, when Black wins.

16 ...	P—R6

Now if 16... P×P? 17. PQ7 B×P (or K×P) 18. PR7 PKt7 19. BR2, and White wins.

17 P—Kt4	

After 17. PR7 BB3 White draws by 18. K×B PR7 19. KKt7, but not by 18. PKt4? KQ2, when the KRP queens.

17 ...	B—Q2

Nor must Black play 17... PR7? 18. PQ7 B×P 19. B×P, when White's disconnected pawns win.

18 P—R7	B—B3
19 P—Kt5	K—Q2

19... PR7? loses after 20. PQ7 K×P 21 B×P even though White's bishop is of the 'wrong colour', for Black's king cannot block the RP.

20 P—Kt6	P—R7
21 P—Kt7	P—R8=Q
22 P—Kt8=Q	Q—B8 ch.
23 Q—B4	Q×Q ch.

24 K×Q	B—R8.

Drawn.

188 Calder-Smith *v.* Katz, London, 1949. Even with so few pieces a combinative finish is sometimes possible.

White to play draws by 1. KK3; but it was Black's move, and the breakthrough 1... PR4 settled matters at once: If 2. K×B PR5 3. BK3 PR6 4. BB1 PB7.

Black to play

If 2. P×P PKt5 3. K×B PKt6 4. PR6 PKt7 queening with check.
If 2. P×P PKt5 3. P×P K×B 4. KKt3 KK6.
If 2. KK3 P×P 3. P×P PB7 4. K×P K×B.

16. TWO MINOR PIECES *v.* TWO MINOR PIECES

With the addition of another piece there are a few cases where the total force may differ significantly from the sum of its parts.

Two bishops are more than twice as strong as one bishop, for between them they control squares of either colour. It is more favourable to have two bishops *v.* bishop and knight than to have bishop *v.* knight. Having the slightest other advantage the bishops often win. A passed pawn or wing majority frequently wins in any event, but with two bishops is overwhelming. As Fine remarks, the two bishops control every square on the queening file, and are a perfect escort for the pawn.

The disparity between two bishops and two knights is even greater, and in very open positions this advantage is alone sufficient for victory.

The bishops drive the knight or knights to inferior positions, even stalemating or trapping them. This is the principle theme of all such endings. The defender draws if the position is blocked, thus limiting the bishops' range; or if he has a strong point in or near the centre which affords a foothold for his knight, which thus exerts its maximum power.

When there are bishops of opposite colour a pawn up often draws. The addition of more pieces always favours the stronger party; not least because there is the possibility of exchanging a bishop for a knight.

189 Trifunović v. Kaila, Helsinki, 1952. The queen's side majority is decisive.

| 1 P—QR3 | Kt—Q6 |
| 2 B—QB3 | P—QR4 |

Both Black's isolated pawns are on Black squares and his bishop is tied to their defence. The bishops could always have forced this, for the pawns could not for long have been defended on white squares.

3 B—K4

All two-bishop endings involve the constriction of the defender's pieces, especially his knight.

| 3 ... | Kt—B5 |
| 4 B—K5 | Kt—R4 |

Making for KB3, which is about as near the centre as practicable. 4... KtK7 ch. 5. KB1 KtQ5, as in the game, fails to 6. B×Kt P×B 7. PQKt4 PB4 8. BB2 P×P 9. P×P, when the united passed pawns win. It is always necessary to consider the possibility of an exchange leading to an ending with bishops of opposite colour.

If 4... Kt—Kt3 (4... PB4 5. B×Kt) 5. B—Q6 (5. B×Kt wins, but keeping the bishop is even better) 5... B—Kt3 (5... BK2 6. BB7 PR5 7. BB2) 6. P—QKt4 RP×P 7. P×PP×P 8. P—B5, and a piece must be given up for White's passed pawn.

5 B—Q6

This fixes Black's bishop on QKt3, for if it goes to QR2 White plays BB7.

| 5 ... | B—Kt3 |
| 6 B—B3 | |

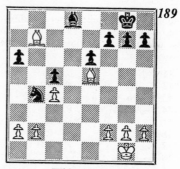

White to play

This forces the knight to retreat before Black can play ... PKB4, which would gain him a little space.

If White resolves the situation at once, 6. PQKt4? RP×P 7. P×PP×P 8. PB5 BR4 9. PB6, the knight comes into play and supports a blockade on his QB2 square, 9... KtB3 10. BB2 KtK1.

In a war of constriction the correct policy is to increase the pressure in every possible way, and not to relieve the tension until a decisive gain is in sight. White has tied down the enemy bishop; next he ties down the knight and its king.

| 6 ... | Kt—B3 |
| 7 B—B6 | |

Preventing ... KtK1.

| 7 ... | P—KR4 |
| 8 P—KR4 | K—R2 |

Black cannot move his knight far, if 8... KtR2 9. BR4 KtB1 10. PQKt4.

9 P—B3   K—Kt3
10 B—R4

The power of the bishops is felt every-
where. Now Black's king cannot get into
play, for if 10... KB4 11. BB2 ch. wins.

10 ...   K—R2
11 K—R2

At this stage, when all the enemy
pieces are tied to their posts, and his
game completely restricted, the usual
plan is to advance the king into the game.
White's king could here enter at Q6 or
QKt5 with decisive results, but he
chooses another plan: to put the knight
out of court so that it cannot return to
the queen's side in time to stop the
passed pawn.

11 ...   K—Kt1
12 K—R3   K—R2
13 B—B6   K—Kt1
14 P—KKt4   P×P
15 P×P   K—R2
16 K—Kt3   K—R1
17 K—B3   K—Kt1
18 P—Kt3

A tempo move forcing Black's king to
the rook's file. He is not without resource
after 18. P—Kt5 Kt—R4 19. P—Kt4
RP×P 20. P×P P—Kt3 21. B×P
(21. P×P BR4 22. BQ7 BKt5) 21...
B×B 22. P×B PB4 23. BQ7 KB2.

18 ...   K—R2
If 18... PKt3 19. BK5.
19 P—Kt5   Kt—R4
20 P—Kt4

At last White makes his passed pawn.
All Black's pieces are badly placed and
he succumbs immediately.

20 ...   RP×P
21 P×P   P—Kt3

If 21... P×P 22. PB5 BR4 23. BR4.

22 B×P   B×B
23 P×B   Kt—Kt2
24 B—Q7   Kt—B4
25 P—B6.

The knight must be given up for the
passed pawn.

190 Taubenhaus *v.* Tarrasch, Monte
Carlo, 1903. When there is no passed
pawn the bishops may yet win if there is
no central foothold for the knight, and
if king-entry is possible. Here Black's
king enters via Q4, K5 and Q6, because
slight pawn weaknesses were created in
the middle-game; but very often the
bishops themselves create such weaknesses, thus making a path for their
king.

Tarrasch was a great believer in the
superiority of the two bishops, and if he
won a bishop for a knight would say he
had won the 'minor exchange'.

1 Kt—B3

White tries to win Black's KRP.
Instead he should try and mobilize his
pawn majority by PKKt4, either here or
on his fourth move.

1 ...   B—Kt8

To weaken White's QRP. This has
meaning in connection with the advance
of Black's king to Q6, when a passed
pawn is more easily forced.

2 P—QR3   B—Q6 ch.
3 K—K1   K—Q4
4 B—B2

This fails because the KRP is not
fixed, but if 4. PR3 PQKt3 5. BB2 KK5.

4 ...   P—R6
5 P—KKt3?

Now 5. PKKt4? KK5 6. KtKt1 loses
material, 6... K×P 7. B×P K×KtP

White to play

8. B×P BKt4; but 5. P×P is better, and although 5... PQKt3 6. BK3 KK5 7. KB2 is good for Black, a win has yet to be demonstrated.

5 ...	P—QKt3
6 Kt—Kt1	B—B4
7 Kt—B3	K—K5
8 Kt—Q2 ch.	

White's bad bishop loses him the game in spite of the bishops of opposite colour after 8. KtKt5 ch. B×Kt 9. P×B KQ6 10. KQ1 BKt5 ch. 11. KB1 KK7.

8 ...	K—Q6
9 Kt—B1	B—K5
10 Kt—K3	B—K2
11 P—KKt4	

This advance comes too late.

11 ...	P—QKt4

Black has advanced his king as far as he can, and cramped White as much as he can, and is ready for the decisive breakthrough.

12 P—Kt5	P—R4
13 K—Q1	P—Kt5
14 BP×P	

Because White's QBP is under attack he is obliged to make this capture, which brings to life Black's dormant pawn-majority.

14 ...	BP×P
15 P×P	P×P
16 Kt—B2	

A neat twist, hoping perhaps for 16... PKt6? 17. KtK1 mate.

16 ...	P—B6
17 P×P	P—Kt6.

White resigns. Black's king's bishop performed well from the base-line, first guarding the KRP and the KKt4 square, and later supporting the advance of the QKtP.

191 Euwe *v.* Pedersen, radio match, 1951. In this wide open position the knights are hounded from pillar to post.

1 B—K5	Kt(Kt2)—K1

After 1... KtK5 2. BR6, or 1... KtB1

2. BR6 KtK2 3. P—QKt5, White wins the QRP by B—QKt8.

2 B—Q3	

Not only preventing ... Kt—K5, but tying Black's king to the defence of his KRP.

2 ...	Kt—KB2

Black gives up a pawn, but hopes to draw by reducing the pawns to one side of the board.

Instead he may guard everything for the time being by 2... Kt—B1 and if 3. B—R6 (3. BQB4 KB2) 3... Kt(K1)—Q3. However, beginning with 3. KB2, White would simply advance his king, Black having no counterplay.

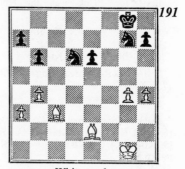

191

White to play

3 B—Kt8	P—QR4
4 B—QB4	

Not 4. P—QKt5? for then Black has a safe place for a knight at Q2, where it is immune from attack by White's KB.

4 ...	P×P
5 P×P	Kt—Q1
6 B—R7	Kt—QB3
7 B×P	Kt×P
8 B×P ch.	

After the struggle Black's knights are scattered, and his king confined. The bishops are so forceful here that they win even with two pawns *v.* one pawn on the same side of the board.

8 ...	K—Kt2

If 8... KB1 9. BB5 ch. winning a

knight; or if 7... KR1   8. BQ4 ch.
KtKt2   9. PKt5, when Black's free
knight is soon run to earth.

| 9 B—Q4 ch. | K—Kt3 |

If 9... KR3   10. BB7 KtQ3   11. PKt5
mate.

10 B—B5 ch.	K—R3
11 B—B5	Kt—Q4
12 B—B8 ch.	Kt—Kt2
13 K—B2	

13. PKt5 ch. KR4   14. B×Kt K×P
15. BB6 also wins, for if 15... PR3
16. BK4.

| 13 ... | Kt—B5 |
| 14 P—Kt5 ch. | |

Best, for Black was threatening
... KtKt3.

14 ...	K—R4
15 B×Kt	K×P
16 B—B6	Kt—R6 ch.

If 16... KR4 (threatening ... PR3)
17. KKt3.

17 B×Kt.

Black resigns, for if 17... K×B
18. KB3 KR5   19. PKt6 ch., but not
19. KB4 KR4   20. KB5? PR3   21. PKt6
stalemate.

192 Robatsch v. Yanofsky, Amsterdam, 1954. The position is partly
blocked, and the knights have a strong-
point at Q4, factors which compensate
for the bishop-pair. Also, Black is
hindered by having to defend his pawn
at K3, for which purpose either his QB
or K must be held back.

Black avoids KB×Kt, for he is left
with a bad bishop; but he welcomes the
chance to play QB×Kt, for then the
B v. Kt ending is favourable to him.

1 P—R4	K—B2
2 Kt(B2)—Q4	B—B4
3 P—KKt3	B—QB1
4 K—Kt2	B—R3
5 K—B2	B—Q6
6 K—K3	B—K5
7 Kt—Kt1	

Best, for other moves give Black a
chance of giving up his QB for a Kt.

| 7 ... | B—Kt7 |

With his bishops alone Black cannot
here tie up the knights. Yanovsky
suggests 7... PKt4, attempting to open
up the position.

8 Kt—K2	B—B8
9 Kt—B3	B—B5
10 Kt—R4	B—Kt5

If 10. BR2   11. PQKt4 threatening
12. KtB5, but 10... BB1 is a better way
to prevent this.

11 Kt—B2

White misses his chance. He should
play 11. PKt3 BR3   12. KtB2 BK2
13. PQKt4. With two strong points for
his knights, QB5 and Q4, he has the
better of it.

11 ...	B—K2
12 Kt—Q4	B—B1
13 P—Kt3	B—B8
14 Kt—B2	B—Kt7

14... BKt4 is also satisfactory. Black
now takes care to prevent PQKt4.

15. Kt—Q4

If 15. PQKt4 BK5.

15 ...	B—K5
16 Kt—B6	B—B7
17 Kt—Q4	B—K5.

Drawn.

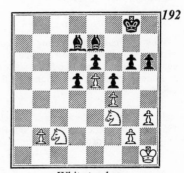

192

White to play

193 Boleslavsky *v.* Kotov, Neuhausen, 1953. If here the knights were exchanged, then the bishops of opposite colour ending would surely be drawn.

1 B—K5

Stalemating the knight, so that if it moves White may play B×Kt, when the Kt *v.* B ending can be won. This is better than 1. P×B? Kt×B, for then White's pawns are very weak.

1 ...   B—B3

Black cannot avoid his queen's side pawns remaining on white squares, for if 1... PKt5 2. P×B, exchanging Kt for B in a different fashion.

2 P—QKt4   P—KR4

Endeavouring to force some pawn exchanges. 2... KKt1, immediately making for K3 so as to try and free his knight, is certainly to be considered.

3 P—B3   K—R2
4 Kt—K2   P—Kt4

If 4... KtB3 White must play 5. B×Kt, but has an easy game after 5... P×B 6. PKR4 fixing Black's KRP on a white square.

5 K—B2   P—R5
6 P—KKt3   P×P ch.
7 P×P   K—Kt3
8 P—Kt4   B—Kt2

If 8... KtB3 9. B×Kt K×B 10. KK3 KK4 11. KtB3 threatening KtK4.

9 K—K3   B—B3
10 Kt—B3   B—Kt2
11 Kt—K4   B—Q4

After 11... BB1 12. KtB5 both pieces are stalemated, and White enters with his king, 12... KB2 13. KK4 KK2 14. KQ5.

12 Kt—B5   K—B2
13 Kt×P   K—K3
14 B—B3   B—R1

The knight cannot escape, for if 14... KtQ3 15. KtB7 ch., or if 14... KQ2 15. KtB5 ch. followed by BK5.

193

White to play

If 14... KB2 15. BK5 KK3 16. PB4 P×P ch. 17. K×P, White wins by advancing the passed pawn, 17... BR7 18. KtB5 ch. KB2 19. KtK4 BKt8 20. KtQ2 BB7 21. KtB3 BQ6 22. KtR4 BB7 23. PKt5 BQ6 24. PKt6 ch.

15 Kt—B5 ch.   K—B2
16 Kt—K4   K—Kt3

If 17... KtB2 18. Kt×P ch., when the united pawns win even with bishops of opposite colour.

17 B—K5   B—Q4
18 Kt—Q2   K—B2.

Black resigns. After 19. KQ4 BK3 20. KB5 BQ2 21. KtK4 KKt3 22. PKt3, a tempo-move forcing Black's king to the KR file, 22... KR3 23. KtB3 and 24. Kt×P, the outside passed pawn wins.

CHAPTER III

ROOK ENDINGS

'. . . and taking aim with a Rook, he dealt him a mortal wound.'*

METELLUS, *A Monk of Tegernsee, c.* 1160.

1. ROOK *v.* PAWN

The pawn falls if blocked by the enemy king. Otherwise the usual question is whether the rook wins or merely draws. The king and rook win if they ultimately control a square which the pawn has yet to cross, although sometimes, especially with RP, this may not be necessary.

The first task for the stronger party is bringing the king nearer to the pawn. The defending king must try to hinder this; and he must also advance his pawn as fast as possible; if he has a choice, it is generally best to advance the pawn ahead of its king.

Unlike the case with a minor piece it makes little difference to the result whether there is a RP or any other pawn, although the play varies.

194 The play against KtP, BP, or Centre P is similar. It is generally best to have the rook behind the pawn, holding it under attack on the file.

When the king and pawn are on their fourth rank or beyond, there are two basic winning processes. In this, method I, White's king tries to approach the pawn from the same side as Black's king.

1 K—K2

Not 1. K—K3? P—Kt7 2. R—B8 ch. (2. KK2 KB7) 2... K—Kt6.

1 ...   K—B7

If 1... P—Kt7 2. K—Q1, but not 2. RB8 ch.? KKt6.

* '. . . et rocho jaculans, mortifere vulnus adegerat.' The translation is by H. J. R. Murray.

2 R—B8 ch.

When the kings are opposed White forces his own king's approach by this check on the file, which also compels Black to obstruct and hold up the pawn.

2 ...	K—Kt7
3 K—Q2	K—R7
4 K—B3	P—Kt7
5 R—R8 ch.	K—Kt8
6 R—QKt8	

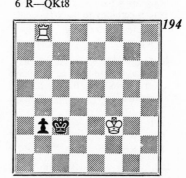

194

White plays and wins
Black plays and draws

There is also a way of winning when the king approaches the pawn from behind, 6. KKt3 KB8 7. RB8 ch. KKt8 8. RB7 KR8 9. RR7 ch. KKt8 10. RR2.

6 ...   K—R8
7 K—B2.

Not 7. R × P? stalemate.

Black to play gets too far forward, 1... P—Kt7 (1... KB7 2. RB8 ch. KQ8, holding off White's king, also draws) 2. K—K2 K—B7 3. R—B8 ch. K—Kt6 (3... KKt8? loses) 4. R—Kt8 ch. K—B7. For White the essential manœuvre is

132

the check on the file, and if his king were here at K3, then 1. RB8 ch. could be played at once.

195 White to play wins by 1. R—B1 ch. K—Kt7 2. K—Q2 K—R7 3. R—B8 (3. KB3? PKt7 4. RB2 KR8 5. R×P stalemate) 3... P—Kt7 4. R—R8 ch.

White plays and wins
Black plays and draws

as before. 1. K—Q1 also wins. White's rook is less effective when on its first rank, for with the move Black draws by 1... KB7 or 1... PKt7, preventing the check on the file.

196 In method II White's king approaches the pawn from the opposite side. This is more favourable, for he can win when his king is one or two ranks farther back than is the case with method I.

White's king here crosses the queening file to the other side of the pawn.

| 1 K—K6 | P—K6 |

If 1... KK6 2. KK5, and White still plays to the opposite side after 2... KQ6 3. KB4, or 2... KB6 3. KQ4.

2 K—Q5	P—K7
3 K—Q4	K—B6
4 K—Q3	K—B7
5 K—Q2.	

With White's king at QR7 (instead of KB7) he fails to win because his rook is not on its best square. 1. K—Kt6 K—K6 (1... PK6? 2. KB5) 2. K—B5 K—Q6

White plays and wins if his king is not on one of the 13 marked-off squares

(opposing White's king as in method I) 3. R—R1 (this is where the rook should have been. If 3. RR3 ch. PK6) 3... P—K6 4. R—R3 ch. K—Q7 (4... KK5? 5. KB4 PK7 6. RR1) 5. K—Q4 (the attack from the rear rarely succeeds, except against RP) 5... P—K7 6. R—R2 ch. K—Q8 7. K—Q3 P—K8=Kt ch. If now 8. K—B3 Kt—B6 9. R—KB2 Kt—K8. With centre P, BP, or KtP, this knight-promotion draws.

With method II it does not make a great difference whether the rook is on the first rank or on the file behind the pawn.

197 There are few subtleties when the rook is behind the pawn. If White's king were on the king's side it would make for K3 or K2 winning by method

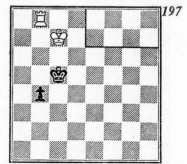

White plays and wins if his king is not on one of the 8 marked-off squares

1. As it is, the king crosses the queening file to the other side of the pawn, method II.

1 R—Kt7

A tempo-move to gain the opposition. Not 1. RKt6? KB5, when White's path across the queening file is obstructed by the rook.

1 ...	K—B5
2 K—Kt6	P—Kt6
3 K—R5.	

198 With the rook on the queening square White has no tempo-move, as shown by Amelung, 1901.

1 K—Kt7

After 1. KQ7 KB5 White's king is too far off for either winning method to succeed. If 1. RB1 ch. KQ5. If 1. RKt2 a tempo is lost after 1... KB5 2. KKt6 KB6.

If 1. RKR1 PKt6; when the pawn is not under attack from the rook it can part company from its king, which is then free to hold off White's king.

1 ...	K—Kt4
2 K—R7	K—R4
3 R—R1 ch.	K—Kt4

(With BP or Centre P Black would here play to the fifth rank.)

4 K—Kt7 P—Kt6.

Black to play also has no tempo-move, and if 1... KKt4 2. KKt7 White wins by

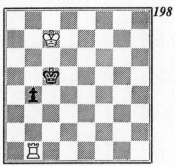
198

White plays and draws
Black plays and loses

method II after 2... KB5 3. KR6, or 2... KR5 3. KB6.

Normally White cannot be forced into Amelung's position, which occurs only when Black's king is on the fourth rank, and his pawn on the fifth. If White's king were here at QR8 (instead of QB7) he would win by 1. K—R7, but not by 1. KKt7? when Black would take the opposition, 1... KKt4.

199 Having the rook elsewhere on the first rank is less effective because the pawn is not under attack, and Black's king is therefore free to fend off White's king.

1 K—Kt4	K—Q5
2 K—B3	K—Q6

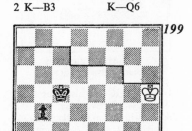
199

White plays and wins if his king is not on one of the 15 marked-off squares

If 2... PKt6 3. KK2 PKt7 4. RQKt1 KB6 5. KQ1, also if 2... KB6 3. KK2; but after the text move White gets his rook to a better square without loss of time.

3 R—QKt1	K—B6
4 K—K2	P—Kt6
5 R—B1 ch.	

Winning as method I, but not 5. KQ1? PKt7 when White is in zugzwang. A similar trap may happen with BP or RP, but not with Centre P, for then the rook could lose a move.

If White's king is at KR6 (instead of KR5) a draw follows 1. KKt5 PKt6 2. KB4 KQ5 fending off White's king, for now 3. RQKt1 does not gain a tempo (3... KB6).

This horizontal fending-off would not be possible if White's rook were at Q1 (instead of KR1), and in that event White would win with his king at KR6.

Finally, there is the vertical fending-off which combats method II. If in this example White's king were at QR8 (instead of KR5), Black would draw after 1. K—Kt7 P—Kt6 (1... KKt4? 2. RQKt1) 2. K—R6 K—Kt5.

200 Other ways of winning occur less frequently. The pawn may be intercepted at an earlier stage; or the rook may help the king to get within the square of the pawn, as here shown by Maizelis, 1950.

200

White plays and wins

1 K—Kt5

Bringing the king into play is almost invariably the first thing to do. The rook with its greater mobility can rapidly be deployed later on, when it is easier to determine its best position.

1 ...	P—Kt5
2 K—B4	K—Q5
3 K—B3 ch.	K—B6
4 K—K2	P—Kt6
5 K—Q1	P—Kt7
6 R—R3 ch.	K—Kt5
7 K—B2.	

201 Against a RP method I wins. As before, it is best for White to have the rook behind the pawn.

1 K—Q2

1 KQ3? KKt7 2. RKt8 ch. KB8 draws, but not here 1... PR7? 2. RKt8 ch. KR6 3. KB2 PR8=Kt ch. 4. KB3 winning the knight.

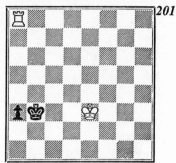

201

White plays and wins
Black plays and draws

1 ...	K—Kt7
2 R—Kt8 ch.	K—R7
3 K—B3	K—R8
4 R—Kt7	K—R7

If 4... PR7 5. RQ7 KKt8 6. RQ1 mate.

5 R—QR7.

And White mates in three.

Having the move Black draws by advancing either piece. After 1... KKt7 2. KQ2 PR7 3. RKt8 ch. KR8 the stalemate threat cannot be circumvented.

202 Slastenin *v.* Shustov, 1951.

1 R—B4 ch.   K—Kt6?

The fending-off move 1... KKt4 draws, for after 2. KQ5 PR6 White is a move too late for method I.

2 K—B5

The checking sequence, method III, wins only against a RP, because in that case a knight-promotion does not save Black.

2 ...   P—R6
3 R—B3 ch.

For this winning method White wants to have the rook checking on the ranks.

202

Drawn

| 3 ... | K—Kt7 |
| 4 K—Kt4 | |

After the check White's king attacks the pawn. This would not have been possible if Black had kept the pawn ahead of the king—see the note to his first move.

4 ...	P—R7
5 R—B2 ch.	K—Kt8
6 K—Kt3	P—R8=Kt ch.
7 K—B3.	

White wins the knight.

If in the diagram position White's king were at KB5 (instead of Q6) he could win by method I, but should attend to his king's position before moving the rook. 1. K—K4 (1. RQR6? draws) 1... P—R6 (1... KB6 2. RR6 KKt6 3. KQ3) 2. K—Q3 P—R7 3. R—Kt6 ch. K—R4 4. R—Kt8 K—R5 5. K—B2.

203 Black cannot expect to draw when neither his king nor pawn is beyond the third rank.

| 1 ... | K—Kt4 |

If 1... PR4 2. RR5 PR5 3. KKt7 PR6 4. RR3 as in the text.

| 2 R—Kt7 ch. | |

After 2. K—Kt7? (2. RR7? PR4) 2... P—R4 3. K—B6 P—R5 4. K—K5 K—B5 5. R—R7 K—Kt6 White's king does not arrive in time for method I.

With the text-move White deploys the rook without loss of time, a finesse

possible whenever Black's king is ahead of the pawn. If the pawn were in front a check would most likely improve the position of Black's king.

| 2 ... | K—B4 |
| 3 R—R7 | K—Kt3 |

Method I now wins after 3... KKt4 4. KKt7 PR4 5. KB6.

203

White wins

4 R—R8	K—Kt2
5 R—K8	P—R4
6 R—K5	

6. KKt7 also wins. The idea behind the text-play, winning method IV, is to cut Black's king off from the pawn. It applies especially when the defending king is on the third rank or farther back.

6 ...	K—Kt3
7 K—Kt7	P—R5
8 K—B6	P—R6

If 8... KB3 9. RQR5.

Otherwise White simply brings up his king.

| 9 R—K3 | P—R7 |
| 10 R—QR3. | |

The pawn is lost.

2. ROOK v. TWO PAWNS

White wins easily if his king is in front of the pawns, but otherwise it is not simply a question of whether the rook wins or draws, for sometimes the pawns may win; the result mostly depending on the White king's position.

2 ROOK *v.* TWO PAWNS

The rook is ill adapted for combating united pawns, but, in contrast to the minor piece, it is in its element against disconnected pawns, the farther apart the better because the enemy king is less able to defend them.

204 United pawns are best for Black not least because they support one another's advance. When neither king is present the pawns win if they are on the sixth, and lose if they are not.

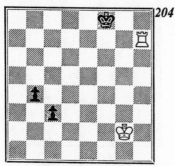

Whoever plays wins

White plays 1. R—B7 (the rook plays behind the most advanced pawn, not 1. RR3? PB7) 1... K—K1 2. R—B4 K—Q2 3. R×KtP K—Q3 4. R—QB4. The pawns win after 1... K—Kt6 (or 1... PB7) 2. K—B3 (the rook cannot stop them, if 2. RB7 PKt7, or if 2. RQKt7 PB7) 2... P—Kt7 3. R—QKt7 P—B7.

205 In the absence of his king White only saves the day against advanced pawns if he has mating threats, or if Black's king is so placed that White may capture a pawn with a check or a pin. These are popular themes for composers, but the ideas have occurred more than once in play. This study is by Salvioli, 1887.

   1 K—B4   K—Kt7
   2 R—Kt1

It is always important to select the right pawn for attack. 2. RQR1? loses

after 2... PKt7 3. RKt1 KB7 4. KK4 KK7 5. KQ4 KQ7 6. KB4 KB7.

   2 ...   P—R7

If 2... P—Kt7 3. K—K3 K—Kt6 (Black's king is awkwardly placed on the seventh rank, for if 3... PR7? White captures the KtP with check) 4. R—Kt1 ch. K—R7. 5. R—QKt1 K—Kt6, with repetition of moves.
If Black plays his king to the KR file, White draws by threatening mate, e.g. 2... P—Kt7 3. K—K3 K—Kt6 4. R—Kt1 ch. K—R6 5. K—B3 K—R5 (after 5... KR7? 6. RKt1 both pawns' fall) 6. K—B4 etc.

   3 R—QR1   K—B7

Not 3... KR7? 4. KB3 PKt7, when 5. R×P pins the KtP.

   4 K—K4   K—K7

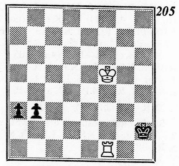

White plays and draws

If 4... K—Kt6 5. R—Kt1 ch. K—R7 (5... KR6 6. KB3 or 5. KR5 KB4 with mating threats) 6. R—R1 K—Kt6 with repetition, for if 6... KKt7? 7. KQ3, and the pawns fall.

   5 K—Q4   K—Q7

Here too if 5... KB6? 6. KB3 winning the pawns.

   6 K—B4   K—B7
   7 K—Kt4   K—Kt7
   8 R—R1   P—R8=Q
   9 R×Q   K×R
  10 K×P.

It is of course sometimes possible to win, directly or indirectly, by such mating threats.

206 More frequently Black's king is out in the open, as here. The positions of this and the next example, and the variations therefrom, are those most likely to occur in practice. If the diagram position were moved one file to the right or one or two files left, the results would be similar.

The rook is best placed behind the pawns; by checks on the file it may help White's king to approach, for this is his main problem.

1 K—Kt4

1. RQB8 PQ7 2. R×P ch. KK4 3. RB8 also draws.

1 . . .   K—K6

The alternative is 1... P—B6 2. R—K8 ch. K—Q5 (2... KQ4 3. RQ8 ch. KB5 4. KB4) 3. K—B4 (not 3. KB3? PB7 4. RQ8 ch. KK4) 3... P—B7 (if 3... PQ7 4. RQ8 ch. KB5 5. KK3) 4. R—Q8 ch. K—B6 (4... KB5 5. RB8 ch. KQ4? 6. KK3) 5. R—B8 ch. K—Q7 (5... KKt7 6. KK3) 6. K—K4 K—K7 7. K—Q4 P—Q7 8. R×P.

2 R—K8 ch.   K—Q7

Black must obstruct his pawns. If 2... KB7 3. RQ8 KK7 4. RK8 ch. KQ8 5. RQB8.

3 K—B3

White draws only by playing to this square, from where he moves either to K4 or K2 according to Black's play.

3 . . .   P—B6
4 R—QB8.

The rook plays behind the un-obstructed pawn.

If 4... K—B7 5. R—Q8 P—Q7 6. K—K2, or if 4... PB7 5. KK4.

Black to play:

1 . . .   K—K6

Not 1... P—B6? 2. R—K8 ch. K—B6 3. R—B8 P—B7 (3... PQ7 4. R×P ch. KK5 5. RB4 ch. KK4 6. RB8) 4. K—B5

K—Kt6 (if 4... PQ7 5. RB3 ch. and 6. R×P pinning the last pawn) 5. R—B3 K—B7 (after 5... KR5? 6. KB4 the mating threats win for White, for if 6... KR4 7. KK3, or if 6... PQ7 7. R×P PQ8=Q 9. RR2 mate) 6. K—K4 K—K7, with a draw.

2 R—K8 ch.   K—Q7
3 K—B4   P—B6
4 R—QB8   K—B7
5 K—K3   P—Q7.

206

White plays and draws
Black plays and wins

If in this example White's king were on a square other than KKt5 the following results are obtained:

White K at KKt4. White plays and wins, 1. R—K8 ch. K—Q5 2. K—B3 K—B6 (2... PB6 3. RQ8 ch. KB5 4. KK3 PQ7 5. KK2 KKt6 6. KQ1) 3. R—QB8 (3. KK3? KB7 4. RQ8 PB6 5. R×P KKt7 draws) 3... K—Q5 4. K—B2 P—B6 5. K—K1, and when White's king is in front of the pawns they are helpless, 5... P—B7 6. K—Q2 K—K5 7. R—B3.

White K at KKt3 (KKt2, KKt1). White plays and wins, 1. K—B2. Black plays and wins, 1... P—B6 2. R—K8 ch. K—B4, disengaging his king.

White K at KB6 (QKt6, QB6, Q6). White plays and draws, his king attacking the pawns from the rear, 1. RK8 ch. KB6 2. RQ8 KK7 3. RK8 ch. KQ7 4. KK5 (QB5) PB6 5. KQ4, and now 5... KB7 6. KB4, or 5... PB7 6. RQB8. Black plays and wins, 1... PB6.

2 ROOK v. TWO PAWNS

White K at KR1, KR2, KR6, KKt6, K6, QR6, or on 7th or 8th rank, Black wins, playing ... PB6 as soon as possible.

White K at KR5, KR4, KR3. Black plays and wins, 1... PB6. White plays and draws.

White K at QR5, QKt5, QB5. Whoever plays wins.

When White's king is on other squares than these it can block the pawns and win.

207 To have the pawns the other way round, as it were, is much more drawish. Here White to play at least draws wherever the king is.

1 K—Kt7	K—Q6

The attempt 1... PQ6 is answered here and in other contexts by the finesse 2. RB4 ch. followed by 3. R × P; but not by 2. R × P? PQ7, when the pawn queens, 3. RB4 ch. KK4 4. RB5 ch. KK3 5. RB6 ch. KQ2.

White plays and draws
Black plays and wins

2 K—B6	K—B7
3 K—K5	P—Q6
4 K—Q4	P—Q7
5 R × P ch.	

Black to play wins by 1... KQ6, etc.

White too has fewer winning chances. If his king were at KKt1 (instead of KR8) it would not be able to block the pawns, e.g. 1. KB2 KQ6 2. KK1 KB7.

White wins if his king is at QR4 (instead of KR8). 1... K—Q6 2. K—Kt3

K—Q7 3. R—KR8, when the kings are on opposite sides of the pawns the rook may operate rank-wise, 3... K—B8 (3... PQ6 4. RR2 ch.) 4. R—R4 P—Q6 (4... PB7 5. RR1 ch.) 5. R—R1 ch. K—Q7 6. R—R2 ch.

208 A study after Schultz, 1946.

1 K—Kt4

He may also win by 1. R—QB5 (White must not attack the wrong pawn, 1. RKt5? PB6 2. R × P KQ4 3. RKt8 KQ5 draws) 1... P—B6 2. K—Kt4, but not 2. RB4? KQ4 3. R × KtP PB7 4. RKt5 ch. KQ3 5. RKt6 ch. KB2, for it is more important to get the king back than to snatch pawns.

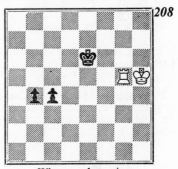

Whoever plays wins

1 ...	P—B6

If 1... KQ3 2. KB3; or if 1... PKt6 2. RKt5 KQ3 3. KB3.

2 R—QB5

Black must not be permitted to get his pawns to the sixth.

2 ...	K—Q3
3 R—B8	

Here too the attempt to win a pawn by 3. RB4? is incorrect.

3 ...	K—Q4
4 K—B3	K—Q5
5 K—K2.	

And White blocks the pawns.

Black to play must be careful as to which pawn he advances:

139

| 1 ... | P—B6 |

1... P—Kt6? 2. R—Kt5 K—Q3 (or 2... PKt7 3. R×P KK4) 3. K—Kt4 K—B3 4. R—Kt8 K—Q4 5. K—B3 K—Q5 draws, as noted in the preceding example.

2 R—QB5	K—Q3
3 R—B8	K—Q4
4 K—Kt4	K—K5

Only this move, fending off White's king, wins; for if 4... KQ5? 5. KB4.

| 5 K—Kt3 |

If 5. RK8 ch. KQ6 6. RQ8 ch. KB7 7. KB3 PKt6; or if 5. RB4 ch. KQ6 6. R×P PB7 7. RKt3 ch. KQ5.

5 ...	K—Q6
6 K—B3	P—Kt6
7 R—Q8 ch.	K—B7
8 K—K3	P—Kt7.

209 Tarrasch v. Janowski, Ostend, 1907. Colours reversed.

| 1 ... | P—B5 |

Foreseeing an ending of two united pawns v. a rook, Tarrasch advances the BP, and indeed 1... PKt5 is far less promising.

| 2 R×P | K—Q3 |
| 3 R—R5? |

White now threatens both R×P and RKt5, and probably hoped for 3... PB6? 4. RKt5 R×R 5. K×R PB7 6. PKt8=Q PB8=Q ch. with a drawish

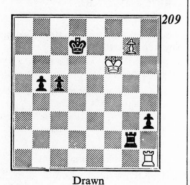

Drawn

queen ending. However 3. R—R8 R×P (4... PB6 is no better) 4. K×R P—B6 5. R—QB8 P—Kt5 6. K—B6 draws, Example 206.

| 3 ... | R×P |
| 4 K×R | P—B6 |
| 5 R—R8 |

The pawn cannot be stopped after 5. R×P PB7.

| 5 ... | P—Kt5 |
| 6 R—QB8 | K—K4 |

If White's king were at KKt6, then this fending-off manœuvre would be essential; but here 6... KQ4 suffices.

| 7 K—Kt6 | K—Q5 |

The more consistent 7... KK5 8. RB4 ch. KQ6 9. R×P PB7 also wins.

| 8 K—B5 | P—Kt6 |

The simpler way is 8... KQ6, Example 206.

| 9 R—Q8 ch. | K—K6 |

9... KB5? 10. KK4 draws.

| 10 R—QKt8 |

Janowski resigned after 10. RK8 ch. KQ6 11. RQ8 ch. KB7.

| 10 ... | P—Kt7 |

Avoiding the trap 10... PB7? 11. R×P ch. KQ5 12. RKt4 ch. KQ4 13. RKt8 PB8=Q? 14. RQ8 ch.

| 11 K—K5 | K—B6 |

Both 11... KQ7? 12. KQ4 and 11... PB7? 12. RKt3 ch., draw.

| 12 K—B5 | K—K7 |

Not 12... K—Kt6? 13. R—Kt3 K—R5 (13... KB7 14. KK4) 14. R—Kt4 ch. K—R4 15. R—Kt8, when the mating threats draw.

13 K—K4	K—Q8
14 K—Q3	P—B7
15 R—KR8	P—B8=Kt ch.
16 K—B3	P—Kt8=Q.

210 In the absence of kings disconnected pawns one file apart lose if Black cannot get either of them beyond the sixth rank. The rook combats un-

supported isolated pawns from the rank:
1. R—B2 (1. RQB8? PR7 2. RQR8
PB7) 1... K—Kt6 2. R—B2 and both
pawns fall. Not here 1. K—Kt6? P—R7
(the choice of pawn is important, for if
1... PB7? 2. RB1, White wins after
2... KKt6 3. KB5 KKt7 4. RB1, or
2... PR7 3. KB6 KKt6 4. KK5) 2.
R—B1 K—Kt6 3. K—B5 K—Kt7
4. R—QR1 K—B6 5. R×P K—K6,
with a draw.

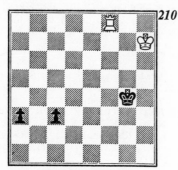

White plays and wins
Black plays and draws

Kockelkorn, 1888, shows the drawing
idea here.

| 1 ... | P—R7 |

1... PB7 is also sound, but not 1...
KKt6?, for with his king on the sixth
rank there is a danger of White attacking
from the rear and capturing a pawn with
check, 2. RB8 PR7 3. R×P ch.

2 R—B1	P—B7
3 K—Kt6	K—Kt6
4 K—B5	K—Kt7
5 R—QR1	K—B6

When Black's king is on the seventh
rank there is a danger of the rook capturing one pawn and pinning the other, if
5... KB7? 6. R×P.

| 6 K—K5 | K—K6 |
| 7 K—B5 | |

Black wins after 7. KQ5? KQ6 8.
KK5 KB6 9. KK4 KKt7 10. KQ3
PB8=Q.

7 ...	K—Q6
8 K—B4	K—B6
9 K—K3	K—Kt7
10 K—Q2	K×R
11 K—B1 stalemate.	

211 When Black's king is near, and
White's is far off, the rook should be
behind the pawns, because checks on the
ranks may be answered by a pawn
advance. However far away his king,
White draws if the pawns are not yet
both on the sixth (or one on the seventh
and the other on the fifth). His drawing
chances are better here than against
united pawns.

| 1 R—Q7 ch. | K—B7 |
| 2 R—QR7 | |

When the king shelters behind one
pawn, the rook attacks the other.

| 2 ... | K—Kt6 |
| 3 R—Kt7 ch. | |

When the king emerges, the rook
checks on the file.

| 3 ... | K—R7 |
| 4 R—QB7. | |

If Black's king goes away altogether,
4... KKt6 5. RKt7 ch. KB5 6. RB7 ch.
KQ5 7. RQ7 ch. KK5, the rook attacks
the foremost pawn, 8. RQB7.
When the pawns are on the sixth
White sometimes draws if his king is not
too far away, as shown by Chéron (1945)
after 1. K—B5 P—R6:

| 2 R—Q7 ch. | |

Not 2. KK4? PB7 3. RQ7 ch., and
now that the pawns are sufficiently
advanced, Black's king simply gets out
of the way, 3... KK8 (taking cover from
checks) 4. RQB7 PR7.

| 2 ... | K—K8 |

If 2... K—B8 blocking his BP, White
brings up the king 3. K—K4 P—B7
(3... PR7 4. RQR7) 4. K—Q3 P—R7
(4... KQ8 5. RKR7) 5. R—KR7
K—Kt8(7) 6. R—Kt7 ch. K—B8
7. R—KR7, with repetition.
If the king goes to the seventh, 2...

K—K7, then 3. RQB7 PR7 4. RQR7
PB7 5. R×P pinning the BP.

If the king goes to the sixth, 2...
K—K7 3. R—QB7 K—Q7 4. R—Q7
ch. K—K6, then 5. RQR7 PB7 and the
rook captures with check.

3 R—K7 ch.   K—B8
4 R—KR7

When Black's king moves away from
the pawns, the rook attacks rank-wise.
If it cannot do this, as would happen
if this position were moved one file to
the right, then the pawns win.

4 ...   P—B7

If 4... PR7 5. RR1 ch. KK7 6. RR1.
If 4... KKt8 5. RKt7 ch., whilst 4...
KKt7? loses after 5. RQR7.

5 R—R2   P—R7
6 R—R1 ch.   K—K7
7 R—R1   K—Q6
8 K—B4.

211

White plays and draws
Black plays and wins

Drawing by stalemate, as in the preceding example.

Pawns on the sixth supported by their
king win if the enemy king is too far
away, as happens with Black to play:

1 ...   P—R6

1... P—B7 also wins, 2. R—Q7 ch.
K—B8 (2... KK8 3. RK7 ch. KB8?
4. RQB7) 3. R—QR7 P—R6 transposing to the text-play.

2 R—Q7 ch.

White has no real plan; he merely
harrasses Black as much as possible with
checks, pins, and skewer-threats.

2 ...   K—B8

The quickest way, although no harm
comes from the detour 2... K—K8
3. R—K7 ch. K—B8 (not 3... KB7?
4. RQR7 drawing, for if 4... PB7?
5. RQB7, White winning) 4. K—B5
P—B7 (4... PR7? 5. RKR7) 5. R—
KR7 K—Kt8 6. R—Kt7 ch. K—B8
7. R—KR7 K—K7 (7... PR7? 8. RR1
ch. KK7 9. RR1 draws) 8. R—K7 ch.
K—Q6 9. R—Q7 ch. K—B6 10. R—B7
ch. K—Kt6.

3 R—QR7   P—B7

The text continuation is by Selesniev,
1921. Berger and Kockelkorn, 1888,
show an alternative win: 3... ·KKt7
4. RKt7 ch. KR8 5. RQB7 PR7 6. KB5
KKt7 7. RKt7 ch. KR6 8. RR7 ch.
KKt6 9. RKt7 ch. KB5 10. RQR7 PB7
11. KK4 KKt4, but not 11... KB4?
12. KQ3.

4 K—B5

If 4. R×P KKt7.

4 ...   K—Kt7

Now that the pawns are far enough
forward Black simply wants to get his
king out of the way.

5 R—Kt7 ch.   K—B6
6 R—B7 ch.   K—Kt6
7 K—K4

If 7. RKt7 ch. KR5 8. RQB7 PR7;
but after the text-move Black takes
cover from checks at K8.

7 ...   K—Kt7

A curious draw follows 7... P—R7?
8. K—Q3 K—Kt5 (8... PR8=Q 9.
RKt7 ch. KR2 10. RR7 ch.) 9. R—Kt7
ch. K—B4 10. R—QR7 K—Kt3 (10...
PB8=Q? 11. RB7 ch.) 11. K×P K×R
12. KKt2.

8 R—Kt7 ch.   K—B6
9 R—B7 ch.   K—Q7
10 R—Q7 ch.   K—K8.

If 11. RKR7 PB8=Q, and if 11. RQB7
PR7.

212 White wins if his king can block one of the pawns; but when his king is far away he has winning chances against the pawns, supported by their king, only when they are not beyond the fourth rank.

Here White's king is about as badly placed as it could be. The text play is given by Maizelis, 1950.

1 K—R7

White plays and wins
Black plays and draws

White first gets his king into play. The rook can wait until its best position is apparent; indeed, the attempt to snatch a pawn by 1. R—B7? P—K4 2. R×Pch. draws after 2... KB4 3. KB7 PK5 4. RK6 KB5 because the rook obstructs the king.

1 ...   P—K4

If 1... PB4 2. KR6; or if 1 KKt4 2. RK7 (gaining time) 2... KB4 3. KR6.

2 K—R6   K—B4

If 2... PK5, White cuts off the king, 3. RR5.

3 K—R5   P—K5
4 K—R4

First one should deal with the most advanced pawn, here the KP. Later there is time for mopping-up.

4 ...   K—B5
5 R—B7 ch.

The familiar check on the file forces the approach of his king.

5 ...   K—K6
6 K—Kt3   P—B4

If 6... KQ6 7. RQ7 ch. KK7 8.RQB7.

7 R—B7   K—Q5
8 K—B2   P—B5
9 K—K2   K—B6

After 9... PB6 this pawn is lost.

10 K—K3   K—Kt6
11 K×P   P—B6
12 K—Q3.

With the move Black draws by 1... P—K4 2. K—R7 K—Kt4, but not by 1... PB4? 2. RB7 KK4 3. R×P ch. KQ5 4. RB1 PK4 5. RQ1 ch. (getting the rook to the queening square without loss of time) 5... KB6 6. RK1 KQ5 7. KB7, when White wins.

213 When the disconnected pawns are further apart their chances of winning diminish. Drawing chances are about the same, because in most cases only one pawn can be rapidly advanced, and the other is almost an onlooker, so that it amounts to a R *v.* P ending, the result mostly depending on the White king's position.

Here a draw by repetition follows 1... KK6 2. RKt1 KQ6 3. RKt1.

The rules for dangerously advanced pawns when White's king is absent are as follows:

Pawns on the sixth rank two or more files apart *v.* rook on the second rank: Black cannot win.

Drawn

Pawns on the seventh rank 2 or 3 files apart *v.* rook on the first rank: Black usually wins if his king is nearer than White's, but not otherwise.

Pawns on the seventh rank 4 or more files apart *v.* rook on the first rank: Black cannot win.

Finally, if White's king is better placed, i.e. it prevents Black's king from aiding his pawns, then White wins easily.

3. ROOK *v.* THREE PAWNS

United Pawns are best for Black, and they win if White's king is unable to confront them. When White's king gets in front of the pawns his rook attacks from the side or rear and forces a blockade. If then one of the pawns is on the sixth or seventh the game is normally drawn; but White wins if the pawns are blocked farther back.

White usually wins against isolated pawns if his king is not farther away than Black's king.

214 Fazekas *v.* Klein, Buxton, 1950. After 1. K—B6 ch. K—K3 (1... KKt3 2. KQ5 KR3 3. KK4 leaves Black helpless) 2. R×P (breaking up the pawns) 2... P—B4 3. K—B5 K—K4 4. R—K7 ch. K—B5 5. K—Q4 P—R6 6. R—R7 K—Kt6 7. K—K3 P—B5 ch. (7... PR7 8. RKt7 ch. KR6 9. KB2) 8. K—K2 K—Kt7 White mates in six. But in the game it was Black's move.

1 ...	P—Kt4
2 K—B6 ch.	K—K3
3 K—B5	

Once again it is pointed out that White should first attend to his king's position. He actually played 3. R—R1? and should have lost—see Variation A.

3 ...	K—K4
4 K—B4	K—K5
5 R—K7 ch.	

As usual, the check on the file forces the king's approach. If now 5... KB6 6 RKB7.

5 ...	K—B5
6 K—Q3	P—Kt5
7 K—K2	K—Kt6

Or 7... P—Kt6 8. K—B1 P—R6 (8... KB6 9. RKB7) 9. R—QR7 (9. RKR7 also draws) 9... P—B4 10. K—Kt1 K—Kt5 11. R—R4 ch. P—B5 12. R—R3 P—R7 ch. 13. K—R1 (not 13. KKt2? PB6 ch.) 13... K—R6 14. R×P ch.

Black does best to advance a pair of pawns. For the over-ambitious 7... P—B4? see Variation B.

8 R—KB7	P—R6
9 R×P	K—Kt7
10 K—K3	P—Kt6
11 R—KR6	K—R7
12 R—KKt6.	

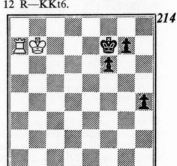

White plays and wins
Black plays and draws

Variation B (1... P—Kt4 2. K—B6 ch. K—K3 3. K—B5 K—K4 4. K—B4 K—K5 5. R—K7 ch. K—B5 6. K—Q3 P—Kt5 7. K—K2 P—B4?).

| 8 K—B2 | K—Kt4 |

Black suddenly finds himself on the defensive. After 8... PKt6 ch. 9. KKt2 KKt5 10. RKR7 PB5 11. RKt7 ch. KB4 he loses because his pawns are blocked, 12. R—Kt8 K—K5 13. RKt4.

8... P—R6 also loses, 9. R—KKt7 K—K4 (9... KK5 10. KKt3, and now 10... KK6 11. RK7 ch., or 10... PB5 ch. 11. K×P) 10. K—Kt3 K—K3 11. K—B4 K—B3 12. R—Kt5 K—K3 13. R—R5.

| 9 R—KR7 | P—R6 |

White normally wins if his king gets in front of three united pawns on their fifth rank because they can be blockaded: 9... PB5 10. KKt2 PR6 ch. 11. KR2 KKt3 12. RR8 KKt4 13. RKB8 PB6 14. KKt3 KKt3 15. RB4.

10 R—KR8   K—Kt3
11 R—KB8

Not 11. KKt3? KKt2 12. RQR8 KB2 13. KB4 KKt2, the standard drawing line for all chains of three when the pawns are on the fourth, fifth, and sixth ranks. If White captures the BP Black's other pawns advance.

Black keeps his king on KR2, KKt2, or KR2 when the rook is on its eighth rank, or on KB3, KKt3, or KR3 when the rook is on its seventh rank.

Black keeps his king on KB2 or KKt2 when the rook is on its sixth rank: 14. R—R6 K—B2 (14... KR2? 15. KKt5 KKt2 16. RKt6 ch. KB2 17. RKR6 KKt2 18. RR5) 15. R—KR6 K—Kt2 16. R—R5 K—Kt3 17. R—Kt5 ch. K—R3 18. R—Kt8 K—R2.

White keeps his king on KKt3 or KR3 when Black's rook is on its fifth rank.

11 ...   K—Kt4
12 K—Kt3   K—Kt3
13 K—B4

White now wins after 13... K—R3 14. R—B6 ch. and 15. R×P.

The position after White's 13th move is also won with White to play: 14. KKt3 KKt4 15. RKt8 ch. KR3 16. KB2 KR4 17. KK3 KR3 18. KK2! KR4 19. KB2, and now 19... PB5 20. RR8 ch. KKt4 21. KKt1 KB4 22. KR2, or 19... KR5 20. RKt7 KR4 21. KKt3 KR3 22. RKt8 KR4 23. KB4 (Kopaiev).

Variation A. (1... P—Kt4 2. K—B6 ch. K—K3).

3 R—R1?

Unless the pawns are really menacing, the rook should bide its time.

3 ...   P—Kt5

The winning idea is to get a pair of advanced united pawns as quickly as possible, and winning chances are better here with the KtP advanced ahead of the RP, Example 206.

In the game Black could not avoid moving the RP ahead, and consequently he drew: 3... K—K4? 4. R—K1 ch. K—B5 5. R—B1 ch. K—K5 6. R×P P—R6 (6... PKt5 7. RR6) 7. R—Kt6 K—B5 8. K—Q5 P—Kt5 9. R—KR6, Example 207.

4 K—B5

If 4. R—K1 ch. K—B4 5. K—Q5 (5. RB1 ch. KK5 6. R×P PKt6, Example 206) 5... P—Kt6 6. R—B1 ch. (6. KQ4 PR6 7. KK3 KKt5) 6... K—Kt5 7. K—K4 P—Kt7 8. R×P P—R6 9. R—Kt6 ch. K—R4 10. K—B5 P—R7 11. R—Kt8 K—R3 12. K—B6 K—R2 13. R—Kt7 ch. K—R1, a fascinating variation!

4 ...   K—K4
5 K—B4   K—K5

Not 5... PKt6? 6. KQ3 KB5 7. KK2 PR6 8. RR4 ch. KKt4 9. KB3, with a blockade to follow.

6 R—K1 ch.   K—B6
7 K—Q3

Of course if 7. RB1 ch. KK7 8. R×P PKt6, Example 206.

7 ...   P—Kt6
8 R—B1 ch.   K—Kt7
9 R—QR1

Black meets a few awkward threats because his pawns are on the edge of the board.

If 9. R×P PR6 or if 9. RK1 PR6 10.KK3 PR7 11. KB4 KB7 12. RKR1 PB4 with zugzwang.

9 ...   K—B7

Not 9... PR6? 10. KK3 PR7 11. KB4 KR6 12. RR8.

10 K—K4   P—Kt7

Not 10... PR6? 11. RR2 ch.

11 R—R2 ch.   K—Kt6
12 R—R1   K—R7
13 K—B4   P—Kt8=Q
14 R×Q   K×R
15 K—Kt4   K—Kt7
16 K×P   K—B6.

215 If White's king is satisfactorily placed, then isolated pawns lose even when far advanced, as in this ending won by Tartakower, Paris, 1933. Colours reversed.

1 R—Kt1	K—Kt5
2 K—Q2	K—B6
3 R—QR1	P—B5
4 R—QB1	P—R5
5 R—QR1	P—B6 ch.
6 K—Q3	

White cannot prevent the pawns' advance; but rather he welcomes it, for the sooner will Black run out of moves, and be forced to move his king away.

6 ...	P—B7
7 K—Q2	P—R6
8 R—KB1	P—R7
9 R—QB1?	

215

White plays and wins

9. KQ3 is correct, keeping Black's king away from the queen's side, and edging him away from the KBP, 9... KKt7 10. KK2 KKt6 11. RQB1 KKt7 12. RQR1 KKt6 13. RKB1, and Black is in zugzwang.

9 ...   K—Kt7?

Black should play 9... K—K5 10. K—K2 (if 10. K×P KK6, or 10. RKB1 KQ5 11. K×P KK6, supporting the KBP) 10... K—Q5 11. K—Q2 (11. K×P KB6 12. KK2 KKt7 supporting the QRP) 11... K—K5, with a draw by repetition.

10 K—K2   K—Kt6

11 R—KB1	K—B5
12 K×P	K—K5
13 K—K2	

Black resigns.

Four united pawns may well defeat a rook; but if they are far back, and if White's king is nearby, a draw is to be expected. If the four pawns are not connected White's chances improve, but Black generally has sufficient drawing resources. The principles are the same: White's king must be brought to the scene, and the more advanced pawns dealt with first; as to Black, he should value his connected pawns more than his isolated pawns, and his best plan is often that of forcing a pair of advanced united pawns.

4. ROOK AND PAWN v. ROOK

This ending is normally drawn when the pawn is blocked by Black's king. Against a KtP he should not allow his king to be driven away. Against a Centre P or BP Black may permit his king to be driven to the short side of the pawn, when the result should still be a draw.

When Black's king cannot block the pawn White's chances are more promising than is the case with minor pieces, because there is no question of the defender sacrificing his rook for the pawn.

By controlling all the squares on a file or a rank the rook may set up a barrier cutting off the defending king, and preventing its approach. For KtP, BP, or Centre P the following rules apply when the defending king is cut off on the file:

A pawn on the fifth or beyond wins if the enemy king is cut off by one file. Exceptions occur with BP or Centre P when the defending king is on the short side of the pawn.

A pawn on the fourth wins if the enemy king is cut off by two files. An exception is the KtP, for which three files are necessary.

A pawn on the third wins if the enemy king is cut off by three files.

A KtP on the second wins if the enemy king is cut off by five files, whilst four files are enough for a BP.

There are also good winning chances if the defending king is horizontally cut off, behind the pawn, and cannot get back to block it.

Unlike the similar case with minor pieces, the RP is very drawish. White cannot easily protect his king from checks, his RP providing no cover.

A RP on the fifth wins for certain only when the enemy king is cut off by four files, and a RP on the fourth if the enemy king is cut off by five files. Black generally draws when the pawn is farther back.

White in all cases tries to keep Black's king at a distance, Black to bring it nearer. Black uses his rook to attack the pawn, and to drive White's king away whenever it takes up an aggressive position and/or is about to help the advance of the pawn. The rook moves to the limit of the board, or as far as possible, so that its checking-distance is at a maximum, and thus the opposing king has less chance of escaping a series of checks.

There are two files on what is called the short side of the BP, and five on the long side; with a Centre P the difference is less marked. In either case it is important for the defender, who wants to have his king on the short side, and the long side left clear for his rook; for if his rook is on the short side the checking-distance is not long enough.

The KtP, BP, and Centre P are considered first; and the RP later.

216 When the king is blocking the pawn, Philidor laid down the drawing method against a pawn on any file: Black's rook stays on the third rank, preventing the advance of White's king. When, and if, the pawn moves to the sixth, Black's rook moves to the eighth, threatening a series of checks on the files.

1 ...	R—Kt3

Against a KtP, but not against a BP or Centre P, the rook on the first rank

draws. Here Black may safely play 1... RKt1.

2 R—KB7	

If 2. RR8 ch. KKt2.

2 ...	R—R3
3 P—Kt6	R—R8
4 K—R6	R—R8 ch.

216

Drawn

The checks may be avoided by 5. KKt5 RKt8 ch. 6. KB5 RB8 ch. 7. KQ4 RQ8 ch. 8. KB3, but then the pawn falls, 8... RQKt8 9. RB6 KKt2.

White has winning chances if his king can move to the sixth before his pawn, because he then has mating threats:

1 K—R6	R—Kt1

Against a KtP Black loses if his rook stays on the eighth rank, 1... R—QKt8? (or 1... KB1? 2. RR8 ch. KQ2 3. PKt6) 2. K—Kt6 (2. RR8 ch. KB2 leads nowhere) 2... K—B1 (or 2... RQB8 3. RR8 ch. RB1 4. R×R ch.) 3. R—R8 ch. K—Q2 4. R—QKt8, guarding the pawn, 4... R—Kt7 5. K—R7 K—B2 (5... RR7 ch. 6. KKt7) 6. P—Kt6 ch. K—B3 7. R—B8 ch. K—Q2 (7... KKt4 8. PKt7 RR7 ch. 9. KKt8 KKt3 10. RB1 RR7 11. RKt1 ch. KB3 12. RQR1) 8. P—Kt7 (while assisting the pawn's advance, White's king is safe from checks on the rank), 8... R—R7 ch. 9. K—Kt8 R—R8, and there remains the task of extricating the king, which is shown by Salvio in Example 219.

2 P—Kt6	R—KB1.

White has no way of breaking Black's wholly passive defence.

217 A position by Cheron, 1944. Against a BP (or Centre P) passive defence fails:

1 K—Kt6

It is this dangerous advance that Philidor's method is designed to prevent.

1 ...   K—Kt1

It is too late to move the rook to the eighth, 1... RKt8 2. RR8 ch. KQ2 3. PB6 ch. KQ3 4. RQ8 ch. KK2 5. PB7 RKt8 ch. 6. KR5.

2 P—B6	R—KB1
3 R—R7	R—K1
4 R—Kt7 ch.	K—B1
5 R—QR7	

White wins because, unlike the case with the KtP, his rook can operate on the other side of the pawn.

5 ...	K—Kt1
6 P—B7 ch.	K—B1
7 R—R8 ch.	

When Philidor's simple method is not practicable, Black draws against a BP (or Centre P) by having his rook on the eighth rank:

1 ...   R—Kt8

Not 1... KB2? 2. RR7 ch. KB1 3. KKt6, when 3... RKt3 ch. is answered by 4. PB6.

2 K—B6

For 2. K—Kt6 see Variation A.

2 ...   K—Kt1

When the kings are opposed Black avoids mate by moving his king to the short side of the pawn (obviously not possible with a KtP). Here the king is out of the way of his rook which, by pressure on the queening file combined with threats of checking on the rank, prevents the pawn's advance. If 2... KQ1? 3. RR8 ch. KK2 4. KB7 and 5. PB6.

| 3 R—R8 ch. | K—R2 |
| 4 R—Q8 | |

From here Black interposes his rook to parry the checks on the rank, for if 4. RQB8 RKt3 ch., or if 4. KB7 RKt2 ch.

4 ...   R—QB8

When a series of checks is not available Black's rook attacks the pawn from behind. Here this prevents 5. KB7.

5 K—Q6   K—Kt2

Whenever possible Black's king returns to block the pawn. His rook now assists in preventing 6. PB6 ch.

6 R—Q7 ch.	K—B1
7 R—B7 ch.	K—Kt1
8 R—KR7	R—B7
9 P—B6	R—Q7 ch.

White cannot avert checks on the file without deserting his pawn.

217

White plays and wins
Black plays and draws

Variation A (1... R—Kt8):

2 K—Kt6   R—QB8

The rook attacks the pawn from the rear.

3 K—B6

After 3. RR8 ch. KQ2 White cannot advance his pawn because it is under attack.

3 ...   K—Kt1

Playing to the long side loses, 3... K—Q1? 4. R—R8 ch. K—K2, for here Black's king prevents checks on the ranks, 5. R—QB8, and White's rook, freed from the necessity of parrying checks, guards the pawn, 5... R—B7 (5... RQKt8 6. KB7) 6. K—Kt7 K—Q2 7. P—B6 ch. K—Q3 8. R—Q8 ch. K—B4 9. P—B7 R—Kt7 ch. 10. K—B8 K—B3 11. R—Q1 R—KR7 12. R—B1 ch. K—Q3 13. K—Kt7 R—Kt7 ch. 14. K—R6.

4 R—R8 ch.	K—R2
5 R—QB8	

When the rook guards the pawn it cannot also parry the checks on the ranks; but if 5. RQ8 Black temporizes by 5... RB7; and if 5. KQ6 Black's king returns, 5... KKt2.

5 ...	R—KR8
6 K—Q7	R—R2 ch.
7 K—B6	R—R3 ch.
8 K—Kt5	K—Kt2
9 K—Kt8	K—B2
10 R—Kt7 ch.	K—B1.

Arriving at Philidor's position.

218 With a Centre pawn the short side, which is not quite so short, is on occasion long enough for checks on the rank, so that Black may sometimes play his king to the long side. Even so, it is always wiser and simpler for him not to do so. The following analysis is after Cheron, 1944.

1 K—Q6

The alternative is 1. K—B6 R—Q8, attacking the pawn, 2. K—Q6, after which Black may move his king either way, e.g. 2... K—K1 3. R—R8 ch. K—B2 4. R—Q8 (his pawn being under attack there is nothing better, if 4. KB6 KK2, or if 4. RB8 RQ7) 4... R—QR8 5. K—B7 (5. KB6 KK2) 5... R—R2 ch. 6. K—Kt6 K—K2 7. R—KR8 R—QR8 8. R—R6 K—Q2. The short side is here long enough for Black's rook.

1 ...	K—B1

Moving to the long side now loses, 1... KK1? 2. RR8 ch. KB2 3. KQ7 RQR8 4. PQ6 RR2 ch. 5. KB6 RR3 ch. 6. KB7 RR2 ch. 7. KKt6; the checking distance is too short, and if 7... RQ2 8 KB6 RR2 9. PQ7.

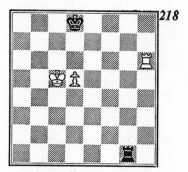

Drawn

2 R—R8 ch.	K—Kt2
3 K—K7	R—Kt2 ch.

White's rook occupies the remote (KR) file, so that the long side is in effect shortened—from the point of view of Black's rook. Because of this more care is necessary, and if 3... RKt4? 4. PQ6, the pawn on the sixth wins, as in Examples 221 and 264.

4 K—Q8

If 4. KK8 KB2 5. RR6 RKt1 ch. 6. KK7 RKt2 ch. 7. KK6 RQ2 8. RR5 RQ3 ch.

4 ...   R—Kt3

Preventing the pawn's advance.

5 R—R5

If 5. RR7 ch. KKt3 6. RQ7 KB4 7. KB7 RQR3 8. RQ8 RR2 ch. 9. KKt8 RR3.

5 ...	R—Q3 ch.
6 K—K7	K—B2
7 R—K5	R—Q2 ch.
8 K—K6	R—Q3 ch.
9 K—B7	R—Q2 ch.
10 R—K7	K—Q3.

219 The general case with a pawn on the fifth and Black's king cut off by one file is shown here with White to play. This example is the key to most rook and pawn endings.

1 P—Kt5	K—Q2
2 K—R5	

Not 2. KKt4? RB1 3. R×R (else Black's king crosses the QB file) 3... K×R 4. KR5 KKt2.

2 ...   R—R1 ch.

Against a pawn on the fifth the checking distance is too short, and the checks run out.

3 K—Kt6	R—Kt1 ch.
4 K—R6	R—R1 ch.
5 K—Kt7	R—R7
6 P—Kt6	R—QKt7
7 K—R7	R—R7 ch.
8 K—Kt8	R—QKt7
9 P—Kt7	R—QR7
10 R—B4	

In this position* White's king extricates itself by sheltering behind the rook. 10. R—B5 also wins.

219

White plays and wins
Black plays and draws

10 ...   R—R8

If 10... KQ3 11. KB8, or if 10... RR7 11. RQR4 RQKt7 12. KR7.

11 R—Q4 ch.   K—K3

If 11... KB3 12. KB8.

12 K—B7	R—B8 ch.
13 K—Kt6	R—Kt8 ch.
14 K—B6	R—Kt7

* For no good reason this is often called Lucena's position. It was first published on p. 69 of Salvio's book *Il Puttino, altramente detto, il cavaliero errante del Salvio . . .*, Naples, 1634, where the author attributes the analysis of the position to Scipione Genovino.

If 14... RB8 ch. 15. KKt5 RKt8 ch. 16. RKt4.

15 R—K4 ch.   K—B2

If 15... KB3   16. RK8 RB7 ch. 17. KQ5.

16. R—K5.

The threat of 17. RQKt5 is unanswerable.

Black to play must prevent PKt5:

1 ...   R—R1 ch.

If at once 1... K—Q2? hoping to oppose rooks, then 2. R—B4 (2. PKt5? RQB1) 2... R—R1 ch. (2... RQB1 3. R×R) 3. K—Kt5 R—Kt1 ch. 4. K—R6 R—R1 ch. 5. K—Kt7 followed by PKt5.

2 K—Kt3

White's king and pawn cannot advance unaided, 2. KKt5 RKt1 ch. 3. KR5 RR1 ch. 4. KKt6, because of 4... RKt1 ch. and White must retreat or lose his pawn. Against a pawn on the fourth the checking distance is sufficient, and in order to advance White must at some stage guard his pawn with the rook.

2 ...   K—Q2

The simplest way.

2... RQKt1 preventing the pawn's advance also draws.

2... R—R1 is sound, and if 3. P—Kt5 R—R5 when both kings are cut off from the pawn. The result then depends on how far Black's king is from the queening square. Here it is near enough, and a draw follows 4. R—B3 (4. RB8 KQ2 5. RB1 RKt5 6. KB3 RKR5 7. PKt6 RR3, or 4. PKt6 KQ2 5. PKt7 RR1) 4... K—Q2 5. K—R3 R—KB5 6. P—Kt6 R—B3 7. R—QKt3 K—B1, when Black blocks the pawn.

3 R—B4	R—QB1
4 R×R	K×R
5 K—R4	K—Kt1

If White advances Black takes the opposition.

The position of this diagram moved one or two files to the left gives the same results. The winning idea shown by

Salvio applies equally to a BP or Centre P when Black's king is on the long side of the pawn, but not otherwise.

220 Black's king is favourably placed, on the short side. On the long side his rook has a sufficient checking distance on the ranks. The play relates to Example 218.

1 P—K5   K—Kt2

The king on the short side is best placed on the second rank.

220

Drawn

2 K—Q5	R—QR1
3 P—K6	R—R4 ch.
4 K—B6	R—R3 ch.
5 K—Q7	R—R2 ch.
6 K—Q8	R—R1 ch.
7 K—B7	R—R2 ch.
8 K—Kt8	R—K2.

The position of this example moved one file to the right is also drawn.

221 Javelle v. Griesmann, Charleville, 1952. Colours reversed. When Black's king is on the short side of the pawn on the fifth White has winning chances only if his king is well forward, on the fifth or sixth rank, and if the defending rook is badly placed, as here.

1 R—R1

This prevents Black moving his rook away, if 1... RQR5 2. RKt1 ch. KR2 3. KB6. White wins if his king has access to the KB file, for his pawn then covers

221

White plays and wins

the checks on the rank, 3... RR3 ch. 4. PK6.

Griesmann played 1. RQ7? when Black draws by 1... R—K5, attacking the pawn from behind (1... RQR5 also draws) 2. R—Q1 K—Kt2 3. K—Q6 K—B2, Example 218.

1 ...	R—Kt6
2 R—R1	R—Kt7
3 R—R8	K—Kt2
4 K—K7	R—Kt7

Black's rook is freed a move too late. If it were his turn to play he could draw by checking on the ranks; but after White's next move the checking distance is too short, White's rook having occupied the remote (QR) file.

5 P—K6	R—Kt2 ch.
6 K—Q6	R—Kt3 ch.
7 K—Q7	R—Kt2 ch.
8 K—B6	R—K2
9 K—Q6	R—Kt2
10 P—K7.	

222 When Black's king is on the short side of a BP, the long side is always long enough for the defending rook, and White's winning chances are therefore more slender than is the case with a centre pawn. Such endings are usually drawn, but here, with every factor in his favour, White just wins. An understanding of this position is the key to the notorious R+BP+RP v. R ending, Examples 248-250.

1 R—K6 ch.

1 PB6? RQR8 2. KB8 KKt3 3. PB7 KB3 draws.

1 ...	K—R2
2 P—B6	R—QR8
3 K—B8	

The essential winning manœuvre, holding off Black's king. Neither 3. KK8? RR1ch. 4. KK7 KKt3, nor 3. RK8? RR2 ch. 4. KB8 KKt3 suffices.

3 ...   K—Kt3

If 3... R—R1 ch. 4. R—K8 R—R8 (4... RR2 5. RK7 ch.) 5. P—B7 R—R2 6. R—Q8.

222

White plays and wins
Black plays and draws

4 P—B7 ch.	K—R2
5 R—KB6	R—K8
6 R—B2	R—K6
7 R—R2 ch.	K—Kt3
8 K—Kt8.	

Black to play simply prevents White's manœuvre, 3. KB8:

1 ...	R—QR8
2 R—K6 ch.	K—R2
3 P—B6	R—R1

Not 3... RR2 ch.? 4. KB8 KKt3 5. PB7 ch. This discovered check is the point of White's having his rook on the sixth.

4 R—K8

If 4. RK1 RR2 ch. 5. KB8 KKt3, or if 4. KK7 KKt3 5. PB7 ch. KKt2 6. RKB6 RR2 ch. 7. KK8 RR1 ch.

4 ...   R—R2 ch.

Checks are permissible when White's rook is no longer on the sixth rank.

5 R—K7

If 5. KB8 KKt3.

5 ...	R—R1
6 R—Q7	R—QKt1
7 R—Q1	R—Kt2 ch.
8 K—K8	K—Kt3
9 P—B7	R—Kt1 ch.
10 K—K7	R—Kt2 ch.
11 K—K6	R—Kt3 ch.

With a BP on the fourth or farther back, Black should always draw if his king is on the short side of it.

223 Black draws by keeping his king on either K4 or K3.

1 R—Q2

A tempo-move. White's king and pawn cannot advance against the enemy rook, 1. KB4 RB1 ch. 2. KKt5 RKt1 ch. 3. KB5(R5) RB1(R1) ch. 4. KKt6 RKt1 ch.—Black checks the White king whenever it threatens to support the advance PKt5.

1 ...   K—K3

With 1... KK5? Black ventures too far forward, and is cut off on the rank 2. R—Q6 (2. RQ7 also wins) 2... K—K4 3. R—QR6 K—Q4 4. K—R4 R—KR1 (4... KB5 5. RB6 ch. KQ4 6. PKt5) 5. P—Kt5 R—R8 6. R—QB6, Example 219.

223

Drawn

4 ROOK AND PAWN v. ROOK

2 R—Q4

An ideal square for the rook from which it holds off Black's king, and also guards the pawn.

2 ...   K—K4

It is essential to dislodge the rook. If 2... KK2? White's king may advance because the pawn is now defended by the rook, 3. KB4 RB1 ch. 4. KKt5 RKt1 ch. 5. KR6 KK3 6. PKt5.

3 R—Q1   K—K3
4 R—Q2   K—K4.

Here too 4... K—K2? loses, 3. R—Q4 K—K3 (3... RQ1 4. R×R) 4. K—B4 R—B1 ch. (4... KK4 5. RQ5 ch. KK3 6. PKt5) 5. K—Kt5 K—K4 (5... RKt1 ch. 6. KR6) 6. R—QB4 R—Kt1 ch. 7. K—R6 K—Q4 8. R—R4 K—B3 9. P—Kt5 ch. K—B4 10. R—R5 ch. K—Q3 11. P—Kt6, when Black's rook is misplaced.

4... RKt2?, shortening the checking distance, also loses, 5. KB4 RB2 ch. 6. KKt5 RKt2 ch. 7. KB5 RB2 ch. 8. KKt6 RB1 9. PKt5.

224 White wins because he can move up his king on the two open files (QR, QKt) where it does not obstruct his pawn.

1 K—Kt4   R—Kt1 ch.
2 K—R5   R—QB1
3 K—Kt5   R—Kt1 ch.
4 K—R6   R—QB1
5 R—QB1

White wins

This is the other way (contrasted with R—K4) in which White's rook may guard his pawn, and thus free his king. Black's king returns, but finishes up on the long side of the pawn.

5 ...   K—K3
6 K—Kt7   R—B4
7 K—Kt6   R—B1
8 P—B5   R—Kt1 ch.

If 8... KQ2 9. RQ1 ch., Example 219.

9 K—B7   R—Kt7
10 P—B6.

The position of this diagram moved one file to the right is also won for White.

225 Black's king is on the short side. White wins in quite a different way, by means of mating threats when Black's king is on R3 or R5.

1 ...   K—R5

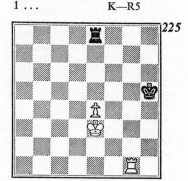

White wins

Black is in zugzwang.

If 1... RK2, shortening the checking distance, 2. KQ4 RQ2 ch. 3. KB5 RK2 4. KQ5 RQ2 ch. 5. KK6 and 6. PK5.

If 1... KR3 2. KB4 RB1 ch. 3. KK5 RK1 ch. 4. KB6, the mating threat indirectly guards the KP, 4... RB1 ch. 5. KK7, and 6. PK5.

Even if Black could get his king to R2, he would lose in a similar way; whilst if he could get his king to R7, White would win by RKKt5 followed by KKB4.

2 P—K5

153

White cannot win as in the preceding example by 2. KQ4 RQ1 ch. 3. KB5 RK1 4. KQ5 RQ1 ch. 5. KB6 RK1 6. RK1? because the checks on the rank draw after 6... KKt4 7. KQ7 RK4 8. KQ6 RR4 9. PK5, Example 220. For the same reason there is little point in 1. RKt6, attempting to cut Black off on the rank.

2 ...   R×P ch.

If 2... KR4 3. KK4, and, if necessary, White's king escapes from checks on the rank by playing to the KB file.

3 K—B4.

White wins a rook.

226 A position analysed by Grigoriev, 1937.

1 R—K2

A tempo-move which puts Black in zugzwang, for his king stands on its best square.

White's king and pawn cannot yet advance against Black's rook: 1. K—B3 R—B1 ch. 2. K—Q4 R—QKt1 3. K—B4 R—B1 ch. 4. K—Q5 R—QKt1, and if White is to make progress his rook must guard the pawn from either the rank or the file:

5. R—K3 K—B4 6. K—Q6? (better to retreat) 6... K—B5 7. R—R3 K—B4 8. K—B7 R—Kt5 9. K—B6 (threatening KB5 and PKt4) 9... R—Kt1 10. K—B5 R—B1 ch. 11. KKt4 RKt1 ch. 12. KB3 KK3; or

5 R—QKt1? K—K2 6. K—B6 R—Kt5 7. R—K1 ch. K—Q1 8. R—K3 R—KR5 9. R—K5 R—R3 ch. 10. K—Kt7 R—R2 ch. 11. K—Kt8 K—Q2 12. R—QB5 R—R5 13. R—QKt5 K—B3 14. R—Kt7 K—B4.

In either case Black's king returns, moving via K2 or KB4 according to White's play.

1 ...   K—B2

After this White's rook protects his pawn from the rank; but if instead 1... K—B4, then after 2. K—B3 R—B1 ch. 3. K—Q4 R—QKt1 4. K—B4 R—B1

ch., 5. K—Q5 R—QKt1, White finesses to force Black farther away, 6. R—B2 ch. K—Kt3, and guards his pawn from the file, 7. R—QKt2, when Black's king cannot get back in time, 7... K—B2 8. P—Kt4 K—K2 9. K—B6 K—Q1 10. R—Q2 ch. K—K2 (10... KB1 11. RKR2) 11. P—Kt5.

Neither can Black temporize, for if 1... RKt2, shortening the checking distance, 2. K—B3 R—B2 ch. 3. K—Q4

226

White wins

R—QKt2 4. K—B4 R—B2 ch. 5. K—Q5 R—QKt2 6. R—K3 K—B4 7. K—B5 K—B5 8. R—R3 K—Kt5 9. R—Q3, Black must lose time with his rook, 9... R—Kt1 (for if 9... KB5 10. PKt4 KK5 11. RQ8) 10. P—Kt4 R—B1 ch. 11. K—Kt5 R—Kt1 ch. 12. K—B4 R—B1 ch. 13. K—Kt3 R—QKt1 (or 13... RK1 14. PKt5 RK5, cutting off White's king but his own is too far away, 15. KR3 KB4 16. PKt6) 14. R—Q6, cutting Black off on the rank and winning after 14... KB5 15. RQR6 KK4 16. KR4 KQ4 17. PKt5 KB4 18. RB6 ch.

Finally, if 1... R—Q1 2. R—K3 (not 2. PKt4? RQ6 when White too is cut off from the pawn, and he can only draw) 2... K—B4, so as to dislodge White's rook, 3. P—Kt4 K—B5 4. R—K1 R—Q6, cutting off White's king, but Black now loses because his own king is too far forward, 5. KB2 RQR6 6. PKt5 RR4 7. PKt6 RB4 ch. 8. KQ3 RQKt4 9. RK6 KB4 10. KB4 and White's king rejoins his pawn, whilst Black's is cut off on the rank.

2 R—K3	K—B3
3 K—B3	R—B1 ch.
4 K—Q4	R—QKt1
5 K—B5	

Threatening 6. P—Kt4.

5 ...	R—B1 ch.
6 K—Q6	R—QKt1
7 R—B3 ch.	

This finesse forces Black's king farther away.

| 7 ... | K—Kt4 |
| 8 K—B5 | K—Kt5 |

After 8... RB1 ch. 9. KQ4 RQ1 ch. 10. KB3 RB1 ch. 11. KKt2 RQKt1, White's journey has not been in vain, for Black's king is cut off by four files, and after 12. RB2 KKt5 13. KB3 RB1 ch. 14. KQ4 RQKt1 15. KB4 RB1 ch. 16. KQ5 RQKt1 White guards the pawn from the rear 17. R—Kt2, when Black's king cannot get back in time.

| 9 R—Q3 | K—B4 |

If 9... RB1 ch. 10. KKt6 RKt1 ch. 11. KB7 RKt5 12. KB6 RKt1 13. RQ4 ch. KB4 14. PKt4 KK4 15. RR4.

| 10 P—Kt4 | R—B1 ch. |

If 10... KK5 11. RQ6 cutting Black off on the rank.

11 K—Q5	R—Q1 ch.
12 K—B4	R—B1 ch.
13 K—Kt3	R—QKt1

If 13... RKR1 14. PKt5, when Black may cut off White's king 14... RR5, but his own king is too far away, 15. KR3 KK3 16. PKt6 RR2 17. RKt3 RQKt2 18. KR4.

14 R—Q6.

Black is cut off on the rank as in the notes to Example 223.

With a BP or Centre P on the third rank the win is easier, White's king moving forward on the files on the short side, and in due course playing his rook behind the pawn.

227 A position given by Fine, 1941.

1 K—B2

Similar play follows 1. RKt1, for if 1... RQ1 2. PKt3 RQ7 White's king is cut off but Black's is too far off, 3. KR1 RKB7 4. PKt4 RB5 5. RKt1 KKt4 6. KR2 KB3 7. KKt3 KK2 8. RQ1 RB1 9. RQ4, Example 223.

White's simplest win is to cut Black off on the rank, 1. RB5 KKt5 2. RB5 KB5 3. KB2 KK5 4. KB3, followed by 5. PKt4.

1 ...	R—B1 ch.
2 K—Q3	R—QKt1
3 K—B3	R—B1 ch.
4 K—Q4	R—Q1 ch.

White wins

If 4... RQKt1 5. RQKt1 KKt4 6. PKt4 KB3 7. KB5 as in the preceding example.

| 5 K—B5 | R—B1 ch, |
| 6 K—Q6 | R—QKt1 |

If 6... RQ1 ch. 7. KB7 RQ6 8. PKt4 RQKt6 9. RB4 ch.

| 7 R—QKt1 | R—Kt6 |

This is the idea behind Black's plan of enticing White's king forward.

8 K—B5	K—Kt4
9 K—B4	R—Kt1
10 P—Kt4.	

Winning as in the examples given. Black to play:

| 1 ... | K—Kt4 |

If 1... KKt6 2. RB5. If 1... KKt5 2. RB6, and now 2... RKR1 3. RQR6, or 2... KKt4 3. RB2.

2 R—B2	K—Kt5
3 K—B1	

Kopaiev's subtle discovery, putting Black in zugzwang. 3. KB2? RB1 ch. draws; White could advance his king to QR7 but Black's king could subsequently attack the white rook, breaking the barrier on the KB file. Whilst if 4. KKt1 RKR1 5. PKt3 KKt6 6. RB6 RR7 7. PKt4 RR5 8. PKt5 RKt5 ch. By playing the text-move White avoids this check.

3 ...	R—KR1

If 3... RB1 ch. 4. RB2 RKR1 5. RB5 RR7 White moves his king to QR3 and then plays PKt4. If 3... KKt4 (moving farther from White's rook) White wins by 4. KB2, advancing to QR7.

4 P—Kt3	K—Kt6
5 R—B6	R—R7
6 P—Kt4	K—Kt5

If now 6... RR5 the pawn advances.

7 P—Kt5	K—Kt4
8 R—B8	R—R2
9 R—QKt8	K—B3
10 P—Kt6	K—K3
11 P—Kt7	R—K2

White wins by advancing his king.

228 With a BP White's king moves up on the files on the short side, as shown by Cheron, 1923.

1 K—Kt2	R—Kt1 ch.
2 K—R3	R—QB1
3 K—Kt3	R—Kt1 ch.
4 K—R4	R—QB1

If 4... R—R1 ch. 5. K—Kt5 R—Kt1 ch. 6. K—R6 R—R1 ch. (6... RQB1 7. RQB1 RB6 8. KKt5 KKt3 9. KKt4 RB1 10. PB4) 7. K—Kt7 R—R6 (7... RR5 8. RQB1), and now the ingenious 8. RKt8 wins, 8... R—QB6 9. R—QB8 R—B6 10. P—B4.

5 R—QB1	K—Kt3
6 P—B4	K—B3

White wins

7 K—Kt5	R—Kt1 ch.
8 K—B6	

To hold off Black's king.

8 ...	K—K2
9 R—K1 ch.	K—Q1
10 R—Q1 ch.	K—K2

If 10... KB1 11. RKR1.

11. P—B5.

229 When Black's king is in White's half of the board he is in danger of being cut off (from the queening square) on the rank, which is quite as lethal as being cut off on the file. This and the following position are by Cheron, 1944.

1 R—QR4	R—KR1

If 1... RQB1 2. KR2 RB5 3. R×R.

2 K—R2	R—R7

White plays and wins
Black plays and draws

If 2... R—R8 (2... KB7 3. RB4 ch. KQ6 4. PKt3) 3. P—Kt3 K—B6 4. R—B4 ch. K—Q6 5. R—B8 K—Q5 6. K—R3 R—R8 ch. 7. K—Kt4 R—R2 8. R—Q8 ch. K—K4, and White's rook is misplaced, 9. KB5 RB2 ch. 10. KKt6.

3 R—KKt4	R—KB7
4 K—R3	R—B8
5 P—Kt4	K—B6
6 K—R4	

A step by step process with king and pawn.

6 ...	R—R8 ch.
7 K—Kt5	R—R1
8 R—Kt3 ch.	K—Q5

8... KKt7, attacking from the rear, fails because the checking distance on the files is too short, 9. KB6 RB1 ch. 10. KKt7. Compare Example 231.

9 K—B6	R—B1 ch.
10 K—Kt7	R—B8
11 P—Kt5.	

Black to play draws by 1... RQR1 hemming in White's king. If then 2. PKt3 KB6.

The position of this diagram moved one file to the right gives the same results.

230 Cutting Black off on the rank may be less effective with a centre pawn, his rook having checks on the ranks.

1 R—B4

If 1 RR4 RQB1 restricting White's king.

Drawn

1 ...	R—QR1
2 K—B2	R—R7 ch.
3 K—B3	R—R6 ch.
4 K—Kt2	

If 4. KQ4 KK7, or 4. KKt4 RQ6 5. RB3 KK5.

4 ...   R—QR1.

All the rook has to do is to force White's king from the QB file to the QKt file. Now if 5. PQ4 KK5, or 5. PQ3 KK6, or if 5. KB2 or 5. KB3 Black checks on the rank; finally, if 5. KKt3 KK7 6. PQ4 KQ6.

231 A position after Fine, 1941. Black's king is in danger of being cut off on the rank. He draws by an attack on two fronts, the king from the rear and the rook from in front. Usually this works only if the pawn is not beyond the third rank, when the checking distance is of sufficient length.

1 R—R2 ch.   K—Kt8

Drawn

Not 1... KQ6? 2. RR4 RKt1 ch. (2... KB7 3. KR3) 3. K—R3 K—B6 4. R—B4 ch. K—Q6 5. K—Kt2, when Black is effectively cut off on the rank, and if 5... RKR1 6. RKKt4 RR7 ch. 7. KR3 KB6 8. PKt4 RR1 9. RKt5.

2 R—R5

Unless this rook is moved up White cannot parry the threatened checks on the file, being unable to play to QKt2 as in the last note, e.g. 2. KB5 RB1 ch.

3. KQ5 RQ1 ch.   4. KB6 RQKt1   5. RR3 KKt7.

2 ...   K—Kt7.

Not 2... RKt1 ch.? 3. KR4 RR1 ch. 5. RR5 followed by PKt4. But after the text move, attacking the pawn from the rear, White can make no progress.

232 Black usually draws against a RP if he can get his king to the nearer bishop's file, here QB1, QB2, or even QB3.

With an advanced pawn on any other file White finds it preferable to have his king in front of rather than behind the pawn; but with the RP White has some difficulty extricating his king, as here shown by Karstedt, 1909.

1 R—QB2

White opposes rooks on the QKt file as soon as he can.

White plays and wins
Black plays and draws

1 ...   K—K2
2 R—B8.

Now if 2... KQ2 White escapes via QB5, 3. RQKt8 RKR8 4. KKt7 RKt8 ch. 5. KR6 RR8 ch. 6. KKt6 RKt8 ch. 7. KB5.

Whilst if 2... KQ3 White escapes via QB8, 3. RQKt8 RKR8 4. KKt7 RKt8 ch. 5. KB8 RB8 ch. 6. KQ8 RKR8 7. RKt6 ch. KB4 8. RB6 ch. KKt4 9. RB8.

Black to play keeps White imprisoned.

When Black's rook is driven off the QKt file, his king takes over the guard duties:

1 ...   K—K2
2 R—KR2   K—Q2
3 R—R7 ch.   K—B3
4 R—R8   K—B2

Not 4... RKt7? 5. RB8 ch., forcing the king off the QB file, and 6. RQKt8.

5 R—QKt8   R—KR8
6 R—Kt7 ch.   K—B3.

6... KB1 7. RKt4 RQB8 also draws.

233 Where Black's king is nearer (to the QRP) than the KB file White wins only if the arrangement of the pieces is in some way favourable to him. In this study by Cheron, 1944, White's rook is ideally placed on the QKt file, and on the

White wins

fourth rank. In fact Black to play would in most cases draw if White's rook were anywhere else. Black's rook, on the other hand, would be better placed where it could sustain a series of checks; if it were at KR1, the game would be drawn after 1... KB2 2. RKt7 ch. KB1.

In the following variations White's king avoids blocking his pawn:

1... R—QR1 2. R—KR4 R—KKt1 (2... KB3 3. RR7 transposes) 3. P—R7 K—B2 4. R—R7 ch. K—B3 5. K—R6 R—KB1 6. R—R1 R—KKt1 7. RB1 ch.

1... R—KR1 2. P—R7 K—B2 3. R—Kt6 R—R4 ch. (3... RKR8 4. RQR6 or 3... RKKt1 4. KR6 RKR1

5. RKt7 ch. and 6. RKt8) 4. K—R6
R—R7 5. R—B6 ch. K—Q2 6. K—Kt7
R—R7 7. R—QKt6.

1... R—B4 ch. 2. K—Kt6 R—B3 ch.
3. K—Kt5 K—B2 (3... RB2 4. RKR4)
4. P—R7 R—Kt3 ch. 5. K—R5 R×R
6. P—R8=Q.

1... R—B8 (or 1... KB2) 2. P—R7.

234 White's rook cuts off Black's
king by three files. When the pawn is on
the fifth or beyond, Black's rook is best
placed on the eighth rank.

White to play wins only because his
rook is on Q4, its best square: were it on
Q3 or Q2 the game would be drawn.

1 P—R6	R—Kt8 ch.
2 K—B5	

2. KR7? draws. White should not
voluntarily block his pawn.

2 ...	R—QR8
3 K—Kt5	R—R7
4 R—QR4	R—Kt7 ch.
5 K—R5	R—Kt1
6 P—R7	R—QR1
7 K—Kt6.	

Black to play draws against the pawn
on the fifth although his king is three
files away.

1 ...	R—Kt8 ch.
2 K—B5	

Blocking the pawn also draws, 2. KR7
RKt7 3. PR6 RKt8 4. KR8 RKt7
5. PR7 RKt8, Example 232.

White plays and wins
Black plays and draws

2 ...	R—QR8
3 K—Kt5	R—Kt8 ch.
4 R—Kt4	R×R ch.
5 K×R	K—Q2.

With a RP an exchange of rooks is
frequently possible because the pawn
ending offers so many drawing chances.

235 A position after Cheron, 1926.

1 K—Kt4	R—Kt1 ch.
2 K—B5	R—QR1
3 K—Kt5	R—Kt1 ch.
4 K—B6	R—QR1
5 R—QR1	K—K2
6 P—R5.	

And White wins. Once the pawn is on
the fifth Black's rook is misplaced in
front of it.

White plays and wins
Black plays and draws

Unlike the cases with the pawn on
other files, Black draws by offering an
exchange of rooks, for which purpose
the second rank is the best place for his
king.

1 ...	K—B2

When Black's king is properly placed
he draws against a RP on the fourth,
although cut off by four files.

2 K—Kt4	R—K1
3 R—Q1	

If 3. R×R K×R 4. KKt5 KQ2
5. KKt6 KB1.

3 ...	K—K2
4 P—R5	R—Q1

5	R—QB1	K—Q2
6	P—R6	R—QB1
7	P—R7	R—QR1
8	R—QR1	K—B2
9	K—Kt5	K—Kt2.

If Black's king were cut off by five files then the RP on the fourth wins. An exchange of rooks is not then practicable for it would leave Black's king outside the square of the pawn.

236 A study by Grigoriev. Black's king attacks from the rear, and the rook checks on the ranks: a counter-attack especially effective against the RP, because this pawn provides no shelter for the king.

1 ...	R—KR7
2 P—R6	

If 2. R—Kt1 ch. K—R5, maintaining the attack on the pawn, 3. P—R6 R—R3 ch. 4. K—Kt7 (4. KB5 RR4 ch. 5. KQ4 RR5 ch. 6. KK5 RR4 ch. 7. KK4 RR5 ch. 8. KB5 RR1) 4... R—R2 ch. 5. K—R8, the king is driven in front of the pawn, 5... K—R4.

2 ...	R—R3 ch.

The play should be contrasted with Example 231. Here the checking-distance on the ranks is at its maximum regardless of the rank the RP is on. Black's king behind the pawn in no way obstructs his rook.

3 K—B7	R—R2 ch.
4 K—Q6	R—R3 ch.
5 K—K5	

236

Black plays and draws

If 5. KK7 RR2 ch. 6. KB6 RR2. White must move to the king's side to escape the checks.

5 ...	R—R4 ch.
6 K—B6	R—R1

Not 6... RR3 ch.? 7. KKt7, when the pawn cannot be stopped.

7 P—R7	R—R1
8 K—K6	K—B4

The only move, holding off White's king. Seyboth, 1899, shows that after 8... K—Kt4? the mating threats are fatal, 9. K—Q6 K—Kt3 10. R—Kt1 ch. K—R3 (10... K×P 11. KB7) 11.K—B7 R×P ch. 12. K—B6.

9 K—Q7	K—Kt3
10 R—Kt1 ch.	K—B4

Not 10... KR3? 11. KB7.

11 R—Kt7	R—R1
12 K—K6	

If 12. RKt8 RR7 ch.

12 ...	R—R1
13 K—Q7	R—R1.

An amusing draw by repetition.

237 White's rook is poorly placed in front of the pawn, a not uncommon situation with the RP. With a KtP as in Example 241, or any other pawn, Black's king is usually able to cross the board so that the position is resolved one way or the cther.

Black must do something about White's threat of moving his rook.

1 ...	R—QR6

Not 1... RK2? 2. RKt8 ch. K×R 3. PR8=Q ch.

After 1... R—K4 ch.? the checking distance is too short, 2. K—Kt6 R—K3 ch. 3. K—B7 R—QR3 (3... RK2 ch. 4. KQ6 RKB2 5. RKt8 ch.) 4. K—Kt7, guarding the pawn, 4... R—R8 5. R—Q8 R—Kt8 ch. 6. K—B6 R—B8 ch. 7. K—Kt5 R—Kt8 ch. 8. K—B4.

1... RB6 ch.? is also a careless check, for after 2. KKt4 Black's rook cannot play to the QR file, and if 2... RB2 3. RKt8 ch.

The text-move follows the simple rule:

237

Black plays and draws

when not checking the rook must be on the QR file attacking the pawn from the rear.

2 K—Kt6   R—Kt6 ch.

Another rule: when White's king guards the pawn, threatening to free his rook, Black must give check. Usually he checks on the file.

3 K—B5   R—QR6

Not 3... RB6 ch.? 4. KKt4.

4 K—Kt4   R—R8
5 K—Kt3   R—R3.

Black's rook must stay on the QR file. Black's king is tied to the squares KKt2 and KR2. If 5... KKt3? 6. RKt8 ch. KR2 7. PR8=Q, or if 5... KB2? 6. RR8 R×P 7. RR7 ch. winning Black's rook. It is because of this skewer check that Black's king cannot cross the intervening KB, K, and Q files to approach the pawn.

Black draws this kind of position by checks on the ranks only when his rook is moving up and down the KB file; or, with his king at KR2, the KKt file. If White's king moves towards the rook to put a stop to the checks, then Black's rook plays to the QR file behind the pawn. Checks on the ranks are useless if Black's rook is on either the K or Q files because the checking distance is too short, as noted above; whilst if Black's rook is on the KR file then checks on the rank cease when White plays his king to the seventh.

Finally we note that an extra white pawn on the KR or the KKt file would not alter the result in any way; but an extra white pawn on the KB file could eventually play to KB6, decoying Black's king from the safe square, KKt2.

The diagram position moved one file to the right is also drawn.

238 The RP on the seventh is defended from the rank, which is better for White than having the rook in front of the pawn. White wins if his king can penetrate the queen's side, via QKt6, QB6, or Q6. Black draws if his king gets to QB3, preventing White's design.

1 K—K4   K—K3

1... R—R4, temporarily cutting off White's king also fails by a tempo, 2. K—Q4 K—K3 3. K—B4 K—Q3 4. K—Kt4 R—R8 5. K—Kt5, when White's king gets to the eighth and wins, 5... R—Kt8 ch. 6. K—R6 R—R8 ch. 7. K—Kt7 R—Kt8 ch. 8. K—B8 (not 8. KR8? blocking the pawn, 8... KB3) 8... R—B8 ch. 9. K—Kt8 R—Kt8 ch. 10. R—Kt7.

2 R—R6 ch.

The skewer-threats are fatal, as is often the case when Black's king ventures to the K-file.

238

White plays and wins
Black plays and draws
The same with White king on KB3, K3, K2, or Q2

2 ...   K—Q2(B2)
3 R—R8   R × P
4 R—R7 ch.

Black to play draws by 1... KK3 2. KK4 KQ3 3. KQ4 KB3.

White king on K3: White wins by 1. KQ4 KK3 2. KB5. Black draws by 1... RR5 cutting off White's king on the rank, 2. KQ3 KK3 3. KB3 KQ3 4. KKt3 RR8 5. KKt4 KB3.

White king on K2: White wins by 1. K—Q3 R—R5 (1... KK3 2. KB4) 2. K—B3 K—K3 3. K—Kt3 R—R8 4. K—Kt4 K—Q3 5. K—Kt5. Black draws by 1... KK3. Black may instead interpose the moves 1... KKt3 2. RQKt7 reaching a position which brings about the same result for although 2... KB3 appears to lose time, after 3. KQ3 KK3 4. KB4 KQ3 White must give back the tempo by 5. RKR7 in order to make way for his king, or draw by 5. KKt5 RKt8 ch.

When White's king is to the right of these positions, the game is drawn.

When White's king is to the left of the squares listed on the diagram he wins with or without the move, e.g. White king at QB2, 1... K—K3 (1... KK4 2. KKt2 RR3 3. KKt3 KQ4 4. KKt4 KB3 5. RR6 ch.) 2. K—Kt2 (2. KKt3? draws) 2... R—R4 (if 2... RR3, 3. RR6 ch. skewers the rook) 3. K—Kt3 K—Q3 4. K—Kt4, gaining a tempo, 4... R—R8 5. K—Kt5, winning as before.

239 The pawn is better stopped on the sixth rank when the rook is in front of it, because this leaves a hole for the king at R7.

1 ...   R—K3

The rule in this case: when not giving check the rook attacks the pawn from the rank.

If the rook attacks from the file 1... R—QR6? (1... RB6 ch.? is bad for the same reason) then White's king runs to cover at R7, 2. K—Kt6 R—Kt6 ch. 3. K—R7, winning after 3... K—B2

4. R—QKt8 R—R6 5. K—Kt7 R—Kt6 ch. 6. K—R8 R—QR6 7. P—R7.

White's main threat is transposing to Example 238, which can happen when his pawn is not under attack, 1... KR2? 2. RR7 ch. KKt3 3. RQKt7 followed by PR7.

Careless checks must be avoided. If 1... R—K4 ch.? 2. K—Q6, and Black can neither give check nor attack the pawn from the rank. He therefore loses, although the win in this particular case is somewhat recondite: 2... R—KB4 (2... RQR4 3. KB6, or 2... RKR4 3. KB7) 3. R—K8 R—QR4 (3... RB3 ch. 4. RK6 RB2 5. KB6) 4. R—K7 ch. K—B1 5. R—QR7 (and not 5. PR7?

239

Black plays and draws

RR3 ch., the point of Black's defence) 5... R—KB4 (Black prepares for checks on the ranks as White is threatening RR8 ch. and KB6) 6. K—K6 (at this point Black cannot reply with RB3 ch.) 6... R—QR4 (6... RKR4 7. RB7 ch. KKt1 8. PR7) 7. R—R8 ch. K—Kt2 8. K—Q7, and if 8... R—KB4, relinquishing the attack on the pawn, then 9. R—K8 R—QR4 10. R—K6.

2 K—Kt5

If 2. RR7 ch. KKt3.

2 ...   R—K4 ch.

Black must check on the rank when White's king guards the pawn; otherwise White's rook is freed.

3 K—Kt6

When, and if, White plays PR7 Black must either play his rook behind the pawn, 3. KKt4 RK3 (the check on the rank is also sound) 4. PR7 RQR3 5. KKt5 RR8, Example 237; or give checks on the rank from the KB file, 3. KKt4 RKB4 4. PR7 RB5 ch. 5. KKt5 RB4 ch. 6. KKt6 RB3 ch. 7. KB7 RB2 ch. 8. KQ6 RB3 ch. and if 9. KK5 RQR3, Example 237.

| 3 ... | R—K3 ch. |
| 4 K—B7 | R—B3 |

The best file for the rook. On the KKt or KR files its king obstructs it, whilst on the K or Q files the checking distance is too short, e.g. 4... RK2 ch.? 5. KQ6 RKB2 6. RK8.

| 5 K—Kt7 | R—B2 ch. |
| 6 K—B6 | |

The hole at QR7 does not shield White from checks on the ranks.

| 6 ... | R—B3 ch. |
| 7 K—Q5 | R—B4 ch. |

Either 7... RQKt3 or 7... KR2 is also playable.

| 8 K—Q4 | R—B3 |

Not 8... RB5 ch.? 9. KK5 RB3, because of the trap 10. RKt8 ch.

| 9 P—R7 | R—QR3. |

Example 237.

240 This position by Romanovsky, 1950, relates closely to the preceding examples.

Black wants to get his rook on the ranks for a draw as in Examples 237 and 239; whilst White hopes to transpose to Example 238.

| 1 K—Q3 | R—R5 |

Temporarily cutting off White's king, which is trying to get to QR7.

If Black's rook leaves the QR file, 1... R—KB8, the RP is not under attack, so White transposes to Example 238, 2. R—R7 ch. K—B3 (or 2... KKt3 3. RQKt7) 3. R—R7 R—QR8 4. P—R7.

Black's king cannot cross to the queen's side, 1... KB2 2. KB4 KK2,

because of the skewer threats, 3. PR7 KQ2(B2) 4. RR8 R×P 5. RR7 ch.

| 2 K—B3 | R—KR5 |

This prevents White's playing R—KR7 on his fourth move.

| 3 R—R7 ch. | |

White usually regroups as soon as Black's rook leaves the QR file.

| 3 ... | K—B3 |
| 4 K—Kt3 | |

If at once 4. RQKt7? (the natural 4. RKR7 is not possible) 4... RR5 5. PR7 KK3 6. KKt3 RR8 7. KKt4 KQ3 8. RKR7 (losing a tempo, but if 8. KKt5 RKt8 ch.) 8... KB3.

| 4 ... | R—R8 |
| 5 R—R8 | |

240

White plays and wins
Black plays and draws
The same with White king on K6, KB5, KB4, K3, KB3, or Q2

Making a hole for his king, and threatening PR7 thus preventing the approach of Black's king.

5 ...	R—QR8
6 K—Kt4	R—Kt8 ch.
7 K—B5	R—B8 ch.
8 K—Kt6	R—Kt8 ch.
9 K—R7	K—K2
10 R—QKt8	R—Q8
11 K—Kt7	R—Q2 ch.

If 11... RKt8 ch. 12. KR8 RKR8 13. PR7 KQ2, Example 232.

III ROOK ENDINGS

12 K—Kt6	R—Q3 ch.
13 K—R5	R—Q4 ch.
14 R—Kt5.	

Black to play draws because he need not fear the transpositions, 1... RQKt8 2. KQ2 RKt3, Example 239; or 1... R—QKt8 2. R—R7 ch. K—B3 3. R—R7 (3. KQ3 KK3) 3... R—QR8 4. P—R7, Example 238.

White king on K6: Black draws by 1... R—R8 (1... RKB8? 2. KK5 RB3 3. RKt8 ch.) 2. K—Q7 (after the natural 2. RR7 ch. KKt1 3. RQKt7 the pawn is skewered, 3... RR3 ch. Even worse is 2. RR7 ch. KKt1 3. RKB7 RR8 4. PR7? RR3 ch.) 2... R—R3, attacking the pawn from the rank, 3. K—B7 (3. RR7 RKB3) 3... R—B3 4. P—R7 R—B2 ch., and Black's rook is on the correct (KB) file for his checks on the ranks.

White king on KB5(KB4): Black draws by 1... R—R4 ch. (1... RB8 ch.? 2. KK5 preventing 2.... RB3) 2. K—K4 (White is cut off on the rank; for 2. KK6 RR4 see above) 2... R—QB4 3. R—R7 ch. K—B3 (or 3... KKt3) 4. R—KR7 R—QR4 5. P—R7 K—Kt3 (5... KK3? 6. RR6 ch. KQ2 7. RR8) 6. R—Kt7 K—B3 7. K—Q4 K—K3 8. K—B4 K—Q3 9. K—Kt4 K—B3.

White king on KB3: White wins by 1. K—K4 R—R4 2. K—Q4 R—KR4 (2... RKB4 3. RR7 ch. KB3 4. RKR7 RQR4 5. PR7) 3. K—B4 (not yet 3. RR7 ch.) 3... R—R3 4. K—Kt5 R—R4 ch. 5. K—B6 R—R3 ch. 6. K—Kt7, and the checks on the rank cease. Black draws by 1... RB8 ch. 2. KK4 RB3, Example 239.

When White's king is to the right of these positions the game is drawn. If it is on KKt5 there may follow: 1. RR7 ch. (ineffective whilst Black's rook is on the QR file) 1... KB1 2. KB6 KK1 3. KK6 KQ1 4. KQ6 RQ8 ch. 5. KB6 RB8 ch. 6. KKt7 RB2 ch.

When White's king is to the left of the squares listed on the diagram, he wins regardless of the move. If White's king is on QB2 there follows: 1... R—KR8

(1... RB8 2. RR7 ch. KKt3 3. RKt7 RQR4 4. PR7 KB3 5. KKt2, Example 238) 2. R—R7 ch. K—B3 3. K—Kt3 (the immediate 3. RQKt7 RR8 4. PR7 draws) 3... R—Kt8 ch. 4. K—B4 R—B8 ch. 5. K—Kt5 R—Kt8 ch. 6. K—B6 R—B8 ch. 7. K—Kt7 R—Kt8 ch. (7... KK3 8. RR8 KQ3 9. RQ8 ch. KK2 10. RQ5, Example 234) 8. K—B8 R—QR8 (8... RKt3 9. RR7) 9. R—R8 R—B8 ch. (9... KK3 10. KB7 RB8 ch. 11. KKt6 RKt8 ch. 12. KB5) 10. K—Kt7 R—Kt8 ch. 11. K—R7 K—K3 12. R—QKt8 R—QB8 13. K—Kt7 R—Kt8 ch. 14. K—R8 R—QR8 15. P—R7, Example 232.

241 This position with a KtP is otherwise comparable to the preceding examples, but the play is simpler. Black draws because the KtP is not so far from his king, which crosses the board with less fear of the skewer threats that dogged him in the case with the RP.

1 K—K3	K—B2
2 K—Q4	

If 2. PKt7 KKt2 drawing as Example 237.

Drawn

2 ...	K—K2
3 K—B5	

After 3. PKt7 KQ2 4. RKR8 R×P the skewer check is harmless.

3 ...	K—Q2

This ending depends on the kings' positions. If Black can get his king to

164

Q2, keeping White's out of QKt7, he draws.

4 R—KR8   R—Kt7.

Not 4... RB8 ch.? 5. KKt5, and if 5... RKt8 ch. 6. KR6 RR8 ch. 7. KKt7, or if 5... RQR8 6. PKt7, winning in either case.

5. ROOK AND TWO PAWNS v. ROOK

United pawns win except for some, but not all, blocked positions. RP+KtP is the most difficult because White's king can less easily hide from checks, and most blockades with these pawns can be drawn under suitable circumstances.

With disconnected pawns White wins by getting one pawn to the fifth and abandoning the other so that after its capture Black's king is cut off by at least one file, Example 219.

This plan does not work with KtP+BP one file apart, for after White has sacrificed the RP Black's king is left on the short side of the pawn, Example 222.

The ending with KRP+QRP is often, but not always, drawn; after the sacrifice of either pawn White is left with the notoriously drawish R+RP v. R. ending.

Doubled pawns normally draw.

Sometimes White finds the pawns hard to defend, or his rook is boxed in. Draws from these causes are nearly always associated with the ending RP+KtP, as indicated in the note to White's third move, Example 247.

Finally, the stronger party · should beware of stalemate, which is certainly more common here than in endings with minor pieces and/or pawns.

242 The effectiveness of a blockade depends upon which files and which ranks the pawns are on, the positions of the rooks, and, most important of all, whether White's king is in contact with his pawns. White's chances are not less promising than in the similar case with minor pieces.

When White's king is not cut off the blockade may often be lifted.

With KtP+BP White wins if the KtP is ahead of its companion.

242

White wins

1 ...	R—Kt7
2 R—B1	R—Kt6
3 R—Q1	R—R6
4 K—B1	R—Kt6

After 4... RR1 5. RQ3 ch. KKt5 6. KKt2 White's king is safe from checks.

| 5 R—Q3 ch. | R×R |
| 6 P×R. | |

As Example 64.

243 A study by Cheron, 1926, shows that when the BP is ahead of the KtP White's king is exposed to checks on the ranks. Even with the BP on the sixth White may not win.

1 K—B4

If 1. RB4 RKKt1 2. RQ4 RKt4; or if 1. PB7 RQB1 2. RB6 ch. KKt2 3. KR5 RR1 ch. 4. KKt4 RQB1 5. KB5 R×P 6. KQ6 RKR2.

1 ...	R—R5 ch.
2 K—Q5	R—R4 ch.
3 K—K6	R—R3 ch.
4 K—B7	R—R2 ch.
5 K—B6	

If 5. KKt8(Kt6) RQB2 6. RQKt2 RB1.

| 5 ... | R—R1. |

Drawn

The rook plays to the first or second rank, anticipating White's threat of PB7. When White's king threatens to help the BP, Black checks on the rank.

244 With BP+Centre P the ideas are similar. If the BP is ahead of the Centre P, White has a sheltered space for his king, which then supports the further advance of the BP. If the Centre P is ahead White is likely to win only if it is on the sixth rank, as here shown by Cheron, 1926.

| 1 ... | R—R5 ch. |

If 1... RR4 2. PQ7.

| 2 K—B3 | R—R1 |

The capture 2... K×P here loses after 3. PQ7 (but would draw if the pawns were farther back).

White wins

3 K—Q4	R—R5 ch.
4 K—K5	R—R4 ch.
5 K—B6	R—R2
6 R—Q1	K—Q2

Black is in zugzwang. The checking distance is too short for the rook to make a tempo-move, if 6... RR3 ch. 7. KKt7, if 6... RQ2 7. KK6 followed by 8. PQ7, or if 6... RR1 7. PQ7 KB2 8. PB6.

7 R—K1	K—B3
8 R—K7	R—R3 ch.
9 K—Kt7	R—R4
10 R—B7 ch.

Getting the rook to this square is the most usual way of relieving a blockade.

With a pair of centre pawns White often wins if one is on the sixth, but often draws if they are farther back.

245 Black has far better drawing chances if his rook cuts off White's king on the side adjoining his rearmost pawn, as here shown by Cheron, 1951. If, on the contrary, White's king is on the side of the board (here the queen's side) adjoining his more forward pawn he often wins, his chances corresponding approximately to those of the preceding examples.

| 1 R—R5 |

For White there are two principal winning ideas: getting his rook to K7; or manœuvring his king to help the advance of his QP, which Black's rook here prevents.

| 1 ... | R—B4 |

Black wants to answer White's RQB5 by ... RKB1, and in the meanwhile he keeps his rook on KB2 or KB4.

After 1... R—B1? 2. R—B5 Black is in zugzwang, 2... R—B8 (2... RB4 3. PQ7 RB1 4. RB8) 3. R—B8 (threatening RK8 ch. and RK7) 3... R—Kt8 ch. (3... K×P 4. PQ7, or 3... RB2 4. RB7 followed by RK7) 4. K—B3 R—B8 ch. 5. K—K2 R—B2 6. R—B5 (not 6. RB7? R×R, whilst if 6. RK8 ch. KQ2) White's king rejoins his pawns, and in due course assists the advance of his QP.

2 R—Q5   R—B2
3 R—Q3

If 3. R—QB5 R—B1 White cannot lose a tempo, and after 4. K—Kt5 (4. KKt3 RB4) 4... R—B4 ch. 5. K—Kt6 R—B1 6. K—Kt7 R—B2 ch. 7. K—Kt8 R—QR2 he is just as effectively cut off on the rank, 10. RB7 RR1 ch. 11. KKt2 K×P.

3 ...   R—B1

When White plays his rook to the queen's file Black answers RKB1, anticipating PQ7, and threatening ... K×P.

245

Drawn

3 R—K3

After 3. R—KB3 R—QR1 4. R—B5 R—R5 ch. White's king advances, but can do nothing on this side of the pawns, 5. K—Kt5 R—R1 6. K—Kt6 R—Kt1 ch. 7. K—R7 R—R1 8. R—Kt5 R—R8 (8... RQKt1? 9. RKt8 RKt2 ch. 10. RKt7 RKt1 11. RK7 ch.) 9. K—Kt8 (9. RKt8 K×P 10. PQ7 RR2 11. RKt7 RR1) 9... R—R2, cutting White off on the eighth rank, 10. K—R8 (10. KB8 RR1 ch. 11. KKt7 RR2 ch. 12. KKt6 RR1 13. KR6 RR3 14. KR5 RR1 15. KKt4 RKB1) 10... R—R1 ch. 11. R—Kt8 (11. KR7 RR8) 11... R—R2 12. R—K8 ch. (12. RKt7 RR1 ch.) 12... K—B2 13. R—B8 K—K3 14. R—B5 (14. RB7 RR1 ch.) 14... R—Q2 15. K—Kt8 R—QR2 16. K—B8

R—QKt2, and the mating threats prevent White's king travelling along the back rank.

4 ...   R—B4

In order to answer 5. RB3 by 5 R×P.

5 R—K2   R—B1
6 K—Kt5   R—B4 ch.
7 K—Kt6   R—B1
8 R—Q2   R—Kt1 ch.

Not 8... K×P? PQ7.

9 K—R7   R—Q1
10 R—K2   R—Q2 ch.
11 K—Kt8   R—QR2.

White's king is still cut off from his pawns.

The position of this diagram moved one file to the left or right is also drawn

246 Horwitz and Kling, 1851. With KtP+RP blockades often draw, except when the KtP is on the seventh.

1 K—R5   R—R4 ch.
2 R—Kt5   R—R1
3 R—Kt6

The key move, which would be in-effective if the pawns were farther back. Not 3. RQB5? RR3.

3 ...   R—R4 ch.
4 K—Kt4   R—R5 ch.
5 K—B5   R—R4 ch.
6 K—Q4   R—R5 ch.
7 K—K5   R—R4 ch.
8 K—B4   R—R5 ch.

246

White wins

9 K—Kt5	R—R1
10 R—QB6	

Threatening RB8.

10 ...	K—Kt1
11 K—Kt6	R—Q1
12 R—B6	K—R2
13 K—Kt7.	

Black cannot meet the threat of RKB8.
The position of this diagram moved
one or two ranks nearer White's side of
the board is drawn.

247 Zukertort *v.* Steinitz, London,
1883. Colours reversed. United pawns
nearly always win if not blocked. With
RP+KtP some care must be taken.

1 R—QKt8	K—Kt3
2 R—Kt5	R—QB6
3 R—K5	

At present if checked White's king
goes to R4; after the text-move he can
interpose the rook.

If at once 3. PR4? RB5 4. KB3 RB6
ch. 5. KK2 RB5 6. RKt5 ch. KR3, the
defence of the pawns ties up his rook:
if White's king guards the KtP, Black
checks on the rank; if 7. RKt8 KR2; or
if 7. RR5 ch. KKt3, or even 7. RR5 ch.
KKt2 8. PKt5 RQB3, well and truly
sealing off White's rook. This kind of
draw less often occurs with united pawns
other than RP+KtP, for if White's king
can manœuvre on either side of the
pawns the rook may be freed.

3 ...	R—QR6
4 P—R4	R—Kt6
5 P—R5 ch.	

Advancing the RP first, making room
at R4 for his king.
If 5. PKt5? KR4 the blockade draws;
this should be compared with Example
246 after 6. RKB5 RR6 7. RB3 RR5
8. RKR3. White can win this kind of
blockade if his king is farther forward,
when he can give up the RP to win with
the KtP.

5 ...	K—R3
6 R—KB5	R—QR6
7 R—B3	R—R8

White wins

If 7... R—R4 8. R—B6 ch. K—Kt4
(Kt2) 9. R—Kt6 ch., but not 8. KKt3?
KKt4 when the blockade draws, for
9. RB5 ch., as in Example 242, does not
win when there is a RP.

8 K—Kt3	R—Kt8 ch.
9 K—R4	R—R8 ch.
10 R—R3	R—KKt8
11 R—R2	

This manœuvre is special to the KtP+
RP ending. Having to move, Black's
rook is forced off the knight's file.

11 ...	R—QR8
12 P—Kt5 ch.	K—Kt2
13 R—KB2	R—R8 ch.
14 K—Kt4	R—Kt8 ch.
15 K—B5	R—KR8
16 P—R6 ch.	K—R2
17 P—Kt6 ch.	

Pointed out by Karstedt. The game
took a longer course after 17. KB6.

17 ...	K—Kt1

If 17... KR1 18. KB6 RR8 19. PKt7
ch., Example 246. If 17... K×P 18. KB6
KR4 19. PKt7.

18 K—B6	R—R8
19 P—R7 ch.	K—R1.

And White mates in three.

248 The ending with RP+BP one
file apart occurs quite often, and,
although theoretically drawn, White
frequently wins in practice. He attempts
to queen the BP, sacrificing the RP as a

5 ROOK AND TWO PAWNS v. ROOK

decoy; but Black's king is thereby left on the short side of the pawn as in Example 222, which closely relates to this ending. The extra pawn does, however, create several new winning stratagems, and the defence is not easy unless the following rules are understood.

Black's rook, whose function is to disrupt the free movement of White's king, should be based on the squares QR7, QR8, and QKt8, thus reserving the option of checking on either the rank or the file.

Black's king occupies KKt2 if possible; it plays to KB2, KB3, KKt3, or KR3, if checked by White's rook. If Black's king is confined to the back rank he often loses, Examples 248, 250. Black may lose if his king is cut off on the rook's file before White's RP is on the sixth, Example 249. Black sometimes loses if he permits his king to be driven to the king's file, on the long side of the BP.

When, and if, White plays P—R6 ch. Black replies with K×RP or KR2.

Black neither can nor need prevent the pawns' advance. The diagram shows a typical position approaching the critical stage. If here Black's rook were misplaced, say at QR5, White could play 1. K—Kt5 followed by R—B7 ch. forcing Black's king to the back rank; but as it is, if White plays 1. K—Kt5 Black's rook can, and must, check on the file.

1 R—Q6

Marking time. We shall follow the play after the 76th move of the game Kotov v. Flohr, U.S.S.R. Championship, 1951. Colours reversed.

If 1. PB5, Black checks on the files, attacking the pawns after driving off White's king.

If 1. K—Kt5 (the 87th move of the game Gligorić v. Smyslov, Moscow, 1947) 1... R—Kt8 ch. (essential) 2. K—B5 R—QR8, the check followed by an immediate return to base is a typical manœuvre, 3. R—B7 ch. K—R3 4. R—K7 R—QKt8 5. R—K8 K—Kt2 6, R—K6 R—QR8 7. P—R6 ch., K—R2

8. R—Q6 R—QKt8 9. K—Kt5 R—Kt8 ch. (essential) 10. K—B6 (10. KB5 RQR8) 10... K×P (Black must be prepared to capture the RP when it is on the sixth) 11. K—K7 ch. K—R2 12. P—B5 R—K8 ch. 13. R—K6 R—QR8 14. P—B6 R—R1, example 222.

Finally, 1. RKt6 ch. KB2 leads nowhere: 2. RKt5 KB3; or 2. KKt5 RKt8 ch. 3. KB5 RQR8.

1 ...   R—R4

Black's simpler course is to temporize, 1... RQKt8.

2 R—Kt6 ch.

This check now has some point, because of a tempo-gain on his next move.

2 ...   K—B2

Or 2... K—R2 3. P—B5 R—R8 4. K—Kt5 R—Kt8 ch. (4... RQKt8 5. RQ6 KKt2 6. RQ7 ch.) 5. K—B6 R—QR8 6. R—Kt7 ch. K—R3 7. R—K7 R—R3 ch. 8. R—K6 R—R2; but not here 7... K×P? 8. KKt7, nor 7... RKB8 8. RK8 KR2 9. KK6 RK8 ch. transposing to the position which occurs after the 20th move of the next example.

3 R—Kt5   R—R8
4 P—R6   R—Kt8 ch.

A useless check, after which Black's king gets confined to the back rank. The temporizing 4... R—QKt8 is simpler.

Drawn

169

5. KB5 RKt4 ch. 6. KKt4 RKt8.
5. RR5 KKt1 6. PR7 ch. KR1.
5. RKt7 ch. KB3   6. RQ7 KKt3
7. PR7 RKR8.
5. PR7 RKt8 ch.   6. KB3 RKR8
7. RQ5 KKt3.

5 K—B5	R—KR8
6 R—Kt7 ch.	K—B1
7 K—Kt6	R—Kt8 ch.
8 K—B6	

If 8. KR7 RKB8   9. RQB7 R×P
10. KKt6 RKt5 ch.

8 ...	R—KR8
9 R—Kt6	R—R7
10 P—B5	R—R8
11 K—K6	R—R7
12 K—Q7	K—B2
13 R—K6	R—Q7 ch.?

White was threatening 14. PR7 R×P
15. RKt7 ch.; but the way to prevent
this is to return the rook to its base,
13... R—QR7, when a draw is soon
evident, 14. P—R7 (14. R—K7 ch.
KB3   15. PR7 RR1) 14... K—Kt2
15. P—B6 ch.   (15. RK7 ch. KR1)
15... K×P 16. K—K7 (16. KK8 RR1
ch.) R—R1 17. K—B7 (17. PB7 KKt2
or 17. RQ6 KKt3   18. PB7 ch. KKt2)
17... R—QKt1, Example 222.

14 R—Q6	R—KR7

If now 14... RQR7   15. PR7 KKt2
16. PB6 ch. K×P 17. KK8 RR1 ch.
18. RQ8.

15 K—Q8	K—B1

If 15... R—R8   16. P—R7 (the idea
behind his 13th and 15th moves) 16...
K—Kt2   17. R—Q7 ch. K—R1   18.
P—B6 R—KB8 19. K—K7 R—K8 ch.
20. K—B7 (20. KB8? RK1 ch.) 20...
R—QR8 (20... K×P 21. RQ2) 21.
RK7 RR7 (21... K×P 22. KB8 ch.
KKt3 23. PB7) 22. RK8 ch. K×P 23.
K—B8 K—Kt3   24. P—B7 R—KB7
25. R—K6 ch., K—R2 26. R—K1.
If 15... R—R7 16. P—R7 R—R1 ch.
(16... KKt2 17. PB6 ch. K×P 17. KK8,
or 16... RR7   17. RQ7 ch. KB3   18.
KK8) 17. K—B7 R—R1 (17... KKt2
18. RQ8) 18. R—KR6.

16 R—B6 ch.	K—Kt1
17 K—K7	R—R7
18 R—Q6	R—K7 ch.
19 K—B6	K—R2

If 19... R—QR7 20. R—Q7, Black is
confined to the back rank, and loses,
20... R—R8 21. R—K7 R—R7 (21...
RKR8 22. KK6 R×P ch. 23. PB6 or
21... RR3 ch. 22. KKt5 RR8 23. PB6
when White's king goes to K8) 22.
K—K5 R—K7 ch. 23. K—Q6 R—Q7
ch. 24. K—K6 R—K7 ch. 25. K—Q7
R—Q7 ch. (25... RKB7 26. RK8 ch.
KR2 27. KK6) 26. K—K8 R—KB7
27. R—K5 K—R2 (25... RQR7 28.
PB6, or 27... RB8 28. KK7) 28. K—B7
(28. KK7? K×P 29. RK6 ch. KKt2
30. PB6 ch. KKt3 draws) 28... K×P
29. R—K6 ch., Example 222, and not
29. PB6? RQR7 30. KB8 KKt3 31.
PB7 KB3.

20 K—B7	R—QR7

A move too late.

21 R—K6	R—R1

If 21... RR8 22. PB6 RR1 23. RK8
RR2 ch. 24. KK6 RR3 ch. 25. KB5
RR4 ch. 26. RK5 RR8 27. PB7 RB8 ch.
28. KK6 KKt3 29. RKt5 ch. K×R
30. P—R7.

22 R—K8	R—R2 ch.
23 K—B8	K×P

24. R—K7 ch. was threatened. If 23...
R—R3 24. R—K7 ch. K—R1 (24...
K×P 26. RK6 ch.) 25. R—K6 R—R1
ch. 26. R—K8 R—R3 27. P—B6 (the
point of White's apparently aimless
moves ; if 27... R×P ch. 28. KK7 ch.
and the despised RP prevents ... KKt2)
27... K—R2 28. P—B7 K×P 29.
K—Kt8.

24 R—K6 ch.	K—Kt4
25 P—B6	K—Kt3
26 P—B7 ch.	K—R2
27 R—K1	R—R1 ch.
28 K—K7	R—R2 ch.
29 K—B6.	

And Kotov resigned.

249 This position arose after the
62nd move of the game Keres v. Sokol-

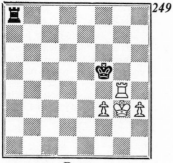

249

Drawn

sky, Moscow, 1947, and the play shows what happens if Black's king gets cut off on the rook's file before White's RP is on the sixth.

1 P—R4	R—R8?

An instructive error. Black knows that this is theoretically the correct place for the rook, but plays it there too soon. At this stage the checking distance on the files is not long enough. He should play 1... RR1 2. RKt5 ch. KB3 3. KKt4 RR1 4. PR5, and now that White's king is on the fourth rank Black threatens checks from the rear, 4... RR8.

2 P—R5	R—R3

It is always unsatisfactory to block a pawn with a rook; but the check from the rear, 2... RKt8 ch., is answered by 3. KR2, when Black's prospects are even worse.

3 R—KR4	R—R3
4 R—B4 ch.	K—Kt4
5 R—Kt4 ch.	K—B4
6 K—R4	R—R1

If 6... RR3 7. RKt5 ch. KB5 8. RKt6 RR8 9. RB6 ch. KK4 10. RB8, Black's king is cut off on the K-file, and White advances his RP.

7 R—Kt5 ch.	K—B3

If 7... K—B5 8. R—Kt7 K—B4 9. R—B7 K—B3 (9... RR3 10. RB7 ch.) 10. K—Kt4 R—Kt1 ch. 11. K—B4 R—KR1 12. P—R6 K—Kt3 13. P—R7.

8 K—Kt4	K—B2
9 R—B5 ch.	K—Kt2
10 K—Kt5	R—KKt1
11 R—B6	K—R2 ch.

Now Black's king is cut off on the rook's file. This loses when the RP is only on the fifth, for Black has not time to capture it.

12 R—Kt6	R—QR1
13 P—B4	R—R8
14 R—K6	R—Kt8 ch.
15 K—B6	R—KB8
16 P—B5	R—B7
17 R—K5	R—KR7

If 17... KR3 18. KB7 K×P 19. PB6 ch.

18 R—K7 ch.	K—R3
19 R—K8	K—R2
20 K—K6	R—K7 ch.
21 K—B7	R—QR7
22 P—B6	R—R3
23 K—K7	R—R2 ch.
24 K—B8	R—R3
25 P—B7	R—R2
26 R—B8	R—R8
27 K—K7.	

And Black resigned.

250 Faulty rook-moves are usually the cause of Black's downfall in this ending, and here too Black draws easily enough by playing 1... R—QKt8 holding his rook in readiness for checks on the ranks if necessary.

1 ...	R—R8?

250

Drawn

A mistake made at Leningrad, 1941, on his 78th move, by Bondarevsky, whose opponent Smyslov failed to find the win, which had previously been shown by Panov in his defeat of L. Steiner, Moscow, 1936. In both cases Black had the pawns.

2 P—B6 ch.	K—B2
3 P—R6	R—R6
4 R—Kt2	

White juggles his rook with the idea of shortening Black's checking distance on the files.

4 ...	R—R8
5 R—Kt3	R—R7
6 R—Kt1	R—R6
7 R—QR1	R—Kt6 ch.
8 K—R4	R—Kt7
9 P—R7	R—R7 ch.
10 K—Kt5	R—Kt7 ch.
11 K—B4	R—KR7
12 R—R8	R×P
13 R—R7 ch.	

251 Smyslov v. Bondarevsky, Moscow, 1940. Black draws against the two RPs if one of them has to be defended by its rook in front of it, as here. Black's rook then operates on the ranks, very much as in Example 239.

1 P—R6 ch.

If 1. RKt6 ch. KB2 2. RKt5 RR5 3. RKt2 RR5.

1 ...	K—R2
2 P—R4	

Obviously White must attempt to queen the QRP. He may at once give up his KRP, 1. R—K6 R—R5 2. R—K2 K×P, when Black draws although his king is on the far side of the board, 3. R—KKt2 (3. KK3 KKt4 4. KQ3 KB4 5. KB3 RR1) 3... K—R4 4. K—K3 K—R5 5. K—Q3 K—R6 6. R—K2 (6. RQ2 KKt5 7. KB3 KB4, Example 235) 6... R—R1 7. K—B3 K—Kt5 8. K—Kt3 R—Kt1 ch. 9. K—B4 R—QR1 10. K—Kt5 R—Kt1 ch. 11. K—B6 R—QR1 12. K—Kt7 R—R6.

2 ... R—QKt5

White's inactive rook takes little further part. The struggle is between Black's rook and White's king. Whenever the king threatens to guard the QRP, Black checks on the rank; otherwise Black's rook holds the QRP under attack on the rank. Black cannot free his rook: it is the same idea as Example 239, for White's KRP makes no real difference.

3 K—K3	R—QB5
4 K—Q3	R—QKt5
5 K—B3	R—KB5
6 K—Kt3	R—B6 ch.
7 K—B4	R—B5 ch.
8 K—Q5	R—QKt5

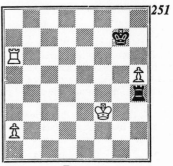
251

Drawn

Not 8... R—B4 ch.? 9. K—K6 R—B5 (9... RKR4 10. RQ6 RR4 11. RQ4 K×P 12. KQ6) 10. P—R5 for Black can no longer attack the pawn from the rank, and after 10...R—QR5 (10... RK5 ch. 11. KQ6 RQ5 ch. 12. KB6) 11. K—Q7 R—R8 12. K—B7 R—R7 13. K—Kt7 R—R8 14. R—R8 K×P 15. PR6, White wins.

9 K—B6	R—KB5
10 K—Q7	R—Q5 ch.

10... RQKt5 also draws, but not 10... RB2 ch.? 11. KK6 RB5 12. PR5.

11 K—B7	R—KB5
12 P—R5	R—B4

The attack on the pawn must be maintained, else White frees his rook.

13 K—Q7	R—Q4 ch.
14 K—K7	R—K4 ch.
15 K—B6	R—B4
16 R—R8	R—QKt4
17 P—R6	R—Kt3 ch.
18 K—K7	R×KRP
19 K—B7	R—QKt3
20 R—R7.	

Here a draw was agreed.

252 Suetin *v.* Cholmov, Kiev, 1954. Doubled pawns are not appreciably stronger than a single pawn. A few extra threats may be conjured up but Black is in no real difficulty.

1 R—Q5	R—Kt3

Philidor's drawing method, Example 216, is quite applicable to this ending.

Drawn

2 K—K5	K—Kt2
3 R—Q7 ch.	K—B1
4 R—Q6	R—Kt2

Not 4... RKt8? 5. KB6 threatening mate.

With only one pawn Black could draw by exchanging rooks; as it is he must find another way of preventing White's king maintaining a foothold on its sixth rank.

5 K—B6	R—B2 ch.
6 K—Kt5	R—Kt2 ch.
7 R—Kt6	R—QR2
8 R—B6 ch.	K—Kt2
9 R—Kt6	R—QB2
10 R—Kt8	R—R2

Returning to the third rank, 10... RB3? would lose after 11. PB6 ch.

11 R—K8

With a cunning threat of 12. RK7 ch. R×R 13. PB6 ch.

11 ...	K—B2
12 R—KR8	K—Kt2
13 R—KR6	

The threat of 14. PB6 ch. KKt1 15. KKt6 RKt2? 17. PB7 ch. is not real, for Black has the stalemate resource 15... RKt2 ch.

13 ...	K—B1
14 P—B6	R—R8

As in Philidor's method, Black's rook goes to the eighth when White plays his pawn to the sixth. Now if 15. KKt6 RKt8 ch.

15 R—R8 ch.	K—B2
16 R—R7 ch.	K—B1
17 K—B5	R—QKt8

Not 17... RR4 ch.? 18. KKt6.

18 R—Q7	R—QR8
19 P—B7	R—QR3

With the pawn on the seventh White cannot avoid the stalemate threats.

20 K—Kt5	R—Kt3 ch.

A draw was agreed. If 21. K—B5 R—B3 ch. 22. K—K5 R—QR3 23. P—B5 R—QKt3 24. R—R7 (24. KB4 RKB3) 24... R—QB3 25. P—B6 R×P.

6. ROOK AND PAWN *v.* ROOK AND PAWN

When each player has a pawn a draw is to be expected. If one player's pawn is more advanced, he may win a rook for it; and an incorrect assessment of the resultant R. *v* P ending is one of the commonest faults, even having occurred in important matches such as Morphy *v.* Lowenthal, 1858, and Alekhine *v.* Bogoljubow, 1929.

253 Gilg *v.* Tartakower, Semmering, 1926.

1 ...	R—Kt8

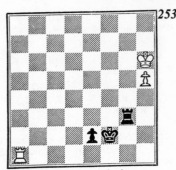

Black plays and wins

1... PK8=Q? 2. R×Q K×R 3. KR7 KB7 4. PR6 KB6 5. KR8 KB5 6. PR7 KKt4 7. KKt7 draws.

| 2 R—R2 | K—B6 |
| 3 R—R3 ch. | |

If now 3. R×P Black wins by a tempo, 3... K×R 4. KR7 KB6 5. PR6 KB5 6. KR8 KB4 7. PR7 KKt3 8. KKt8 KR3 ch.

3 ...	K—B5
4 R—R4 ch.	K—Kt6
5 R—R3 ch.	

If 5. RK4 PK8=Q 5. R×Q R×R, Black wins as in Example 202.

5 ...	K—R5
6 R—R4 ch.	R—Kt5
7 R—R1	R—K5
8 R—R1 ch.	K—Kt5
9 R—Kt1 ch.	K—B4
10 R—K1	K—B3
11 K—R7	K—Kt4
12 P—R6	R—K2 ch.

White resigns.

7. ROOK AND TWO PAWNS v. ROOK AND PAWN

A draw is normal when there is no passed pawn.

An outside passed pawn may do no more than draw unless the stronger party also has some positional advantage, however slight.

Also when there are two disconnected passed pawns the game is as often drawn as not.

On the other hand united passed pawns, which are much more effective than disconnected pawns, frequently win. If there is any choice, this is the ending the stronger party should aim for.

In most cases an exchange of pawns takes place; and White times this, if possible, so that he gets a favourable R+P v. R ending.

254 Chekover v. Kazakevich, Odessa, 1949. When there is no passed pawn the defender must not play too passively, but should try and get his lone pawn to the third rank. There are winning chances for the stronger party only if he gets both pawns to fifth, and not even then with KtP+RP.

| 1 ... | R—B2 |

If 1... PKt3 ch. 2. KR6 P×P 3. PKt6 ch. KB3 4. PKt7 RR1 5. RKt6 ch. KK4 6. RKt6 PB5 7. PKt8=Q R×Q R×R, Example 196.

If 1... RR3 2. RKt7 ch. KKt1 3. RKt8 ch. KB2 4. PKt6 ch. KK2 5. RKt8 KB3 6. RB8 ch. KK4 7. PB6 R×P 8. RB7 (very neat) 8... RB4 ch. 9. KKt4 RB3 10. KKt5 KK3 11. R×P, Example 219.

If 1... RR1 2. RKt7 ch. KKt1 3 KKt6 RR3 ch. 4. PB6 P×P 5. P×P RR1 6. RKt7 ch., and Black loses because his rook is on the first rank, Example 217.

White wins

2 R—Kt8	R—R2
3 P—Kt6 ch.	K—B3
4 R—B8 ch.	K—K4
5 P—B6	

The pawn sacrifice is the key in all variations.

5 ...	P×P
6 K—R6	R—R8
7 P—Kt7	R—R8 ch.
8 K—Kt6	R—Kt8 ch.
9 K—B7.	

Black resigns.

255 Flohr *v.* Szabo, Budapest, 1950. The other kind of winning chance occurs when Black's king is cut off. White's chances are better than in the comparable case of R+P *v.* R because Black's last pawn is hard to defend.

1 ...	K—K3
2 R—Q2	R—R4
3 K—Kt3	R—R5
4 R—Q8	

Threatening RQKt8.

255

White wins

4 ...	K—K2
5 R—Q5	R—Kt5

If 5... KK3 6. RQKt5.

6 K—B3	R—KR5
7 P—Kt3	R—KKt5
8 R—Q4	R—Kt6 ch.
9 K—B4	R—Kt4
10 R—Q5	R—Kt5 ch.

If 10... RKt6 11. PR4 RR6 12. PKt4

RKKt6 13. KKt5 RKt5(Kt6) 14. PR5 P×P 15. K×P, Example 219.

11. K—Kt5	R—Kt6
12 P—Kt4	R—Kt3

If 12... R×P 13. K×P, Example 219.

13 K—R6	R—R3
14 P—Kt5.	

Black resigns because of 15. PR4, 16. KR7, 17. PR5 P×P and 18. PKt6.

256 Hooper *v.* Newman, British Championship, Hastings, 1953. White's outside passed pawn wins easily because he also has many positional advantages: his pawns are well forward, and of the right kind—there are no RPs; his rook is more active; his king is centralized. The unpassed pawns are on the same file; this is a fine point, but when they are on adjoining files Black has more chances of counter-attack or pawn-exchange.

1 R—Kt5	K—Kt2
2 P—Kt5	R—Kt3
3 P—Kt4	K—B2
4 R—K5	R—Q3 ch.
5 K—B4	

White's king usually assists the advance of whichever pawn is not held up by Black's king, here the QKtP.

5 ...	R—Kt3
6 K—Kt5	K—B1
7 K—R6	K—B2
8 P—Kt5	K—B1
9 K—Kt7	

256

White wins

White finesses. The immediate 9.
RB5 ch. KK2 10. RB6 R×P 11. R×P
KQ2 12. RQB6 also wins, Example
219.

9 ...	K—B2
10 K—B7	K—B1
11 K—Q7	K—B2
12 R—B5 ch.	K—Kt2
13 K—B7.	

Black resigns (14. RB6 follows).

This is the normal winning idea,
White exchanging pawns at a moment
chosen by himself so as to get a won
R+P ending. Thus the relevance of
having one's pawns well forward, so that
one can finish up with a pawn on the
fifth, when the enemy king needs to be
cut off only by one file.

257 Donner v. Euwe, The Hague,
1950. Colours reversed. The most important positional factor is the situation of
the rooks. A rook is a great deal more
powerful behind a passed pawn—one's
own or one's opponents—than in front
of it.

White to play backs up the passed
pawn with his rook and wins easily,
1. RKt3 RK7 2. PKt5 RK2 3. PKt6
RKt2, Black's rook is forced into a
passive role, 4. KB5 KB2 5. PKt4 KK2
6. KKt6 KK3 7. RKB3.

In the game Black took the active
rook position behind the pawn, and
should have drawn:

1 ...	R—QKt7
2 R—B4	K—Kt3
3 K—B4	P—B4

White threatened PKt4, when his rook
guards both pawns, thus freeing his king
which then assists the QKtP. Anyway
the text-move is good, for Black should
keep White's pawns as far back as he
can.

4 R—B6 ch.	K—B2
5 R—QKt6	R—Kt6
6 P—Kt5	K—K2

If Black's king moves too far from the
passed pawn, 6... KKt2?, an exchange
of pawns leads to Example 219, 7. K×P

R×P 8. KK5 KB2 9. KQ5 KK2
10. RQB6.

7 R—Kt8	K—K3
8 R—K8 ch.	K—B3
9 R—B8 ch.	K—Kt3
10 R—QKt8	K—B3?

This leads to a curious zugzwang on
his next move, whereas after 10... KB2
11. PKt6 KB3 White can win Black's
KBP only by advancing his QKtP to the
seventh, 12. PKt7 KKt2 13. K×P,
which brings about the well known draw
of Example 237, White's KKtP making
no significant difference.

257

White plays and wins
Black plays and draws

11 P—Kt6	R—Kt5 ch.

This releases White's king but there
is nothing better:
11... KKt2 12. K×P, Example 219.
11... KKt3 12. KK5 RKt8 (if the rook
moves off the file White advances the
KtP) 13. KQ6, as in the game.
11... KK3(K2) 12. PKt7 KQ2 13.
RKt8 R×QKtP 14. RKt7 ch., and
White wins the pawn ending.

12 K—K3	K—Kt2

The position correlates to Example
241, if 12... RKt6 ch. 13. KQ4 and
Black dare not capture, 13... R×KKtP
because of 14. PKt7.

13 K—Q3	K—B3

Marking time, for if 13... RKt6 ch.
14. KB4 R×KKtP White still plays 15.
PKt7, when Black's rook cannot move

behind the passed pawn, and if 15...
RKt5 ch. 16. KB5.

Similar difficulties follow 13... P—B5
14. P×P (14. KB3? P×P) 14... R×BP
15. K—B3.

14 K—B3	R—Kt8
15 K—B4	R—B8 ch.
16 K—Kt5	R—Kt8 ch.

White threatens to free his rook. The
best Black can do is to force White's king
in front of the QKtP.

| 17 K—R6 | R—R8 ch. |
| 18 K—Kt7 | R—R6 |

His only counterchance, but it
shortens the checking distance.

| 19 R—B8 ch. | K—K3 |
| 20 R—K8 ch. | K—B3 |

In the game Donner resigned after
20... KB2 21. RK5 KB3 22. RKt5
R×P 23. KB6.

21 K—B6	R—B6 ch.
22 K—Kt5	R—Kt6 ch.
23 K—R5	R—Kt8

The checks cease after 23... RR6 ch.
24. KKt4, and if then 24... RR8 25.
RK3.

24 K—R6

Having driven Black's rook from its
counter-attacking position, White's king
returns to help his pawn.

24 ...	R—R8 ch.
25 K—Kt5	R—Kt8 ch.
26 K—B6	R—B8 ch.
27 K—Q6	R—QKt8
28 K—B7	R—B8 ch.
29 K—Kt8	R—KKt8

Black renews his attack on the KKtP,
but it is too late.

30 P—Kt7	R×P
31 K—B7	R—Kt6
32 P—Kt8=Q	R×Q
33 K×R.	

As example 196.

258 Lasker *v.* Steinitz, 14th match
game, 1896. Black blocks the passed
pawn with his king which is regarded as

the better defence in a general way, but
the positions of the rooks is still likely
to be the deciding factor.

| 1 ... | R—K5? |

His rook is now forced on the defen-
sive. Maintaining its aggressive position
draws, 1... PB5 2. KB2 KB4 3. KQ3
RKt6 ch. 4. KK4 R×QKtP 5. K×P
KQ3 6. RK2 RKt1 7. PKt4 RB1 ch.,
Example 223.

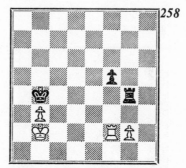

Drawn

2 P—Kt3	R—K4
3 R—B4 ch.	K—Kt4
4 K—R3	R—Q4
5 R—B3	K—R4
6 P—Kt4 ch.	K—Kt4
7 K—Kt3	K—Kt3

If 7... RK4 8. KB3 RQ4 9. RK3.

8 K—B4	K—B3
9 R—Kt3	R—K4
10 P—Kt5 ch.	K—Kt3
11 K—Q4	R—K5 ch.
12 K—Q5	R—K1
13 K—Q6	R—K8

Having advanced his king and pawns
as far as he can, White contrives the
winning pawn-exchange.

14 R—KB3	K×P
15 R×P ch.	K—B5
16 P—Kt4.	

Black resigns, for after 16...KQ5 17.
PKt5 RKKt8 18. KK6 KK5 19. RR5
his king is cut off on the rank.

259 Bondarevsky *v.* Keres, Moscow, 1947. Black's rook is badly placed in front of the passed pawn. Nevertheless, because he has rook's pawns White only draws. He first brings his king to the aid of his passed pawn:

1 R—R3 ch.	K—K5
2 R—R4 ch.	K—B4
3 K—R5	K—K4
4 K—Kt4	K—K3
5 K—B4	K—B3
6 K—K4	K—K3
7 R—R3	K—K2
8 K—K5	K—K1

Drawn

Black's answer to White's tempo moves. Not 8... KB2? 9. KQ5 KK2 10. KB5 KQ2 11. KKt5 RKB3 12. PR6.

9 P—R4	K—K2
10 P—R5	K—K1
11 K—Q5	K—Q2
12 K—B5	K—B2
13 K—Kt5	R—KB3

Not 13... KKt2? 14. RKKt3 RKB3 15. RKt7 ch. driving Black's king to the back rank, 15... KB1 16. RKt6 RB4 ch. 17. KB6 KKt1 18. KKt6 KB1 19. R×P, and White wins.

14 R—B3 ch.	K—Kt2
15 R—B5	R—B8

By giving up a pawn Black's rook achieves freedom, whilst White's rook becomes confined.

16 P—R6 ch.	K—R2

17 R—B7 ch.	K—Kt1
18 R—B6	K—R2
19 R×P	R—B4 ch.

Black draws by checking on the rank, and otherwise maintaining his attack on the KRP, as in Examples 239 and 251. His king remains on QR2 rendering of no account White's QRP.

260 Spielmann *v.* Capablanca, Moscow, 1925. Colours reversed. Black's king blocks one pawn, and his rook, strongly placed behind the other, cuts off White's king. In these circumstances the disconnected passed pawns cannot win.

1 ...	K—B2

If 1... KQ1? 2. RR6 KK1(K2) 3. PB7, and if 3... KB2 4. RR8; but not 2. RQ6 ch.? KK2 3. R×P R×P, and although 4. RKB5 cuts off Black's king he draws by 4... RB5 in turn cutting off White's king, as noted in Example 219.

2 R—R6	K—Kt2
3 R—Q6	K—R2
4 K—B3	K—Kt2
5 K—K3	K—R2
6 K—Q3	K—Kt2

Black's QP is not useless; on the contrary it supports his rook on an ideal square.

7 R—Q7 ch.	K—Kt3
8 P—B7	K—R4

Not 8... K×P? 9. R×P ch., nor 8... RB3? 9. KQ4.

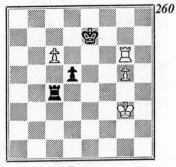

Drawn

7 ROOK AND TWO PAWNS v. ROOK AND PAWN

If this position were moved one file to the right Black would be in zugzwang, but as it is the text-move saves him.

9 R—Kt7

It is often difficult to protect isolated pawns without getting the rook into an inactive position.

| 9 ... | K—Kt5 |
| 10 R—Kt8 | |

If 10. RQ7 KR4.

10 ...	R × P
11 K—Q4	K—B4
12 K × P	R—Q2 ch.

A draw was agreed.

261 Najdorf *v.* Tartakower, Dubrovnik, 1950. The alternative defence is to make something of the lone passed pawn, and here too Black needs to have his rook aggressively placed.

1 P—R5

As the pawn advances White's rook is progressively restricted.

1 ...	P—B6
2 K—Q3	K—B5
3 P—R6	R—R8
4 P—R7	

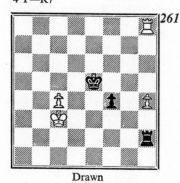

261

Drawn

After 4. RB8 ch. KK4 the exchange 5. R × P R × P draws.

| 4 ... | P—B7 |
| 5 K—Q4 | |

If 5. R—B8 ch. K—K4, but not 5... K—Kt6? 6. K—K2 R—K8 ch. (6...

R × P 7. RB3 ch. KKt5 8. R × P, Example 224) 7. K—Q2 R—KR8 8. R—Kt8 ch. K—B6 9. P—R8=Q.

5 ...	K—B6
6 R—B8 ch.	K—K7
7 R—K8 ch.	K—Q7.

Not 7... KB6? 8. PR8=Q. A draw was now agreed after 8. RKB8 KK7.

262 Mikenas *v.* Poliak, Leningrad, 1947. Colours reversed. Black often draws against passed pawns one file apart if his king obstructs them, even though White has the better rook position, as here.

| 1 ... | R—R8 |

1... RR7 2. KB5 PR6 3. RR7 ch. KB1 4. KB6 RB7 ch. 5. KKt6 PR7 is simpler. The pawn on the seventh guarded by the rook on the rank draws easily.

| 2 K—B5 | P—R6? |

262

Drawn

His king is now driven to the back rank. Instead he should play 2... R—B8 ch. 3. K—Kt5 (3. KQ5 RQKt8) 3... R—KR8, after which White makes progress only by advancing his QP, 4. P—Q5 (4. RR7 ch. KQ3) 4... P—R6 5. P—Q6 ch. K—Q2 6. K—Kt6 R—QKt8 7. P—Kt5 R—Kt6 8. K—R6 R—R6 ch. 9. K—Kt7 R—QKt6 10. P—Kt6 R—R6 11. K—Kt8 R—QKt6 12. P—Kt7 R—QB6. Black's pawn on the sixth guarded by the rook on the rank draws here, but loses in the game

179

continuation because White there holds back his QP, which later provides a vital tempo-move (14. P—Q5).

3 R—R7 ch.	K—B1
4 K—B6	R—B8 ch.
5 K—Kt6	R—B5

Black loses when the pawn on the seventh is guarded by the rook in front of it, 5... RKR8 6. PKt5 PR7 7. RB7 ch. KQ1 8. RB2 KQ2 9. RR2, threatening KR6 and PKt6.

6 R—R8 ch.

This leads to an interesting finish but is unnecessary, as the immediate 6.¦PKt5 wins, 6... R×P 7. R×P RQ1(Q3 ch.) 8. KR7 RQ2 ch. 9. KR8 KB2 10. RR6.

| 6 ... | K—Q2 |
| 7 P—Kt5 | R—B6 |

If 7... R×P 8. R×P KB1 9. RR8 ch. KQ2 10. KKt7.

8 R—R6	R—R6
9 K—Kt7	R—QKt6
10 P—Kt6	R—R6
11 K—Kt8	R—QKt6
12 R—R7 ch.	K—Q1

If 12... KQ3 White's king extricates himself via Q8, 13. PKt7 RQB6 14. PQ5 (this tempo-move decides) 14... RR6 15. KB8 RB6 ch. 16. KQ8, and now 16... RQKt6 17. RR6 ch. K×P 18. KB7 RB6 ch. 19. KKt6 RKt6 ch. 20. KR7 RR6.ch. 21. RR6.

| 13 P—Kt7 | R—QR6 |
| 14 P—Q5 | P—R7 |

Black is in zugzwang.
If 14... RQKt6 15. KR7, and, White's king extricates itself via Q6.
If 14... KK1 15. KB8 RB6 ch., and because Black's pawn is only on the sixth, White can play 16. RB7.

15 R×P   K—Q2

Black resigned six moves later. White sacrifices the QP to get Salvio's position, Example 219.

263 Kieninger v. Richter, Munich, 1941. Colours reversed. Here Black does not block the pawns. His king and pawn counterbalance White's rook; and his rook fights two pawns as in Example 211.

White plays and wins
Black plays and draws

White wins by getting one pawn to the seventh, the other to the fifth, 1. PKt7 RKt5 2. KB6 RKt8 3. PK5 RB8 ch. 4.KK7 RKKt8 5.KB7 RB8 ch. 6.KKt8, and if 6... RK8 7. PK6 R×P 8. KB7.
Black plays and draws by 1... RR8 2. PKt7 RKKt8 3. KB6 RB8 ch. 4. KK7 RKKt8 5. KB7 RB8 ch. 6. KKt8 RK8.

264 Bergkvist v. Zapata, Dubrovnik, 1950, shows the customary winning procedure when White has united pawns.

1 ...	K—Kt3
2 K—B2	K—B4
3 K—B3	P—Kt4
4 R—K8	

White's rook plays to its best position, behind the passed pawn.

4 ...	R—Kt8
5 R—B8 ch.	K—K3
6 K—K4	R—K8 ch.
7 K—Q3	R—Q8 ch.
8 K—B4	P—Kt5
9 K—B5	P—Kt6
10 R—KKt8	R—KKt8
11 P—B4	P—Kt7

When Black's rook is in front of the pawn on the seventh, White wins if his united pawns are on the fourth.
White cannot advance the pawns

White wins

without leaving one of them unguarded, which invites a transposition to a R+P v. R ending. Such an ending would be drawn if the pawns were further back.

12 P—Q5 ch.	K—Q2
13 R—Kt7 ch.	K—K1

Unlike the case with disconnected pawns, White's mating threats force Black's king out, for after 13... KQ1 14. KQ6, or 13... KB1 14. KB6, the pawns' advance continues unmolested.

14 K—Q6

White cannot avoid a pawn exchange, but may choose instead to win with the BP, 14. PQ6 KB1 15. PQ7 RQ8 16. R×P R×P 17. KB6.

14 ...	R—QB8
15 R×P	R×P
16 R—K2 ch.	K—Q1

Now Black's rook turns out to be awkwardly placed, but if 16... KB1 17. KQ7, Example 219.

17 R—KR2	K—B1
18 R—R8 ch.	K—Kt2
19 K—Q7	R—B2 ch.
20 K—K6	R—Kt2
21 P—Q6	

The game continuation 21. RQ8? should draw after 21... RKt3 ch. 22. KB7 KB2.

21 ... R—Kt3 ch.

The checking distance is too short (Example 221), but if 21... KB3 22. RB8 ch. KKt2 23. PQ7.

22 K—K7	R—Kt2 ch.
23 K—B6	R—Q2
24 K—K6	R—Kt2
25 P—Q7.	

265 Alekhine v. Bogoljubow, 8th match game, 1934. Colours reversed. In sharp contrast to Example 262, having the pawn on the seventh guarded by the rook on the rank is the least favourable arrangement for Black. White may win even when the united pawns are as far back as the second rank, unless Black's king can support its pawn, making it a real counterthreat.

1 R—R1

It is better for White to place his rook behind the KRP. Because this is not possible Black has more counterplay than usual. After 1. RB1? Alekhine drew, 1... RQB7 2. RB1 ch. KKt6 3. KQ5 KKt7 4. RKt1 PR8=Q 5. R×Q K×R, Example 207. The text-move is given by Klein (1934).

1 ... K—B4

White plays and wins

The counter-attack fails, 1... K—Kt6 (or 1... KB6 2. KB3 KK6 3. PB7) 2. K—B3 R—KKt7 3. P—B7 R—Kt8 4. P—B8=Q.

The rook alone cannot halt the pawns, 1... R—QB7 2. KQ5 KK6 3. PQ4 RQ7 4. PB7 R×P ch. 5. KB5 RQ7 6. RQB1 RQB7 ch. 7. R×R PR8=Q 8. PB8=Q.

2 K—B5 R—B7 ch.

181

If 2... K—K3 (2... R×P 3. R×P)
3. R—K1 ch. K—B3 4. P—B7 R×P
5. K—B4 R—Q7 (5... RK6 6. PB8=Q)
6. K—B3.

3 K—Q5	K—B3
4 P—Q4	K—K2
5 R—K1 ch.	K—Q1
6 K—Q6	R—B6

If 6... RK7 7. R×R PR8=Q 8.
PB7 ch.

7 R—QR1	K—K1
8 R—R8 ch.	K—B2
9 R—R8	R—B7
10 P—B7.	

266 Kostić *v.* Reti, Gothenburg,
1920. Colours reversed. The most favourable position for the defender's rook is behind his pawn. White cannot win unless he gets both pawns to the sixth, and not even then with KtP+RP.

1 K—Kt4

A sly move, which entraps his unwary opponent.

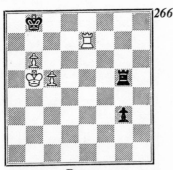

Drawn

1 ...	P—Kt7?

1... R—Kt3 draws by preventing the alignment of White's pawns on the sixth, 2. K—Kt5 R—Kt4 3. K—B6 (if 3. KR6 R×P 4. RK8 ch. RB1, but not 3. PKt7? PKt7 when Black wins) 3... R—Kt1 4. R—Kt7 ch. K—R1 5. R—R7 ch. K—Kt1 6. K—Q6 (6. KKt5 RKt4) 6... R—Kt3 ch. 7. K—Q5 R—Kt4 ch. 8. K—B4 P—Kt7 9. P—B6 R—B4 ch.

2 P—B6	R—Kt1

The mating threats are Black's undoing. If 2... RKt5 ch. 3. KKt5 RKt4 ch. 4. KR6.

3 R—Kt7 ch.	K—B1

If 3... KR1 4. RR7 ch. KKt1 5. PB7 ch. KB1 6. RR8 ch.

4 R—QR7	R—Kt5 ch.
5 K—Kt5	K—Q1
6 R—Q7 ch.	K—K1
7 P—Kt7.	

Black resigns.
Black to play forces an immediate draw by 1... PKt7 2. KR6 R×P.

267 A position from the game Henneberger *v.* Schonmann, Correspondence, 1937-38. Black's rook is powerfully placed behind the pawn, but White wins in a different way, blocking it with his king.

1 ...	P—R6 ch.
2 K—R2	K—Q6
3 P—B5	K—K7
4 P—B6	R—KB8
5 R—K6	

Not 5. K×P? R×P.

5 ...	K—B6
6 P—K4	

And certainly not 6. K×P? RR1 mate.

6 ...	K—Kt5
7 P—K5	R—QR1

White wins

8 P—B7	R—R7 ch.
9 K—Kt1	P—R7 ch.
10 K—R1	K—Kt6
11 R—Kt6 ch.	K—R6
12 R—Kt1	

This ingenious combination is the only way to win.

| 12 ... | P×R=Q ch. |
| 13 K×Q | R—R1 |

If 13... KKt6 14. PB8=Q.

14 K—B2

Not 14. PK6? KKt6, when the mating threats draw.

14 ...	K—Kt5
15 P—K6	R—KB1
16 K—K3	K—B4
17 P—K7.	

White wins.

268 Thomas *v.* Alekhine, Hastings, 1922. Colours reversed. Here Black's pieces are so placed that they halt the advance of the united pawns, and in the following continuation he prevents White's king directly blocking the lone pawn.

1 K—R2

White cannot lose a move. If he moves his rook Black's king takes up a more favourable position blocking the pawns, 1. R—KKt7 (or 1. RR8 KKt2 2. RKKt8 KR3 3. RKt5 RQR6 4. RKt5 KKt2 and now if 5. KB2, then 5... RB6 ch. 6. KK2 RB1 much as in the text) 1... K—Kt4 2. R—Kt5 ch. K—R3 3. R—KB5 (if 3. KB2 RB6 ch., and 4... RB1, which the text-move prevents) 3... R—QR6 (it would not be correct to give up the lone pawn 3... RKt7 ch?. 4. KKt3 RKt6 ch. 5. K×P, for although White's blocked pawns are the comparatively unfavourable RP+KtP he can here manœuvre his king to the aid of his KtP) 4. K—B2 R—QKt6 5. K—K2 R—QR6 6. K—Q2 P—Kt6 7. K—K2 R—R7 ch. 8. K—B1 R—QKt7 9. R—B8 R—QR7 (9... K×P? 10. RR8 ch.) 10. R—R8 ch. K—Kt2 11. R—R7 ch. K—Kt1, with a draw (Cheron).

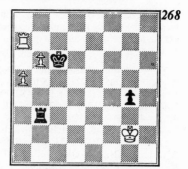

268

White plays and draws
Black plays and loses

| 1 ... | R—R6 ch. |

Forced, but adequate. If Black moves his king, or moves his rook off the QKt file, White wins by PKt7; whilst if the rook temporizes on the QKt file, 1... RKt5? White's king confronts the pawn and wins, 2. KKt3.

| 2 K—Kt1 | R—Kt6 ch. |

Not 2... RQKt6? 2. KKt2, and White has lost a move.

| 3 K—B2 | R—B6 ch. |
| 4 K—K1 | |

To avoid repetition White plays to the K file, where his king is cut off from the pawn. 4. KK2 is no better, 4... RB1 5. PKt7 PKt6 6. RR8 RB7 ch.

| 4 ... | R—B1 |
| 5 R—KKt7 | |

If 5. PKt7 PKt6 6. RR8? PKt7.

5 ...	K—Kt4
6 R—Kt5 ch.	K—R3
7 K—Q2	P—Kt6
8 K—B3	P—Kt7
9 K—Kt4	R—B5 ch.
10 K—B3	R—B4
11 R×P	R×P.

In the game continuation White cannot be prevented from directly blocking Black's pawn, and in consequence he wins:

| 1 ... | P—Kt6 |

There is no way for Black to lose a move. 1... RKt7 ch. 2. KKt3 RKt5

III ROOK ENDINGS

3. KR4 comes to the same thing. If he
moves his king, or if he moves his rook
off the file, then 2. PKt7 wins quickly.

2 K—R3   P—Kt7 ch.

There is nothing better. After 3. K×P
R—Kt7 ch. 4. K—B3 R—Kt6 ch. 5.
K—K4 R—Kt8 6. K—K5 R—K8 ch.
7. K—B6 R—QKt8 8. K—K7 R—KR8
9. R—B7 ch. K—Kt4 10. P—Kt7
R—R1 11. K—Q6 (11. RB8? RR2 ch.)
11... K—R3 12. R—Q7 (12. RB8?
RR3 ch.) 12... R—QKt1 13. K—B6
K—R2 14. P—R6, Example 246,
Thomas resigned.

8. MORE PAWNS: MATERIAL ADVANTAGE

When White has no positional disadvantage a pawn up is not less likely to
win than is the case with other pieces;
but the practical problems are difficult,
and for this reason rook endings are
often said to be drawish, when it would
be more precise to say that they are so
difficult that chances of a draw may well
arise.

The most important of all the positional factors is the situation of the
rooks. There is a vital distinction
between an aggressively posted rook and
one on the defensive. An aggressive rook
is one that is behind a passed pawn; or
one that attacks an unpassed pawn
which has to be defended by a rook; or
one that occupies the seventh rank or an
important open file.

A knight or queen may be badly
placed, but, given time, its position may
be improved; it is less often so with the
rook. Other pieces may retain much of
their power whilst blocking a passed
pawn, but the rook is a poor defender.
A rook controlling the only open file, or
the seventh rank, is an advantage often
worth a pawn.

Examples 269-279 shows how different
positions of the rooks affect the results in
those comparatively simple endings
when there is just one outside passed
pawn.

Examples 280-284 show the kind of
play when there is a pawn-majority; it is
usually possible for the stronger party
to ensure for himself the better rook
position before he permits a simplification, so that when he makes a passed
pawn his rook will be satisfactorily
placed.

Examples 285-287 show some of the
possibilities in cases where the pawns are
on one side of the board, on four or
fewer files, when a pawn up cannot win
unless one also has other advantages—
as is also the case in queen or bishop
endings.

The final example is an amusing
reminder that in rook endings stalemate
is a not uncommon drawing resource.

There are, as usual, other kinds of
positional disadvantage, such as isolated
or doubled pawns, etc., which may
sufficiently counterbalance a material
advantage.

269 Alekhine *v.* Capablanca, 34th
and final match game, Buenos Aires,
1927.

White wins if his passed pawn is on or
beyond the fourth rank with Black's
rook in front of it. The defending rook
is passively placed, and cannot disturb
the White king's advance.

1 R—R4

The first step is to get the rook
actively placed. Unlike the case with the
king, the knight, or the queen, there is
no question of 'centralizing' the rook.
Its best position is determined by the
pawn structure. A rook is not weaker on
the edge of the board but rather it is
stronger so placed, for the checking
distance (when relevant) is then at a
maximum.

The text move is best; but 1. RQ5 does
not jeopardize the win, for Black's rook
is still badly placed in front of the pawn.

1 ...   K—B3
2 K—B3

Next the king advances, via the centre,
with the intention of supporting the
passed pawn.

2 ...	K—K4
3 K—K3	P—R4
4 K—Q3	K—Q4

Black sometimes draws this kind of ending by counter-action on the king's side as in the next example; here this is not possible, and therefore he loses.

5 K—B3	K—B4
6 R—R2	

White makes a tempo-move with his rook.

6 ...	K—Kt4

After this White's king invades the king's side, but if 6... KQ4 7. KKt4 KB3 8. KB4 KQ3 9. KKt5, dislodging Black's rook.

269

White to play

If Black moves his rook the QRP advances.

If Black moves his pawns he weakens them; he cannot win the tempo struggle, for White can make any number of waiting moves with his rook.

7 K—Q4	R—Q3 ch,

The pawn ending is lost after 7... R × P. If 7... K—Kt5 8. R—R1 K—Kt6 9. K—B5 K—Kt7 10. K—Kt5 R—KB3 (10... RK3 11. RQ1) 11. P—R6.

8 K—K5	R—K3 ch.
9 K—B4	K—R3

By thus reversing the roles of his pieces Black frees his rook which, however, cannot in the long run defend the king's side.

10 K—Kt5	R—K4 ch.
11 K—R6	R—KB4

If 11... RK2 12. KKt7 RQ2 13. RR3 RB2 14. PB4 RQ2 15. KB6 RB2 16. PB5 P×P 17. K×P RQ2 18. KB6 RB2 19. RKB3 K×P 20. RB5 ch.

12 K—Kt7

The game took a longer course after 12. PB4.

12 ...	R—B6
13 K—Kt8	

White triangulates, winning at once; but if this resource were not available, there would be other ways of breaking up Black's king's side.

13 ...	R—B4
14 P—B4	R—B3
15 K—B8	R—B4
16 K—Kt7.	

Black is in zugzwang. White wins the KBP and the game.

270 Botvinnik v. Borisenko, U.S.S.R. Championship, 1955. Colours reversed.

Black draws because he brings about some favourable pawn exchanges on the king's side.

1 ...	R—R4

The passed pawn should be stopped as far back as possible.

2 K—Kt4?

Already the decisive error. White can win by 2. K—Kt2.

2... P—B3 3. K—B2 P—R4 (3... PKt4 4. PR5) 4. K—K3 P—Kt4 5. K—Q4 P×P 6. P×P K—B2 7. K—B4 K—K3 8. K—Kt4, and if 8... RKB4 9. PR5.

2... K—Kt2 3. K—B2 K—B3 4. K—K3 P—R4 (4... KK4 5. KQ3 KQ4 6. KB3, Example 269) 5. P—B4 K—B4 6. K—Q4 K—Kt5 7. R—R3 P—B3 8. K—B4 P—Kt4 9. BP×P P×P 10. P×P K×P 11. K—Kt4 R—R1 12. P—R5.

2 ...	P—B3
3 K—B4	

185

If 3. PB4 KB2 4. KB3 KK3 5. KK4
PR4 6. KQ4 PKt4 7. BP×P P×P
8. KB4 KQ3, Black's king is within
reach of the QRP and he may free his
rook, 9. KKt4 RK4 10. RQB2 P×P
11. P×P RK8, with play as in Example
259. But this offers White better chances
than the game continuation.

3 ...   P—Kt4 ch.
4 P×P

Black to play

After 4. KK3 P×P 5. P×P KB2
6. KQ3 KK3 7. KB3 KQ3, Black's king
is in time to stop the QRP, 8. KKt4 RR4
9. RR2 RKB4 10. RR3, and White's
rook is defensively placed.

4 ...   P×P ch.
5 K—K4

Black now gets a passed pawn, and
sufficient counterplay. White's best
chance is 5. K—Kt4 K—Kt2 6. K—R5
K—Kt1 7. K—R6 K—R1 8. P—Kt4
(8. PB4 P×P 9. P×P KKt1 10. PB5
KB2) 8... K—Kt1 9. R—R3 K—R1
10. R—K3 R—R3 ch. 11. K×P.

5 ...   P—R4
6 K—Q4   P—R5
7 P×P   P×P
8 K—K3

White retreats, for if 8. KB4 PR6
9. KKt4 RR4 10. RR2 his rook is
defensively placed, 10... RR5 ch. 11.
KKt5 RR4 ch. 12. KKt6 RR3 ch.
13. KKt7 RR4.

8 ...   P—R6
9 K—B2   R—KKt4
10 K—B1   R—KB4.

A draw was agreed after 11. K—Kt1
(11. RR3 RKKt4) 11...R×P 12. K—R2
R—B2 13. P—R5 R—QR2 14. K×P
K—B2 15. K—Kt4 K—K3.

271 Botvinnik v. Boleslavsky, Moscow, 1941. The passed pawn is a QKtP,
and because it is not so far away (as
compared with the QRP of the preceding
examples), Black's king has some chance
of capturing it and returning in time to
save his pawns. It is also to Black's
advantage that there are fewer pawns on
the king's side, for when White's king
attacks them it will gather a smaller
harvest.

In spite of these factors, and a backward king, White wins.

1 R—QKt1   K—B2
2 P—Kt5   K—K3
3 P—Kt6

By his advance White pins down the
enemy rook.

3 ...   R—B1
4 P—R3

White to play

4. KKt1 KQ4 5. KB2 is a more direct
way of bringing the king into play.

A passed pawn should be advanced,
not as far as is possible, but as far as is
necessary. 4. PKt7? draws, 4... RQKt1
5. KKt1 KQ3 6. KB2 KB2 7. KKt3

R×P 8. R×R ch. K×R 9. KB4 KB3 10. KK5 KQ2.

4 ...	R—QKt1
5 K—R2	K—Q2
6 K—Kt3	K—B3
7 K—Kt4	K—Kt2

If 7... RKt2 White's simplest method is to oppose the kings, 8. KB4 KQ4 9. KK3 KK4, as in Example 269.

8 R—K1	R—KKt1
9 R—K6	K—R3

If 9... KKt1 10. RK7.

10 K—Kt5	K—Kt2
11 P—R4	

Next White breaks through on the king's side.

11 ...	K—R3
12 P—R5	K—Kt2
13 P—Kt4	K—R3
14 K—R4	K—Kt2
15 P—R6	P×P
16 R×P	R—Kt2
17 K—R5.	

After the game continuation 17... KR3 18. RQB6 RK2 19. RB7 RK4 ch. 20. PKt5 K×P 21. R×P, or the alternative 17... RK2 18. PKt5 RKB2 19. RKB6 RK2 20. KR6 RQ2 21. RB8 K×P 22. RKR8 KB3 23. R×P, White wins as Example 219.

272 This position may be compared with Example 269. The game is normally drawn when White's rook is in front of

272

White to play

the passed pawn, and when each player has three or fewer pawns on the other side.

1 P—R6	P—R4
2 K—B3	K—B3
3 K—K4.	

After 3. PR7 White's king cannot profitably advance because of checks on the files; whereas after the text move Black draws by 3... R×P, or by 3... KK3 4. KQ4 KB4 5. KB5 KKt5 6. KKt6 RKt7 ch. (driving the king in front of the pawn) 7. KR7 R×P, and if 8. RQB8 K×P 9. RB4 RQKt7 10. KR8 PB3 11. PR7 PKt4, for in either case he gets sufficient compensation on the king's side.

273 Black sometimes has difficulties with his counter-attack if the pawns are partly or wholly blocked. If his king is exposed he must also guard against White's playing PR7 with the threat of moving the rook and queening the pawn, e.g. if here 1... RR6 2. KQ2 KB2 3. KB2 KK3? then 4. PR7.

1 ...	R—R6

Black's rook must try to curb the activities of White's king, which would be liberated after 1... R—R7 ch? when White wins, 2. K—Q3 R—R6 ch. 3. K—Q4 R×KtP 4. R—QB8 R—QR6 5. R—B7 ch. K—B3 6. P—R7 (White has improved the position of his rook) 6... K—K3 7. K—B5 R—R8 8. K—Kt6 R—Kt8 ch. (8... KQ4 9. RB5 ch. KK5 10. RR5) 9. K—B6 R—QR8 10. K—Kt7 K—Q4 11. R—K7 (cutting off Black's king from the pawns) 11... K—Q3 12. R—K5, and if 12... P—Kt4 13. RP×P P—R5 14. R×P P—R6 15. R—B6 ch. K—Q2 16. R—QR6 R—Kt8 ch. 17. R—Kt6.

·2 K—Q2	

White may indirectly guard his KKtP by 3. PR7, but if he then advances his king it has no shelter from checks.

2 ...	R×KtP
3 R—Kt8	R—QR6

273

Black to play

| 4 R—Kt7 ch. | K—B3 |
| 5 R—Kt6 ch. | |

If 5. PR7 KK3 6. KB2 KQ4 7. KKt2 RR3 8. KKt3 KK5 attacking White's pawns, and if here 8. RK7 KQ3.

| 5 ... | K—Kt2 |
| 6 K—B2 | P—Kt4 |

This sacrifice creates a passed pawn which provides sufficient counterplay. Not 6... RR5? 7. KKt3 R × BP 8. PR7.

7 BP×P	P—B5
8 K—Q2	P—B6
9 R—Kt7 ch.	K—Kt3
10 P—R7	R—R7 ch.
11 K—K1	K—B4.

Either 12. RB7 ch. KKt3 13. R × P R × P 14. RB6 ch. KKt2 15. KB2 RR6 16. RKR6 RQKt6 17. R × P RKt3, or 12. RKKt7 RK7 ch. 13. KB1 RQR7 14. RB7 ch. KKt3 15. RQKt7 KB4 16. RKt7 KKt5, draws.

274 Black's blocked pawns are weak, but he draws because his active rook can curb the White king's activities.

| 1 ... | R—R6 |
| 2 K—B1 | |

After 2.PR7 RR8 3.PB4 P×P e.p.ch. 4. K×P PR5 Black draws quickly, Example 237.

| 2 ... | R—R7 |
| 3 P—R7 | |

If 3. KK1 KR2 4. KQ1 R×P, and Black obtains enough counterplay. After

the text-move White's king advances with the hope of sheltering from the checks by playing to KKt5 or KR4.

3 ...	R—R8 ch.
4 K—K2	R—R7 ch.
5 K—K3	R—R5

White's king must be kept out of KB4.

6 K—Q3	R—R6 ch.
7 K—Q4	R—R4
8 K—B4	R—R5 ch.
9 K—Q5	R—R4 ch.
10 K—K6	R—R7

Not 10... RR3 ch.? 11. K×P RR4 ch. 12. KB4 RR5 ch. 13. KKt5 RR4ch. 14. KR4, and if 14... KR2 15. PR3 RR5 16. P×P P×P 17. KR5 KKt2 18. RKt8 R×P 19. RKt4.

274

Black to play

11 R—K8

If 11. K×P R×P ch. If 11. KK5 RK7 ch.

11 ...	R×RP
12 RK7 ch.	R×R ch.
13 K×R	K—Kt3.

The pawn ending is drawn, 14. KK6 KKt4 15. KB7 PB5 16. KK6 PR5.

275 Unzicker *v.* Lundin, Amsterdam, 1954. All of these examples with the rook in front of the QRP relate closely to Examples 237-240.

1 P—R7

In general this advance should be made only when it gains a clear advantage as here; for now Black's king, which

275

White to play

cannot get to the safe squares KKt2 and KR2, dare not move, else White checks with the rook and queens the pawn.

| 1 ... | R—R7 ch. |

It is a struggle between White's king and Black's rook, and White wins because his king has a safe square at KR6.

2	K—Q3	R—R8
3	K—Q4	R—R4
4	K—B4	R—R6
5	K—B5	R—R8
6	K—Q6	R—R6
7	K—K7	R—R3
8	K—B7	R—R6
9	K—Kt7	R—R8
10	K—R6	R—R3
11	R—QKt8	R×P
12	R—Kt5 ch.	K—K3
13	K×P	R—R1
14	K×P	R—KKt1
15	P—Kt4	R—R1 ch.
16	K—Kt6.	

Black resigns, for if 16... R×P 17. RKt6 ch.

276 Bisguier v. Udovčić, Zagreb, 1955. When each player has four or more pawns on the king's side White has better winning chances. He can make new threats (e.g. a passed KP); his king can more easily find or create safe squares amongst the Black pawns; and it is less likely that all his king's side pawns will be exchanged off.

| 1 | K—R2 | R—R8 |
| 2 | P—Kt4 | |

The alternative is 2. PKt3 followed in due course by PB4.

2 ...	P×P
3	P×P	R—R5
4	P—R7	

This advance, which indirectly secures White's king's side pawns (e.g. 4... R×KP 5. RQKt8), is justified because White's king can find safety at K6 or KB5.

4 ...	R—R7 ch.
5	K—Kt3	R—R6 ch.
6	K—B2	R—R7 ch.
7	K—K3	R—R6 ch.
8	K—Q2	K—Kt3

If 8... PKt3 White makes available his KB5 square by 9. PR5 P×P 10. P×P, when the counter-attack 10... PB4 11. P×P is inadequate.

| 9 | P—R5 ch. | K—Kt4 |
| 10 | P—R6 | |

276

White to play

This forces Black's king to retreat, for either 10... K×RP 11. RR8 ch., or 10... P×P 11. RKt8 ch., loses at once.

10 ...	K—Kt3
11	P×P	K×P
12	K—B2	R—R7 ch.
13	K—Kt3	R—R8
14	K—Kt4	R—R7
15	K—Kt5	

Black's rook cannot prevent White's king reaching KB5, with a decisive attack on the Black pawns.

15 ...	R—Kt7 ch.
16 K—B6	R—QR7
17 K—Q6	R—R3 ch.
18 K—K7	R—R4
19 K—K6	R—R6
20 P—Kt5	P×P
21 K—B5	R—B6 ch.
22 K×KtP.	

Black resigned after 22... RB2 23. RKt8 ch.; if instead 22... RQR6 23. KB5 RR4 24. KK6 KR2 25. KB6, when the KP falls.

277 Lissitzin *v.* Stoliar, Leningrad, 1955. Here White's king cannot easily get at Black's pawns. Instead White makes two 'clearance sacrifices' to open up lines for his rook.

1 K—Q8	K—B2

White threatened 2. KK8.

2 K—Q7	R—R7

If 2... R—R3 3. K—B7 R—R8 (3... KK3 4. KKt7) 4. K—B6.

3 K—B6	K—K3
4 P—K4	P×P

White to play

If 4... RB7 ch. 5. KKt6 RKt7 ch. 6. KB5 RB7 ch. 7. KKt4 RQR7 8. P×P ch. KQ2 9. PQ6 P×P 10. RR8 R×P 11. R×P ch., the familiar skewer.

5 P—Q5 ch.	K—B2
6 P—Q6	

Clearing the seventh rank before Black can play his king to the safe square KKt2.

6 ...	P×P

If 6... PK6 7. PQ7 PK7 8. PQ8=Q PK8=Q 9. QKt8 mate.

7 R—R8	K—K3

If 7... R×P 8. R×P ch.

8 P—R8=Q	R×Q
9 R×R.	

Black resigned after 9... KB4 10. KQ5 PK6 11. KQ4, for if 11... K×P 12. RB8 ch. K×P 13. K×P KKt5 14. KB2 PR4 15. RQ8.

278 Lipnitsky *v.* Smyslov, U.S.S.R. Championship, 1952.

When White's rook is at the side of the pawn, and Black's behind it, a draw is the usual outcome unless the pawn is already on the seventh rank.

1 ...	R—B8 ch.
2 K—K2	R—QR8
3 R—Q4	

Black to play

White chooses this in preference to 3. RQ8 ch. KB2 4. RQR8, Example 272.

3 ...	R—R6
4 K—Q2	

White has only two winning ideas: either his king attacks Black's king's side which is here, and in general, impracticable; or his king moves over to support the passed pawn, and because of Black's better rook position this takes longer than in Example 269, so that meanwhile Black gets sufficient play on the king's side.

190

4 ...   K—B2

Before capturing the KKtP Black improves his king's position.

5 K—B2   K—Kt3
6 K—Kt2   R×KtP
7 P—R5   K—R4

Neatly clearing a square for his rook.

8 P—R6   R—Kt3
9 P—R7

Also after 9. RR4 RKt3 ch. 10. KB3 RKt1 11. PR7 RQR1 Black has enough counterplay on the king's side, 12. KQ4 K×P 13. KK5 KKt5 14. RR1 PKt4 15. RKt1 ch. KB6.

9 ...   R—QR3

White has got his pawn to the seventh, but Black's counterplay is too far advanced. Compare Example 291, and the note to Black's first move, Example 273, for other instances of the pawn on the seventh guarded by the rook on the seventh.

10 R—Q7   P—Kt3
11 R×P ch.   K—Kt5
12 K—Kt3   R—R8
13 K—Kt4   K×P
14 K—Kt5   K—Kt6
15 K—Kt6   P—B5
16 P—R5   P×P
17 R×P.

The draw was agreed after 17... PB6 18. RKt5 ch. KR7 19. RR5 R×R 20. K×R PB7 21. PR8=Q PB8=Q.

279 Szabo *v.* Ivkov, Wageningen, 1957. As in the parallel cases with the White rook in front of the pawn, Black may lose if his king's side pawns are blocked or weak, making counterplay difficult or ineffective.

1 K—B3   R—K8
2 R—K4   R—QR8
3 K—K3   R—R6 ch.
4 K—Q2   R—R7 ch.
5 K—B3

White must sacrifice a pawn if he is to make progress.

White to play

5 ...   R×BP
6 P—R5   R—QR7
7 K—Kt4   K—B4
8 R—B4 ch.   K—K4
9 K—Kt5   R—R6
10 P—R6   R×KtP
11 R—R4   R—Kt1
12 P—R7   R—QR1
13 K—Kt6   P—B4
14 K—Kt7   R×P ch.
15 K×R

White in turn must give up his rook for a pawn, but wins because he is able to retain one pawn on the king's side.

15 ...   P—B5
16 R—R5 ch.   K—K5
17 R×P   P—B4

If 17... PB6 18. RR5 PB7 19. RR1 KB5 20. KKt6.

18 R—Kt5   P—B6
19 R—Kt1   P—B7
20 R—KB1   K—K6
21 P—R5   K—K7
22 R×P ch.   K×R.

There follows 23. PR6 PB5 24. PR7 PB6 25. PR8=Q, Example 307.

280 Tartakower *v.* Balogh, Bartfeld, 1926. When there is no passed pawn White normally has a majority on one wing or the other, and can eventually make a passed pawn.

Deploying the rook is the first and most important thing to do. Not only does White seek the best and most

191

aggressive position for his own rook, but he must also prevent Black's rook from taking an aggressive position. If it were Black's move here, then 1... R—QB1 (or 1... RQ1) followed by playing the rook to the seventh would offer him excellent drawing chances.

1 R—B1

Of one or more open files the remoter is, in general, more important.

1 ...   K—Q3

In preventing the invasion of his second rank (1... RQ1 2. RB7 ch. KK3 3. PKt3) Black is forced to block the queen's file which his rook might otherwise have occupied.

2 P—B4

White next brings his king into play.

2 ...   P—QR4

If 2... RK1 3. RQ1 ch. KB3 4. KB2, when the king's file is not of much use to Black.

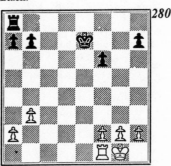

280

White to play

3 K—B2   P—QKt4

Black hopes for pawn exchanges or counterplay on this wing; however, these advances leave the pawns more vulnerable to attack later on.

4 P—QR3

White may now answer 4... PKt5 by 5. PQR4, or 4... PR5 by 5. PQKt4.

4 ...   P—B4
5 K—B3   R—K1
6 R—Q1 ch.

White next makes a passed pawn, first driving Black's king farther away.

6 ...   K—B4

It would be better for Black if his king could oppose the pawn-majority, but after 6... KK2 White exchanges rooks.

7 P—KKt4   P×P ch.
8 K×P   R—Kt1 ch.

Sooner or later, in most cases, the defender's rook obtains active play, and White's task is to delay this for as long as possible. This he has done, and the powerful passed pawn, from which Black's king is cut off, more than outweighs an aggressive advance on the file, for if 8... RK6 or 8... RK7, 9. PB5.

9 K—B3   R—KB1
10 R—Q7   P—R3
11 R—QR7

Another finesse, pushing Black's king farther away.

11 ...   K—Kt3
12 R—K7   K—B4
13 R—K5 ch.   K—B3
14 P—B5   R—B3
15 K—K4   R—B1
16 P—Kt4   P×P
17 P×P   P—R4
18 R—B5 ch.   K—Q3

After 18... KKt3 White's king supports the advance of the KBP, eventually winning the rook for it. Because of this threat Black gives up another pawn.

19 R×P   R—K1 ch.
20 K—Q4   R—K7
21 R—Q5 ch.   K—B2
22 P—B6   R—KB7

If 22... R×P White places his rook behind the KBP, 23. RKB5.

23 K—K5   P—R5
24 K—K6   R×P
25 P—B7.

Black resigns.

281 Najdorf v. Kottnauer, Amsterdam, 1950. In the preceding example the extra pawn was itself a decisive threat. The player with the extra pawn also has

the advantage (as was the case with minor pieces) that he may improve his position by offering an exchange of rooks.

1 R—Q3

White prepares to contest the remoter (QB) file.

1 ...   K—K3

If 1... RQB1 2. RQB3.

2 K—B3

Naturally White brings up his king. It is generally wrong to mobilize the pawns before the pieces, and if White plays indifferently, e.g. 2. PKR4, then Black seizes the QB file 2... RQB1, for if 3. RQB3? R×R 4. P×R KQ4.

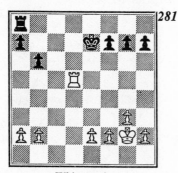

White to play

2 ...   R—QB1

Black's king gets in the way on the central files, as in Example 280. Instead he should play 2... P—Kt3 making a hole for it; and play might continue 3. P—KR4 R—QB1 4. R—B3 R—Q1 5. R—B6 ch. (if 5. RK3 ch. KB3 6. RQ3 RQB1 7. RB3 RQ1 8. RB6 ch. KKt2) 5... K—Q2 6. R—B2 K—K3 7. K—B4, when White may mobilize his majority, or his king may invade the king's side.

3 R—B3   R—Q1
4 R—K3 ch.

A finesse.

4 ...   K—B3

If 4... KB4 5. RK7 RQ7 6. R×P ch. winning another pawn.

5 R—Q3   R—QB1
6 R—B3   R—Q1
7 R—B6 ch.

Not 7. RB7? RQ7 when all the queen's side pawns will most likely be exchanged.

After the text-move Black resigns because of 8. RB7.

282 Konstantinopolsky *v.* Shaposhnikov, Sochi, 1952. When both sides have a wing majority, which implies a more unbalanced pawn structure, White wins more easily; for he can set up two united passed pawns which are much superior to the single passed pawn that Black is likely to obtain on the other wing. Compare Examples 264 to 268.

1 R—QKt5   P—QKt3
2 R—Kt2   K—K3
3 K—Kt2   K—Q4

After 3... P—KKt4 4. K—R3 P—KR4 5. P—B4 K—B3 (5... RB4 6. PQR4 threatening 7. RKt5) 6. R—Kt5 P—Kt5 ch. (6... RB4 7. R×R) 7. K—R4 R—B7 8. R×P R×P ch. 9. K×P R×P 10. P—K4, White wins the race to queen because his pawns are more advanced, and not because they are more numerous.

4 R—Q2 ch.   K—B3

Black plays the king here because it supports the advance of his own majority. If 4... KK5 5. RQ7.

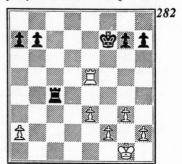

White to play

5 P—B4	P—QR4
6 K—B3	P—QKt4
7 P—B5	P—R5
8 P—K4	R—B8

If 8... PKt5 9. PK5 PKt6 10. P×P P×P 11. PK6 RB7 12. PK7.

9 P—K5	R—K8

If 9... RB8 ch. 10. KK4 RK8 ch. 11. KQ4.

10 R—K2	R—B8 ch.
11 K—Kt4	K—Q2
12 K—Kt5	P—R6

12... PKt5 13. PK6 ch. KK1 14. RQKt2 PR6 15. R×P comes to the same thing.

13 P—K6 ch.	K—K1
14 R—QB2	P—Kt5
15 R—B8 ch.	K—K2
16 R—QR8	

Anticipating the breakthrough sacrifice, PKt6.

16 ...	R—K8
17 R—R4	R—K7

If 17... RK5 18. RR7 ch.

18 R×KtP	R×QRP
19 R—Kt7 ch.	K—B1
20 R—B7 ch.	K—Kt1
21 R—QR7	K—B1
22 P—R4	R—R8
23 P—R5.	

And the threat of PKR6 forced Black's resignation. If 23... PR7 24. PR6 P×P ch. 25. KB6; if 23... PR7 24. PR6 RKKt8 White mates in three; and if 23... PR3 ch. 24. KKt6 PR7 25. PK7 ch. KK1 26. K×P RKB8 27. PB6.

283 Prins v. Stahlberg, Trencianske-Teplice, 1949. The defender may draw if he has a positional advantage, especially that of a better placed rook. Here Black's rook, awkwardly obstructing his pawns, contrasts sadly with White's aggressive rook on the seventh.

1 P—Kt4	

White endeavours to liquidate the queen's side pawns.

1 ...	P—R3

Here (or on the next move) 1... RB5, attempting to improve the rook's position, is to be considered; but it seems doubtful whether Black can win after 2. PKt5 ch. KKt3 3. RKt7 RB3 4. KK4.

2 P—R4	P—Kt4

If 2... PKR4 3. PQ5 ch., or 3. PKt5 ch.

3 R—B6 ch.	K—Q4
4 R×QRP	R—R6 ch.

Black is at a disadvantage inasmuch as his united pawns are RP+KtP. Here a blockade follows 4... P×P 5. R×QRP RK5 ch. 6. KB3 R×P 7. RR1 R×P 8. RR1 RKt3 9. KKt4.

283

White to play

5 K—B2	P×P
6 R×QRP	K×P

Black seems to have no inkling of what is to come; but he cannot avoid the draw by 6... K—K5, because of 7. P—Kt5 R—QKt6 8. P—Q5 ch. K—K4 (8... K×P 9. RR6) 9. P—Q6 R×P 10. P—Q7 R—Kt1 11. R—R6 P—R4 12. R—R5 ch. K—B3 13. R—R6 ch. K—K2 14. R—R5 R—KKt1 15. P—Q8=Q ch.

7 K—Kt2	R—R4

If 7... RR5 8. PKt5 ch., or if the rook moves off the KR file, then 8. RR6.

8 P—Kt5 ch.	K—B4
9 R—KKt4	K×P
10 R—K4.	

A draw was agreed, for Black cannot free his rook.

284 Stahlberg *v.* Keres, Budapest, 1950. The better position of White's king, which threatens to penetrate the holes on the queen's side, largely compensates for the pawn minus. A forced win for Black cannot be demonstrated.

1 ...	K—B2
2 K—B5	R—R1
3 R—Q2	

White prevents Black freeing his rook. Not 3. PQKt4? RQ1 4. R×P RQ4 mate!

284

Black to play

3 ...	R—QB1

Not 3... RQ1? 4. R×R K×R 5. KKt6.

4 R—Q6	K—Kt2 ch.
5 K—Kt4	R—B7

If Black wants to win he must take his chance with this move, which gives the rook active play.

6 P—B4	

Not 6. R—Q7 ch.? K—Kt2 7. R—Q6 ch. (7. R×P PR4 ch. 8. KR3 PKt5 ch. 9. KR4 RR7 mate) 7... R—B3 8. R—Q7 P—R4 ch. 9. KR3 RB2, when Black has freed his queen's side pawns.

6 ...	R×P
7 R—Q7 ch.	K—B3

If 7... KKt3 8. RQ6 ch.

8 R×P	R—K5 ch.

9 K—R5	R—K6
10 K×P	

After 10. KKt4 KKt3 11. R×P PR4 ch. 12. KR3 PR5 Black's united passed pawns lead to a win.

On the sixth move, here, and later on, Keres makes clever use of tactical threats against the White king on the edge of the board, and thus delays the imminent annihilation of his king's side pawns.

10 ...	R×QKtP
11 K—R5	R—Kt7
12 P—R3?	

White overlooks Keres' subtle mating threat. The obvious move, 12. R×P, is now best, and after the scramble for pawns, 12... R×P 13. RK7 RK7 14. KKt4 PR4 15. RKR7 RK5 ch. 16. KB3 RK6 ch. 17. KQ4 R×P 18. R×P, a draw is the probable result.

12. ..	R—K7
13 R—B8	

If 13. R×P RK5, threatening RR5 mate! If 13. KKt4 RK5 ch. 14. KB3 RK6 ch. 15. KQ4 R×P.

13 ...	R—K6
14 P—Kt4	R×P
15 R—B8 ch.	K—Q4
16 R—B7	P—Kt3
17 K×P	R—Kt6 ch.
18 K—R4	R—KB6
19 R×P	R×P ch.
20 K—Kt3	R×P.

White resigned after 21. KB3 KK5 22. KQ2 RKt7 ch. 23. KK1 PKt4 24. KB1 RQR7 25. RKKt7 PKt5.

285 Capablanca *v.* Yates, Hastings, 1930-31. When 3 pawns are opposed by 2 pawns on one side of the board, and there is no passed pawn, the game is normally drawn. To have any winning chances at all White must have a centre pawn as here (and as Examples 286, 287, and 300).

1 ...	R—K8?

This position should be compared with Example 254. Here too Black should not allow White to get his pawns to the fifth rank, but should play 1... P—B3 2. K—Kt2 R—K8 3. K—B3 (3. PK5 P×P 4. R×P R×R 5. P×R PR4) 3... R—B8 ch. 4. K—K3 R—KKt8, with a perpetual attack on White's pawns.

2 P—K5	R—K6 ch.
3 K—Kt2	R—QR6
4 R—B6 ch.	K—Kt2
5 R—QKt6?	

5. RQ6 is correct, and if 5... RR5 6. KB3 RR6 ch. 7. KK4 RR5 ch. 8. R—Q4.

| 5 ... | R—K6? |

In 1957 Kopaiev showed the following draw: 5... RR5 6. KB3 RR6 ch. 7. KK4 RR5 ch. 8. KB5 RB5 9. RKt3 RR5 10. RK3 RR3 11. KK4 RR5 ch. 12. KB3 RR3 13. PB5 KB1 14. RKt3 RR8 15. RKt8 ch. KK2 16. PB6 ch. KK3 17. RK8 ch. KQ4 18. PK6 RR3.

| 6 R—Kt4 | R—QB6 |
| 7 K—B2? | |

White hesitates; and Black could now draw: 7... P—R4! 8. P—Kt5 (8. P×P RKR6) P—R5 9. R—Kt7 K—Kt3 10. R—Kt6 ch. K—Kt2 11. R—KR6 P—R6 12. P—B5 (12. KKt1 RKB6) R—B4 13. P—B6 ch. K—Kt1 14. P—Kt6 P×P 15. R×P ch. K—B2 16. R—Kt7 ch. K—B1 17. R—K7 R—B2 ch. 18. K—Kt1 P—R7 ch. 19. K—R1 R—K7. 7. R—Kt8, as in the game, is correct.

| 7 ... | R—QR6? |
| 8 R—Kt7 | K—Kt1 |

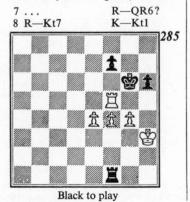

285

Black to play

White threatened PK6. The KBP is, as Reinfeld puts it, the Achilles heel of Black's position.

If 8... KKt3 9. PB5 ch. KKt4 10. R×P K×P 11. PK6.

| 9 R—Kt8 ch. | K—Kt2 |

If 9... KR2 10. PB5 RR4 11. RK8.

| 10 P—B5 | |

White now threatens 11. P—B6 ch. K—Kt3 (11... KR2 12. PK6) 12. R—Kt8 ch. K—R2 13. R—Kt7 ch. winning the KBP.

| 10 ... | R—R7 ch. |

Permitting White's king to advance, but there is nothing better. If 10... KR2 11. PB6 RB6 12. PK6.

11 K—K3	R—R6 ch.
12 K—K4	R—R5 ch.
13 K—Q5	R—R4 ch.

If 13... R×P 14. PB6 ch. KR2 15. RKB8 KKt3 16. RKt8 ch. KB4 17. R×R K×R 18. PK6.

| 14 K—Q6 | R—R3 ch. |
| 15 K—B7 | |

If White's rook were at Q8 he would be able to play 15. KK7 here.

| 15 ... | K—R2 |

If 15... R—R8 (15... RR2 ch. 16. KKt6 RR8 17. PB6 ch.) 16. P—B6 ch. K—R2 17. R—KB8 R—R2 ch. 18. K—Q8 K—Kt3 (18... RKt2 19. KK8) 19. R—Kt8 ch. K—R2 20. R—Kt7 ch. K—R1 21. P—Kt5 P×P 22. K—K8 R—R4 23. R×KtP R—R2 24. P—K6.

| 16 K—Q7 | R—R2 ch. |
| 17 K—Q6 | K—Kt2 |

If Black continues checking White plays his king to KB6.

| 18 R—Q8 | |

See note to White's fifth move. If now 18... RR3 ch. 19. KK7 RR2 ch. 20. RQ7.

18 ...	R—R4
19 P—B6 ch.	K—R2
20 R—KB8	R—R2

21 K—B6	K—Kt3
22 R—Kt8 ch.	K—R2
23 R—Kt7 ch.	K—R1
24 K—Kt6	

White's king now outwits Black's rook. Not at once 24. PK6? because of RR3 ch. 25. KQ7 R×P 26. R×P RR3 with a draw.

24 ...	R—Q2
25 K—B5	R—B2 ch.
26 K—Q6	R—R2
27 P—K6	R—R3 ch.
28 K—K7	R×P ch.
29 K×P	R—K5
30 P—Kt5	P×P
31 K—Kt6.	

Black resigns, for if 31... R—QR5 (31... RK3 32. RK7) 32. R—R7 ch. K—Kt1 33. P—B7 ch. K—B1 34. R—R8 ch.

286 Gligorić v. Euwe, Zurich, 1953. The ending 4 pawns v. 3 pawns should also be drawn under normal circumstances; but Black's king must cover a front four files wide, not always an easy task.

1 P—Kt5

Instead of the text-move White might have played 1. KKt3, with the idea of following with PB3, PK4, and KB4; Black could answer this by 1... P×P 2. R×P PR3 followed by ... PB3, drawing as noted in the preceding example.

1 ...   P×P

Black must prevent White's threatened PR6.

The alternative is 1... PR3, when the double exchange of pawns brings about an easily drawn position.

2 R—R6

White prevents the liberating move, PKR3.

2 ...   R—Kt6

After this Black has a difficult, maybe a lost, game. Instead he should pursue the policy of simplification by 2... R—K2 (2... RKt5 3. PB3) 3. K—Kt3 (3. RR6

RK4 6. R×P KKt3) 3... R—K3 4. R×R (4. RR7 PR3) 4... P×R 5. K—R4 K—Kt3 6. P—B3 P—R3 7. P—B4 P—K4.

3 R—R6	R—R6
4 K—Kt3	R—R8
5 P—K4	

If 5. R×P KKt3.

5 ...	R—Kt8 ch.
6 K—B4	R—KR8
7 P—K5	P—R5 ?

Perhaps this move is the decisive error, for it frees the square KKt4 for White's king, and the advanced RP is doomed. Instead, Black should simply mark time by 7... RR7 8. PB3 RR8 9. KB5 RR7 10. PB4 RR8, and if 11. RQB6 RK8.

8 K—Kt4

In masterly fashion Gligoric now demonstrates the win. First he eliminates the advanced KRP.

8 ...	R—Kt8 ch,
9 K—B5	

The pawn ending is drawn after 9. K×P? RR8 ch. 10. KKt4 R×R 11. P×R ch. K×P 12. KB5 KKt2 13. PB3 PR3 14. PB4 PR4 15. KKt5 PB3 ch.

9 ...	R—KR8
10 P—B4	P—R6

If 10... KKt1 11. KB6 White has mating threats, 11... PR6 12. PB5 PR7 13. RR4.

11 K—Kt4	R—Kt8 ch.
12 K—B3	

12. K×P? draws, 12... RR8 ch. 13. KKt4 R×R 14. P×R ch. K×P 15. PB5 KKt2 16. KKt5 PB3 ch.

12 ...	R—B8 ch.
13 K—Kt3	R—Kt8 ch.
14 K—B2	R—KR8
15 R—KB6	

A tempo-move which forces Black's king to KKt1.

15 ...   R—R8

If 15... KKt1 16. KKt3 KKt2 17. KKt4 KKt1 18. RKR6, as in the text.

286

White to play

| 16 K—Kt3 | R—R8 |
| 17 K—Kt4 | K—Kt1 |

If 17... RR7 18. RKR6.

18. R—KR6   P—R7

Now the pawn ending is lost after 18... R—Kt8 ch. 19. K×P R—R8 ch. 20. K—Kt4 R×R 21. P×R, although White must play carefully after 21... P—B3 22. P×P (either 22. KB5? P×P, or 22. PK6? KB1 23. PB5 draws) 22... K—B1 23. K—B5 K—B2 24. K—K5 K—K1 25. K—K6 K—B1 26. K—Q7 K—B2 27. K—Q8 K—B1 28. P—B7 K×P 29. K—Q7, and White has the horizontal opposition, Example 69.

19 K—Kt3	R—Kt8 ch.
20 K×P	R—Kt5
21 R—KB6	K—Kt2
22 K—R3	R—Kt8
23 K—R4	R—R8 ch.

White now has the following winning plan: he plays his rook to Q7 or QB7 threatening to win the pinned KBP by PK6, and Black must either use his rook to prevent PK6, or retreat his king to the first rank; then White plays PB5 which renews the threat of PK6, and also threatens PB6, with the possibility of mate on the back rank.

White's problem is that he must avoid both perpetual check, and the loss of his advanced pawns, after he has played PB5.

If Black checks on the files White's king shelters at QB8 or Q8, e.g. 23...

R—Kt7 24. K—R5 R—Kt6 25. R—QB6 R—Kt8 26. R—B7 K—B1 (if 26... KKt1 White's king later plays to K7) 27. P—B5, and after the checking series 27... R—R8 ch. 28. K—Kt4 R—Kt8 ch. 29. K—B4 R—B8 ch. 30. K—K4 R—K8 ch. 31. KQ5 RQ8 ch. 32. K—B6 R—B8 ch. 33. K—Q7 R—Q8 ch. White takes cover by 34. K—B8, and if 34... R—Q4 35. P—B6, when the mating threats decide, 35... R×P 36. KQ7 RQ4 ch. 37. KB6 RQ1 38. RQ7 RR1 39. KKt7 RK1 40. KB7, forcing off the rooks and winning the pawn ending.

| 24 K—Kt4 | R—Kt8 ch. |
| 25 K—B5 | R—KB8 |

If Black checks on the ranks, White covers with his rook, e.g. 25... R—QR8 26. R—B6 R—R5 27. R—B7 K—B1 28. K—Kt4 R—R4 (for 28... RR8 29. PB5 see above note) 29. PB5 R—R6 ch. 30. K—K4 R—R5 ch. 31. K—K3 R—R6 ch. 32. K—Q4 R—R5 ch. 33. R—B4, and next advances his KBP, 33... R—R8 34. P—B5 R—KKt8 35. K—Q5 R×P 36. P—B6, and again the mating threats are decisive, 36... KK1 37. KQ6 KQ1 38. RQR4 KB1 39. RR8 ch. KKt2 40. RKB8.

| 26 R—B6 | K—B1 |
| 27 R—B8 ch. | |

Black's rook is ideally placed, for White can neither advance his king (27. KB6 R×P ch.), nor advance his KBP because of the checks on the files (27. KKt4 RKt8 ch.).

27 ...   K—Kt2
28 R—Q8

This tempo-move forces Black's rook to move from its best square (KB1).

28 ...   R—B7

If 28... RQR8 29. RQ7 KB1 30. KB6 RR3 ch. 31. RQ6 RR1 32. PB5 threatening 33. PK6.
If 28... RQR8 29. RQ7 RR3 30. KKt4 KB1 31. PB5.
Finally if 28... PR3(4) 29. P×P ch. K×P 30. RKKt8 KR2 31. RKKt4

cutting off White's king from the KBP, which soon falls.

29 R—Q1   R—B6

After this the checking distance on the files is too short, but if 29... RQR7 30. RQ7, etc.

30 K—K4   R—B7
31 K—K3   R—QR7
32 P—B5

At last White makes this decisive advance.

32 ...   R—KKt7

If 32... RR6 ch. 33. KK4 RR5 ch. 34. RQ4.

33 R—Q7   R×P

If 33... KB1 34. PB6, with mating threats which drive out Black's king, 34... KK1 35. RK7 ch. KB1 36. RB7 KK1 37. RB8 ch. KQ2 38. RB8 KK3 39. RK8 ch. KB4 40. PK6.

34 K—B4   R—Kt8
35 P—K6   R—B8 ch.
36 K—K5   R—K8 ch.
37 K—Q6   P—R4
38 R×P ch.   K—Kt1
39 K—K7.
Black resigns.

287 Botvinnik *v.* Najdorf, Moscow, 1956. White wins because he can force a passed KP, and because of the hole at KKt6.

1 R—R5   R—B2
2 R—Q5   R—R2
3 P—K5   P×P
4 P×P   K—K2

White was threatening 5. RQ7 ch. R×R 6. PK6 ch. with a won pawn ending.

5 P—K6   R—R5

If 5... RR3 6. RQ7 ch. KB1 7. KKt6 R×P ch. 8. KR7, when Black loses both pawns.

6 P—Kt5

Not 6. RQ7 ch. KB1 7. PKt5? RR4 ch.

6 ...   R—R2

The game continued 6... P×P 7. R—Q7 ch. K—B1 8. R—B7 ch. K—Kt1 9. K—Kt6 (Black's doubled pawn protects White's king from checks) 9... P—Kt5 10. P—R6 P×P (if 10... PKt6 11. PR7 ch. KR1 12. RB8 mate, or if 10... RR1 11. P×P PKt6 12. PK7 PKt7 and White mates in 2) 11. P—K7 R—R1 (now if 11... RR3 ch. White interposes the rook) 12. R—B6, and Black resigned, for if 12... RK1 13. RQ6 threatening RQ8.

7 R—K5

White plays the rook behind the passed pawn. He does not relieve the tension by exchanging pawns, for Black's KKtP may yet prove a vulnerable target.

Botwinnik's intended exchange, 7. P×P? P×P, followed by guarding the pawn from the side, 8. R—Kt5 R—B2 9. R—Kt6, draws as shown in a fine analysis by Kopaiev, 9... R—B4 10. K—Kt6 R—K4 (White must be forced to cede the KP as soon as possible, if 10... RKt4 ch.? 11. K×P RKt8 12. KR7 RKt7 13. PR6, etc.) 11. K×P K—B3 12. R—R6 R—KB4, holding the KRP under attack, 13. R—R1 K×P 14. K—Kt6 R—B3 ch. 15. K—Kt7 R—B2 ch. 16. K—Kt8 R—Kt2 17. R—KB1, White prevents Black's playing his king to the KB file, 17... R—Kt4 18. P—R6 R—Kt4 ch. and White must try 19. K—B8 for he draws if his king blocks the RP, 19... R—KR4 20. R—QR1, the pawn can otherwise be protected only by blocking

287

White to play

it with the king, 20... R—B4 ch. 21.
K—K8 R—QKt4 22. R—R6 ch. K—B4
23. P—R7 R—Kt2 24. R—R6 R—Kt1
ch. 25. K—Q7 (25. KK7 RKt2 ch.)
25... R—KR1 26. K—K7 K—Kt4
27. R—R1 K—Kt3, reaching the same
position as after Black's 9th move,
Example 236.

7 ...	P×P

If 7... R—R3 (7... KQ3 8. P×P
P×P 9. KB6) 8. K—Kt6 attacking the
KtP, 8. R×P ch. (8... KB1 9. KR7)
9. R×R ch. K×R, when 10. P×P
draws, but 10. K×P wins.

8 K×P	R—R8

If 8... K—Q3 (8... RR3 9. KKt6, or
8... KB1 9. KKt6 RK2 10. PR6 P×P
11. KB6) 9. K—B5 (9. RK1? RR4 ch.
10. KKt6 KK2) 9... R—R1 10. P—K7
R—K1 11. P—R6 P×P 12. K—B6.

9 K—Kt6	R—KB8

If 9... RKt8 ch. 10. RKt5 RKB8
11. K×P.

10 K×P	R—Kt8 ch.
11 K—R6	R—Kt7
12 R—Kt5	R—KB7
13 K—Kt7	K×P
14 P—R6	R—B2 ch.
15 K—Kt8	R—QR2
16 P—R7.	

And White wins.

288 Cherdev v. Baranov, Moscow,
1949. The greater the positional advan-

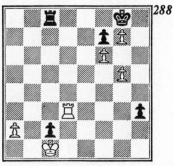

Black to play

tage, the more one is likely to overlook
tactical resources.

1 ...	R—Kt1
2 K×P	

Not 2. P—Kt6? P—R7 3. R—KR3
P—R8=Q ch. (3... RKt8 ch.? 4. K×P
PR8=Q 5. RR8 ch. and White wins)
4. R×Q R—Kt8 ch., and Black wins.

2 ...	P—R7
3 R—KR3	P—R8=Q
4 R×Q	R—Kt7 ch.

5. K×R gives stalemate. If 5. KQ3
RKt6 ch. 6. KK4 RKt5 ch. 7. KB3
RKt6 ch. 8. KKt4 RKt6 ch., but not
8... RKt5 ch.? 9. KR5.

9. MORE PAWNS: POSITIONAL ADVANTAGE

Endings with minor pieces are often
decided by the pawn configuration, as to
whether there is a passed pawn or a pawn
majority. In rook endings these factors
are also important but not so decisive;
such cases, as Examples 289-295, almost
inevitably develop into a race between
rival passed pawns, and to be sure of a
win one needs more than a head start,
although the odds favour the player with
the remote passed pawn, or the farther
wing majority.

In Examples 296 and 297 the pawn
majorities are less significant than the
pawn weaknesses.

The positions of the rooks frequently
determine the result, and this factor is
linked with that of pawn weaknesses, as
in Examples 297-302. A pawn that is
weak is one that can be attacked; and a
pawn that cannot be attacked is not
weak, although it may be isolated, backward, or doubled.

In Example 297 both players have
weak pawns in the formal sense, but
Black's rook is defensively placed, and it
might be said that White's pawns are not
weak because they cannot be effectively
attacked. Whereas in Example 301
White's weak pawns can be attacked,
and his rook must defend them, and thus

9 MORE PAWNS: POSITIONAL ADVANTAGE

his opponent's rook is able to maintain an aggressive position.

The importance of striving for the better rook position cannot be overstressed. There is hardly a parallel in endings with other pieces, excepting perhaps those cases of the bad bishop and the weak colour complex.

A stratagem common to all endings is the making of further points of attack as on moves 6 and 9 of Example 289, or move 5 of Example 299. A stratagem peculiar to rook endings is the advance of a pawn to make a strong point on the file for the rook, as moves 6-8 of Example 293, or move 25 of Example 301.

289 Euwe *v.* Stahlberg, Neuhausen, 1953. Even though White can place his rook behind his powerful QRP, it is doubtful whether he can force a win. When his king moves to support the passed pawn Black in turn makes a dangerous passed pawn on the king's side, and the pawn race is started.

White first places his rook in its best position, and then centralizes his king.

1 R—QR4	K—B1
2 K—Kt2	K—K2
3 K—B3	K—Q2

3... K—K3 4. K—K4 P—R4 5. K—Q4 K—Q2 transposes, but Black must not play 5... PKt4 6. PR6 RR2, permitting an invasion by White's king, 7. KB4 KQ2 8. KKt5 KB2 9. RB4 ch.

4 K—K4	R—R2
5 K—Q5	P—R4
6 P—B4	

White endeavours to create further points of attack, and this pawn establishes a wedge at KB5, fixing Black's KBP as a target.

| 6 ... | R—R3 |

It is a sound principle to stop the passed pawn as far back as possible. As it happens however Black could force a drawn position by making a passed pawn at once, 6... P—B3 7. P—R6 (or 7. RR3 PKt4 8. PB5 PR5 9. P×P P×P 10. KK4 PR6 11. KB3 PQ4 12. KKt3

KQ3 13. K×P KK4) 7... P—Kt4 8. P—B5 P—R5 9. P×P P×P 10. K—K4, White's king is forced back, for an exchange of RPs draws, 10... K—B3 11. K—B4 K—Kt4, gaining time by attacking White's rook, 12. R—R3 R×P 13. R×R, and the pawn ending is drawn.

7 P—K4

The alternative is to move the rook out of reach of Black's king, 7. R—R1, but Black appears to have sufficient resource, 7. P—B3 8. R—R3 (8. PK3 PKt4 9. RR3 PR5 10. P×RP P×RP 11. KK4 KB3 12. KB3 KKt4) 8... P—Kt4 9. P—B5 P—R5 10. P×P P×P 11. K—K4 K—B2 12. K—B4 R—B3, and Black's rook is freed for active service, e.g. 13. PR6 KKt1 14. PK4 KR2 15. RQ3 R×P 16. KKt4 KKt2 17. K×P KB2, or 13. KKt4 RB5 ch. 14. KR5 RK5.

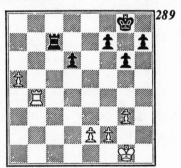

White to play

7 ...	P—B3
8 R—R2	P—Kt4
9 P—B5	P—R5
10 P×P	P×P
11 K—B4	R—R1 ?

Black runs into tactical difficulties through permitting White's QRP to reach the seventh rank (see notes to Black's 13th and 17th moves). The skewer check is a recurrent theme in endings with a passed RP, as already shown in Examples 238, 240, 277, and 287.

11... R—R2 offers excellent drawing chances, 12. P—R6 (if 12. KKt5 RKt2 ch. 13. KR6 RKt5—White's king wants to support his QRP but not to block it) 12... K—B3 13. K—Q4 (13. RR3 PR6 14. R×P R×P 15. RR6 KQ2 16. RR7 ch. KK1 17. KQ5 RR4 ch. 18. K×P RK4) 13... P—R6 14. R—R3 P—R7 15. R—R1 K—Q2 16. K—Q5 P—R8=Q 17. R×Q, and the rook captures the pawn when it is on the sixth rank, 17... R×P, and if 18. R—R7 ch. K—K1 19. K—K6 P—Q4 ch.

| 12 P—R6 | K—B3 |
| 13 P—R7 | P—R6 |

After 13... K—Kt2 14. R—R2 R×P 15. R×P K—B3 16. R—R6 Black's king cannot get back because of the skewer check (16... KQ2 17. RR7 ch.), whilst Black's rook is driven on the defensive after 16... R—KB2 17. R—R8 R—K2 18. K—Q4 R—KB2 19. RKKt8, and he is slowly stifled.

14 K—Q4	K—B2
15 K—Q5	K—Q2
16 R—R3	P—R7
17 R—R1	R—K1

The skewer check again foils Black after 17... P—R8=Q (17... KK2 18. KB6) 18. R×Q R×P 19. R—R7 ch.

18 R—R1	R—K4 ch.
19 K—Q4	R—QR4
20 R×P	K—B3
21 R—R7	R—R5 ch.

After 21... PQ4 the breakthrough sacrifice wins, 22. PK5 RR5 ch. 23. KB3 P×P 24. PB6.

22 K—K3	R—R6 ch.
23 K—B4	R—R8
24 R—B7	K—B4
25 R×P	R×P
26 R—K6	R—R8
27 P—B6	K—B3
28 K—B5	K—Q2
29 R—K7 ch.	K—Q1
30 K—K6.	

Black resigns.

290 Bronstein *v.* Boleslavsky, 7th match game, 1950. Black loses because his king is badly placed. Black's rook is in consequence forced into a passive role, stopping the QRP; whilst White's rook becomes extremely active.

| 1 P—R5 | R—QR2 |

If the rook attempts aggressive action, 1... R—K2 2. R—Q3 R—K8 (2... RK5 3. RQ4), the result is even more calamitous, 3. R—Q8 ch. K—Kt2 4. R—Q7 ch. K—B1 5. P—R6 R—QR8 6. P—R7, threatening RQ8 ch., and if 6... K—K1 7. R—R7, threatening 8. PR8=Q and 9. RR8 ch.

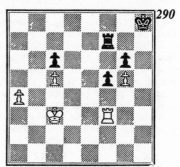

White to play

| 2 K—Kt4 | K—Kt2 |
| 3 R—QR3 | R—R3 |

White was threatening PR6 followed by KR5 and KKt6.

| 4 R—Q3 | |

White now has the open files all to himself.

| 4 ... | K—B2 |

If 4... RR1 5. RQ7 ch. KKt1 6. RQ6.

5 R—Q6	K—Kt2
6 R—Q7 ch.	K—Kt1
7 K—R4	

A subtle clearance of the QKt file.

| 7 ... | K—B1 |
| 8 R—QKt7 | P—B5 |

This unfortunate pawn falls at the first fence, and there is no race, but if

8... RR1 9. RKt6 RB1 10. PR6 KB2
11. KR5 PB5 12. PR7 RQR1 13. KR6.

9 R—Kt4	K—K2
10 R×P	K—K3
11 R—B6 ch.	K—Q4
12 K—Kt4.	

Black resigns.

291 Smyslov v. Goldenov, U.S.S.R. Championship, 1952. A wing majority is not in itself a winning advantage. White's rook is less aggressive than it seems, for Black's king will not be confined to the back rank; whilst Black's rook is not badly placed, for it controls the queen's file, cutting off White's king from his majority.

1 K—B1	P—R4
2 K—K2	P—K4
3 P—QR4	K—R2
4 P—QKt4	K—Kt3
5 P—KR4	

If White makes a passed pawn, 5. P—R5 P×P 6. P×P, he cannot get his rook behind it, and after 6... R—R3 (not 6... RQ5? 7. PR6 RR5 8. PR7 and with the pawn already on the seventh White is ahead, 8... KR3 8. KQ3 PKt4 10. KB3 PB4 11. KKt3 RR8 12. KB4) 7. R—Kt5 K—B4, Black's counter-attack is in full swing. It would be better for White if his KKtP were at Kt2.

With the text-move White delays the start of the pawn race, perhaps hoping for 5... KB4? 5. R×KKtP RQ5 6. PKt4 ch. forcing a passed KRP; but the advance of White's KRP further weakens the king's side.

5 ...	K—R3
6 K—K3	

White is still trying to fix points of attack on the king's side, but this does not prove practicable.

The alternative is 6. P—R5 P×P 7. P×P R—R3 8. R—Kt5.

6 ...	P—Kt4
7 P×P ch.	

If 7. PR5 P×QRP 8. P×RP P×RP 9. RKt6 R×R 10. P×R PR6.

White to play

7 ...	K×P

Not 7... P×P? 8. RK7, and the KP falls.

8 P—R5

The race is started, but Black can now make a passed pawn which is as dangerous as White's.

8 ...	P×P
9 P×P	R—Q5
10 P—R6	R—R5
11 P—R7	P—K5

Not at once 11... PR5? 12. P×P ch. K×P 13. RKt4 ch.

12 R—K7	K—B4

12... PB4 may be played at once.

13 K—Q2

White can make progress only by moving his king to the queen's side.

13 ...	K—Kt4
14 K—B3	P—B4
15 K—Kt3	R—R8
16 K—B4	P—R5
17 P×P ch.	K×P
18 R—KKt7	K—R4

Black's play is too slow. He should make a passed pawn by 18... PB5 19. KQ4 RR5 ch. 20. KB5 PK6 21. P×P P×P, and if 22. RK7 PK7 23. KKt6 RKt5 ch. 24. KR5 RKt7.

19 K—Kt5	K—R3?

The decisive error. 19... PB5 20. RK7 PK6 21. P×P P×P 22. KKt6 RKt8 ch. 23. KB7 RQR8 24. KKt8 RKt8 ch. draws.

20 R—QB7   K—Kt4

If 20... PB5 21. RB6 ch. and 22. RQR6.

21 K—Kt6   K—B5

If 21... KKt5 22. RB5 R×P 23. K×R PB5 24. RB3.

22 R—B5.

Black resigns because there is no answer to White's threat of RQR5.

292 Alekhine v. Euwe, 27th Match game, 1935. Besides his pawn-majority White has three very small advantages: his king is nearer the centre; he has the move; Black has a doubled pawn. Lacking any one of these the game is drawn, e.g. with a Black pawn at KR3 instead of KKt3 Black could mobilize his own majority more quickly.

1 R—Q7   R—QB1

Black makes active play for his rook. 1... RQR1 would be hopeless.

The alternative 1... PR4 also loses, 2. P×P P×P 3. KK3 RKt1 (seizing the remote open file) 4. RR7 RKt7 5. R×RP R×KtP 6. RR8 ch. KR2 7. PQR4 R×P 8. PR5 RR7 9. PR6, and if Black now had a KRP he would probably draw, but after 9... PKt4 10. PQB4 White wins the queening race.

2 R×RP   R×P
3 R—R8 ch.?

White wastes a check. Instead he can win by sacrificing his king's side pawns, 3. KK2 RB7 ch. 4. KQ3 R×KtP 5. KB4 R×KRP 6. KKt5 PKt4 7. K×P RR6 8. PKt5 R×P 9. KB5 PKt5 10. PKt6 PKt6 7. PKt7, and White queens with check; because of the doubled pawn it takes Black longer to make a passed pawn.

3 ...   K—R2
4 P—QR4

Relatively best, for the correct reply is difficult to find.

After 4. K—K2 R—B7 ch. 5. K—Q3 R×KtP 6. K—B4 R×KRP 7. K—Kt5 P—Kt4 8. K×P R—R6 9. P—Kt5

R×P 10. K—B6 P—Kt5 11. P—Kt6 P—Kt6 12. R—R8 ch. K—Kt3 13. R—R1 R—B7, there is a number of critical variations, but in them all Black holds his own.

4 ...   R—Kt6?

After 4... RB7 ch.? 5. KK3 R×P 6. RR6 RR7 7. KQ4 White wins.

A fine analysis by Grigoriev and Dr. Lasker shows that Black can make sufficient counterplay with his pawn majority, 4... P—K4 5. P—Kt5 (5. KK2 PB4 6. KQ2 RB5 7. PKt5 PK5, or 5. PKt4 PKKt4 6. PKt5 PKt3 7. RR6 RR6 8. KK2 PB4 9. KQ2 PK5) 5... P—B4 6. R—K8 (to prevent ... PK5)

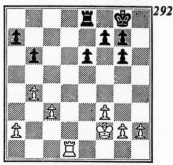

White to play

6... R—B5 7. R×P R×P 8. R—K6 R—R7 ch. 9. K—Kt3 P—Kt4 10. R×P R—Kt7 (cp. Examples 272-275) 11. R—Kt8 K—Kt3 12. P—Kt6 K—B3 13. P—Kt7 K—Kt3 14. P—B4 R—Kt6 ch. 15. K—B2 P×P 16. P—R4 K—R2 17. P—R5 P—Kt4 18. P×P e.p. ch. K—Kt2 19. K—K2. White can win the remaining Black pawns, but the position is a book draw, Example 241.

5 P—Kt5	P—Kt4
6 K—K2	P—K4
7 K—Q2	P—B3
8 K—B2	R—Kt5
9 K—B3	R—Q5
10 R—R6	K—Kt3
11 R×P	R×P
12 R—R6	R—Q5
13 P—Kt6.	

Black resigns, for his rook is lost for the QKtP after 13... RQ8 14. RR2, or 13... RQ1 14. KB4.

293 Fuster *v.* Bronstein, Moscow-Budapest match, 1949. Here White's doubled pawn completely cripples his pawn-majority. In effect Black is a pawn up, and having no weaknesses he therefore wins. His task is all the easier because his rook can occupy the remote open file.

1 ...	R—Kt1
2 R—Q2	K—B1
3 K—K2	K—K2
4 K—Q3	P—QB4
5 K—B2	K—Q3
6 R—K2	P—QR4

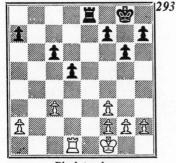

293

Black to play

Having centralized his pieces Black next prepares a point of entry on the QKt file for his rook.

7 K—B1

If 7. PQR3 PR5 followed by ... RKt6. If 7. PQR4 PQ5 8. PQB4 RKt5.

7 ...	P—R5
8 R—Q2	

The pawn ending is an easy win after 8. RKt2 R×R 9. K×R PB5, for if 10. KR3 PQ5 11. P×P PB6.

8 ...	P—R6
9 P—QB4	

White tries to block the position.

9 ...	P—Q5
10 K—B2	P—Kt4

Black could exchange rooks by 10... RKt7 ch., but this leaves no king-entry. In any event there is no good reason why he should ease the pressure, as White cannot attempt anything.

11 K—Q3	P—B4
12 K—B2	P—R4
13 K—Q3	P—R5
14 P—R3	R—Kt8
15 P—Kt4	

Desperation!

15 ...   R—QB8

Threatening RB6 ch. followed by R×QBP, making a pair of united passed pawns.

16 P×P	K—K4
17 R—B2	R×R
18 K×R	K×P
19 K—Q3	K—B5
20 K—K2	P—Q6 ch.

White resigns.

294 Barcza *v.* Smyslov, Moscow, 1956. Besides his pawn majority White has three advantages: his king is nearer the centre; his rook is better placed than in Example 291, for here White has good chances of getting the rook in its best position behind the passed pawn which he creates on the queen's side; Black's king's side pawns are rather weak, a factor which counts for little as in any event White is several lengths ahead in the queening race.

1 K—K3

Not 1. RB7? RQ7 2. R×RP R×P 3. PQR4 RR7 and Black draws, Example 272 et seq.

1 ...	R—Q4
2 P—QKt4	K—Kt2

If Black attempts to defend as in Example 291, 2... P—K4 3. P—QR4 P—QR3 (so that if 3. RB6? RQ5), then White places his rook behind the KtP, 4. R—B3 P—B4 5. R—Kt3 R—Q3 6. P—Kt5 P×P 7. P×P R—QKt3 8. K—Q3.

If 2... PQR4 3. RB5.

3 P—QR4	P—K4
4 P—Kt5	R—Q1

If 4... R—Q2 (preventing 5. RB7) 5. P—R5 R—Kt2, and again White places his rook behind the pawns, 6. R—Kt4.

5 R—B7	P—R3
6 P×P	R—Q5
7 P—R7	R×P

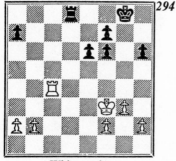
294

White to play

Black has defended so that White's rook is on the side of the pawn, which is however already on the seventh. In the event Black loses because his counter-attack is too slow.

8 K—Q3

White's king begins its customary trek, to support his passed pawn.

8 ...	P—B4
9 K—B3	K—B3
10 K—Kt3	R—R8
11 K—Kt4	K—Kt4

Black's king must keep off the open ranks, if 11... KK3 12. KKt5 KQ3 13. RB6 ch. KQ4 14. RR6, when follows 14... RKt8 ch. 15. KR5 KB4 16. RB6 ch. KQ4 17. RB8, or here 16... KQ5 17. KR6.

12 K—Kt5	K—R4

Here too if 12... KKt5 13. RB4 ch. and 14. RQR4.

13. K—Kt6.

Black resigns.

The result in most of these examples

with pawn majorities generally depends on whether the player with the outside majority, here White, can get his king over to help his passed pawn before his opponent can develop dangerous counterplay on the other wing.

295 Averbach v. Stahlberg, Salts-jobaden, 1952. When rival groups of passed pawns already exist a hectic race ensues. The advantage tends to lie with the player having the outside majority, here White, because his king can obstruct Black's pawns. On the other hand, Black's united passed pawns may assist in weaving a mating net for White's king. A parallel case with knights is Example 165.

1 ...	R—Q2

The rook seeks active play; anything else loses miserably.

2 R×RP?

White expects to win quickly, under-estimating Black's resources. Instead he should play 2. R×BP, at once bringing his rook into play, 2... R—Q6 ch. (2... RQ7 3. PK5 R×P 4. RB7 ch. KR3 5. RB7) 3. K—Kt4 P—B6 4. K×P P—B7 5. R×P ch. K—R2 6. R—KB6.

2 ...	R—Q6 ch.
3 K—K2	

Already White has no more than a draw. If 3. K—Kt4 (3. KB2 RQ7 ch. 4. KKt1 RQ8 ch. 5. KB2) 3... P—B6 4. K—Kt3 P—Kt5 5. R×P (5. PR3 PB7 ch. 6. K×BP P×P 7. R×P PKt4 8. RB7 ch. KR3 9. RB8 KKt2 10. RB7 ch.) 5... R—Q7 6. K×P (not 6. PK5? RKt7 ch. 7. KR4 PB7 8. RB6 KR3 9. PR3 PB8=Q 10. R×Q PKt4 mate) 6... P—B7 7. R—B7 ch. K—Kt1 8. R—B8 ch. with perpetual check.

3 ...	R—KR6
4 P—Kt5	R×P ch.
5 K—Q3	R—R6 ch.
6 K—Q4	

White is still trying to win, else he would take the draw by 6. KK2 RR7 ch. 7. KQ3.

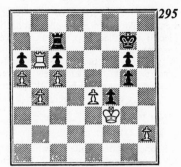

295

Black to play

6 ...	P—Kt5
7 R—R7 ch.?	

Driving Black's king to a better position.

After 7. P×P P—Kt6 8. P—B7 R—R1 (8... PKt7 9. PB8=Q) 9. R—Kt6 R—QB1 10. P—R6 P—Kt7 11. R—Kt1 R×P White's king is able to block the enemy pawns, 12. P—K5 (12. RQR1? RQ2 ch.) 12... P—Kt4 13. R—Kt1 P—B6 14. K—K3 P—Kt5 15. K—B2, and if 15... R×P 16. RQR1.

7 ...	K—B3
8 P—K5 ch.	

After this Black's king supports his own pawns; but if 8. P×P P—Kt6 9. P—B7 R—R1 10. R—Kt7 R—QB1 11. P—R6 P—Kt7 12. R—Kt1 R×P White's king cannot get back in time, for if 13. PK5 ch. KB4, or if 13. RKt1 RQ2 ch., whilst if 13. KQ3 KKt4 14. RKt1 PB6 15. KK3 KKt5 16. KB2 R×P 17. RQR1 RB7 ch. 18. KKt1 KKt6, with threats of mate.

8 ...	K—Kt4
9 P×P	P—Kt6
10 P—B7	R—R1
11 R—Kt7	P—Kt7
12 R—Kt1	K—Kt5
13 P—R6	P—B6
14 P—R7	P—B7
15 P—R8=Q	R×Q
16 R—Kt8	R×R
17 P×R=Q	P—B8=Q

White resigns, for Black gets another queen after 18. QB8 ch. KKt6.

296 Najdorf v. Bronstein, Budapest, 1950. Black has three advantages: White's advanced pawns are weak; Black's rook, aggressively poised, can attack them; after breaking up the centre Black wins because of his outside passed pawn.

1 ...	R—Q7
2 P—Q6 ch.	K—K3
3 R—B4	

If 3. RB6 ch. K×P 4. R×BP R×P.

3 ...	R—Q4

Not, of course, 3... K×P? 4. R×P ch. K×P when the pawns are reduced to one side of the board.

4 R—K4	P—B3
5 P×P ch.	K×BP
6 P—Kt4	

Naturally White tries to exchange off as many pawns as he can.

6 ...	R×P
7 P×P	P×P
8 R—QB4	R—Q4

The ending is won because Black's pawns, both guarded by his rook, cannot be effectively attacked, whilst White's rook must soon accept a defensive role.

9 K—K2	K—K3

The standard procedure—Black's king supports his passed pawn.

10 K—K3	K—Q3
11 R—QR4	K—B3
12 R—R1	

296

Black to play

If 12. KK4 RQ8, threatening 13...
KKt4 and 14... RQ5 ch.

12 ...   R—Q5
13 R—R1

As so often happens, the weaker party
is forced to accept the defensive rook
position.

13 ...   K—Q4
14 K—K2   P—B5
15 K—K3   K—B4
16 R—R2   P—B6
17 R—R2

Clearly White must free his rook, else
Black's BP cannot be stopped.

17 ...   R×P
18 R—R8   R—R6 ch.
19 K—K2   K—B5
20 K—Q1   R—R8 ch.
21 K—B2   R—R7 ch.
22 K—B1   P—R5
23 R—B8 ch.   K—Q5
24 R—Q8 ch.   K—K5
25 R—K8 ch.

If 25. RQB8 RR8 ch. 26. KB2 PR6
27. R×P PR7 28. RKR3 RR8 followed
by the familiar skewer check.

25 ...   K—B6
26 R—B8 ch.   K—Kt6
27 R—B8   R—KB7.

White wanted to be shown, and
resigned after 28. R×P ch. KKt7 29.
KQ1 PR6 30. RB8 PR7 31. RKt8 ch.
KB8 32. RKR8 KKt8 33. KK1 RKKt7.

297 Botvinnik *v.* Smyslov, 14th
match game, 1958. The pawn majorities,
which are under restraint, do not play a
significant part. White has some but not
a winning advantage. His rook can attack
Black's pawns, notably the KRP, which
may be attacked on the file from KR8,
or on the rank from Q4.

The position of the diagram shows the
following points of attack: Black's
pawns at KR5 and KB4 (isolated), at
QB2 (base of chain), and at QR3 (tem-
porary); White's pawns at QR4, QB4,
and KR3 (isolated), and at KB2 (base
of chain).

What makes some of the pawns
weaker than others is the position of the
pieces; and Black's pawns are weaker
because, and only because, White's rook
is aggressively placed. Reciprocally,
Black's rook is defensively placed
because it must guard his 'weak' pawns.

1 R—KR8   K—Kt4

Not 1... PKt4? 2. RR6 ch.

2 K—Q4

Sooner or later White can win Black's
KRP, as he could here, by 2. PB4 ch.
KKt3 3. R×P; but as matters stand
Black replies 3... PKt4 with active
counterplay.

White's strategy here, and in all such
positions, is to maintain and increase the
pressure, and to curb or prevent
attempts by Black to get freedom for his
rook.

2 ...   R—B4

Almost the only hope of freedom for
Black's rook is to play to QR4 with
attack on White's QRP—

3 R—R7

—and White therefore holds Black's
rook to the defence of his QBP. If 3.
PB4 ch. KKt3 4. R×P RR4, and Black's
rook becomes active, 5. RR8 R×P
6. RQB8 PB4 ch. 7. KQ5 RR6.

3 ...   K—Kt3?

Probably the decisive error.

Instead he should play 3... R—B3
4. R—Q7 (4. PB4 ch. KKt3 5. R×RP
RB4 6. RR8 RR4, or 6. KB3 PKt4, with
counterplay) 4... K—B3 5. R—Q5
K—K3 6. K—B3 (threatening 7. RQ4)
6... R—Q3. At this particular moment
Black could offer an exchange of rooks
because he could draw the pawn ending;
and if White avoided this exchange,
Black's rook would get active play.

4 R—Q7   K—B3
5 R—Q5

For the time being White's rook prevents Black's playing either P—Kt4 or
R—B4—QR4.

5 ...   R—B3

Now 5... R×R ch. leads to a lost pawn ending.

| 6 K—B3 | R—K3 |

5... RQ3 7. R×R P×R also loses; and if 5... KK3 6. RQ4.

7 R—Q4	K—Kt4
8 R—Q7	R—QB3
9 K—Kt4	

This move anticipates the Black counterthreats of P—Kt4 and R—QB4 —QR4.

| 9 ... | K—B3 |

If 9... R—B4 10. R—Q8 K—B3 11. R—KR8 K—Kt4 12. R—QR8, a manœuvre which, by inducing Black to advance the QRP deprives him of counterplay on this wing, 12... PR4 ch. 13. K—B3 R—B3 14. R—QB8, and White wins a pawn, 14... KKt3 15. RKR8 KKt4 16. RR7 RB4 18. PB4 ch. KKt3 19. R×RP, or 14... RB4 15. RKt8 ch. KB3 16. RKR8 KKt4 17. PB4 ch.

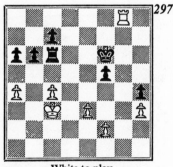

297

White to play

10 R—Q4	K—Kt4
11 R—Q8	R—K3
12 R—QB8	P—B5

When both players have weak pawns it is often possible for the defender to sacrifice a pawn so as to get his rook into play, when he may exploit his opponent's weaknesses.

Here this plan is insufficient, although it offers practical chances. The alternative is 12... RK2, to which White replies

13. KB3; he then threatens RQR8 forcing the Black QRP to advance, and follows this by a re-centralization of his rook and king.

| 13 P×P ch. | |

Not 13. RKt8 ch.? KB4 14. RB8 ch. RB3 15. PK4 ch. KK4 16. R×R, for the pawn ending is drawn.

13 ...	K×P
14 R×P	K—B6
15 R—KR7	R—K5
16 R—R6	P—Kt4

After 16... KKt7 17. R×KtP K×RP 18. R×P White may, in due course, give up his rook for Black's KRP, and win as Example 211.

17 P×P?

Pawn exchanges are imminent, and the result depends on the kind of basic ending which comes about. It is a matter of knowledge rather than judgment. It so happens White wins by 17. R×QRP P×BP (17... P×RP 18. R×P K×P 19. RR3) 18. R—QB6 P—B6 ch. 19. K—Kt3 K×P 20. R×P, e.g. 20... KKt7 21. PR5 RK4 22. KKt4 RK5 ch. 23. KB5 RK4 ch. 24. KKt6 RK3 ch. 25. KB7 RK4 26. RR3, placing the rook behind the pawn, 26... RR4 27. PR6 RR2 ch. 28. KQ6 RR3 ch. 29. KK5 RR1 30. PR7 RR1 31. KQ6 KR7 32. KB6 P×P 33. R×R K×P, and now the rook confines Black's king, a method possible only against a RP (compare Example 202), 34. RKKt7 KR7 35. KQ5 PR6 36. KK4 KR8 37. KB3 PR7, and White can win by 38. KKt3, or mate in 2 by 38. RQR7.

| 17 ... | P×P |
| 18 R—B6 ch. | |

This drives Black's king where it wants to go, but is White's best chance, for 18. K×P K×P draws fairly quickly.

| 18 ... | K—Kt7 |
| 19 K×P | R—K7? |

Black advances his rook and threatens checks on the files. He also hopes to bring pressure on the KBP, but in fact that very pawn obstructs the rook from carrying out an interesting drawing manœuvre.

19... R—K8 is correct, 20. P—B5 K×P 21. R—B4 R—Kt8 ch. 22. K—R6 (22. RKt4 R×R ch. 23. K×R KKt7 24. PB6 K×P) 22... R—R8 ch. 23. K—Kt6 R—Kt8 ch. 24. K—B7 R—KR8, protecting the KRP, and freeing the king, after which the advanced KRP ensures the draw.

20 P—B5   R—Kt7 ch,

Now if 20... K×P 21. RB4 RKt7 ch. 22. KR6 RR7 ch. 23. KKt7 RKt7 ch. 24. KB7 RKt8, and Black has lost a decisive tempo, 25. PB6 RKR8 26. KQ6, and White wins.

21 K—R6   R—R7 ch.
22 K—Kt7   R—Kt7 ch.
23 R—Kt6   R—B7

If 23... R×P 24. RKt3 RB6 25. R×R.

24 P—B6   K×RP
25 P—B7   K—Kt7

If 25... KKt5 26. PB8=Q ch. R×Q 27. K×R KB6 28. RKR6.

26 P—B4.
Black resigns.

298 Chekover *v.* Budo, U.S.S.R. Championship, Tiflis, 1937. A case of the aggressive rook and the weak pawn. Black consistently strives to win the isolated QP.

1 ...   R—Kt5
2 R—Q2   K—K2
3 K—K3   K—B3
4 P—B4   K—B4
5 K—B3   P—KR4
6 P—Kt3

This gives Black a new point of attack, which he immediately exploits. The alternative is 6. P—KR3 when Black plays 6... P—KKt4, attempting to free the square K4, so that he may attack the QP with his king, and if 7. P×P K×P, or if 7. PKt4 ch. P×P ch. 8. P×P ch. KB3 9. PB5 RB5 ch. 10. KKt3 RQ5.

6 ...   P—R4
7 R—Q3

If White attempts counterplay by 7. RK2 PQR5 8. P×P R×P 9. RK7, Black plays 9... RR6 ch.

7 ...   P—QR5
8 P×P   R×P
9 P—QR3

Now White has two weak pawns instead of one.

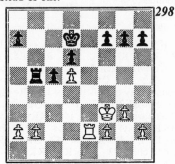
298

Black to play

9 ...   P—Kt4
10 P×P   K×P
11 K—K2   K—B4
12 K—Q2

If 12. RB3 ch. KK5 13. R×P R×P —Black is always ahead.

12 ...   K—K5
13 K—B2   P—B5
14 R—QB3   K×P
15 R—B3   K—B3
16 K—Kt2   R—R2
17 R—B5   P—Q4
18 R×RP

White has avoided loss of material, but Black's united passed pawns win easily.

18 ...   R—Kt2 ch.
19 K—B2   R—Kt6
20 R—R6 ch.   K—B4
21 R—R6

If 21. RKB6 R×RP 22. R×P RR7 ch.

21 ...   R—KB6
22 P—KR4   R×KtP

9 MORE PAWNS: POSITIONAL ADVANTAGE

22... KQ5 is also good.

| 23 | P—R5 | R—R6 |
| 24 | P—R6 | P—B3. |

An amusing touch. After 25. R×P R×QRP 26. RB8 RR6 27. RKR8 KQ5 28. PR7 RR7 ch. Black wins as Example 264.

299 Kotov v. Pachman, Venice, 1950. White's isolated pawn at QB5 seems to be in much the same predicament as the White pawn at Q5 in the preceding example; but the positions of the rooks alter the situation entirely, and it is White's active rook that decides matters.

1 ...		K—Q2
2	R—KR8	K—K3
3	R—Q8	K—K2

White next forces an entry for his king. Black could not prevent this for if 3... KK4 4. RK8 mate! And if 3... RQB2 4. RQ6 ch. KK4 5. KK2 PKt4 (White was again threatening mate) 6. P×P P×P 7. KQ3 RB1 8. RQ7 PR3 9. RQ6, winning a pawn.

| 4 | R—Q6 | R—R3 |
| 5 | P—Kt5 | |

Not only freeing K5 for his king, but fixing Black's KRP as a backward pawn. The creation of more points of attack is of course the prerogative of the player with the initiative—and is in fact an important part of the winning method.

299

Black to play

5 ...		P×P
6	P×P	K—B2
7	K—Kt3	

White advances with caution, for if 7. KB4 RR5 ch. 8. KK5? RK5 mate.

7 ...		K—K2
8	P—B3	R—R6
9	K—B4	R—R5 ch.
10	K—K5	R—R6

Black must find play for his rook, or be crushed. If 10... RR3 11. RK6 ch. KQ2 12. KB6.

| 11 | R×BP | R×P ch. |
| 12 | K×P | R—Q6 ch. |

If 12... R×P 13. RB7 ch. KK1 14. R×P RB4 ch. 15. KK6, threatening mate, 15... KQ1 16. KQ6 KB1 17. PB6.

13	K—K4	R—B6
14	P—B4	R—B8
15	R—B7 ch.	K—Q1

Black also loses the king's side pawns after 15... KK3.

| 16 | R×P | R×P |
| 17 | R—KB7 | |

Black resigns, for if 17... RB3 18. RB6 R×R 19. P×R KK1 20. KQ5 KB2 21. KK5 KB1 22. KK6 KK1 23. PB7 ch. KB1 24. KB6 PKt4 25. K×P.

300 Lyskov v. Selesniev, Moscow, 1956. Another case where Black can assume the aggressive rook position because White must defend his weak QP with a rook.

1	R—B8	R—Q6
2	R—Q8	P—B4 ch.
3	K—R3	R—Q7
4	R—QR8	

White cannot avoid losing a pawn, but the ending three pawns against two pawns on the same side of the board is usually drawn. In the event Black has winning chances because he can exchange his KtP for White's KBP, thus getting a passed centre pawn (compare Examples 285 to 287).

211

It is better to leave Black with dis-connected pawns, 4. P—Kt4 (not 4. KR4? when he is mated in 2; whilst if 4. RQ7 KK1) 4... R—Q6 ch. 5. K—R4 R—KB6 6. P×P R×P ch. 7. K—Kt3 R×P 8. P—Q6 P—K3 9. K—Kt4 R—Q4 10. K—B4 P—Kt4 ch. 11. K—Kt4, and Black cannot make pro-gress, e.g. 11... KKt2 12. KR5, or 11... RQR4 13. RQKt8 threatening PQ7, or 11... KKt3 12. RKt8 ch.

4 ...	R×P
5 R—R6	R—Q5
6 R—Kt6	

White cannot prevent the impending exchange. If 6. KR4? RQ8 7. KKt5 RKKt8 8. RR3 RKR8, threatening mate, and winning both pawns after 8. PKt4 RKKt8

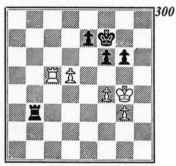

300

White to play

6 ...	P—Kt4
7 P×P	R—KKt5
8 K—Kt2	R×P
9 K—B3	R—Kt5
10 R—QR6	P—K3
11 R—Kt6	R—QR5
12 R—Kt3	K—B3
13 K—K3	P—K4
14 R—Kt3	K—Kt4
15 R—Kt8	

Now that the pawns are advancing, White moves his rook to the rear for checks on the files.

15 ...	R—R6 ch.
16 K—Kt2	

The wrong plan. White should block the passed pawn with his king, and guard the KtP with his rook. After 16. KB2 PK5 17. RKt8 ch. Black cannot success-fully attack the KtP, neither can his king enter on the king's side.

16 ...	P—K5
17 R—KB8?	

This should lose. 17. RKt8 ch. is correct, 17... K—B3 18. K—B2 K—K4 19. K—K2 R—R7 ch. 20. K—K3 R—KKt7 21. R—K8 ch. (21. RKt5? R×P ch.) 21... K—Q4 22. R—KKt8.

17 ...	R—R7 ch.
18 K—R3	

If 18. KB1 KKt5.

18 ...	P—K6
19 P—Kt4	

White ingeniously breaks up Black's pawns. If 19. R—K8 P—K7 20. R—K3 White gets into zugzwang, 20... K—B3 21. R—K8 R—Kt7, for if 22. RK3 PB5 23. P×P RKt6, or if 22. KR4 PK8=Q 23. R×Q RR7 mate.

19 ...	P×P ch.?

This draws because White's king blocks the KKtP, and Black's king cannot assist the KP.

Instead Black wins by 19... KB5 stealing through to the aid of his KP, (19... PB5? 20. RB5 ch.) 20. R×P ch. K—K5 21. R—B8 (21. KKt3 RR8, or 21. RB1 PK7 22. RK1 KB6 23. KR4 KB7) 21... P—K7 22. R—K8 ch. (22. PKt5 RR4 threatening RK4) 22... K—B6 23. R—B8 ch. (23. PKt5 RR5) 23... K—K6 24. R—K8 ch. K—B7 25. R—B8 ch. K—Kt8 26. R—K8 R—R6 ch. 27. K—R4 K—B7 28. R×P ch. K×R.

20 K—Kt3	R—K7
21 R—K8	R—K8
22 R—K5 ch.	K—B3
23 R—K8	K—B4
24 R—K7	R—Kt8 ch.
25 K—R2.	

The game continued oddly 25... RKB8 26. RB7 ch. KK5 27. R×R PK7 28. RQR1 KK6 29. KKt2 KQ7, and a draw was agreed, for if 30. KB2 PKt6 ch.

301 Smyslov *v.* Keres, Leningrad, 1941. White's weak QP, and vulnerable KRP and QKtP are his undoing. Needless to say Black has, or soon will have, the aggressive rook position.

1 ...   R—QKt4

This fixes Black's rook on the second rank, where it potters about for the rest of the game.

2 R—K2	R—Kt6
3 K—B2	K—B3
4 K—K1	P—R3

This waiting move leaves White in zugzwang, for if 5. KQ1 RQ6 ch., or if 5. KB2 RQ6 6. RK4 RK7 ch.

5 R—Kt2

Black's king can now cross the king's file.

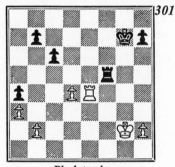

Black to play

5 ...	K—K3
6 K—Q1	K—Q4
7 K—B2	R—R6

White having brought his king to defend the QKtP, Black promptly attacks the KRP, keeping White's rook on the defensive. There is no hurry for Black to capture the queen's pawn, which is doomed anyway.

8 R—Q2	K—B5
9 K—Kt1	P—R4
10 K—R2	R—R5
11 R—B2	K×P
12 R—B7	P—Kt4
13 R—B2	

Black has won a pawn without appreciably freeing White's rook—which is as it should be.

13 ...	R—R6
14 R—Q2 ch.	K—B4
15 R—B2 ch.	K—Kt3
16 R—B2	P—B4

Black intends to break through on the queen's side by ... PB6.

17 R—B6 ch.	K—R4
18 R—B2	P—B5
19 R—Kt2	

If 19. R—B2 (to prevent PB6) then 19... PKt5 20. P×P ch. K×P followed by PR6 getting a passed QBP.

19 ...	P—B6
20 P—Kt4 ch.	P×P e.p. ch.
21 K×P	P—B7 ch.
22 K×P	R×QRP
23 K—Kt2	R—KB6
24 R—K2	P—R5
25 R—Q2	P—R6

Black makes an advanced point at KKt7 for his rook, so that he may invade the seventh rank.

26 R—K2	K—R5
27 K—Kt1	R—B8 ch.
28 K—B2	P—Kt5
29 K—Q3	R—Q8 ch.
30 K—B2	R—KKt8

White resigns because of the threatened ... R—KKt7.

302 Euwe *v.* Barcza, Budapest, 1940. White has the better rook position, controlling the remote open file. A scramble for pawns ensues, and the odds are with White, because Black's queen's side is indefensible, whereas White's king can obstruct Black's rook to some extent.

1 R—B7   R×QP

1... R×P ch. 2. KK3 is even worse.

2 K—K3

Not 2. R×KtP? RQ7 ch. followed by capturing White's QKtP.

2 ...   R—K5 ch.
3 K—Q3

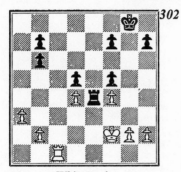

302

White to play

Not 3. KB3 ? PQ5 4. R × KtP RK6 ch.
5. KB2 RQKt6.

White wants to retain both his queen's
side pawns, for a single passed pawn can
be held up by an enemy rook, but united
passed pawns cannot.

3 ...   R × P

Black prefers sudden death to the
slower defeat which follows 3... RK3
4. R × KtP KKt2 5. KQ4.

4 R × KtP	R—B7
5 R × KtP	R × KKtP
6 P—R4	R × KRP
7 P—R5	R—R8
8 R—Kt3	R—R6 ch.

If 8... RR8 9. RR3 RQ8 ch. 10. KK2
RQB8 11. PR6 RB1 12. PR7 RQR1
13. PKt4 KB1 14. PKt5 KK2 15. PKt6
KQ2 16. PKt7.

9 K—B2	R—R7 ch.
10 K—Kt1	R—K7
11 P—R6	R—K2
12 R—QR3.	

Placing the rook behind the passed
pawns is better than 12. R—Kt7?
R—K8 ch. and now 13. KR2 RK3
14. PR7 RR3 ch. 15. KKt1 KKt2 16.
PKt4 PB5 17. PKt5 PB6, or 13. KB2
RQR8 14. PR7 KKt2 15. PKt4 PB5
16. KQ2 PQ5 17. KK2 RR7 ch.

After the text-move Black resigns
because of 12... RR2 13. PKt4 PB5
14. PKt5, when his four isolated pawns
are not of the slightest use.

CHAPTER IV

QUEEN ENDINGS

'With her fals draughtes dyvers,
She stal on me and took my fers
And Whan I sawe my fers away,
Allas! I couthe no longer play
But seyde, "Farwel swete y-wis,
And farwel all that ever there ys!" '

CHAUCER, *The Boke of the Duchesse*, 1369.*

Exchanges of pawns often lead to perpetual check before their numbers are greatly reduced. The endings of the first three sections are usually the consequence of a pawn ending in which one or both players promote.

In contrast to endings with the other pieces the main defensive idea is perpetual check, and in the simpler cases stalemate.

1 QUEEN *v.* PAWN

The queen wins in every case against a KtP or Centre P, provided always she can at first check or pin or otherwise prevent the immediate promotion of the pawn.

A BP or RP on the seventh draws unless White's king is within a specified distance of the pawn.

If the pawn is on the sixth or farther back, only the BP offers drawing chances—and those rarely.

303 The queen approaches by means of checks and pins, or by attacking, or threatening to block, the pawn. Periodically a close-ranged check forces Black's king in front of his pawn, thus giving White's king time to approach.

1 Q—R2   K—Q6

If 1... K—B8 (1... KQ8 2. KQ5, or

* Fers: queen. draughtes: moves.

1... KB6 2. QK2 KB7 3. KQ5) 2. Q—B4 K—B7 3. Q—B4 ch.

2 Q—R5   K—B7

White threatened 3. QQ1.

3 Q—K2   K—B8
4 Q—B4 ch.

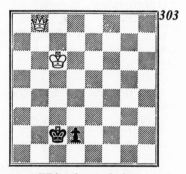

303

White plays and wins

The queen always needs access to certain squares, here QB4, and on the ninth move K4. Although of no account in the basic ending this fact may be relevant when there are other pawns on the board, as in the final position of Example 80.

4 . . .   K—Kt7
5 Q—Q3   K—B8
6 Q—B3 ch.

The king must now obstruct his pawn.

6 ...	K—Q8
7 K—Q5	K—K7
8 Q—B2	K—K8
9 Q—K4 ch.	K—B7
10 Q—Q3	K—K8
11 Q—K3 ch.	K—Q8
12 K—Q4	K—B7.

With the aid of his king White mates in four, 13. Q—B3 ch. K—Q8 (13... KKt8 14. Q×P KR8 15. KB3) 14. K—K3, etc.

The play against a knight's pawn is the same.

304 White wins against a BP on the seventh only if his king is near enough to capture it, or if there is a mating finish after the pawn queens. If White's king were here at K2, then the pawn falls after 1. KQ2 KR1 2. K×P, but not 2. Q×P? stalemate.

With White's king within one move of Kt3 as diagrammed, he mates:

1 Q—R8 ch.   K—R7

If 1... KKt8 2. KKt3 PB8=Q 3. QR7 ch. KR8 4. QR7 ch, KKt8 5. QR2 mate.

2 Q—R2

Not 2. QB3? PB8=Q 3. Q×Q stalemate.

2 ...	K—Kt7
3 Q—Q2	K—Kt8
4 K—Kt3	

White plays and wins if his king is within the marked-off area

When Black's king is on the short side of the BP he cannot be forced to block it, for if 4. QKt4 ch. KR7 5. QKt3 ch. Black goes to the corner, 5... KR8, when 6. Q×P? stalemates. This is what happens if White's king is farther away.

4 ...   P—B8=Q
5 Q—R2 mate.

305 To have the king on the long side of the pawn, as in the finish of the game Albin v. Charousek, Example 28, is less favourable for Black.

| 1 Q—Kt2 | K—Q8 |
| 2 K—B3 | |

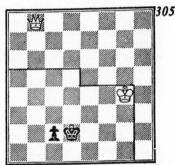

White plays and wins if his king is within the marked-off area

This combination depends on White's king being able to guard K2 in one move, and now if 2... PB8=Q 3. QK2 mate.

2 ...	K—Q7
3 K—B2	K—Q8
4 Q—Q4 ch.	K—B8
5 Q—QKt4	K—Q8
6 Q—K1 mate.	

If White's king were here at QKt5 there follows 1. QB4 ch. KQ8 2. QQ4 ch. KK7 3. QB3 KQ8 4. QQ3 ch. KB8, and White gains a tempo for bringing up his king, 5. KR4 KKt7 6. QQ2, winning as in the preceding example.

If instead White's king were at KB5, he may try 1. QKt2 KQ8 2. QKt3 KQ7 3. QR2, when 3... KB6 draws, but Black

must not fall for the cunning trap 3...
KQ8? 4. KK4 PB8=Q 5. KQ3.

306 In general White cannot win
against a RP on the seventh if his king
is too far off, and after 1. QKt8 ch.?
KB7 the queen may zigzag towards the
pawn, 2. QR7 KKt8 3. QKt6 ch. KB7
4. QR5 KKt8 6. QKt4 ch. KB7 7.
QR3 KKt8, but now 8. QKt3 ch. is
answered by 8... KR8, and White cannot
circumvent the stalemate threat.

When the king is nearer there are
mating combinations after the pawn
queens.

1 K—Q5 ch.

White plays and wins

This is the more usual finish, White's
king making for Kt3 as in Kashdan *v.*
Flohr, Example 112.

Alternatively the king may control B2,
1. K—K4 ch. K—Kt8 2. Q—KR1 ch.
K—Kt7 3. Q—Kt2 ch. K—Kt8 (3...
KKt6 4. QKt7) 4. K—Q3 P—R8=Q
5. Q—B2 mate.

1 ...	K—Kt8
2 Q—KR1 ch.	K—Kt7
3 Q—R2 ch.	K—Kt8
4 Q—Kt1 ch.	K—Kt7
5 Q—Q4 ch.	K—Kt8
6 K—B4	P—R8=Q
7 Q—Q1 ch.	K—Kt7
8 Q—Q2 ch.	K—Kt8

If 8... KR6 9. QKt4 ch. KR7 10.
QKt3 mate.

9 K—Kt3.

And the mating threats are fatal.

Leaving out of account checks by
discovery, White wins only if his king is
within the marked-off area shown on the
diagram.

307 The stalemate defences with BP
and RP on the seventh are no longer
available when the pawn is on the sixth.

1 Q—K4

Any other legal move except 1. Q—
QB8? wins.

The alternative is to get the king into
the winning area of Example 305, permitting the pawn to reach the seventh,
1. KB6 PB6 2. KKt5.

1 ...   P—B6
2 Q—QKt4

This simple manœuvre, which consists
of pinning the pawn on one of the two
available diagonals, brings Black to a
standstill.

2 ...   K—Q6
3 K—Q6.

The point: if Black advances the pawn
3... PB7, it is blocked after 4. QK1.

White plays and wins
Black plays and draws

Black to play draws after 1... PB6
because White can neither prevent
... PB7 with his queen, nor get his king
within the winning area. This is an
improbable situation, which happens in
fewer than 50 of the many thousands of
possible positions.

A RP on the sixth cannot even be defended temporarily, as shown in Example 32.

2 QUEEN v. TWO OR MORE PAWNS

The queen is not worth a certain number of pawns. She may defeat eight on the fourth rank, but draw against one on the seventh. Everything depends on how far advanced they are.

When White's king is near enough to take part there is nearly always a mating finish.

When White's king is far away two united pawns on the sixth or beyond usually draw; two disconnected pawns are weaker, but if both are on the seventh Black may draw if his king supports a BP or RP, or if White's queen cannot reach one of the queening squares.

When only one of the disconnected pawns is on the seventh Black frequently loses: if it is a KtP or Centre P the other pawn rarely saves him; whilst if he has a BP or RP on the seventh, then extra pawns are a liability impairing his stalemate chances.

308 Yates *v.* Marshall, Carlsbad, 1929. Even without his KBP White could win, because his king is nearby.

1 Q—B5 ch.	K—Kt6
2 Q—B4 ch.	K—R6
3 Q—Q3 ch.	

308

White plays and wins

Not 3. QKt5? PKt8=Q 4. Q×Q stalemate.

| 3 ... | K—R7 |
| 4 Q—B2 | |

Incredible as it may seem the game was drawn, 4. KB4? PKt8=Q 5. Q×Q ch. K×Q 6. KKt4 KKt7 7. K×P KB6.

| 4 ... | P—R6 |
| 5 K—B4 | |

The most precise. In view of his extra pawn he might also win by 5. KB3 KR8 6. KKt3 PKt8=Q 7. Q×Q ch. K×Q 8. K×P.

| 5 ... | K—R8 |
| 6 Q—B3 | K—R7 |

If 6... PR7 7. KKt3.

7 Q—Kt3 ch.

White wins the QRP.

309 Neither of the pawns could draw if the other were lost. White places his queen on a queening square.

1 Q—R7 ch.	K—B8
2 Q—R6 ch.	K—B7
3 Q—B6 ch.	K—Kt8

Or 3... KQ8 4. QQKt6 KB7 5. QB2 ch. and 6. Q—Kt1.

4 Q—QKt6	K—R7
5 Q—R7 ch.	K—Kt6
6 Q—Kt1.	

Next White brings up his king; if 6... KR7 7. Q×P.

If in the diagram position Black had a pawn at Q7 instead of at KKt7, White to play would win a similar manner: 1. Q—R7 ch. K—B8 2. Q—B7 ch. K—Q8 3. Q—QKt6 K—B8 (3... KK1 4. QK3 ch. KB8 5. QB4 ch. KK7 6. QK4 ch. or 5... KKt7 6. QKt4 ch.) 4. Q—B6 ch. K—Q8 5. Q—K4 K—B8 6. Q—B4 ch. K—Kt8 7. Q—Kt3 K—R8 (7... KB8 8. QB3 ch.) 8. Q—R4 ch. K—Kt8 9. Q—Q1 ch.

If in the diagram position Black had a pawn at K7 instead of at KKt7, White could not win. His queen could not force its way to a queening square, 1. Q—R7 ch. K—B8 2. Q—B7 ch. K—Q8 3. Q—Q6 ch. K—B8 (not 3... KK8? 4.

QQ3 KB7 5. QB5 ch. KKt7 6. QKt1 and White wins) 4. Q—B5 ch. K—Q8 (not 4... KKt8? 5. QB3 KR7 6. QR5 ch.) 5. Q—Q4 ch. K—B8 6. Q—B3 ch. K—Q8 7. Q—Q3 ch. K—B8.

The normal results when Black's king is near one of his two isolated pawns on the seventh, and White's king is far off, may be summarized:

Pawns one file apart: drawn, except for KtP + Centre P as shown.

Pawns two files apart: drawn.

Pawns three or more files apart: drawn if the black king can support a RP or BP, except for KKtP + QKtP as shown. See Example 310.

309

White plays and wins

In the position White: king at KKt6, queen at KB1; Black: king at K5, pawns at KR7, QB7, and QR7 (Grigoriev, 1933), White to play wins against three 'drawing pawns' because Black's king is not well placed. 1. Q—K2 ch. K—B5 (1... KQ5 2. QQ2 ch. KB5 3. Q×P ch. KKt5 4. QKt2 ch. KB4 5. QR1 KKt5 6. KB5 KKt6 7. KK4 PR8=Q ch. 8. Q×Q, and White's king is in the winning zone) 2. Q—B2 ch. (not 2. Q×P ch? KK6) K—Kt5 3. Q—B1 P—QR8=Q 4. Q×Q K—B6 5. K—B5 K—B7 (after 5... KKt7 6. QKKt7 ch. KB8 7. QR6 KKt7 8. QQ2 ch. KKt8 9. QB1 ch. wins) 6. K—K4 K—Q7 7. Q—Q4 ch. K—K7 8. Q—K3 ch. K—Q8 9. K—Q3 P—B8= Kt ch. 10. K—B3 Kt—K7 ch. 11. K—Kt2 P—R8=Q 12. Q—Q3 ch. K—K8 13. Q—Kt1 ch.

310 If Black's king were at KKt6 supporting the drawing pawn he could score the half-point (1...PKt8=Q 2. Q×Q KKt7). As it is White wins by occupying one of the queening squares.

1 ...   K—B7

There is no time to cross over, if 1... KQ6 2. QR1.

2 Q—Kt2 ch.	K—B6
3 Q—R1	K—Kt6
4 K—Kt7.	

310

White wins

Black can do nothing, whilst White brings up his king.

If in the diagram position Black had a pawn at KB7 instead of KR7 he draws by 1... KQ7 crossing to support it, and abandoning his KtP.

If in the diagram position Black had a pawn at QKt5 instead of KR7, that is doubled KtPs, he loses after 1. Q—B8 ch. K—Kt6 (1... KQ7 2. QKB5 KB8 3. QB5 ch.) 2. Q—KB5 K—R7 3. Q—Q5 ch. K—R6 (3... KR8 4. QR4 ch.) 4. Q—Q1 K—R7 5. Q—R4 ch. Doubled pawns, like isolated pawns, are hard to defend against the queen.

311 With RP (or BP) on the seventh then, unlike the case with KtP or Centre P, the position of White's king in relation to the advancement of Black's other pawn is the critical factor: White's king tries to get into one of the winning areas before Black sacrifices the extra pawn.

1 Q—Kt7 ch.　　　K—B7

Not 1... KR8? 2. KK5 PR7 3. KQ4 PR8=Q 4. Q×Q ch., for White's king is near enough for a win.

2 Q—R6　　　　　K—Kt7(Kt6)

Black keeps his king on the squares Kt6, Kt7, and R6.

311

Drawn

If 2... KKt8? 3. QKt5 ch. KB7 4. QB4 ch. KKt7 5. QKt4 ch. KB7 6. QR3 KKt8 7. QKt3 ch. KR8 8. QB2, when Black's extra pawn deprives him of a stalemate, 8... PR7 9. QB1 mate.

3 Q—Kt5 ch.　　　K—R6

If 3... KB7? or 3... KR8? 4. QB4 (ch.).

4 Q—Q3 ch.　　　K—Kt7

Not 4... KKt5? 5. QQ1 PR7 6. KK5 KR6, when White's king enters the winning area, 7. KQ4.

5 Q—Q2 ch.　　　K—Kt6

Not 4... KR6? 5. QB1 ch., White's queen gets to the first rank without loss of time, 5... KKt6 6. KK5 PR7 7. KQ4.

6 Q—B1

6. QQ3 ch. KKt7 7. QQ4 ch. KKt6 8. KK5 PR7 9. QR1 comes to the same thing.

6 ...　　　　　　P—R7
7 K—K5　　　　　P—R8=Q

8 Q×Q　　　　　K—Kt7.

White might win if his king were nearer, or if the KRP were less forward, or if Black were encumbered by a third pawn.

312 White also cannot win against a BP on the seventh unless his king takes part.

1 K—Kt4

Not 1. QR6 ch.? KKt8 2. QKt6 PB4, for White's queen, unable to use the squares Q4 and QKt4, cannot approach and force Black to block his advanced pawn, 3. QKt6 ch. KR7 4. QR5 ch. KKt7 5. QKt5 ch. KR7 6. QR4 (B4) ch. K—Kt7 7. QKt5 ch. KR7; whilst capturing the rear pawn, which would win in the case of KtP or Centre P, here only draws.

Similar play follows 1. QQ3? PB4 2. QQKt3 KQ7 3. QR2 KQ6 4. QQ5 ch. KK7.

Of course 1. Q×P? KKt7 draws at once.

1 ...　　　　　　P—B4

Black tries to get rid of the rear pawn. If 1... K—Kt7 (1... KKt8 2. QQ3 PB4 3. QKt3 ch.) 2. Q—R8 ch., the only move to win, 2... K—Kt8 (2... KKt6 3. QQR1) 3. Q—Kt8 ch. K—R7 4. Q—R7 ch. K—Kt8 5. Q—Kt7 ch. K—R7 6. Q—R6 ch. K—Kt7 7. Q—Kt5 ch. K—B6 8. Q—B5 ch.

312

White plays and wins
Black plays and draws

K—Kt7 (8... KKt6 9. KB3) 9. Q—Kt4 ch. K—R7 10. Q—B3 K—Kt8 11. Q—Kt3 ch., and because there is no stalemate after 10... KR8 11. Q×P, Black must block his pawn.

2 Q—QKt7

This prevents Black's king going to the short side of the pawn. 2. KB3? KKt7 draws.

2 ...	K—Q8
3 Q—Kt3	P—B5

Grigoriev shows that White's king is near enough for a mating finish against the doubled bishop's pawns on the fifth and seventh ranks.

4 Q—R4	K—Q7
5 Q—R2	K—B6
6 Q—R1 ch.	K—Q7
7 Q—Kt2	P—B6
8 Q—R2	K—Q6

The better chance. If 8... KQ8 9. KB3 PB8=Q 10. QK2 mate.

9 Q—Q5 ch,	K—K7
10 Q—K5 ch.	K—Q7
11 K—B3	P—B8=Kt

He is mated if he queens.

12 Q—R2 ch.	K—Q6
13 Q—B2	Kt—Kt6
14 Q—K2 ch.	K—Q5
15 Q—K4 ch.	K—B4
16 K—K2.	

With the move Black draws by 1... P—B4 threatening ... KKt7, and if 2. Q—QKt7 K—Q7 3. Q—Q5 ch. K—K7, much as in the notes above.

3 QUEEN AND PAWN v. QUEEN

The position of Black's king is the decisive factor.

If it blocks the pawn he draws.

Otherwise his king must be out of the way, and not obstruct his chances of perpetual check. White tries to avoid perpetual check by answering a check with a check, and forcing a queen exchange. This interposed check happens only when both kings are on the same or on an adjoining rank, file, or diagonal; and in this way too the position of Black's king influences the result.

A Centre P or BP on the seventh normally wins, chiefly because White's king has sufficient manœuvring space around it.

A KtP on the seventh almost always wins if supported diagonally by a queen on its fourth rank, e.g. White pawn at KKt7, White queen at Q4.

The RP on the seventh is much less likely to win; even so, the defence can be difficult.

With the pawn farther back results are less clear. Black's king, if not blocking the pawn, cannot improve its position except to move farther away, for his only defence is perpetual check, or on rare occasions stalemate.

Apparently the KtP can be forced to the seventh, but meanwhile Black's king takes up its correct position. There is evidence that under favourable circumstances a BP can be advanced. Less is known about the Centre P. As to the RP, if farther back a draw is certain.

313 A stable position of a kind which might always be obtained, or to which White might return should he make a false start. When unable to check Black pins the pawn.

1 ...	K—B8

White interposes with check on the diagonal if Black's king stands on one of four critical diagonals:

the long diagonal, 1... K—B6 (1... KR8) 2. K—Kt8.

the adjoining white-square diagonals, 1... K—R6 (1... KB7 or Kt8 2. KKt8 QKt5 ch. 3. KR8 QQ5 ch. 4. QKt7 QQ2 5. QKt6 ch.) 2. Q—B6 Q—B4 3. Q—R6 ch. K—Kt6 (3... KKt7 4. KB7 QQ4 ch. 5. QK6 QR4 ch. 6. QKt6 QQ4 ch. 7. KKt7 QKt2 8. QB7 QKt7 ch. 9. KB8) 4. K—B7 Q—B7 ch. (4... QB2 5. KK6 QKt1 6. KQ7, or 4... QB4 ch. 5. QB6 QQ2 or R2 6. KB8, or 4... QR4 ch. 5. QKt6 QB6 ch. 6. KKt8) 5. Q—B6 Q—R2 6. K—B8 Q—B4

7. K—Kt7 Q—Kt8 ch. (7... QR2 or B2 8. QB2 ch.) 8. Q—Kt6 Q—Q5 ch. 9. K—Kt8.

The pinning diagonal, 1... K—R6 2. Q—B6 Q—B4 3. Q—R6 ch. K—Kt5 and now, 4. K—B7 Q—Q4 ch. (4... QR4 ch. or 4... QB4 ch. transposes. If 4... QB7 ch. 5. QB6 QR7 ch. 6. KB8 5. Q—K6 Q—R4 ch. (5... QKt2 6. KB8 QB6 ch. 7. QB7) 6. Q—Kt6 Q—Q4 ch. (6... QB6 ch. 7. KKt7 QB6 ch. 8. QB6 QB2 9. QQ4 ch. KR6 10. KB8) 7. K—Kt7 Q—Q5 ch. (7... QK4 ch. 8. QB6 QB2 9. QQ5 ch. KR6 10. KB8) 8. Q—B6 Q—Kt8 ch. (8... QQ2 9. KB8) 9. K—B7 (not 9... KB8 10. QB4) 9... Q—R2 10. Q—Kt2 ch. K—B5 11. K—B8 Q—B4 12. Q—B2 ch.

There would be similar winning lines if Black's king were on the KR, KKt or KB files.

White wins

2 Q—Q5

With Black's king at QB8 an interposed check cannot be forced as matters stand. White therefore moves his own king to the queen's side, where he threatens to interpose with check on the file. He first centralizes his queen, thus depriving Black's queen of the use of most of the central squares. There are of course other ways in which the same idea may be carried out.

2 ...   Q—B5 ch.

Wherever it is Black's king gets in the way, even on the QR file, 2... K—Kt7

3. K—B7 Q—B5 ch. 4. K—K6 Q—Kt5 ch. (4... QR3 ch. 5. KQ7 transposes) 5. K—Q6 Q—Kt5 ch. 6. K—Q7 Q—Kt5 ch. 7. K—Q8 Q—KR5 8. Q—Q7 K—R8 (8... QKt4 9. KB8 QB4 ch. 10. QB7 QB4 ch. 11. KKt8) 9. K—B8 Q—B5 ch. 10. K—Kt8 Q—B5 ch. 11. K—R8 Q—K5(B6) ch. 12. Q—Kt7.

3 K—Kt7   Q—B2

If 3... Q—Kt6 ch. 4. K—B6 Q—QB6 ch. (4... QB7 ch. 5. KK6 as in the text, or 4... QB5 ch. 5. KKt6) 5. K—B7 Q—B2 6. Q—Q4 (threatening KB8) 6... Q—Kt2 7. Q—B3 ch. K—Q8 8. K—B8, and Black can neither check, nor pin on the diagonal.

4 K—B6   Q—Kt3 ch.

If 4... QB6 ch. 5. KB7, or 4... QB5 ch. 5. KKt6, as before.

5 K—B5   Q—B7 ch.
6 K—K6   Q—Kt3 ch.

If 6... Q—K6 ch. 7. K—Q6 Q—Kt6 ch. 8. K—Q7 Q—Kt5 ch. 9. K—Q8 Q—KR5 10. Q—Q7 K—Kt8 11. K—B8 Q—B5 ch. 12. K—Kt8 Q—B5 ch. 13. Q—B7.

7 Q—Q6   Q—Kt4

If 6... QK6 ch. 7. KQ7 as in the last note. Also if 6... Q—Kt6 ch. 7. K—Q7 Q—R6 ch. (7... QB2 8. KQ8) 8. K—B7 as before.

8 Q—B4 ch.   K—Q8

Else the queens are exchanged, a threat renewed by White's next move.

9 Q—B7   Q—K7 ch.
10 K—Q7   Q—Kt5 ch.
11 K—Q8   Q—KR5
12 K—B8.

To summarize:
If Black's king is already aligned on the relevant diagonals or files White wins by a regrouping of his king and queen around the pawn, as in the notes to Black's first move.

In other cases White boldly moves out his own king, seeking to align it with Black's king, on the file as here, or on the rank as in the next example.

The pin is less effective on the rank

than on the diagonal, and sometimes fails, as in the note to Black's third move. This kind of win is somewhat fortuitous, and depends upon White's having a suitable check, thus regrouping his queen without loss of time.

314 When there is a BP Black's king also has no good square.

| 1 ... | K—Kt6 |

Black hopes for sanctuary on the QR file. As before, the diagonals are unsafe, 1... KKt8 2. KR8, or 1... KB8 2. QKt5 ch. KB7 3. QKt6 ch. KB8 4. KR7 QB2 5. QKt7 QB7 ch. 6. KR8 QR7 ch. 7. KKt8. If Black plays his king to the central files, White wins much as in the preceding example.

2 Q—Kt2	K—R6
3 Q—B3 ch.	K—R7
4 K—Kt7	

In spite of many checks White cannot be prevented from moving his king down the KKt and KR files to KKt1, when Black's checks must have a stop because White threatens to interpose with check on the rank.

314

White wins

4 ...	Q—Q5 ch.
5 K—Kt6	Q—Q3 ch.
6 K—R5	Q—K4 ch.

If 6... QB1 7. QQ5 ch. KR8 8. KKt6 KKt7 9. KR7, and White soon opposes queens, 9... KKt8 10. QK4 ch. KR8 11. QK8, or 9... KB8 10. QKt5 ch. KKt8 11. QKt7.

7 K—Kt4	Q—Kt2 ch.
8 K—R3	Q—R3 ch.
9 K—Kt2	Q—Kt2 ch.

If 9... QB1 10. KB1.

| 10 K—R2 | Q—R3 ch. |
| 11 K—Kt1 | Q—B1 |

If 11... QB8 ch. 12. QB1.

12 K—B1	K—R8
13 Q—B6 ch.	K—R7
14 Q—K6 ch.	K—R8
15 Q—K8.	

The strategy is not profound, but many checks may make it complex. For Black the best checking distance is to have two or three squares between king and queen. White escapes the checks if he pursues a definite plan, and/or his queen is well centralized. Moving his king to a square of a different colour from that occupied by Black's queen often limits her choice of further checks.

315 With a KtP White cannot forcibly manœuvre so as to interpose with check on the diagonal, and consequently Black's king finds a haven in the diagonally opposite corner. White can hope to win only by bringing his king to the QR or QKt file, or to the first or second rank, so that he creates threats of interposing with check on the file or the rank. The question mark, after the caption under the diagram, is intentional for it is not yet known whether or not White can force a win in this way, and the consensus is that the position is drawn.

With the move Black has a new kind of draw because White's king in the corner has less freedom of action: 1... QQ1 ch. 2. PKt8=Q QB6 ch. with perpetual check.

| 1 Q—R2 ch. | K—B8 |
| 2 Q—B7 ch. | K—Kt7 |

This position occurred after 100 moves of the game Pachman *v.* Gligorić, Moscow, 1947, which we shall follow.

| 3 K—Kt8 | |

If White returns his queen, 3. QR2 ch.

IV QUEEN ENDINGS

KR8 4. QR7, Black maintains the pin on the pawn, but must not play 4... QQ1 ch. for his queen is pinned after 5. PKt8=Q QB6 ch. 6. QKt7.

3 ...	Q—Q4 ch.
4 K—B8	Q—KB4 ch.
5 K—K8	Q—K5 ch. ?

After the better move, 5... Q—K3 ch., it would seem that White can avoid perpetual check only by going back to the shelter of his pawn, 6. Q—K7 Q—B1 ch. 7. K—B7 Q—B5 ch. 8. Q—K6 Q—B2 ch. 9. K—B6 (9. KKt6 QKt6 ch. 10. KR7 QR5 ch. 11. QR6 QK5 ch.) 9... Q—B5 ch. 10. Q—B5 (10. KK7 QB2 ch. 11. QQ7 QK4 ch. 12. KB7 QB5 ch. 13. KKt6 QKt6 ch.) 10... Q—Q3 ch. 11. K—B7 (11. KKt5 QKt6 ch. 12. QKt4 QK4 ch.) 11... Q—B2 ch. 12. K—Kt6 Q—Kt6 ch. 13. Q—Kt5 Q—Q6 ch.

This is not to say that there may not be other ways in which White's king may successfully move out and cross the board.

To retain the greatest freedom of movement Black delivers checks, in a general way, from central squares; and here in particular from the squares on his diagonal QKt8-KR7, e.g. KKt6, KB5, etc.

6 K—Q8	Q—R1 ch.
7 K—Q7	Q—Q4 ch.
8 K—B8	Q—Kt1 ch.
9 K—Kt7	Q—Q4 ch.
10 K—R6	Q—R7 ch.

315

Drawn ?

White's pawn makes its little contribution, for if 10... Q—Q6 ch. 11. K—R7 Q—R6 ch. (11... QR2 12. KR8) 12. K—Kt8, and Black cannot check on his KB1 square.

11 Q—R5

With the kings on adjoining files there are two interposed checks. Now if 11. QK3 ch. checking on the rank, 11... QKt6 ch., or if 11... QB5 ch. checking on the diagonal, 11... QKt5 ch.

| 11 ... | Q—Kt1 |

There are five ways in which Black's queen may hinder the KtP from queening: (i) delivering check; (ii) pinning the pawn on the long diagonal; (iii) pinning the pawn on the rank; (iv) occupying the queening square, as here; (v) controlling the queening square. From Black's point of view (i) and (ii) are unquestionably the best defences. (iii) and (iv) are weaker defences, and they sometimes lose; (v) is very weak, and generally loses; e.g. if here 11... QB2 there follows 12. QK5 ch. KB7 13. QR2 ch. K any 14. QKt3(Kt1) ch. followed by 15. PKt8=Q.

12 Q—K5 ch.

White has a minor success, occupying this central square on the long diagonal.

| 12 ... | K—Kt8 |

In a general way it is better to occupy the edge file in this case [or the edge rank if White's king were on the first or second rank] because this leaves Black's queen free to check on the diagonals and on the ranks without fear of a fatal interposed check; Black could therefore try 12... K—R7, although, as his queen is not too well placed, this does not save him. The question also arises as to whether Black might well have played to the QR file at an earlier stage, e.g. on his third move.

13 K—Kt6

According to an analysis by Pospishil and Stepushin-Malishev, 1958, White can win by 13. K—Kt5 Q—Kt6 ch. 14. K—R5 Q—R6 ch. (14... QR7 ch.

224

15. KKt4 QQ7 ch. 16. QB3 QQ3 ch.
17. QB5 QB5 ch. 18. QB4 QKt1 ch.
19. QKt5 QKt6 20. PKt8=Q 21. Q×Q
and White mates in 3) 15. K—Kt6
Q—Kt6 ch. 16. K—B7 (not 16. QKt5
KR8 17. KR6 QK3 ch. and now 18.
QKt6 QB1 ch. 19. QKt7 QB5 ch., or
18. KR7 QK2 ch. 19. QKt7 QK6 ch.
20. KR8 QK1 ch. with a probable draw
in either case) 16... Q—B5 ch. (16...
QB7 ch. 17. KQ8 QQ6 ch. 18. KK8
QKt3 ch. 19. KB8 QKR3, and the pin
on the short diagonal is useless, 20. QB5
ch. KR7 21. KB7; or 16... QB2 ch. 17.
KQ8 QKt1 ch. 18. KK7) 17. K—Q8
Q—R5 ch. 18. Q—K7 Q—Q5 ch. 19.
Q—Q7 Q—B3 ch. (19... QKt3 ch. 20.
KB8 QB4 ch. 21. KKt8 QK4 ch. 22.
KR8) 20. K—B8 Q—B6 ch. 21. Q—B7
Q—R6 ch. (21... QQKt6 22. QKt7
KR8 23. QR1 ch.) 22. K—Kt8 Q—Kt6
ch. 23. K—R8. The final stages are very
like those shown in Example 313.

13 ...   Q—Q1 ch.
14 K—Kt5   Q—Q2 ch.

The mating threats make it difficult
for Black. If 14... QKt1 15. QK4 ch.
KKt7 16. QQ4 ch. KKt8 17. KKt4
QKt1 ch. 18. KR3 QR1 ch. 19. QR4
QQ1 20. PKt8=Q Q×Q 21. QQ1 mate.

15 K—Kt4   Q—Kt2 ch.
16 K—B4   Q—B3 ch.
17 Q—B5   Q—K5 ch.
18 Q—Q4   Q—B3 ch.
19 K—Kt3   Q—KB6 ch.

Here some repetitions of moves are
omitted. White could now win by 20.
KB4 QB3 ch. 21. QB5 QK5 ch. 22.
KKt3 QB6 ch.   23. KR4 QR1 ch.
24. QR5 QKKt1 25. QB5 ch. KB8 26.
QB1 ch. KB7 27. QKt2 ch. KB6 24.
QKt3 ch. KQ5 25. QQKt3.

20 Q—B3 ?   Q—Kt2 ch ?

An oversight. White cannot mate
after 20... QQ4 ch. 21. QB4 QB6 ch.
22. KR4 QR1 ch.

21 Q—Kt4   Q—Q4 ch.

If 21... Q×P 22. QK1 mate.

22 K—R3 ch.

Instead, 22. KB3 ch. mates in 7.

22 ...   K—B7
23 Q—Kt2 ch.
Black resigns.

316 This is a typical winning position with kings on adjoining ranks.
Black's king is misplaced at QR6 and
would be happier at QKt8. White's
queen is centralized on its best square.

1 ...   Q—Kt3 ch.

In a variety of ways White's king and
queen may pair themselves on the second
rank:
1... QK7 ch. 2. QB2.
1... QB3 ch. 2. KB1 QB6 ch. 3. QB2
QQ6(Q8) ch.   4. KKt2 or here 3...
QR6(R8) ch. 4. KK2.
1... QB3 ch. 2. KB1 QB8 ch. 3. KK2
QB7 ch. 4. QQ2.
1... QB3 ch. 2. KB1 QR8 ch. 3. QKt1
QR6 ch. 4. QKt2 QQ6 ch. 5. KKt1
QQ5 ch. 6. KR2.
1... QB3 ch. 2. KB1 QKt4 ch. 3. KK1
QR4 ch. (or 3... QKt8 ch. as in the text-
play) 4. KQ1 QR4 ch. 5. KB2 QR7 ch.
6. QQ2.
Black runs out of checks after 1...
QB3 ch. 2. KB1 QR3 ch. 3. KB2.
Merely controlling the queening
square is usually hopeless, 1... QB1
2. QQ6 ch. KKt7 3. QB6 ch., or here
2... KR5 3. QB4 ch.
Occupying the queening square is a
better defence, but always fails if White's

White wins

king can reach KKt1, and sometimes fails for tactical reasons:
1... QKt1   2. KKt1 KR7   3. QB2 ch. KR8   4. QB8.
1... QR7 ch.   2. QB2 QKt1   3. QB8 ch.

2 K—B1   Q—QKt8 ch.

If 2... Q—B2 ch. (2... QB4 ch. 3. QB2) 3. K—K1 Q—Kt1 (3... QK1 ch. 4. KQ2, or 3... QK2 ch. 4. KQ1, whilst 3... QK3 ch. 4. KQ1 QKt6 ch. 5. KK2 transposes to the text) 4. Q—R7 ch. K—Kt7 5. K—B2 K—Kt8 6. K—Kt1.

3 K—K2   Q—R7 ch.
4 K—K3   Q—K3 ch.
5 K—B4

White escapes the checks after 5... QB2 ch. 6. KKt3 QKt3 ch. 7. QKt4, or 5... QR3 ch. 6. KB5 QR4 ch. 7. KB6 QB6 ch. 8. KKt5 QKt6 ch. 9. QKt4 QK6 ch.   10. KR4 QR3 ch. 11. KKt3 QQ3 ch.   12. KKt2 QQ7 ch. 13. KKt1 QB8 ch.   14. KR2 QQ7 ch. 15. QKt2.

317 Botvinnik *v.* Minev. Amsterdam, 1954. Black's king is badly placed, and Botwinnik wrests a victory, using the two weapons of the interposed check and the centralized queen—for the latter, note moves 2, 14 and 20. He keeps his king clear of the queening corner, thus avoiding the draw of Example 315.

1 Q—B4 ch.   K—R4

1... KR6? 2. QB3 ch.

2 Q—K5 ch.   K—R5
3 P—Kt6   Q—Q8 ch.
4 K—Kt5   Q—Q1 ch.

If 4... QKt8 ch. 5. KB5. In the game a repetition of moves occurred, 5. KB5 QQB1 ch. 6. KB4 QB8 ch. 7. QK3 QB2 ch. 8. QK5 QB8 ch. 9. KB5 QB1 ch. 10. KKt5 QQ1 ch.

5 Q—B6   Q—Q4 ch.
6 Q—B5   Q—Q1 ch.
7 K—R5   Q—K1

Black pins the pawn, for after 7... QR1 ch. 8. KKt4 QKt2 9. QB7 QB6 10. PKt7 QB1 ch. 11. QB5 the checks cease.

8 Q—B4 ch.   K—R4?

If there is a valid defence it surely consists in getting the king to the QR8 corner, 8... KR6.

9 Q—Q2 ch.   K—R5
10 Q—Q4 ch.

White gets to this key square without loss of time.

10 . . .   K—R4

It is too late for 10... K—R6, for after 11. K—Kt5 Q—K2 ch.   12. K—B5 Q—B1 ch.   13. K—Kt4 Q—B1 ch.   14. K—R4 he has no check; and if now 14... Q—K3 (14... KR7 15. PKt7 QKKt1 is no better) 15. P—Kt7, and

White to play

White's king retreats to KKt2, on the adjoining rank to Black's king, 15... Q—R3 ch. (15... QK2 ch. or 15... QK8 ch. lead to the same thing) 16. K—Kt3 Q—Kt3 ch. 17. K—R3 Q—K3 ch. 18. K—Kt2, Example 316.

11 K—Kt5   Q—K2 ch.
12 K—B5   Q—B1 ch.
13 K—K4   Q—R3
14 Q—K5 ch.   K—R5
15 P—Kt7   Q—R8 ch.
16 K—Q4   Q—Q8 ch.
17 K—B5   Q—B8 ch.
18 K—Q6   Q—Q7 ch.

If 17... QR3 ch. 18. KQ5.

As in the preceding examples, White's king marches boldly towards the enemy king.

19 K—K6	Q—R7 ch.
20 Q—Q5	Q—K7 ch.
21 K—Q6	Q—R7 ch.
22 K—B5.	

Black resigns. If 22... QQB7 ch. 23. QB4 ch. KR6 24. PKt8=Q, but not 24. Q×Q? stalemate.

318 A study by Fontana and Roycroft, 1957. Recent analysis by Fontana shows that the case with a RP on or near the seventh, hitherto thought irremediably drawn, can be won if the defending king is wrongly placed.

Ultimately the defender's checks are brought to a stop by White interposing with check, the same motif as before. In a general way White can often do this if Black's king is on the KKt or KB files, or on its own half of the board, as here where it stands on the fourth rank.

The best place for Black's king, if it cannot directly block the pawn, is in or near the corner diagonally opposite the queening square, in which case he draws.

1 P—R7	Q—R6 ch.
2 K—B6	Q—QB6 ch.

If 2... Q×P 3. QR3 mate.

3 K—Kt7

For once interposition fails, for after 3. QB5 ch.? KR5 Black either draws by stalemate, 4. Q×Q, or 4. KQ5 QB6 ch. 5. KB4 QB6 ch. 6. K×Q; or gains the

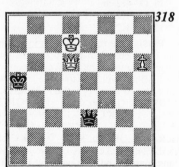

White plays and wins

RP, 4. KQ6 QKt6 ch., or 4. KKt6 QKt6 ch.

3 ...	Q—R1

After 3... QB6 ch. 4. KKt8 QKt6 ch. 5. KB8 QR6 ch. 6. QQ7 QR3 White's queen will find a way to control the queening square, 7. QQ8 ch. KR3 8. QQ3 ch. (8. PR8=Q? QB3 ch. 9. QB7 QK8 ch. 10. Q×Q stalemate) 8... KR2 9. QQ4 ch.

4 Q—Q5 ch.	K—R5
5 Q—Kt8	Q—Kt7 ch.
6 K—R8	Q—R6

An extraordinary resource!

7 Q—B7

Not 7. PR8=Q? for White's queens are bunched at the corner, and he cannot escape perpetual check, 7... KKt4 ch. 8. KKt8 QQ3 ch. 9. KB8 QB3 ch. 10. KQ8 QR1 ch. 11. KK7 QR2 ch. 12. KK6 QR7 ch. 13. KB5 QQB7 ch. 14. KKt5 QKt7 ch.

7 ...	K—Kt4 ch.

Black's king returns to the fourth rank for after 7... KKt5 ch. 8. KKt7 he has no more checks.

8 K—Kt8	Q—Q3 ch.
9 K—B8	Q—B3 ch.
10 K—Q8	Q—R1 ch.
11 K—K7	Q—R6 ch.
12 K—B6	Q—QB6 ch.
13 K—Kt6	Q—Kt6 ch.
14 K—R6	Q—K6 ch.
15 K—Kt7	Q—Kt4 ch.
16 K—Kt6	Q—K2 ch.
17 K—R6	Q—B1 ch.
18 K—Kt5	Q—KR1

Discreetly blocking the pawn. After the valorous 18... QK2 ch. 19. KR5 QK7 ch. 20. KR6 his last bolt is shot.

19 Q—B7	K—R5
20 K—Kt6	K—Kt4

It is too late to run for the corner, if 20... KR6 21. QKt8 QK4 22. QB8 ch. KR7 23. PR8=Q, and there is no perpetual check.

21 Q—B6

If 21. QKt8 QK4 22. PR8=Q? Black has a perpetual check.

21 ...	Q—K1 ch.
22 K—R6.	

Queen and two pawns win against queen if there is no immediate perpetual check, and if the pawns are united, or one or two files apart. In this way the pawns provide sufficient protection for their king.

The farther apart the pawns the greater the difficulty, although the stronger party more often wins than not. A case with the pawns three files apart arises in the next example.

The case of KRP+QRP would surely be drawn in many cases.

4 QUEEN AND TWO PAWNS v. QUEEN AND PAWN

In practice on those occasions when a queen and pawn ending simplifies to this extent perpetual check is highly probable, and queen endings with fewer than 3 v. 2 pawns are therefore frequently drawn.

The game is drawn when there is no passed pawn.

The stronger party has his best but slender chance when there is an outside passed pawn, although perpetual check is the normal outcome.

When all the pawns are passed the extra pawn is not in itself significant. The race is to the swift, and it is a question of who has the most advanced pawn, the other player most likely taking a perpetual check to prevent worse happening.

319 Tolush v. Bronstein, Parnu, 1947. Black has winning chances only because White's QKtP is vulnerable.

1 Q—B7 ch.	K—Kt4
2 Q—Kt7 ch.	K—B4
3 Q—R7 ch.	K—K4
4 Q—R2 ch.	K—Q4
5 Q—R2 ch.	K—B4
6 Q—R5 ch.	K—B5

The kind of pawn influences the result. After 6... QKt4? 7. QB3 ch. K×P 8. Q×P ch. White has good drawing chances against the KtP.

7 K—Q8	K—Q5

Black's king triangulates to lose a move, a manœuvre rarely seen with queens on the board.

Not 7... QQ4 ch.? 8. Q×Q ch. K×Q 9. KB7, when White draws the pawn ending.

319

White to play

8 Q—Kt4 ch.	K—Q4
9 Q—Q2 ch.	K—B4
10 Q—R5 ch.	K—B5
11 Q—R2 ch.	

White is in zugzwang. If 11. KK7 QB4 ch.

11 ...	K—Kt4
12 Q—Kt2 ch.	K—R3
13 Q—R2 ch.	K×P
14 Q—B2 ch.	K—Kt4
15 Q—K2 ch. ?	

Finding the right checks is in general more difficult than the opponent's task of evading them. 15. QKt2 ch. is correct, when Black will have to concede a pawn in order to avoid perpetual check, 15... KB5 16. QB1 ch. KQ6 17. QQ1 ch. KK6 18. QK1 ch. KB6 19. QB1 ch. KKt6 20. QK1 ch. KKt5 21. QKt1 ch. KR4 22. QR2 ch. KKt3 23. QKt3 ch. KB2 24. QKt3 ch. QK3, naturally Black gives up the KtP to keep the BP, 25. Q×P ch. KKt1 26. QKt2 ch. KB1, and

228

4 QUEEN AND TWO PAWNS v. QUEEN AND PAWN

the win, if indeed it is possible, is extremely difficult.

15 ...	Q—B5
16 Q—Kt2 ch.	K—B4
17 K—B7	

If 17. Q×BP QQ5 ch., or if 17. Q×KtP QQ4 ch.

| 17 ... | Q—B5 ch. |
| 18 K×P | |

If 18. KB8 QB4 ch. 19. KQ8 QQ4 ch. 20. KB8 QK3 ch. 21. KQ8 QKt3 ch.

| 18 ... | Q—K5 ch. |

18... QKt5 ch.? 19. Q×Q ch. K×Q 20. KB6 draws.

19 K—R7	Q—R5 ch.
20 K—Kt7	Q—Kt4 ch.
White resigns.	

320 Marshall v. Tarrasch, Ostend, 1907. Realizing that one advanced passed pawn is worth a host of pawns farther back, Black sacrificed two pawns to reach this position, which he should have won.

| 1 Q—R5 ch. | K—K8 |
| 2 P—Kt4 | |

Black wins

White does not hope to queen this pawn, but to open lines for his queen.

| 2 ... | P—K6 |
| 3 Q—QB5 | K—Q8 |

Tarrasch avoids the little trap, 3... PK7? 4. QKt1 mate.

| 4 Q—B5 | P—K7 |

In the game 4... QKB7? 5. QKt1 ch. KK7 6. QKt5 ch. KB6 7. QQ5 ch. KKt6 8. QK5 ch. K×P led to a draw.

5 Q—Kt1 ch.	Q—B8
6 Q—Q3 ch.	K—K8
7 K—Kt2	Q—B3 ch.
8 K—Kt1	Q—B4 ch.
9 K—Kt2	Q—B7 ch.
10 K—R3	K—B8
11 P—Kt5	K—Kt8.

And Black wins.

5. MORE PAWNS: MATERIAL ADVANTAGE

In general a pawn up wins.

When there is an outside passed pawn, or when one can be created because there is a wing majority, White's queen simply escorts it to the eighth, Example 321. Black's only defence is perpetual check, so the result is determined according as White's king is sheltered or not by his pawns.

When the kings are on the same side as the pawn majority, the win is more difficult. The stronger party may advance his king and pawns together, and, because the queen is so powerful a piece, mating threats may be concocted as in Example 324; or his king may move to the other side of the board with a view to advancing the majority without hindrance, and preparing for the transition to a pawn ending, as in Example 322.

The only other defence besides perpetual check is to create a passed pawn, and Examples 323-325 show the kind of play involved. It is not so much the number of pawns as the effectiveness of the passed pawns that decides the game. The stronger party seeks to queen his first, to avoid perpetual check, and to create mating threats; the defender pursues exchanges, endeavours to expose the enemy king, and advances his own passed pawns as fast as he can.

With all the pawns on one side of the board the game is normally drawn; but

229

if there are weaknesses to exploit then the extra pawn may win. Here the theme is mating threats, with the additional weapon of zugzwang; whilst the defender, besides the hope of perpetual check, may also seek stalemate positions.

As in the basic endings, a common stratagem is the centralizing of the queen.

She is very weak when on the edge of the board, but almost any other square may prove good. Note for instance Black's 3rd move, Example 322, or his 7th move, Example 330, for in both cases the queen helps prevent perpetual check.

321 White's queen both supports the advance of the passed pawn and prevents perpetual check.

| 1 P—QKt4 | P—Kt4 |
| 2 P—Kt5 | P—Kt5 |

White to play

Black must try and break open the king's side.

If 2... PR4 3. PKt6 PKt5 4. QB7 ch. KR3 5. PKt7 PR5 6. P×P PR6 7. QB6 ch. KR2 8. PKt8=Q.

| 3 Q—B7 ch. | K—R1 |

If 3... KKt1 4. PKt6 P×P 5. QKt3 ch.

| 4 Q—B8 ch. | K—R2 |
| 5 Q×P. | |

White cannot be prevented from getting his queen back to the KR2-QKt8 diagonal: 5... QKt3 6. QQ7 ch. KR1 7. KR1 KKt1 8. QB6 QQ1 9. PKt6 followed by QQB7; or 5... QQB4

6. QK4 ch. KKt1 7. QK8 ch. KKt2 8. QKt8 followed by PKt6 and QQB7.

322 Stahlberg *v.* Keres. Neuhausen, 1953. White's rooks' pawns offer no protection, so that Black can always reposition his queen without loss of time by means of a series of checks. First Black removes his king to the queen's side.

| 1 ... | P—R5 |

Sealing off White's king, and providing an outpost at KKt6 for Black's queen, thus threatening to win the KRP.

2 Q—K5	Q—B7 ch.
3 K—R1	Q—KB4
4 Q—R8 ch.	K—Kt4
5 Q—Q8 ch.	K—B5

Black's KRP is taboo, for after 6. Q×P ch. KB6 the mating threats are fatal.

| 6 Q—Q2 ch. | |

If 6. QQ6 ch. KK6 7. QKt6 ch. KK7, or 6. QB7 ch. KK5 7. QB2 ch. KQ4.

6 ...	K—K4
7 Q—B3 ch.	K—Q4
8 Q—Kt3 ch.	K—B3
9 Q—QB3 ch.	K—Kt2
10 Q—Kt7 ch.	K—R3
11 Q—B3	Q—B8 ch.
12 K—R2	Q—B7 ch.
13 K—R1	K—Kt3
14 Q—B8	

White cannot avoid a queen exchange or the loss of his KRP. If 14. Q—K5

Black to play

(14. QQ3 QK8 ch.   15. KR2 QKt6 ch.)
14... Q—B6 ch.   15. K—R2 Q—Kt6 ch.
Black returns the pawn but wins the
pawn-ending because his king is ready
to capture White's QRP.

If 14. PR4 QB8 ch., but not 14...
P×P? when White stalemates in 2.

14 ...	Q—K8 ch.
15 K—Kt2	Q—K5 ch.
16 K—Kt1	Q—Q5 ch.

White resigns, for if 17. KKt2 QQ4 ch.
18. KR2 QQ3 ch.   19. KKt2 QB3 ch.
exchanging queens.

323 Szabo *v.* Barcza, Budapest,
1955. When each side has a passed pawn
the result is determined by who gets
there first, and whether perpetual check
can be avoided; and it may be of little
consequence that one player has an
extra pawn.

Of the passed pawns Black's is the less
effective because White's king may block
it. In the event Black draws by com-
bining the advance of the KRP with
threats of perpetual check.

1 Q—K5 ch.	K—Kt1
2 P—Kt5	P—R3
3 K—B2	Q—Kt7
4 Q—QB5	P—R4
5 Q—K5	

Exchanges, as here 5 Q×P? Q×QP
ch., favour the defender because they
improve his chances of perpetual check.

It is however possible at this moment
for White's queen to escort his KtP to
the eighth rank, 5. PKt6 PR5 6. QQB8
ch. KR2 7. PKt7. In practice it is not
always easy to calculate whether perpetual check can be evaded, but it so
happens that White's king can doggedly
make its way to a safe square on the
eighth rank, 7... Q×QP ch.   8. KK1
QR8 ch.   9. KQ2 QQ5 ch.   10. KB2
QR5 ch.   11. KB3 QR4 ch.   12. KB4
QQ4 ch.   13. KKt4, etc., and Black
cannot set up the defence of Example
315 because the extra pawns obstruct
his queen.

5 ...	P—R5
6 K—Kt2	Q—Kt8
7 K—R3	Q—R8 ch.
8 Q—R2	

8. KKt4 may be played at once.

8 ...	Q—QKt8
9 Q—Kt8 ch. ?	

This useless check is the decisive
error. 9. Q—K5 wins after 9... Q—R8
ch.   10. K—Kt4 P—R6 11. Q—Kt3
P—R7 (11... QKt7 12. PKt6) 12.
K—R3 ch.

9 ...	K—R2
10 P—Kt6	

After 10. QK5 QR8 ch.   11. KKt4
PR6 12. QKt3 PR7 13. KR3 White
loses his passed pawn, 13... QB8 ch.
14. K×P Q×P ch.

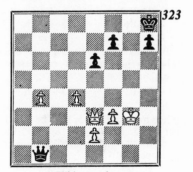

White to play

10 ...	P—B4

Finely calculated.

11 Q—B7 ch.	

If 11. K×P Q—R8 ch.   12. K—Kt3
(better than 12. KKt5? QR3 mate) 12...
Q—Kt8 ch.   13. K—R3 (13. KB4?
QR7 ch.) 13... Q—B8 ch. with perpetual
check.

11 ...	K—Kt3
12 K×P	Q—R8 ch.
13 K—Kt3	Q—Kt8 ch.
14 K—R3	Q—B8 ch.

Not 14... QR8 ch. ? 15. QR2 QB8 ch.
16. QKt2 ch.

15 K—R2	Q—B7 ch.
16 K—R3	Q—B8 ch.
17 K—Kt3	Q—Kt8 ch.
18 K—B4	Q×P ch.
19 P—K4	P—K4 ch.

This seals off the escape route via K5.

20 Q×P	Q—Q7 ch.
21 K—Kt3	Q—K8 ch.

Drawn.

324 Kotov *v.* Steiner, Saltsjobaden, 1948. Black's pawn majority, being farther away, is potentially the more dangerous, and indeed White must avoid a queen exchange which might leave him a lost pawn-ending. But White's KRP is already dangerously advanced, and after 2. PR6 he has a standing threat of QKt7 ch. followed by PR7.

1 P—Kt3	P—R4
2 P—R6	Q—R4 ch.
3 K—Kt2	Q—Q4 ch.

By weakening White's pawns Black enhances his prospects of perpetual check.

4 P—B3	Q—Q7 ch.

4... Q—K4 is the alternative, when White may continue 5. PB4, or 5. QQ3, but not 5. PK4? QB3 6. PB4? PK4 when Black wins because White's queen is trapped.

5 K—R3	Q—B6

5... Q×P, continuing the policy of baring White's king, gives more chances,

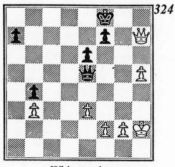

324

White to play

6. Q—Kt7 ch. K—K2 7. P—B4 (if 7. PR7? Q×BP 8. PR8=Q Black has a perpetual check) 7... Q—KB6, and White continues 8. Q—Kt5 ch.

6 Q—K4

By this centralizing move White improves the position of his queen, and threatens QR8 ch. followed by PR7.

6 ...	K—Kt1
7 Q—KB4	P—B4
8 Q—Kt5 ch.	K—R2

If 8... KB2 9. QR5 ch. KKt1 10. QKt6 ch. followed by KR4; also if 8... KB1 9. QQ8 ch. KB2 10. PR7 QR8 11. QKt8 ch. KK2 13. KR4.

9 K—R4

The king takes part in a mating attack, a familiar manœuvre in queen endings.

9 ...	Q—Kt7
10 Q—K7 ch.	

Not 10. KR5? QR7 ch., and Black wins.

10 ...	K—Kt3

10... K×P transposes; whilst if 10... KKt1, or 10. KR1 11. KKt5.

11 Q—K8 ch.

White avoids the trap 11. Q×P ch.? QB3 ch. when he loses the pawn-ending.

11 ...	K×P
12 Q×P ch.	K—Kt2
13 K—Kt5	Q—QB7

There is no saving the game, for the pawns obstruct Black's queen.

14 Q—Q7 ch.	K—B1
15 K—Kt6	P—B5 ch.
16 P—K4.	

Black resigns.

325 van den Berg *v.* Najdorf, Amsterdam, 1950. White permits his queen to be hemmed in, and Black creates mating threats with his king, queen, and central pawns.

1 P—QKt4

White should first centralize his queen

by 1. QQ4, seizing the queen's file, and if necessary block the KP with his king; when it is not easy for Black to capitalize his material advantage, especially as White's protected passed QBP is always to be reckoned with.

1 ...	P—K6
2 Q—K2	Q—K5
3 K—R1	

White is already in trouble. If 3. KB1 QKt8 ch. 4. QK1 QQ6 ch. 5. QK2 Q×P 6. Q×KtP he is mated in 3.

| 3 ... | K—B3 |
| 4 K—Kt1 | Q—Q5 |

Preventing check, and intending to answer 5. KR1 by QQ7.

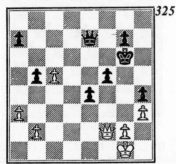

325

White to play

| 5 K—B1 | Q—B5 |
| 6 K—K1 | |

White must not exchange queens and provide Black with another passed pawn.

6 ...   Q—B6 ch.

6... Q×Q ch. leaves a drawn pawn ending, White's powerful QBP balancing his material disadvantage.

7 K—B1   Q—B8 ch.

7... Q×RP is also playable.

| 8 Q—K1 | Q—B5 ch. |
| 9 K—Kt1 | |

If 9. QK2 KK4 10. KK1 QB6 ch. 11. KB1 Q×RP.

| 9 ... | Q—Q5 |
| 10 K—B1 | K—K4 |

| 11 K—K2 | P—B5 |
| 12 Q—Q1 | Q—Kt7 ch. |

Black cannot be induced to exchange queens—

13 K—B3	Q—B7 ch.
14 K—Kt4	Q×KtP ch.
15 K—R5	Q—Q4

—except on his own terms.

16 Q—Kt4.

Black mates in 4.

326 Ciocaltea *v.* Unzicker, Moscow, 1956. White's slightly weakened pawns permit Black's king to enter. With rooks a draw would be in order, but with queens Black wins because of the mating threats concocted by his king and queen.

1 ...   K—B3

Black's queen is already centralized, so his next task is to advance the king, in the direction of KB8.

2 Q—Q8 ch.	K—B4
3 Q—Q7 ch.	K—K5
4 Q—K7 ch.	K—Q6
5 Q—Q7 ch.	K—K7
6 Q—K7 ch.	Q—K3
7 Q—Kt7	P—B4

Here we have omitted some repetitious checks.

The KBP serves a triple function. It provides a strong-point at K5 for Black's queen, it protects Black's king from checks on the KB file, and it becomes the spearhead of the final attack.

8 Q—KKt2 ch.

Either 8. QKt5 ch. KB7 9. QB5 ch. QK6, or 8. QQKt2 ch. KB6 9. QKt2 ch. transposes.

| 8 ... | K—K6 |
| 9 Q—Kt2 | |

After 9. QKt1 ch. KK7 10. QKt2 ch. Black escapes the checks by 10... KQ6 11. QB3 ch. KQ7 12. QB4 ch. KK7.

9 ...	Q—B5
10 Q—R3 ch.	Q—Q6
11 Q—B5 ch.	K—B6
12 Q—B6 ch,	

326

Black to play

After the defensive 12. Q—Kt1 Black breaks up the pawns by 12... P—B5, and soon forces a queen exchange, when the advanced position of his king brings about a winning pawn ending, 13. P×P (13. KR3 KK7 14. QKt2 ch. KK8, or 13. QKt2 ch. KK6 14. QKt1 ch. KQ7 15. P×P QK7 ch.) 13... Q—B7 ch. 14. K—R1 (14. KR3 QB4 ch.) 14... Q—K5 15. Q—Kt5 Q—Kt8 ch. 16. K—R2 Q—B7 ch. 17. K—R1 (17. KR3 QB4 ch.) 17... Q—B8 ch. 18. K—R2 Q×P ch.

12 ...   Q—K5
13 Q—B3 ch.

Black has indirectly protected his KKtP, for if 13. Q×P he mates in 2.

13 ...   K—B7
14 Q—B5 ch.
14 QQ2 ch. KB8 transposes.
14 ...   Q—K6
15 Q—B2 ch.

If White guards his KtP by 15. QB7, then 15... PB5.

15 ...   Q—K7
16 Q—B6   K—B8 ch.
17 K—R3   K—Kt8
18 Q—B5 ch.   Q—B7
19 Q—K3

This stalemate attempt is the only way of postponing mate or an exchange of queens.

19 ...   P—B5.

White resigns, for after 20. Q×Q ch. the pawn ending is lost.

327 Averbach *v.* Suetin, Moscow, 1954. Black cannot defend both the isolated pawn and the mating threats. The win is forced, and not difficult.

1 Q—Q8 ch.	K—B2
2 Q—Q7 ch.	K—Kt1
3 Q—K6 ch.	K—R2
4 Q—B7	Q—K5
5 P—Kt3	Q—K7
6 P—Kt4	Q—Q7
7 K—Kt3	Q—B6 ch.
8 K—R4	Q—Q5
9 Q—B5 ch.	P—Kt3

327

White to play

If 9... KKt1 10. KR5 QQ3 11. PKt5, followed by PKt6, with threats of mate on the back rank, and Black will soon find himself in zugzwang.

10 Q—B7 ch.	K—R3
11 Q—B6	K—R2
12 K—Kt5	Q—Q7 ch.
13 P—B4	P×P

13. Q×P ch. leaves him a lost pawn ending.

| 14 Q—B7 ch. | K—R1 |
| 15 K—R6. | |

Black resigns, for if 15... PB6 ch. 16. PKt5, and mate follows.

6 MORE PAWNS: POSITIONAL ADVANTAGE

By far the most powerful advantage is an advanced passed pawn; for the queen may brush aside all opposition and

escort it to the eighth with alarming
speed, Examples 328 and 329.

When the pawns are balanced one
player may have his queen better placed,
on the seventh, on the open file, or on a
powerful central square. This advantage
does not always win, and may not be a
permanent one if the defender is able to
offer a queen exchange so as to remove
the aggressive queen, or if there are no
specific points of attack. Much depends
on the pawn configuration, and as was
the case with rooks, the factor of the
better queen position is linked with that
of weak pawns.

The same motifs occur in these endings: mating nets, zugzwang, perpetual
check, and stalemate; and the idea of
playing for the pawn ending which is so
frequently the outcome of a queen
exchange.

328 Bannik *v.* Cholmov, U.S.S.R.
Championship, 1956. White's extra
pawn is no compensation for Black's
QRP.

| 1 ... | Q—B1 |

With one fine stroke Black guards his
king's side against threats of perpetual
check, or even mate, and also frees his
QRP.

| 2 K—Kt5 | |

As in Examples 322, 325, and 326, a
vital pawn is indirectly protected by
mating threats, for if 2. Q×P QQ3 ch.
3. KKt5 KKt2, threatening mate by
PB3 or QK4.

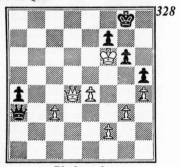

Black to play

2 ...	Q—K2 ch.
3 K—B4	P—R6
4 K—K3	Q—Kt2
5 Q—Q8 ch.	K—R2
6 Q—R5	Q—Kt7
7 Q—B7	Q—Kt6

The same idea as Example 321, Black's
queen both supports the passed pawn
and defends the king's side.

8 P—Kt4	P—R7
9 Q—R5	Q—Kt7
10 Q—B7	K—Kt1

A triangulation exhausts the enemy
threats of perpetual check.

11 Q—Q8 ch.	K—Kt2
12 Q—Q4 ch.	K—R2
13 Q—B4	Q—Kt3 ch.
14 K—K2	Q—R2
15 P×P	P—R8=Q
16 P×P ch.	P×P.

White resigns.

329 Benko *v.* Bilek, Budapest, 1957.
White demonstrates that the blocked
position is not so unassailable as it
seems; and the threat of advancing the
passed QKtP determines the result in his
favour.

| 1 Q—B1 | |

This threatens Q—KB1-KKt2-QR8-
QR6, a remarkable manœuvre!

| 1 ... | P—R3 |
| 2 P—R4 | |

White need not hurry. The text-move
not only makes a new point of attack,
Black's KKtP, but opens a new line for
his queen, the KR file.

2 ...	Q—Q3
3 P×P ch.	P×P
4 Q—Kt1	

A finesse threatening PKt6, and
forcing Black's queen to retreat.

| 4 ... | Q—Kt3 |
| 5 Q—KB1 | P—K5 |

An attempt at counterplay, perhaps
hoping for 6. P×P? PB5.

| 6 Q—R3 | Q—Q1 |

329

White to play

Black might at all events have continued with 6... P×P, or 6... KKt3, not without prospects of making a passed pawn in the centre.

7 Q—R6 ch.	K—K4
8 Q—Kt7 ch.	K—Q3
9 P×P	

Now Black's passed pawn cannot be advanced.

| 9 ... | P—Kt5 |

With a slender hope of 10. Q×P PB5.

10 Q—QKt7

White pursues his main objective, and threatens QB6 ch. followed by PKt6.

10 ...	Q—B2
11 P—K5 ch.	K—Q2
12 Q×Q ch.	K×Q
13 K—B1	P—B5
14 K—K1	K—Kt3
15 K—Q2	K—B4
16 P—B3.	

Black resigns.

330 Marshall *v.* Maroczy, Ostend, 1905. Because of his aggressively placed queen Black is able to fix White's QKtP as a point of attack. The defence of the weak KP will also involve White in further weaknesses.

1 Q—R1

A humiliating position for a queen, and a move that should hardly have been considered. The pawn sacrifice 1.

P—QKt4 Q—Kt7 2. P—KKt3 Q×RP 3. K—Kt2 offers some chances of salvation; and if 3... P—QR4 (better 3... QQ6) 4. P×P P—Kt5 5. P—R6 P—Kt6 6. Q—K3.

| 1 ... | P—QR4 |
| 2 P—KKt3 | |

If 2. PQKt4 P×P 3. P×P QK5 winning a pawn; or if 2. PQR4 PKt5.

| 2 ... | P—R5 |
| 3 P—B4 | |

Sooner or later this move is unavoidable.

| 3 ... | K—Kt1 |
| 4 P—R3 | |

This makes another weakness, the KKtP; but the game is not to be saved. Black has a choice of several winning ideas: bringing the king to the queen's side (QKt6), or penetrating the king's side so as to create mating threats, or advancing his KRP to the fifth with a further weakening of Black's pawns.

330

White to play

4 ...	P—R4
5 P—R4	K—Kt2
6 K—R1	

White is in zugzwang and must lose at least a pawn. If 6. Q—R2 the queen is even more badly placed (6. KB1 QR7) 6... Q—Q8 ch. 7. K—B2 (7. KKt2 QK7 ch. 8. KKt1 QB6 9. KR2 QB7 ch. 10. KR3 QKt8) 7... K—R2 8. K—K3 Q—Kt8 ch. 9. K—B3 Q—B8 ch. 10. K—K3 Q—Kt7.

6 ...	Q—B7
7 Q—KKt1	Q×QKtP
8 Q—B5	P—Kt5
9 P—B5	

White cannot get a perpetual check by 9. Q—K7 because of 9... Q—B8 ch. 10. K—R2 Q—Q7 ch. depriving him of the use of his Q8 square, 11. K—R3 Q—Q8 12. K—R2 P—Kt6, and if 13. P—B5 Q—B7 ch.

9 ...	KP×P

If 9... KtP×P 10. QK3.

10 P—K6	P×RP
11 P×P	K×P
12 Q—Q5 ch.	K—K2
13 Q—B5 ch.	K—K3
14 Q—B6 ch.	K—K4
15 Q×RP	P—R7
16 Q—K8 ch.	K—Q4
17 Q—Q7 ch.	K—K5
18 Q—K6 ch.	K—B6
19 Q—B6 ch.	K—K6
20 Q—B5 ch.	

In the game Black gave up the QRP to exchange queens, 20... QQ5 21. QR3 ch. QQ6 22. QR7 ch. KB6 23. Q×P QB8 ch. 24. KR2 QB7 ch. Instead he could evade the checks and queen the QRP, 20... KK7 21. QB4 ch. KK8 22. QK6 ch. KQ7 23. QQ6 ch. KB7 24. QB5 ch. KKt8.

331 Lissitzin *v.* Capablanca, Moscow, 1935. The defence of White's isolated pawns is irksome, but Black's advantage is not so marked as in the preceding example, and a win cannot be forced.

1 ...	K—B3

Black can do nothing unless his king participates.

2 Q—Kt2	Q—Q4
3 K—K3?	

3. QKt4 holds the position, for then Black's king cannot easily be brought into play.

3 ...	P—K4?

Black hopes for 4. P×P ch. Q×P ch. 5. Q×Q ch. bringing his king to the fourth rank, with a winning pawn-ending; but the player having the advantage should not carelessly bring about pawn-exchanges, which in a general way favour the defender.

3... QB5 is correct, when White is in danger of running out of moves, and Black may in due course bring his king to Q4, whilst if 4. PQ5 ch. PK4, and a pawn is lost.

4 P—B4?

It is not certain that this move is the decisive error, but it leaves Black a useful majority of pawns on the king's side, whilst White still has his weak pawns to defend. 4. Q—Kt4 is best, and after 4... K—K3 (if 4... P×P ch. 5. Q×P ch. QK4 ch. the pawn-ending is drawn) 5. P×P Q×P ch. White can hold the position, having eliminated his weak QP.

Black to play

4 ...	P×BP ch.
5 K×P	K—K3
6 P—R4	

After 6. QK2 ch. KQ3 7. QK5 ch. Q×Q ch. 8. P×Q ch. KQ4 Black wins the KP and the pawn-ending.

6 ...	P—B3
7 K—K3	

If 7. Q—K2 ch. K—Q3 8. Q—K4 P—Kt4 ch. (8... Q×Q ch. draws) 9. P×P Q×P ch. 10. K—B3 Q×P 11. Q—B4 ch. K—Q2.

7 ...	Q—B5

The immediate 7... PKt4 seems more logical.

8 P—Kt3

So as to answer 8... KQ4 by 9. QKt2 ch. Instead White should play 8. QKt1, threatening the KKtP, and giving the queen more scope. It was apparently assumed that 8... Q—B6 ch. 9. Q—Q3 Q×Q ch. 10. K×Q K—Q4 11. K—K3 would leave Black a won pawn-ending because of his wing majority, but, as shown by Grigoriev, if Black attempts to win he loses, e.g. 11... KB5? 12. KK4 K×P 13. KQ5, or 11... PKt4? 12. PKt4.

8 ...	P—Kt4
9 P×P	P×P
10 Q—KR2?	

Hoping for further exchanges, and chances of perpetual check, White overlooks that even with his king in the centre of the board there may be mating threats.

Instead, 10. K—K4 offers stout resistance.

| 10 ... | Q—Kt6 ch. |
| 11 K—K4 | P—Kt5 |

Indirectly guarding the KRP (12. Q×P QB6 mate).

12 Q—K2

White's queen is skewered after 12. KB4 QB6 ch. 13. KKt5 QB3 ch. 14. K×P QR1 ch.

12 ...	Q×KKtP
13 Q—B4 ch.	K—K2
14 Q—B8	Q—B6 ch.
15 K—K5	Q—B3 ch.
16 K—Q5	Q—Q3 ch.

White resigns, for the queens are forced off. An object lesson of the need for the correct evaluation of the pawn endings which may come about.

INDEX OF PLAYERS

INDEX OF COMPOSERS
AND ANALYSTS

INDEX OF PLAYERS

The numbers refer to the examples

INDEX OF PLAYERS

INDEX OF PLAYERS

INDEX OF COMPOSERS AND ANALYSTS

The numbers refer to examples

INDEX OF COMPOSERS

A CATALOGUE OF
SELECTED DOVER BOOKS
IN ALL FIELDS OF INTEREST

A CATALOGUE OF SELECTED DOVER
BOOKS IN ALL FIELDS OF INTEREST

CONDITIONED REFLEXES, Ivan P. Pavlov. Full translation of most complete statement of Pavlov's work; cerebral damage, conditioned reflex, experiments with dogs, sleep, similar topics of great importance. 430pp. 5⅜ x 8½. 60614-7 Pa. $4.50

NOTES ON NURSING: WHAT IT IS, AND WHAT IT IS NOT, Florence Nightingale. Outspoken writings by founder of modern nursing. When first published (1860) it played an important role in much needed revolution in nursing. Still stimulating. 140pp. 5⅜ x 8½. 22340-X Pa. $2.50

HARTER'S PICTURE ARCHIVE FOR COLLAGE AND ILLUSTRATION, Jim Harter. Over 300 authentic, rare 19th-century engravings selected by noted collagist for artists, designers, decoupeurs, etc. Machines, people, animals, etc., printed one side of page. 25 scene plates for backgrounds. 6 collages by Harter, Satty, Singer, Evans. Introduction. 192pp. 8⅞ x 11¾. 23659-5 Pa. $5.00

MANUAL OF TRADITIONAL WOOD CARVING, edited by Paul N. Hasluck. Possibly the best book in English on the craft of wood carving. Practical instructions, along with 1,146 working drawings and photographic illustrations. Formerly titled *Cassell's Wood Carving*. 576pp. 6½ x 9¼. 23489-4 Pa. $7.95

THE PRINCIPLES AND PRACTICE OF HAND OR SIMPLE TURNING, John Jacob Holtzapffel. Full coverage of basic lathe techniques—history and development, special apparatus, softwood turning, hardwood turning, metal turning. Many projects—billiard ball, works formed within a sphere, egg cups, ash trays, vases, jardiniers, others—included. 1881 edition. 800 illustrations. 592pp. 6⅛ x 9¼. 23365-0 Clothbd. $15.00

THE JOY OF HANDWEAVING, Osma Tod. Only book you need for hand weaving. Fundamentals, threads, weaves, plus numerous projects for small board-loom, two-harness, tapestry, laid-in, four-harness weaving and more. Over 160 illustrations. 2nd revised edition. 352pp. 6½ x 9¼. 23458-4 Pa. $5.00

THE BOOK OF WOOD CARVING, Charles Marshall Sayers. Still finest book for beginning student in wood sculpture. Noted teacher, craftsman discusses fundamentals, technique; gives 34 designs, over 34 projects for panels, bookends, mirrors, etc. "Absolutely first-rate"—E. J. Tangerman. 33 photos. 118pp. 7¾ x 10⅝. 23654-4 Pa. $3.00

DRAWINGS OF WILLIAM BLAKE, William Blake. 92 plates from Book of Job, *Divine Comedy, Paradise Lost,* visionary heads, mythological figures, Laocoon, etc. Selection, introduction, commentary by Sir Geoffrey Keynes. 178pp. 8⅛ x 11.　　　　　　　　　　22303-5 Pa. $4.00

ENGRAVINGS OF HOGARTH, William Hogarth. 101 of Hogarth's greatest works: *Rake's Progress, Harlot's Progress, Illustrations for Hudibras, Before and After, Beer Street and Gin Lane,* many more. Full commentary. 256pp. 11 x 13¾.　　　　　　　　　　22479-1 Pa. $7.95

DAUMIER: 120 GREAT LITHOGRAPHS, Honore Daumier. Wide-ranging collection of lithographs by the greatest caricaturist of the 19th century. Concentrates on eternally popular series on lawyers, on married life, on liberated women, etc. Selection, introduction, and notes on plates by Charles F. Ramus. Total of 158pp. 9⅜ x 12¼.　　　23512-2 Pa. $5.50

DRAWINGS OF MUCHA, Alphonse Maria Mucha. Work reveals draftsman of highest caliber: studies for famous posters and paintings, renderings for book illustrations and ads, etc. 70 works, 9 in color; including 6 items not drawings. Introduction. List of illustrations. 72pp. 9⅜ x 12¼. (Available in U.S. only)　　　　　　　　　　23672-2 Pa. $4.00

GIOVANNI BATTISTA PIRANESI: DRAWINGS IN THE PIERPONT MORGAN LIBRARY, Giovanni Battista Piranesi. For first time ever all of Morgan Library's collection, world's largest. 167 illustrations of rare Piranesi drawings—archeological, architectural, decorative and visionary. Essay, detailed list of drawings, chronology, captions. Edited by Felice Stampfle. 144pp. 9⅜ x 12¼.　　　　　　　　23714-1 Pa. $7.50

NEW YORK ETCHINGS (1905-1949), John Sloan. All of important American artist's N.Y. life etchings. 67 works include some of his best art; also lively historical record—Greenwich Village, tenement scenes. Edited by Sloan's widow. Introduction and captions. 79pp. 8⅜ x 11¼.　　　　　　　　　　　　　　　23651-X Pa. $4.00

CHINESE PAINTING AND CALLIGRAPHY: A PICTORIAL SURVEY, Wan-go Weng. 69 fine examples from John M. Crawford's matchless private collection: landscapes, birds, flowers, human figures, etc., plus calligraphy. Every basic form included: hanging scrolls, handscrolls, album leaves, fans, etc. 109 illustrations. Introduction. Captions. 192pp. 8⅞ x 11¾.　　　　　　　　　　　　　　　23707-9 Pa. $7.95

DRAWINGS OF REMBRANDT, edited by Seymour Slive. Updated Lippmann, Hofstede de Groot edition, with definitive scholarly apparatus. All portraits, biblical sketches, landscapes, nudes, Oriental figures, classical studies, together with selection of work by followers. 550 illustrations. Total of 630pp. 9⅛ x 12¼.　21485-0, 21486-9 Pa., Two-vol. set $15.00

THE DISASTERS OF WAR, Francisco Goya. 83 etchings record horrors of Napoleonic wars in Spain and war in general. Reprint of 1st edition, plus 3 additional plates. Introduction by Philip Hofer. 97pp. 9⅜ x 8¼.　　　　　　　　　　　　　　　21872-4 Pa. $3.75

THE EARLY WORK OF AUBREY BEARDSLEY, Aubrey Beardsley. 157 plates, 2 in color: *Manon Lescaut, Madame Bovary, Morte Darthur, Salome,* other. Introduction by H. Marillier. 182pp. 8⅛ x 11. 21816-3 Pa. $4.50

THE LATER WORK OF AUBREY BEARDSLEY, Aubrey Beardsley. Exotic masterpieces of full maturity: *Venus and Tannhauser, Lysistrata, Rape of the Lock, Volpone,* Savoy material, etc. 174 plates, 2 in color. 186pp. 8⅛ x 11. 21817-1 Pa. $4.50

THOMAS NAST'S CHRISTMAS DRAWINGS, Thomas Nast. Almost all Christmas drawings by creator of image of Santa Claus as we know it, and one of America's foremost illustrators and political cartoonists. 66 illustrations. 3 illustrations in color on covers. 96pp. 8⅜ x 11¼. 23660-9 Pa. $3.50

THE DORÉ ILLUSTRATIONS FOR DANTE'S DIVINE COMEDY, Gustave Doré. All 135 plates from Inferno, Purgatory, Paradise; fantastic tortures, infernal landscapes, celestial wonders. Each plate with appropriate (translated) verses. 141pp. 9 x 12. 23231-X Pa. $4.50

DORÉ'S ILLUSTRATIONS FOR RABELAIS, Gustave Doré. 252 striking illustrations of *Gargantua and Pantagruel* books by foremost 19th-century illustrator. Including 60 plates, 192 delightful smaller illustrations. 153pp. 9 x 12. 23656-0 Pa. $5.00

LONDON: A PILGRIMAGE, Gustave Doré, Blanchard Jerrold. Squalor, riches, misery, beauty of mid-Victorian metropolis; 55 wonderful plates, 125 other illustrations, full social, cultural text by Jerrold. 191pp. of text. 9⅜ x 12¼. 22306-X Pa. $6.00

THE RIME OF THE ANCIENT MARINER, Gustave Doré, S. T. Coleridge. Dore's finest work, 34 plates capture moods, subtleties of poem. Full text. Introduction by Millicent Rose. 77pp. 9¼ x 12. 22305-1 Pa. $3.50

THE DORE BIBLE ILLUSTRATIONS, Gustave Doré. All wonderful, detailed plates: Adam and Eve, Flood, Babylon, Life of Jesus, etc. Brief King James text with each plate. Introduction by Millicent Rose. 241 plates. 241pp. 9 x 12. 23004-X Pa. $6.00

THE COMPLETE ENGRAVINGS, ETCHINGS AND DRYPOINTS OF ALBRECHT DURER. "Knight, Death and Devil"; "Melencolia," and more—all Dürer's known works in all three media, including 6 works formerly attributed to him. 120 plates. 235pp. 8⅜ x 11¼. 22851-7 Pa. $6.50

MAXIMILIAN'S TRIUMPHAL ARCH, Albrecht Dürer and others. Incredible monument of woodcut art: 8 foot high elaborate arch—heraldic figures, humans, battle scenes, fantastic elements—that you can assemble yourself. Printed on one side, layout for assembly. 143pp. 11 x 16. 21451-6 Pa. $5.00

THE COMPLETE WOODCUTS OF ALBRECHT DURER, edited by Dr. W. Kurth. 346 in all: "Old Testament," "St. Jerome," "Passion," "Life of Virgin," Apocalypse," many others. Introduction by Campbell Dodgson. 285pp. 8½ x 12¼.   21097-9 Pa. $6.95

DRAWINGS OF ALBRECHT DURER, edited by Heinrich Wolfflin. 81 plates show development from youth to full style. Many favorites; many new. Introduction by Alfred Werner. 96pp. 8⅛ x 11.   22352-3 Pa. $5.00

THE HUMAN FIGURE, Albrecht Dürer. Experiments in various techniques—stereometric, progressive proportional, and others. Also life studies that rank among finest ever done. Complete reprinting of *Dresden Sketchbook*. 170 plates. 355pp. 8⅜ x 11¼.   21042-1 Pa. $7.95

OF THE JUST SHAPING OF LETTERS, Albrecht Dürer. Renaissance artist explains design of Roman majuscules by geometry, also Gothic lower and capitals. Grolier Club edition. 43pp. 7⅞ x 10¾   21306-4 Pa. $3.00

TEN BOOKS ON ARCHITECTURE, Vitruvius. The most important book ever written on architecture. Early Roman aesthetics, technology, classical orders, site selection, all other aspects. Stands behind everything since. Morgan translation. 331pp. 5⅜ x 8½.   20645-9 Pa. $4.00

THE FOUR BOOKS OF ARCHITECTURE, Andrea Palladio. 16th-century classic responsible for Palladian movement and style. Covers classical architectural remains, Renaissance revivals, classical orders, etc. 1738 Ware English edition. Introduction by A. Placzek. 216 plates. 110pp. of text. 9½ x 12¾.   21308-0 Pa. $8.95

HORIZONS, Norman Bel Geddes. Great industrialist stage designer, "father of streamlining," on application of aesthetics to transportation, amusement, architecture, etc. 1932 prophetic account; function, theory, specific projects. 222 illustrations. 312pp. 7⅞ x 10¾.   23514-9 Pa. $6.95

FRANK LLOYD WRIGHT'S FALLINGWATER, Donald Hoffmann. Full, illustrated story of conception and building of Wright's masterwork at Bear Run, Pa. 100 photographs of site, construction, and details of completed structure. 112pp. 9¼ x 10.   23671-4 Pa. $5.00

THE ELEMENTS OF DRAWING, John Ruskin. Timeless classic by great Viltorian; starts with basic ideas, works through more difficult. Many practical exercises. 48 illustrations. Introduction by Lawrence Campbell. 228pp. 5⅜ x 8½.   22730-8 Pa. $2.75

GIST OF ART, John Sloan. Greatest modern American teacher, Art Students League, offers innumerable hints, instructions, guided comments to help you in painting. Not a formal course. 46 illustrations. Introduction by Helen Sloan. 200pp. 5⅜ x 8½.   23435-5 Pa. $3.50

THE ANATOMY OF THE HORSE, George Stubbs. Often considered the great masterpiece of animal anatomy. Full reproduction of 1766 edition, plus prospectus; original text and modernized text. 36 plates. Introduction by Eleanor Garvey. 121pp. 11 x 14¾. 23402-9 Pa. $6.00

BRIDGMAN'S LIFE DRAWING, George B. Bridgman. More than 500 illustrative drawings and text teach you to abstract the body into its major masses, use light and shade, proportion; as well as specific areas of anatomy, of which Bridgman is master. 192pp. 6½ x 9¼. (Available in U.S. only) 22710-3 Pa. $3.00

ART NOUVEAU DESIGNS IN COLOR, Alphonse Mucha, Maurice Verneuil, Georges Auriol. Full-color reproduction of *Combinaisons ornementales* (c. 1900) by Art Nouveau masters. Floral, animal, geometric, interlacings, swashes—borders, frames, spots—all incredibly beautiful. 60 plates, hundreds of designs. 9⅜ x 8-1/16. 22885-1 Pa. $4.00

FULL-COLOR FLORAL DESIGNS IN THE ART NOUVEAU STYLE, E. A. Seguy. 166 motifs, on 40 plates, from *Les fleurs et leurs applications decoratives* (1902): borders, circular designs, repeats, allovers, "spots." All in authentic Art Nouveau colors. 48pp. 9⅜ x 12¼. 23439-8 Pa. $5.00

A DIDEROT PICTORIAL ENCYCLOPEDIA OF TRADES AND IN-DUSTRY, edited by Charles C. Gillispie. 485 most interesting plates from the great French Encyclopedia of the 18th century show hundreds of working figures, artifacts, process, land and cityscapes; glassmaking, papermaking, metal extraction, construction, weaving, making furniture, clothing, wigs, dozens of other activities. Plates fully explained. 920pp. 9 x 12. 22284-5, 22285-3 Clothbd., Two-vol. set $40.00

HANDBOOK OF EARLY ADVERTISING ART, Clarence P. Hornung. Largest collection of copyright-free early and antique advertising art ever compiled. Over 6,000 illustrations, from Franklin's time to the 1890's for special effects, novelty. Valuable source, almost inexhaustible.
Pictorial Volume. Agriculture, the zodiac, animals, autos, birds, Christmas, fire engines, flowers, trees, musical instruments, ships, games and sports, much more. Arranged by subject matter and use. 237 plates. 288pp. 9 x 12. 20122-8 Clothbd. $13.50

Typographical Volume. Roman and Gothic faces ranging from 10 point to 300 point, "Barnum," German and Old English faces, script, logotypes, scrolls and flourishes, 1115 ornamental initials, 67 complete alphabets, more. 310 plates. 320pp. 9 x 12. 20123-6 Clothbd. $15.00

CALLIGRAPHY (CALLIGRAPHIA LATINA), J. G. Schwandner. High point of 18th-century ornamental calligraphy. Very ornate initials, scrolls, borders, cherubs, birds, lettered examples. 172pp. 9 x 13. 20475-8 Pa. $6.00

ART FORMS IN NATURE, Ernst Haeckel. Multitude of strangely beautiful natural forms: Radiolaria, Foraminifera, jellyfishes, fungi, turtles, bats, etc. All 100 plates of the 19th-century evolutionist's *Kunstformen der Natur* (1904). 100pp. 9⅜ x 12¼.   22987-4 Pa. $4.50

CHILDREN: A PICTORIAL ARCHIVE FROM NINETEENTH-CENTURY SOURCES, edited by Carol Belanger Grafton. 242 rare, copyright-free wood engravings for artists and designers. Widest such selection available. All illustrations in line. 119pp. 8⅜ x 11¼.
23694-3 Pa. $3.50

WOMEN: A PICTORIAL ARCHIVE FROM NINETEENTH-CENTURY SOURCES, edited by Jim Harter. 391 copyright-free wood engravings for artists and designers selected from rare periodicals. Most extensive such collection available. All illustrations in line. 128pp. 9 x 12.
23703-6 Pa. $4.50

ARABIC ART IN COLOR, Prisse d'Avennes. From the greatest ornamentalists of all time—50 plates in color, rarely seen outside the Near East, rich in suggestion and stimulus. Includes 4 plates on covers. 46pp. 9⅜ x 12¼.   23658-7 Pa. $6.00

AUTHENTIC ALGERIAN CARPET DESIGNS AND MOTIFS, edited by June Beveridge. Algerian carpets are world famous. Dozens of geometrical motifs are charted on grids, color-coded, for weavers, needleworkers, craftsmen, designers. 53 illustrations plus 4 in color. 48pp. 8¼ x 11. (Available in U.S. only)   23650-1 Pa. $1.75

DICTIONARY OF AMERICAN PORTRAITS, edited by Hayward and Blanche Cirker. 4000 important Americans, earliest times to 1905, mostly in clear line. Politicians, writers, soldiers, scientists, inventors, industrialists, Indians, Blacks, women, outlaws, etc. Identificatory information. 756pp. 9¼ x 12¾.   21823-6 Clothbd. $40.00

HOW THE OTHER HALF LIVES, Jacob A. Riis. Journalistic record of filth, degradation, upward drive in New York immigrant slums, shops, around 1900. New edition includes 100 original Riis photos, monuments of early photography. 233pp. 10 x 7⅞.   22012-5 Pa. $6.00

NEW YORK IN THE THIRTIES, Berenice Abbott. Noted photographer's fascinating study of city shows new buildings that have become famous and old sights that have disappeared forever. Insightful commentary. 97 photographs. 97pp. 11⅜ x 10.   22967-X Pa. $5.00

MEN AT WORK, Lewis W. Hine. Famous photographic studies of construction workers, railroad men, factory workers and coal miners. New supplement of 18 photos on Empire State building construction. New introduction by Jonathan L. Doherty. Total of 69 photos. 63pp. 8 x 10¾.
23475-4 Pa. $3.00

CATALOGUE OF DOVER BOOKS

THE DEPRESSION YEARS AS PHOTOGRAPHED BY ARTHUR ROTH-STEIN, Arthur Rothstein. First collection devoted entirely to the work of outstanding 1930s photographer: famous dust storm photo, ragged children, unemployed, etc. 120 photographs. Captions. 119pp. 9¼ x 10¾.
23590-4 Pa. $5.00

CAMERA WORK: A PICTORIAL GUIDE, Alfred Stieglitz. All 559 illustrations and plates from the most important periodical in the history of art photography, Camera Work (1903-17). Presented four to a page, reduced in size but still clear, in strict chronological order, with complete captions. Three indexes. Glossary. Bibliography. 176pp. 8⅜ x 11¼.
23591-2 Pa. $6.95

ALVIN LANGDON COBURN, PHOTOGRAPHER, Alvin L. Coburn. Revealing autobiography by one of greatest photographers of 20th century gives insider's version of Photo-Secession, plus comments on his own work. 77 photographs by Coburn. Edited by Helmut and Alison Gernsheim. 160pp. 8⅛ x 11.
23685-4 Pa. $6.00

NEW YORK IN THE FORTIES, Andreas Feininger. 162 brilliant photographs by the well-known photographer, formerly with Life magazine, show commuters, shoppers, Times Square at night, Harlem nightclub, Lower East Side, etc. Introduction and full captions by John von Hartz. 181pp. 9¼ x 10¾.
23585-8 Pa. $6.00

GREAT NEWS PHOTOS AND THE STORIES BEHIND THEM, John Faber. Dramatic volume of 140 great news photos, 1855 through 1976, and revealing stories behind them, with both historical and technical information. Hindenburg disaster, shooting of Oswald, nomination of Jimmy Carter, etc. 160pp. 8¼ x 11.
23667-6 Pa. $5.00

THE ART OF THE CINEMATOGRAPHER, Leonard Maltin. Survey of American cinematography history and anecdotal interviews with 5 masters—Arthur Miller, Hal Mohr, Hal Rosson, Lucien Ballard, and Conrad Hall. Very large selection of behind-the-scenes production photos. 105 photographs. Filmographies. Index. Originally Behind the Camera. 144pp. 8¼ x 11.
23686-2 Pa. $5.00

DESIGNS FOR THE THREE-CORNERED HAT (LE TRICORNE), Pablo Picasso. 32 fabulously rare drawings—including 31 color illustrations of costumes and accessories—for 1919 production of famous ballet. Edited by Parmenia Migel, who has written new introduction. 48pp. 9⅜ x 12¼. (Available in U.S. only)
23709-5 Pa. $5.00

NOTES OF A FILM DIRECTOR, Sergei Eisenstein. Greatest Russian filmmaker explains montage, making of Alexander Nevsky, aesthetics; comments on self, associates, great rivals (Chaplin), similar material. 78 illustrations. 240pp. 5⅜ x 8½.
22392-2 Pa. $4.50

HOLLYWOOD GLAMOUR PORTRAITS, edited by John Kobal. 145 photos capture the stars from 1926-49, the high point in portrait photography. Gable, Harlow, Bogart, Bacall, Hedy Lamarr, Marlene Dietrich, Robert Montgomery, Marlon Brando, Veronica Lake; 94 stars in all. Full background on photographers, technical aspects, much more. Total of 160pp. 8⅜ x 11¼. 23352-9 Pa. $5.00

THE NEW YORK STAGE: FAMOUS PRODUCTIONS IN PHOTOGRAPHS, edited by Stanley Appelbaum. 148 photographs from Museum of City of New York show 142 plays, 1883-1939. *Peter Pan, The Front Page, Dead End, Our Town,* O'Neill, hundreds of actors and actresses, etc. Full indexes. 154pp. 9½ x 10. 23241-7 Pa. $6.00

MASTERS OF THE DRAMA, John Gassner. Most comprehensive history of the drama, every tradition from Greeks to modern Europe and America, including Orient. Covers 800 dramatists, 2000 plays; biography, plot summaries, criticism, theatre history, etc. 77 illustrations. 890pp. 5⅜ x 8½. 20100-7 Clothbd. $10.00

THE GREAT OPERA STARS IN HISTORIC PHOTOGRAPHS, edited by James Camner. 343 portraits from the 1850s to the 1940s: Tamburini, Mario, Caliapin, Jeritza, Melchior, Melba, Patti, Pinza, Schipa, Caruso, Farrar, Steber, Gobbi, and many more—270 performers in all. Index. 199pp. 8⅜ x 11¼. 23575-0 Pa. $6.50

J. S. BACH, Albert Schweitzer. Great full-length study of Bach, life, background to music, music, by foremost modern scholar. Ernest Newman translation. 650 musical examples. Total of 928pp. 5⅜ x 8½. (Available in U.S. only) 21631-4, 21632-2 Pa., Two-vol. set $10.00

COMPLETE PIANO SONATAS, Ludwig van Beethoven. All sonatas in the fine Schenker edition, with fingering, analytical material. One of best modern editions. Total of 615pp. 9 x 12. (Available in U.S. only) 23134-8, 23135-6 Pa., Two-vol. set $15.00

KEYBOARD MUSIC, J. S. Bach. Bach-Gesellschaft edition. For harpsichord, piano, other keyboard instruments. English Suites, French Suites, Six Partitas, Goldberg Variations, Two-Part Inventions, Three-Part Sinfonias. 312pp. 8⅛ x 11. (Available in U.S. only) 22360-4 Pa. $6.00

FOUR SYMPHONIES IN FULL SCORE, Franz Schubert. Schubert's four most popular symphonies: No. 4 in C Minor ("Tragic"); No. 5 in B-flat Major; No. 8 in B Minor ("Unfinished"); No. 9 in C Major ("Great"). Breitkopf & Hartel edition. Study score. 261pp. 9⅜ x 12¼. 23681-1 Pa. $6.50

THE AUTHENTIC GILBERT & SULLIVAN SONGBOOK, W. S. Gilbert, A. S. Sullivan. Largest selection available; 92 songs, uncut, original keys, in piano rendering approved by Sullivan. Favorites and lesser-known fine numbers. Edited with plot synopses by James Spero. 3 illustrations. 399pp. 9 x 12. 23482-7 Pa. $7.95

PRINCIPLES OF ORCHESTRATION, Nikolay Rimsky-Korsakov. Great classical orchestrator provides fundamentals of tonal resonance, progression of parts, voice and orchestra, tutti effects, much else in major document. 330pp. of musical excerpts. 489pp. 6½ x 9¼. 21266-1 Pa. $6.00

TRISTAN UND ISOLDE, Richard Wagner. Full orchestral score with complete instrumentation. Do not confuse with piano reduction. Commentary by Felix Mottl, great Wagnerian conductor and scholar. Study score. 655pp. 8⅛ x 11. 22915-7 Pa. $12.50

REQUIEM IN FULL SCORE, Giuseppe Verdi. Immensely popular with choral groups and music lovers. Republication of edition published by C. F. Peters, Leipzig, n. d. German frontmaker in English translation. Glossary. Text in Latin. Study score. 204pp. 9⅜ x 12¼. 23682-X Pa. $6.00

COMPLETE CHAMBER MUSIC FOR STRINGS, Felix Mendelssohn. All of Mendelssohn's chamber music: Octet, 2 Quintets, 6 Quartets, and Four Pieces for String Quartet. (Nothing with piano is included). Complete works edition (1874-7). Study score. 283 pp. 9⅜ x 12¼. 23679-X Pa. $6.95

POPULAR SONGS OF NINETEENTH-CENTURY AMERICA, edited by Richard Jackson. 64 most important songs: "Old Oaken Bucket," "Arkansas Traveler," "Yellow Rose of Texas," etc. Authentic original sheet music, full introduction and commentaries. 290pp. 9 x 12. 23270-0 Pa. $6.00

COLLECTED PIANO WORKS, Scott Joplin. Edited by Vera Brodsky Lawrence. Practically all of Joplin's piano works—rags, two-steps, marches, waltzes, etc., 51 works in all. Extensive introduction by Rudi Blesh. Total of 345pp. 9 x 12. 23106-2 Pa. $14.95

BASIC PRINCIPLES OF CLASSICAL BALLET, Agrippina Vaganova. Great Russian theoretician, teacher explains methods for teaching classical ballet; incorporates best from French, Italian, Russian schools. 118 illustrations. 175pp. 5⅜ x 8½. 22036-2 Pa. $2.50

CHINESE CHARACTERS, L. Wieger. Rich analysis of 2300 characters according to traditional systems into primitives. Historical-semantic analysis to phonetics (Classical Mandarin) and radicals. 820pp. 6⅛ x 9¼. 21321-8 Pa. $10.00

EGYPTIAN LANGUAGE: EASY LESSONS IN EGYPTIAN HIERO-GLYPHICS, E. A. Wallis Budge. Foremost Egyptologist offers Egyptian grammar, explanation of hieroglyphics, many reading texts, dictionary of symbols. 246pp. 5 x 7½. (Available in U.S. only) 21394-3 Clothbd. $7.50

AN ETYMOLOGICAL DICTIONARY OF MODERN ENGLISH, Ernest Weekley. Richest, fullest work, by foremost British lexicographer. Detailed word histories. Inexhaustible. Do not confuse this with Concise Etymological Dictionary, which is abridged. Total of 856pp. 6½ x 9¼. 21873-2, 21874-0 Pa., Two-vol. set $12.00

A MAYA GRAMMAR, Alfred M. Tozzer. Practical, useful English-language grammar by the Harvard anthropologist who was one of the three greatest American scholars in the area of Maya culture. Phonetics, grammatical processes, syntax, more. 301pp. 5⅜ x 8½.   23465-7 Pa. $4.00

THE JOURNAL OF HENRY D. THOREAU, edited by Bradford Torrey, F. H. Allen. Complete reprinting of 14 volumes, 1837-61, over two million words; the sourcebooks for *Walden*, etc. Definitive. All original sketches, plus 75 photographs. Introduction by Walter Harding. Total of 1804pp. 8½ x 12¼.   20312-3, 20313-1 Clothbd., Two-vol. set $50.00

CLASSIC GHOST STORIES, Charles Dickens and others. 18 wonderful stories you've wanted to reread: "The Monkey's Paw," "The House and the Brain," "The Upper Berth," "The Signalman," "Dracula's Guest," "The Tapestried Chamber," etc. Dickens, Scott, Mary Shelley, Stoker, etc. 330pp. 5⅜ x 8½.   20735-8 Pa. $3.50

SEVEN SCIENCE FICTION NOVELS, H. G. Wells. Full novels. *First Men in the Moon, Island of Dr. Moreau, War of the Worlds, Food of the Gods, Invisible Man, Time Machine, In the Days of the Comet.* A basic science-fiction library. 1015pp. 5⅜ x 8½. (Available in U.S. only)
20264-X Clothbd. $8.95

ARMADALE, Wilkie Collins. Third great mystery novel by the author of *The Woman in White* and *The Moonstone.* Ingeniously plotted narrative shows an exceptional command of character, incident and mood. Original magazine version with 40 illustrations. 597pp. 5⅜ x 8½.
23429-0 Pa. $5.00

MASTERS OF MYSTERY, H. Douglas Thomson. The first book in English (1931) devoted to history and aesthetics of detective story. Poe, Doyle, LeFanu, Dickens, many others, up to 1930. New introduction and notes by E. F. Bleiler. 288pp. 5⅜ x 8½. (Available in U.S. only)
23606-4 Pa. $4.00

FLATLAND, E. A. Abbott. Science-fiction classic explores life of 2-D being in 3-D world. Read also as introduction to thought about hyperspace. Introduction by Banesh Hoffmann. 16 illustrations. 103pp. 5⅜ x 8½.
20001-9 Pa. $1.75

THREE SUPERNATURAL NOVELS OF THE VICTORIAN PERIOD, edited, with an introduction, by E. F. Bleiler. Reprinted complete and unabridged, three great classics of the supernatural: *The Haunted Hotel* by Wilkie Collins, *The Haunted House at Latchford* by Mrs. J. H. Riddell, and *The Lost Stradivarious* by J. Meade Falkner. 325pp. 5⅜ x 8½.
22571-2 Pa. $4.00

AYESHA: THE RETURN OF "SHE," H. Rider Haggard. Virtuoso sequel featuring the great mythic creation, Ayesha, in an adventure that is fully as good as the first book, *She.* Original magazine version, with 47 original illustrations by Maurice Greiffenhagen. 189pp. 6½ x 9¼.
23649-8 Pa. $3.50

UNCLE SILAS, J. Sheridan LeFanu. Victorian Gothic mystery novel, considered by many best of period, even better than Collins or Dickens. Wonderful psychological terror. Introduction by Frederick Shroyer. 436pp. 5⅜ x 8½. 21715-9 Pa. $6.00

JURGEN, James Branch Cabell. The great erotic fantasy of the 1920's that delighted thousands, shocked thousands more. Full final text, Lane edition with 13 plates by Frank Pape. 346pp. 5⅜ x 8½. 23507-6 Pa. $4.50

THE CLAVERINGS, Anthony Trollope. Major novel, chronicling aspects of British Victorian society, personalities. Reprint of Cornhill serialization, 16 plates by M. Edwards; first reprint of full text. Introduction by Norman Donaldson. 412pp. 5⅜ x 8½. 23464-9 Pa. $5.00

KEPT IN THE DARK, Anthony Trollope. Unusual short novel about Victorian morality and abnormal psychology by the great English author. Probably the first American publication. Frontispiece by Sir John Millais. 92pp. 6½ x 9¼. 23609-9 Pa. $2.50

RALPH THE HEIR, Anthony Trollope. Forgotten tale of illegitimacy, inheritance. Master novel of Trollope's later years. Victorian country estates, clubs, Parliament, fox hunting, world of fully realized characters. Reprint of 1871 edition. 12 illustrations by F. A. Faser. 434pp. of text. 5⅜ x 8½. 23642-0 Pa. $5.00

YEKL and THE IMPORTED BRIDEGROOM AND OTHER STORIES OF THE NEW YORK GHETTO, Abraham Cahan. Film *Hester Street* based on *Yekl* (1896). Novel, other stories among first about Jewish immigrants of N.Y.'s East Side. Highly praised by W. D. Howells—Cahan "a new star of realism." New introduction by Bernard G. Richards. 240pp. 5⅜ x 8½. 22427-9 Pa. $3.50

THE HIGH PLACE, James Branch Cabell. Great fantasy writer's enchanting comedy of disenchantment set in 18th-century France. Considered by some critics to be even better than his famous *Jurgen*. 10 illustrations and numerous vignettes by noted fantasy artist Frank C. Pape. 320pp. 5⅜ x 8½. 23670-6 Pa. $4.00

ALICE'S ADVENTURES UNDER GROUND, Lewis Carroll. Facsimile of ms. Carroll gave Alice Liddell in 1864. Different in many ways from final Alice. Handlettered, illustrated by Carroll. Introduction by Martin Gardner. 128pp. 5⅜ x 8½. 21482-6 Pa. $2.00

FAVORITE ANDREW LANG FAIRY TALE BOOKS IN MANY COLORS, Andrew Lang. The four Lang favorites in a boxed set—the complete *Red, Green, Yellow* and *Blue* Fairy Books. 164 stories; 439 illustrations by Lancelot Speed, Henry Ford and G. P. Jacomb Hood. Total of about 1500pp. 5⅜ x 8½. 23407-X Boxed set, Pa. $14.95

HOUSEHOLD STORIES BY THE BROTHERS GRIMM. All the great
Grimm stories: "Rumpelstiltskin," "Snow White," "Hansel and Gretel,"
etc., with 114 illustrations by Walter Crane. 269pp. 5⅜ x 8½.
21080-4 Pa. $3.00

SLEEPING BEAUTY, illustrated by Arthur Rackham. Perhaps the fullest,
most delightful version ever, told by C. S. Evans. Rackham's best work.
49 illustrations. 110pp. 7⅞ x 10¾.   22756-1 Pa. $2.50

AMERICAN FAIRY TALES, L. Frank Baum. Young cowboy lassoes
Father Time; dummy in Mr. Floman's department store window comes to
life; and 10 other fairy tales. 41 illustrations by N. P. Hall, Harry Kennedy,
Ike Morgan, and Ralph Gardner. 209pp. 5⅜ x 8½.   23643-9 Pa. $3.00

THE WONDERFUL WIZARD OF OZ, L. Frank Baum. Facsimile in full
color of America's finest children's classic. Introduction by Martin Gardner.
143 illustrations by W. W. Denslow. 267pp. 5⅜ x 8½.
20691-2 Pa. $3.50

THE TALE OF PETER RABBIT, Beatrix Potter. The inimitable Peter's
terrifying adventure in Mr. McGregor's garden, with all 27 wonderful,
full-color Potter illustrations. 55pp. 4¼ x 5½. (Available in U.S. only)
22827-4 Pa. $1.25

THE STORY OF KING ARTHUR AND HIS KNIGHTS, Howard Pyle.
Finest children's version of life of King Arthur. 48 illustrations by Pyle.
131pp. 6⅛ x 9¼.   21445-1 Pa. $4.95

CARUSO'S CARICATURES, Enrico Caruso. Great tenor's remarkable
caricatures of self, fellow musicians, composers, others. Toscanini, Puccini,
Farrar, etc. Impish, cutting, insightful. 473 illustrations. Preface by M.
Sisca. 217pp. 8⅜ x 11¼.   23528-9 Pa. $6.95

PERSONAL NARRATIVE OF A PILGRIMAGE TO ALMADINAH AND
MECCAH, Richard Burton. Great travel classic by remarkably colorful
personality. Burton, disguised as a Moroccan, visited sacred shrines of
Islam, narrowly escaping death. Wonderful observations of Islamic life,
customs, personalities. 47 illustrations. Total of 959pp. 5⅜ x 8½.
21217-3, 21218-1 Pa., Two-vol. set $12.00

INCIDENTS OF TRAVEL IN YUCATAN, John L. Stephens. Classic
(1843) exploration of jungles of Yucatan, looking for evidences of Maya
civilization. Travel adventures, Mexican and Indian culture, etc. Total of
669pp. 5⅜ x 8½.   20926-1, 20927-X Pa., Two-vol. set $7.90

AMERICAN LITERARY AUTOGRAPHS FROM WASHINGTON IRVING
TO HENRY JAMES, Herbert Cahoon, et al. Letters, poems, manuscripts
of Hawthorne, Thoreau, Twain, Alcott, Whitman, 67 other prominent
American authors. Reproductions, full transcripts and commentary. Plus
checklist of all American Literary Autographs in The Pierpont Morgan
Library. Printed on exceptionally high-quality paper. 136 illustrations.
212pp. 9⅛ x 12¼.   23548-3 Pa. $7.95

CATALOGUE OF DOVER BOOKS

YUCATAN BEFORE AND AFTER THE CONQUEST, Diego de Landa. First English translation of basic book in Maya studies, the only significant account of Yucatan written in the early post-Conquest era. Translated by distinguished Maya scholar William Gates. Appendices, introduction, 4 maps and over 120 illustrations added by translator. 162pp. 5⅜ x 8½.
23622-6 Pa. $3.00

THE MALAY ARCHIPELAGO, Alfred R. Wallace. Spirited travel account by one of founders of modern biology. Touches on zoology, botany, ethnography, geography, and geology. 62 illustrations, maps. 515pp. 5⅜ x 8½.
20187-2 Pa. $6.95

THE DISCOVERY OF THE TOMB OF TUTANKHAMEN, Howard Carter, A. C. Mace. Accompany Carter in the thrill of discovery, as ruined passage suddenly reveals unique, untouched, fabulously rich tomb. Fascinating account, with 106 illustrations. New introduction by J. M. White. Total of 382pp. 5⅜ x 8½. (Available in U.S. only) 23500-9 Pa. $4.00

THE WORLD'S GREATEST SPEECHES, edited by Lewis Copeland and Lawrence W. Lamm. Vast collection of 278 speeches from Greeks up to present. Powerful and effective models; unique look at history. Revised to 1970. Indices. 842pp. 5⅜ x 8½. 20468-5 Pa. $8.95

THE 100 GREATEST ADVERTISEMENTS, Julian Watkins. The priceless ingredient; His master's voice; 99 44/100% pure; over 100 others. How they were written, their impact, etc. Remarkable record. 130 illustrations. 233pp. 7⅞ x 10 3/5. 20540-1 Pa. $5.00

CRUICKSHANK PRINTS FOR HAND COLORING, George Cruickshank. 18 illustrations, one side of a page, on fine-quality paper suitable for watercolors. Caricatures of people in society (c. 1820) full of trenchant wit. Very large format. 32pp. 11 x 16. 23684-6 Pa. $5.00

THIRTY-TWO COLOR POSTCARDS OF TWENTIETH-CENTURY AMERICAN ART, Whitney Museum of American Art. Reproduced in full color in postcard form are 31 art works and one shot of the museum. Calder, Hopper, Rauschenberg, others. Detachable. 16pp. 8¼ x 11.
23629-3 Pa. $2.50

MUSIC OF THE SPHERES: THE MATERIAL UNIVERSE FROM ATOM TO QUASAR SIMPLY EXPLAINED, Guy Murchie. Planets, stars, geology, atoms, radiation, relativity, quantum theory, light, antimatter, similar topics. 319 figures. 664pp. 5⅜ x 8½.
21809-0, 21810-4 Pa., Two-vol. set $10.00

EINSTEIN'S THEORY OF RELATIVITY, Max Born. Finest semi-technical account; covers Einstein, Lorentz, Minkowski, and others, with much detail, much explanation of ideas and math not readily available elsewhere on this level. For student, non-specialist. 376pp. 5⅜ x 8½.
60769-0 Pa. $4.50

AMERICAN ANTIQUE FURNITURE, Edgar G. Miller, Jr. The basic coverage of all American furniture before 1840: chapters per item chronologically cover all types of furniture, with more than 2100 photos. Total of 1106pp. 7⅞ x 10¾. 21599-7, 21600-4 Pa., Two-vol. set $17.90

ILLUSTRATED GUIDE TO SHAKER FURNITURE, Robert Meader. Director, Shaker Museum, Old Chatham, presents up-to-date coverage of all furniture and appurtenances, with much on local styles not available elsewhere. 235 photos. 146pp. 9 x 12. 22819-3 Pa. $5.00

ORIENTAL RUGS, ANTIQUE AND MODERN, Walter A. Hawley. Persia, Turkey, Caucasus, Central Asia, China, other traditions. Best general survey of all aspects: styles and periods, manufacture, uses, symbols and their interpretation, and identification. 96 illustrations, 11 in color. 320pp. 6⅛ x 9¼. 22366-3 Pa. $6.95

CHINESE POTTERY AND PORCELAIN, R. L. Hobson. Detailed descriptions and analyses by former Keeper of the Department of Oriental Antiquities and Ethnography at the British Museum. Covers hundreds of pieces from primitive times to 1915. Still the standard text for most periods. 136 plates, 40 in full color. Total of 750pp. 5⅝ x 8½.
23253-0 Pa. $10.00

THE WARES OF THE MING DYNASTY, R. L. Hobson. Foremost scholar examines and illustrates many varieties of Ming (1368-1644). Famous blue and white, polychrome, lesser-known styles and shapes. 117 illustrations, 9 full color, of outstanding pieces. Total of 263pp. 6⅛ x 9¼. (Available in U.S. only) 23652-8 Pa. $6.00

Prices subject to change without notice.

Available at your book dealer or write for free catalogue to Dept. GI, Dover Publications, Inc., 180 Varick St., N.Y., N.Y. 10014. Dover publishes more than 175 books each year on science, elementary and advanced mathematics, biology, music, art, literary history, social sciences and other areas.